BAD GIRLS

ALEX DE CAMPI
VICTOR SANTOS

GALLERY 13

NEW YORK   LONDON   TORONTO   SYDNEY   NEW DELHI

8:00 P.M.

WEDNESDAY 31 DECEMBER 1958

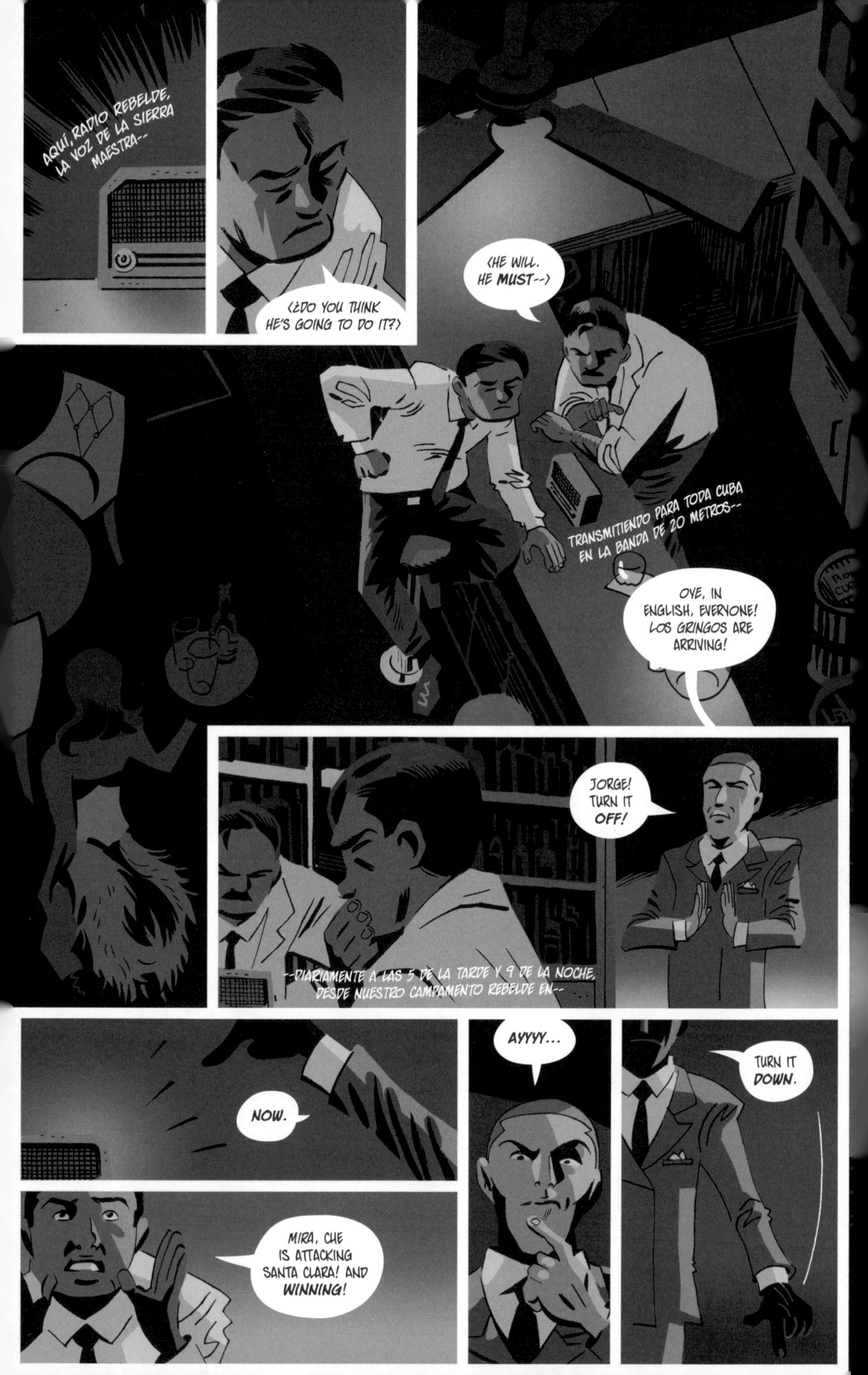
AQUÍ, RADIO REBELDE, LA VOZ DE LA SIERRA MAESTRA--
<¿DO YOU THINK HE'S GOING TO DO IT?>
<HE WILL. HE **MUST**-->
TRANSMITIENDO PARA TODA CUBA EN LA BANDA DE 20 METROS--
OYE, IN ENGLISH, EVERYONE! LOS GRINGOS ARE ARRIVING!
JORGE! TURN IT ***OFF!***
--DIARIAMENTE A LAS 5 DE LA TARDE Y 9 DE LA NOCHE, DESDE NUESTRO CAMPAMENTO REBELDE EN--
NOW.
MIRA, CHE IS ATTACKING SANTA CLARA! AND ***WINNING!***
AYYYY...
TURN IT ***DOWN.***

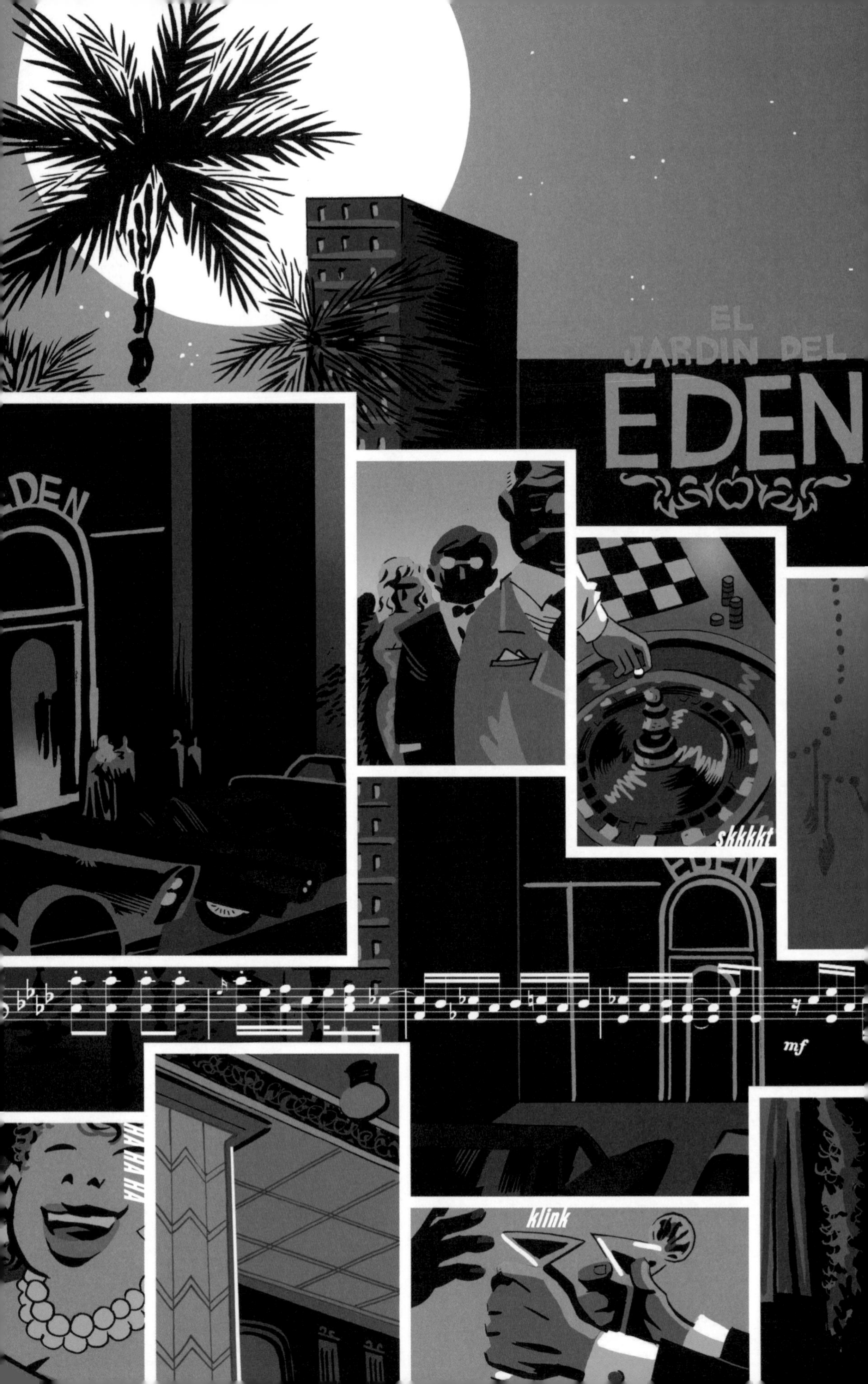
EL JARDIN DEL
EDEN
EDEN
skkkkt
EDEN
mf
HA HA HA
klink

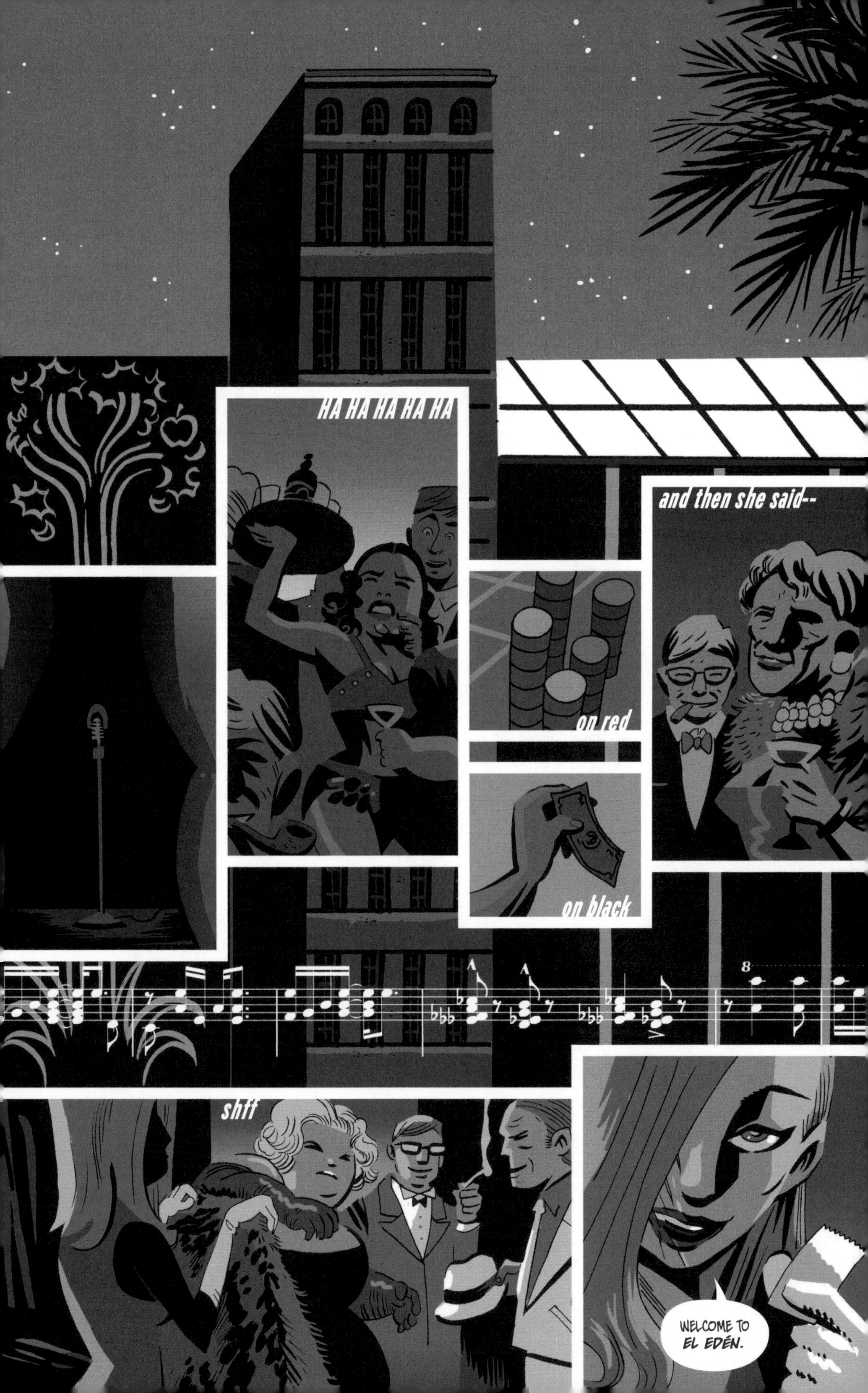
HA HA HA HA HA
and then she said--
on red
on black
shff
WELCOME TO
EL EDÉN.

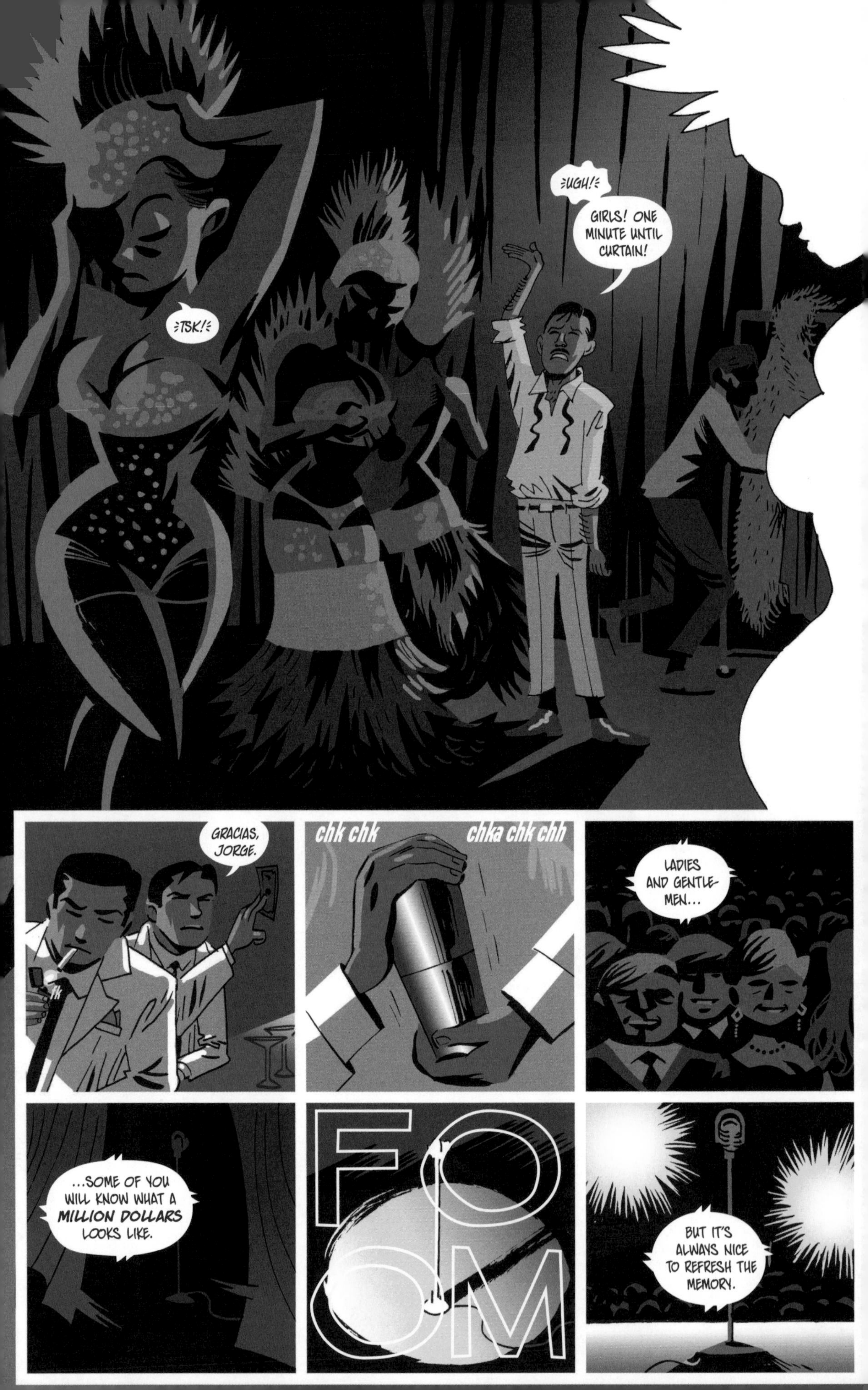

TSK!
UGH!
GIRLS! ONE MINUTE UNTIL CURTAIN!
GRACIAS, JORGE.
chk chk
chka chk chh
LADIES AND GENTLE-MEN...
...SOME OF YOU WILL KNOW WHAT A MILLION DOLLARS LOOKS LIKE.
FOOM
BUT IT'S ALWAYS NICE TO REFRESH THE MEMORY.

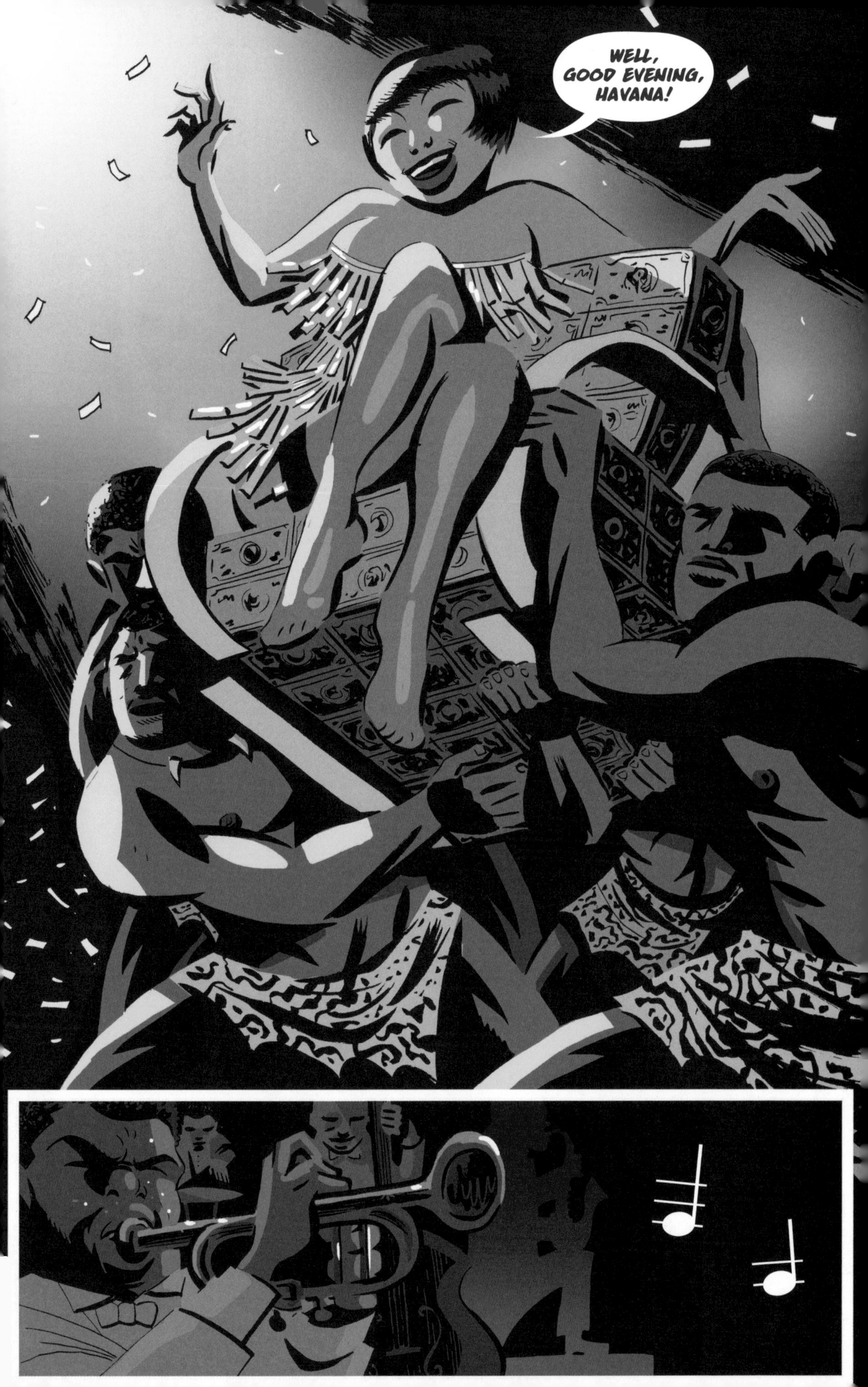
WELL, GOOD EVENING, HAVANA!

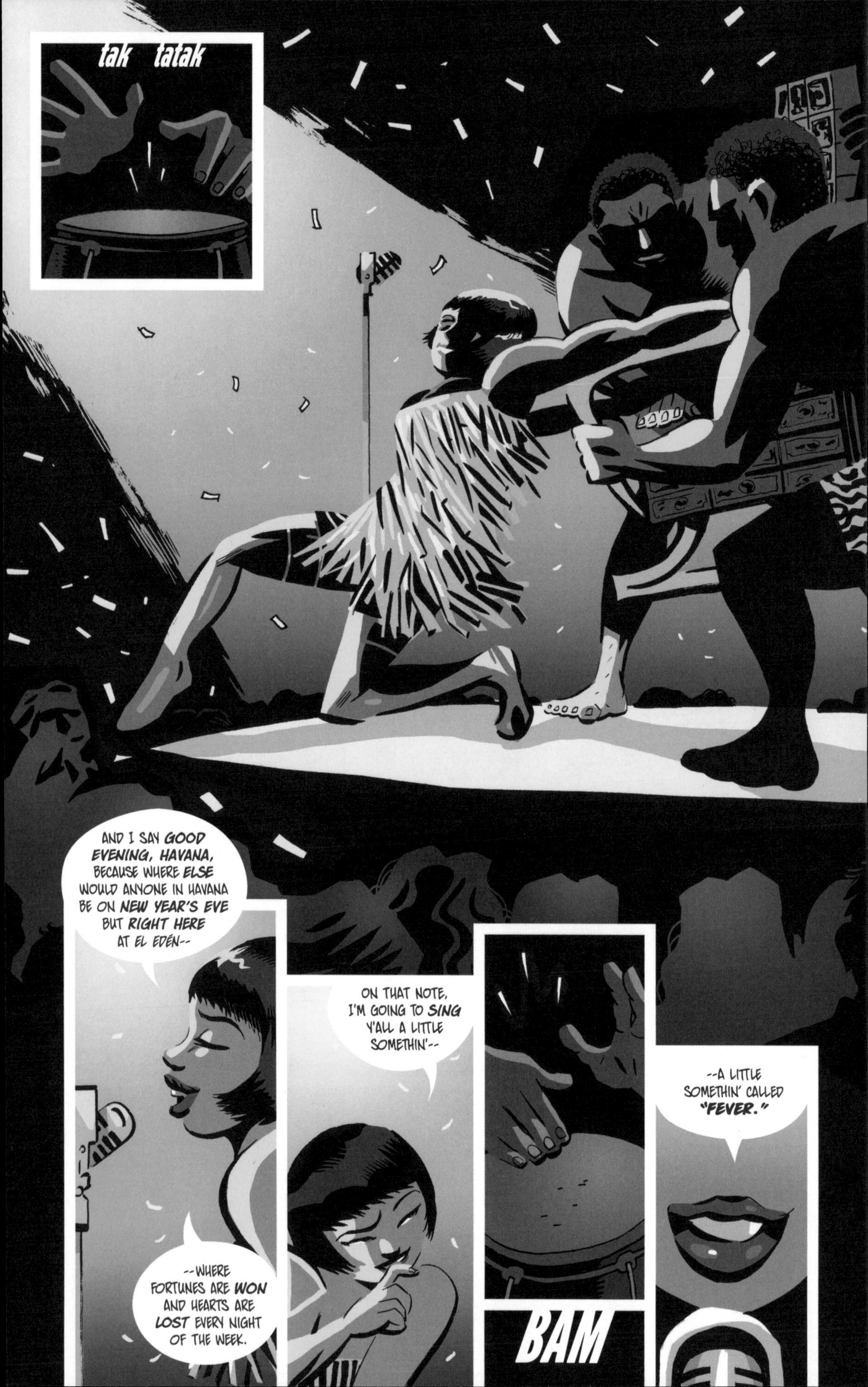

tak tatak
AND I SAY GOOD EVENING, HAVANA, BECAUSE WHERE ELSE WOULD ANYONE IN HAVANA BE ON NEW YEAR'S EVE BUT RIGHT HERE AT EL EDÉN--
--WHERE FORTUNES ARE WON AND HEARTS ARE LOST EVERY NIGHT OF THE WEEK.
ON THAT NOTE, I'M GOING TO SING Y'ALL A LITTLE SOMETHIN'--
BAM
--A LITTLE SOMETHIN' CALLED "FEVER."

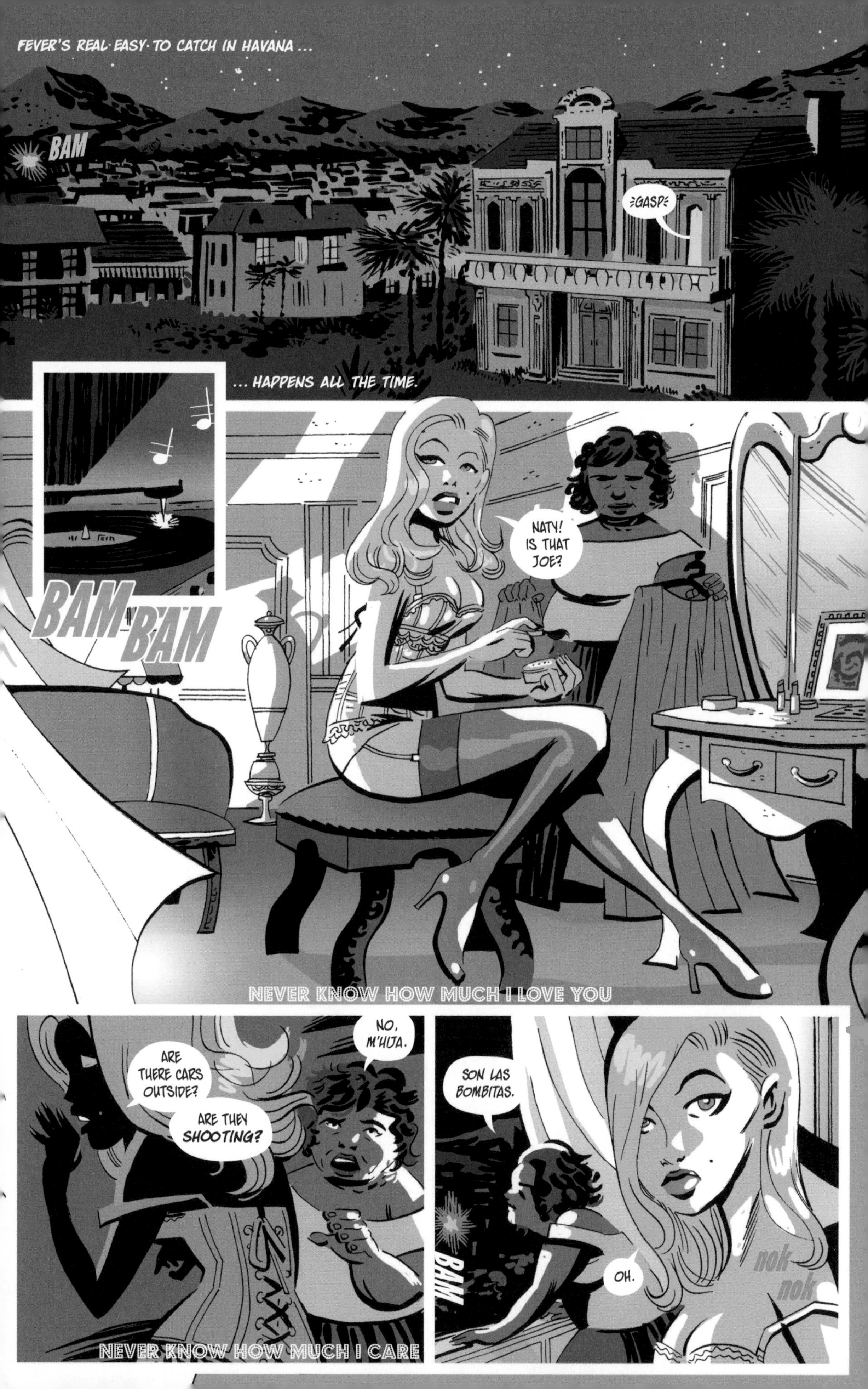
FEVER'S REAL EASY TO CATCH IN HAVANA ...
BAM
GASP
... HAPPENS ALL THE TIME.
BAM BAM
NATY! IS THAT JOE?
NEVER KNOW HOW MUCH I LOVE YOU
ARE THERE CARS OUTSIDE?
ARE THEY SHOOTING?
NO, M'HIJA.
NEVER KNOW HOW MUCH I CARE
SON LAS BOMBITAS.
BAM
OH.
nok nok

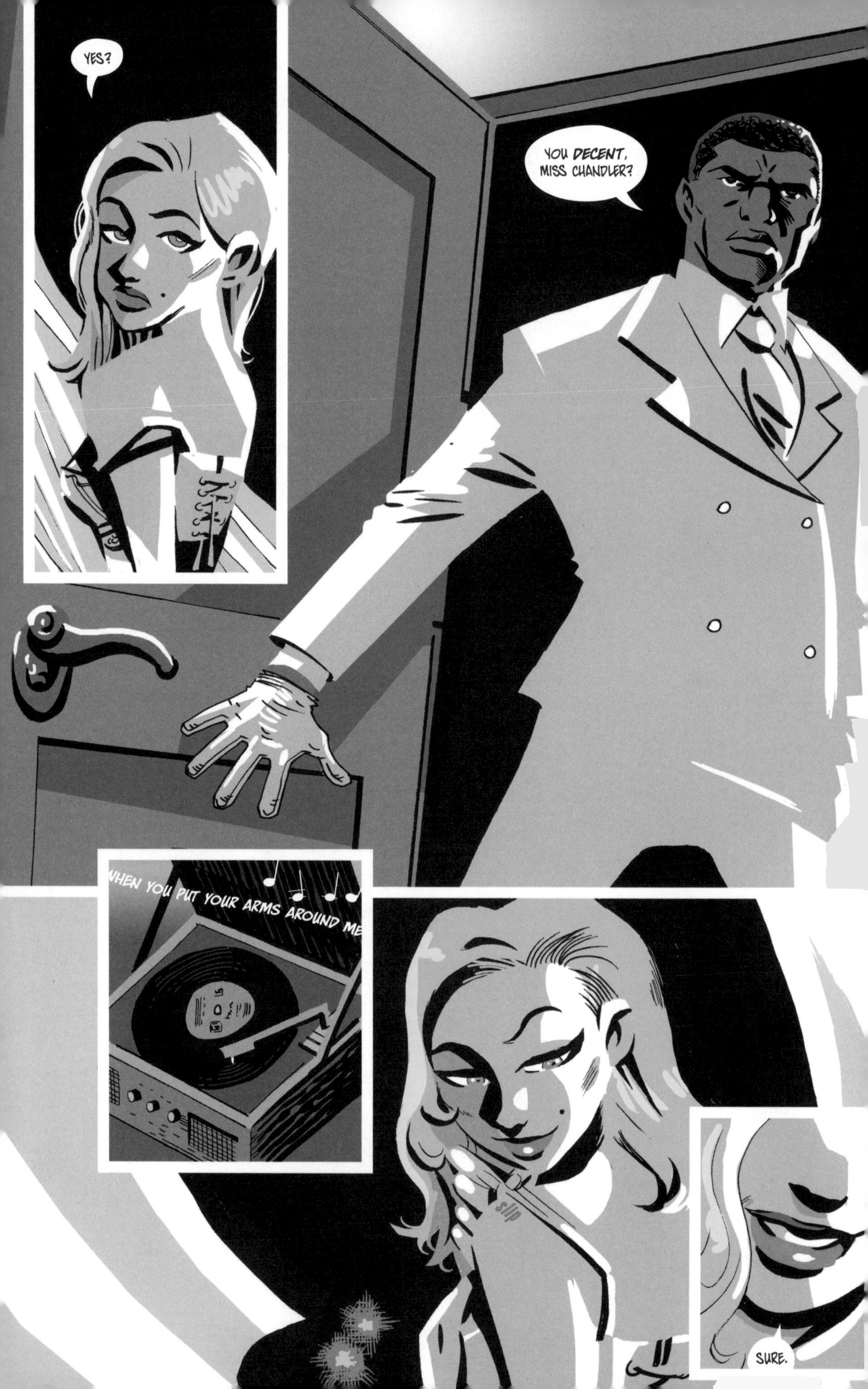
YOU DECENT, MISS CHANDLER?
YES?
WHEN YOU PUT YOUR ARMS AROUND ME
slip
SURE.

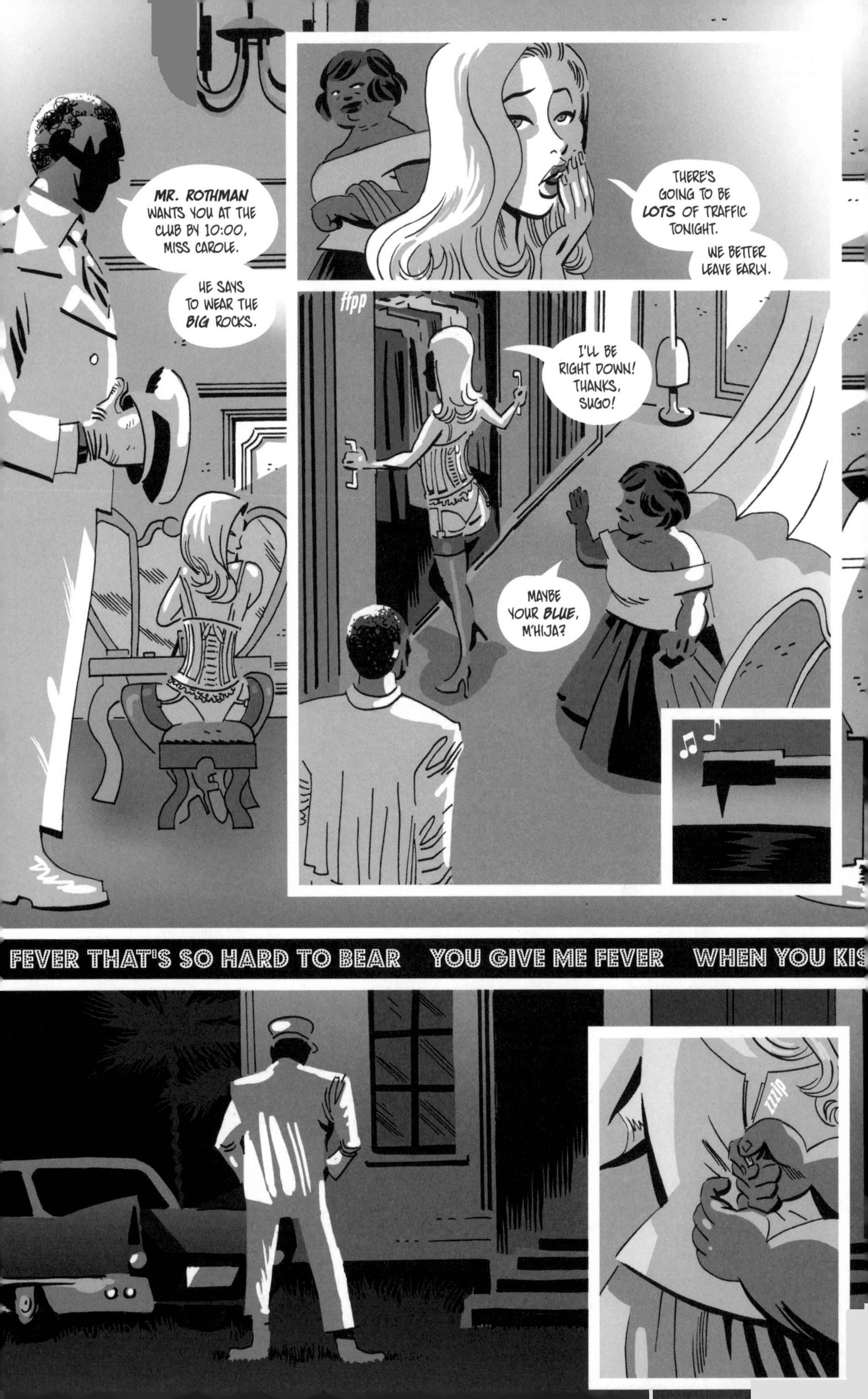
MR. ROTHMAN WANTS YOU AT THE CLUB BY 10:00, MISS CAROLE.
HE SAYS TO WEAR THE BIG ROCKS.
THERE'S GOING TO BE LOTS OF TRAFFIC TONIGHT.
WE BETTER LEAVE EARLY.
ffpp
I'LL BE RIGHT DOWN! THANKS, SUGO!
MAYBE YOUR BLUE, M'HIJA?
FEVER THAT'S SO HARD TO BEAR YOU GIVE ME FEVER WHEN YOU KIS
zzzip

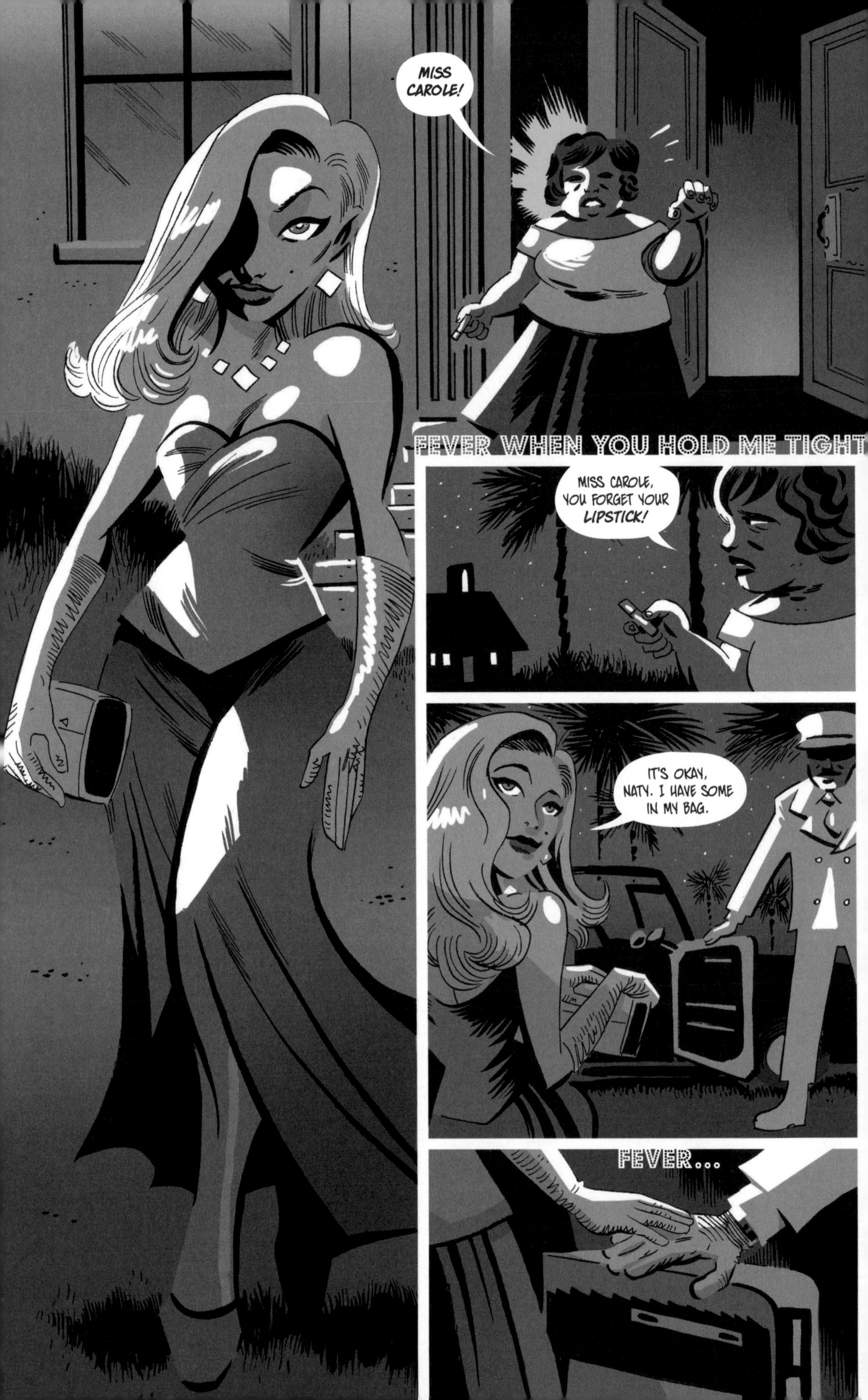
MISS CAROLE!
FEVER WHEN YOU HOLD ME TIGHT
MISS CAROLE, YOU FORGET YOUR LIPSTICK!
IT'S OKAY, NATY. I HAVE SOME IN MY BAG.
FEVER...

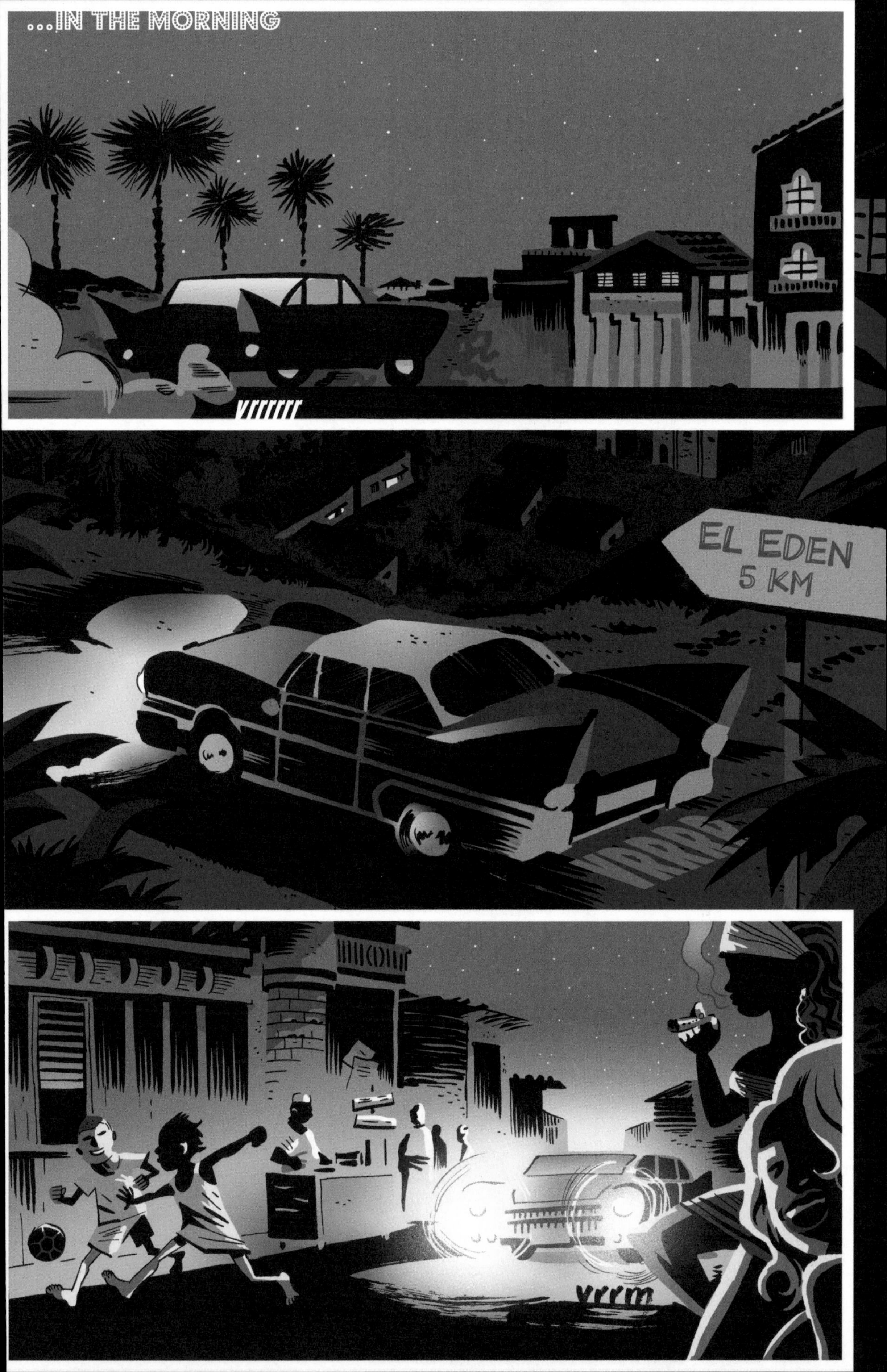
...IN THE MORNING
vrrrrrr
EL EDEN
5 KM
VRRRR
vrrm

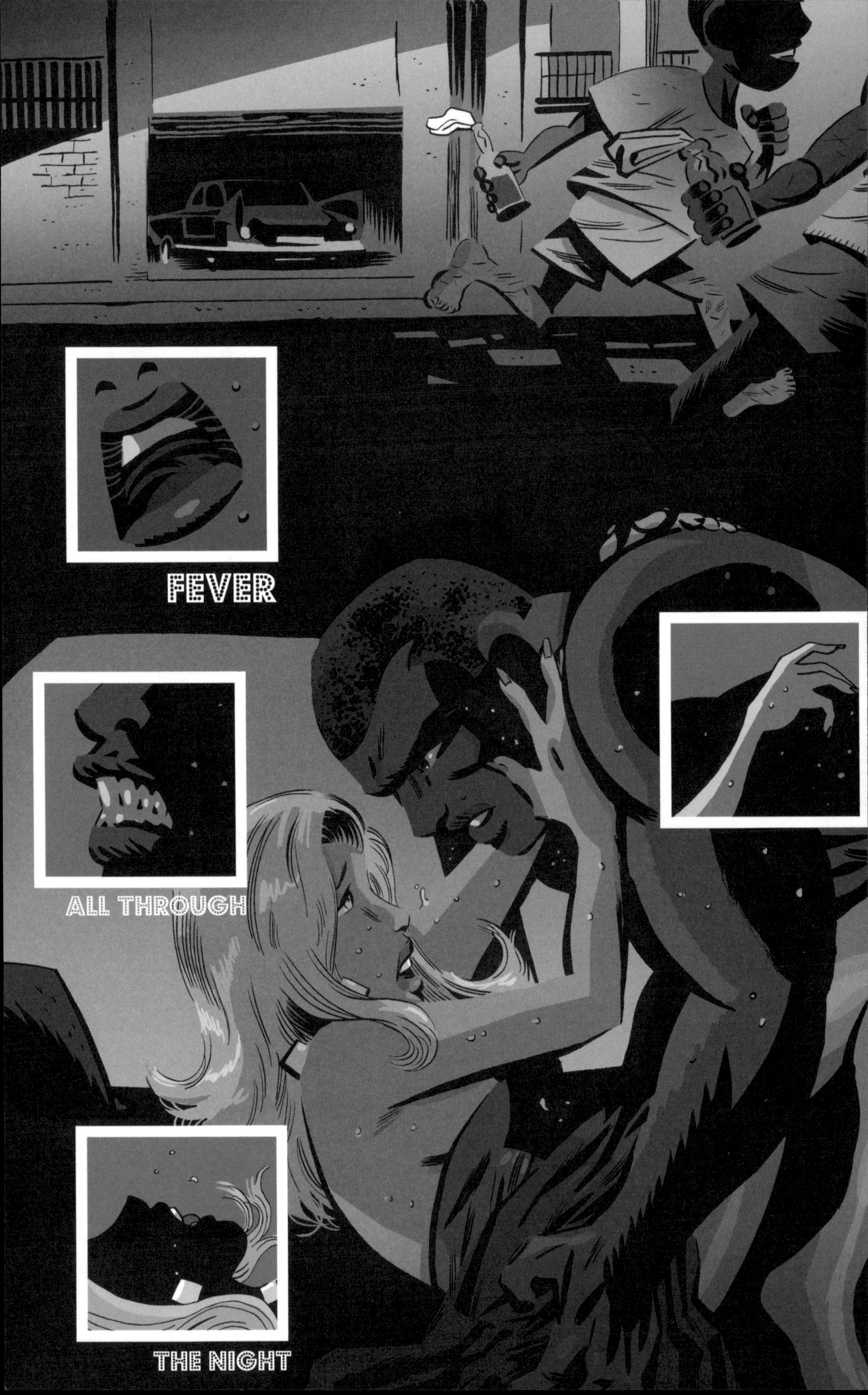
FEVER
ALL THROUGH
THE NIGHT

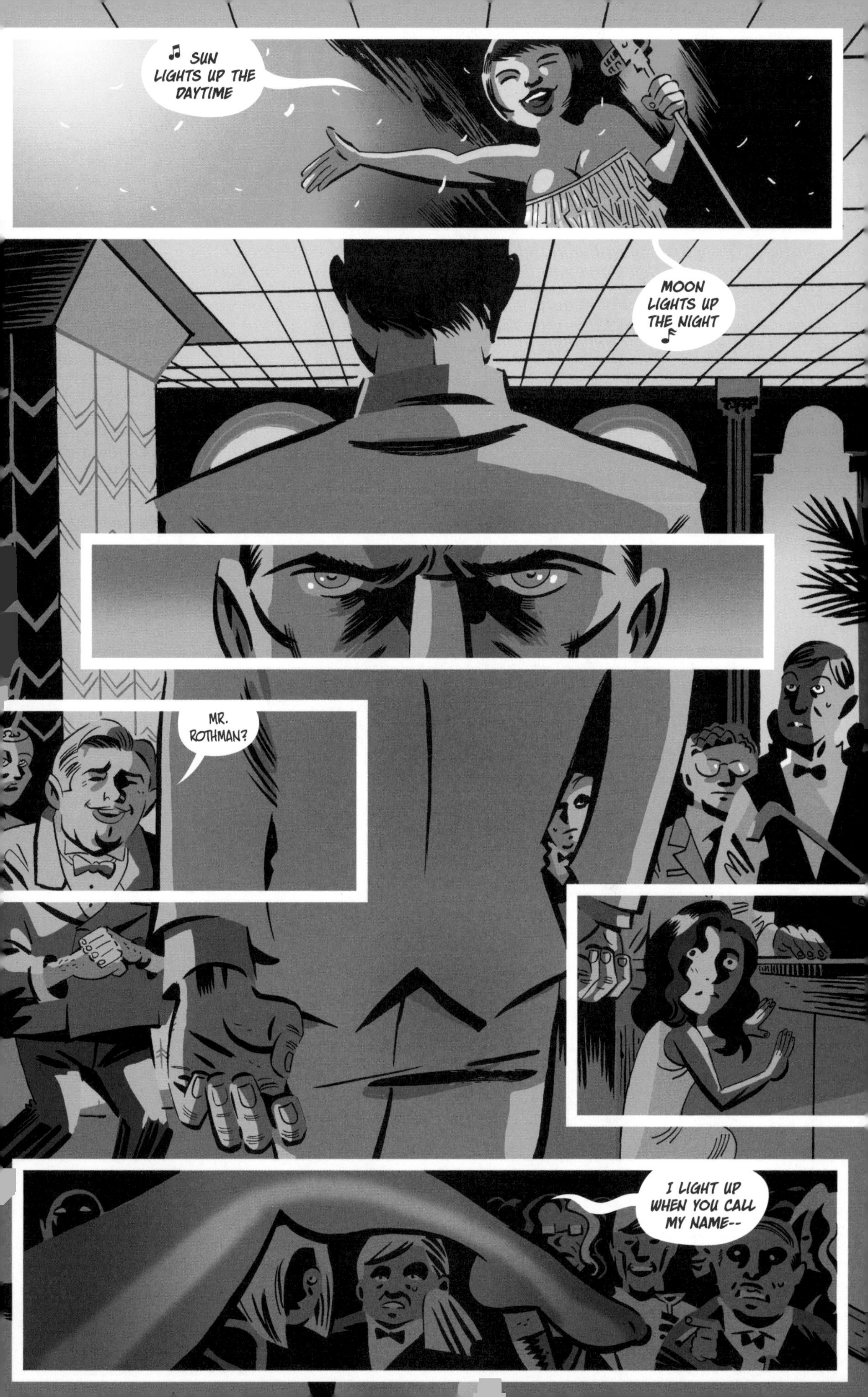
♫ SUN LIGHTS UP THE DAYTIME
MOON LIGHTS UP THE NIGHT ♪
MR. ROTHMAN?
I LIGHT UP WHEN YOU CALL MY NAME--

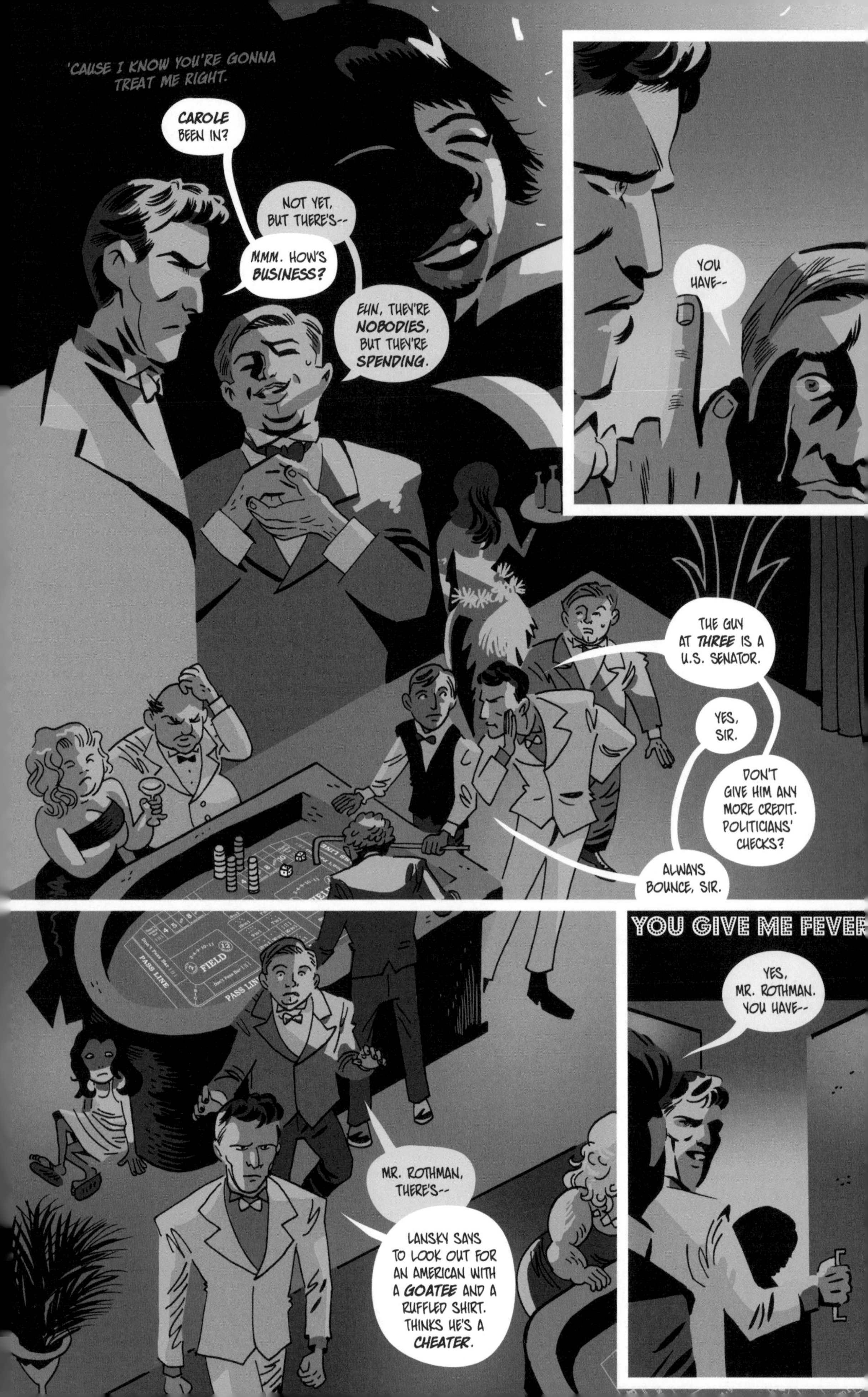
'CAUSE I KNOW YOU'RE GONNA TREAT ME RIGHT.
CAROLE BEEN IN?
NOT YET, BUT THERE'S--
MMM. HOW'S BUSINESS?
EHN, THEY'RE NOBODIES, BUT THEY'RE SPENDING.
YOU HAVE--
THE GUY AT THREE IS A U.S. SENATOR.
YES, SIR.
DON'T GIVE HIM ANY MORE CREDIT. POLITICIANS' CHECKS?
ALWAYS BOUNCE, SIR.
MR. ROTHMAN, THERE'S--
LANSKY SAYS TO LOOK OUT FOR AN AMERICAN WITH A GOATEE AND A RUFFLED SHIRT. THINKS HE'S A CHEATER.
YOU GIVE ME FEVER
YES, MR. ROTHMAN. YOU HAVE--

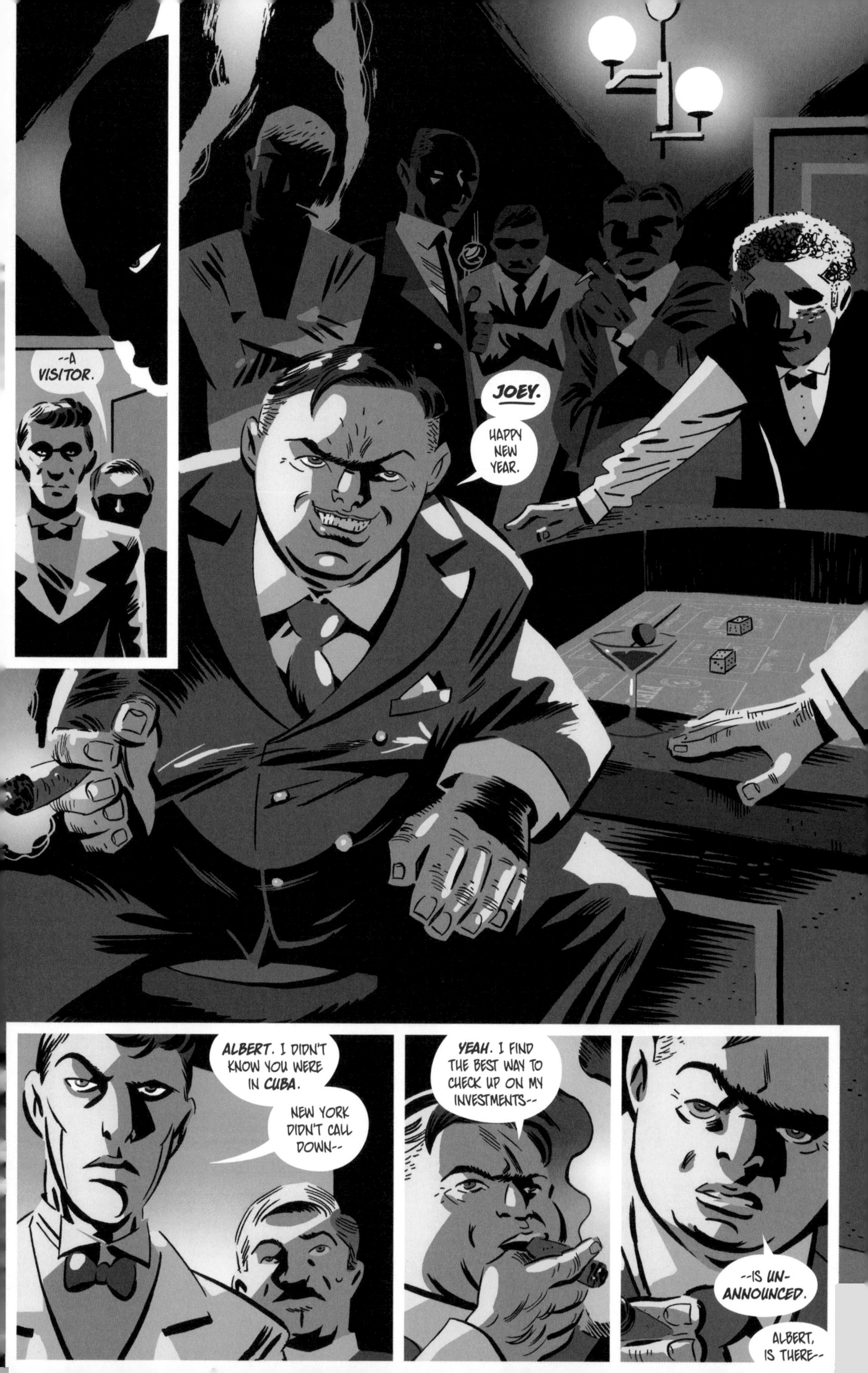
--A VISITOR.
JOEY.
HAPPY NEW YEAR.
ALBERT. I DIDN'T KNOW YOU WERE IN CUBA.
NEW YORK DIDN'T CALL DOWN--
YEAH. I FIND THE BEST WAY TO CHECK UP ON MY INVESTMENTS--
--IS UN-ANNOUNCED.
ALBERT, IS THERE--

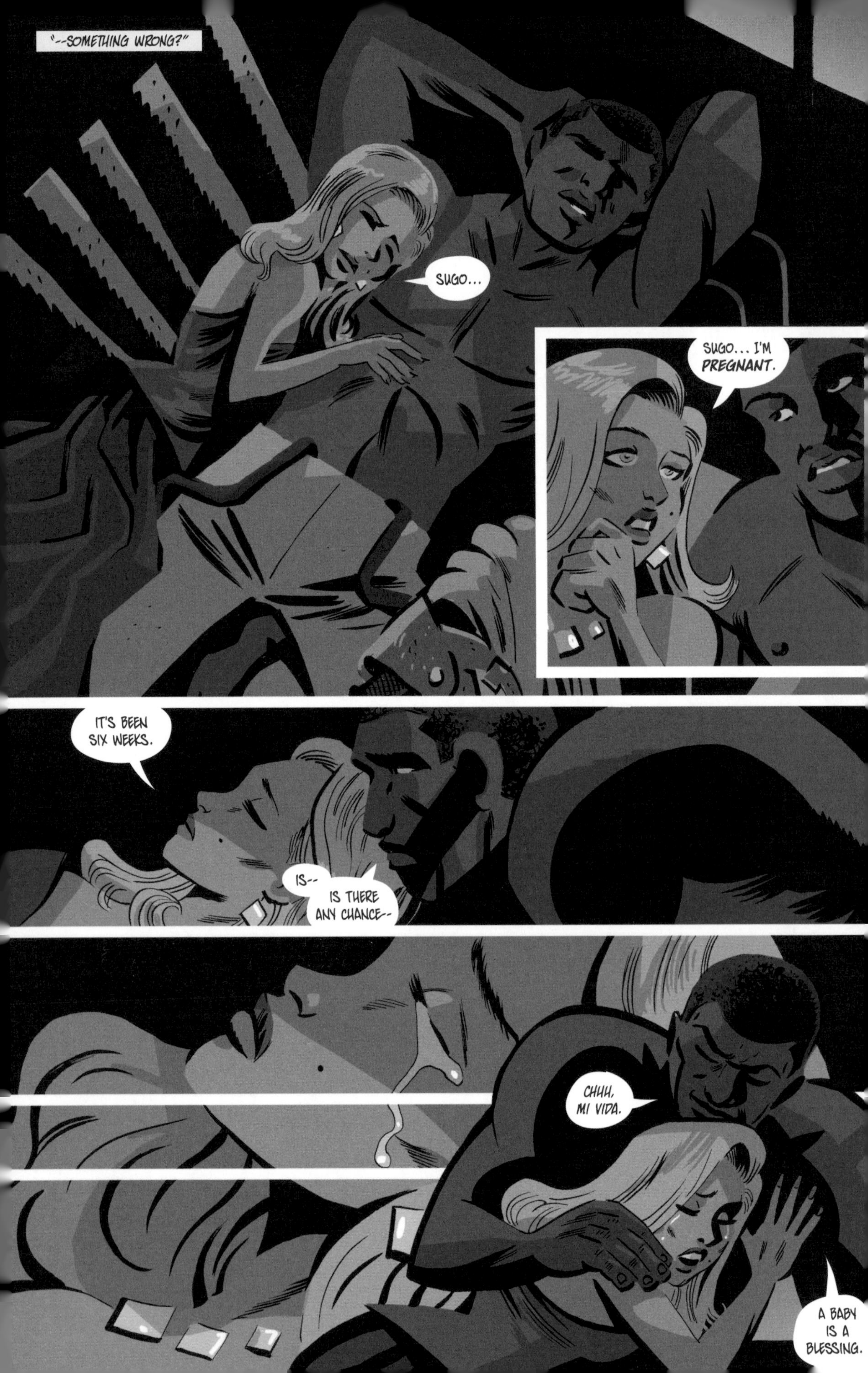
"--SOMETHING WRONG?"
SUGO...
SUGO... I'M PREGNANT.
IT'S BEEN SIX WEEKS.
IS--
IS THERE ANY CHANCE--
CHUU, MI VIDA.
A BABY IS A BLESSING.

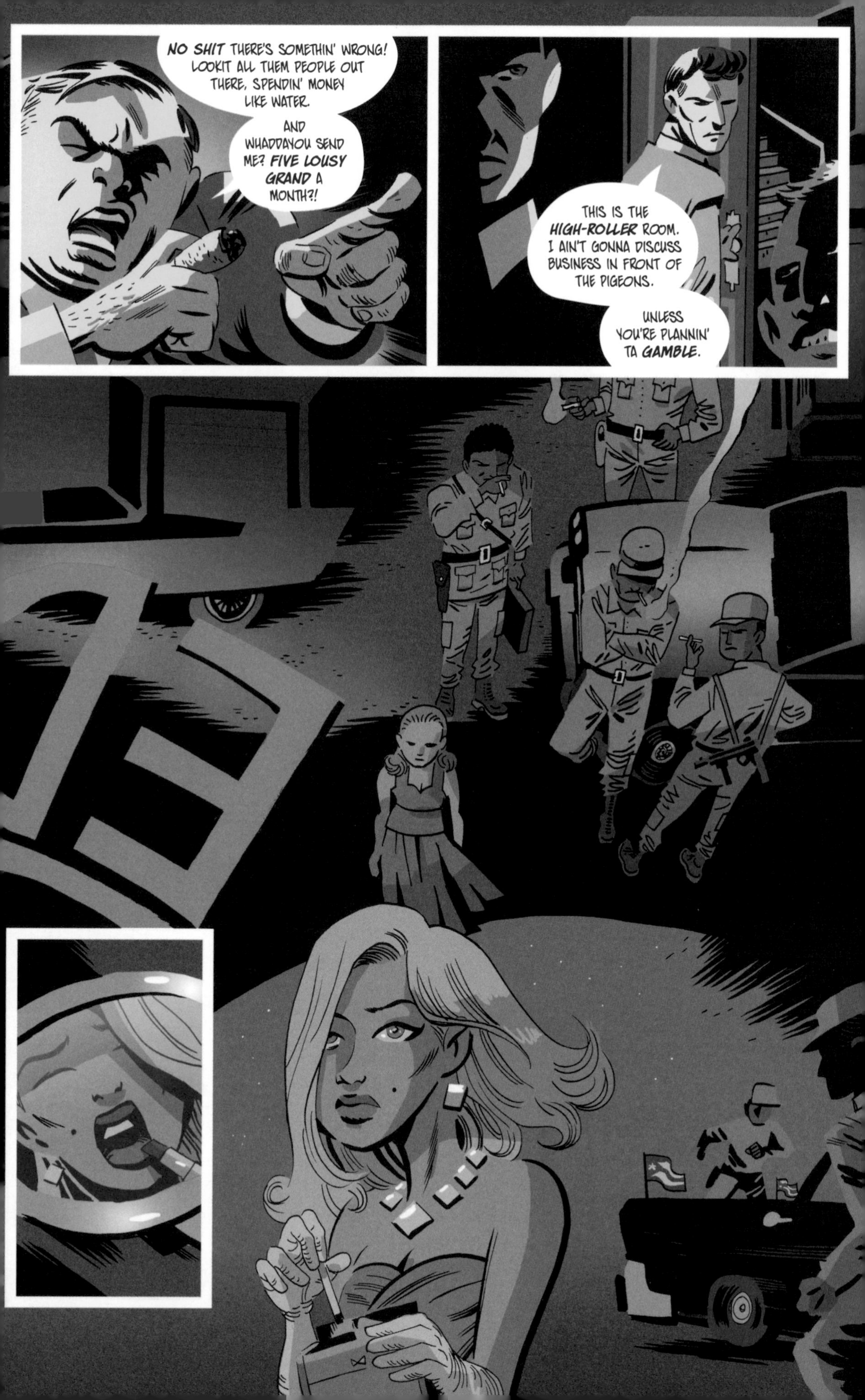
NO SHIT THERE'S SOMETHIN' WRONG! LOOKIT ALL THEM PEOPLE OUT THERE, SPENDIN' MONEY LIKE WATER.
AND WHADDAYOU SEND ME? FIVE LOUSY GRAND A MONTH?!
THIS IS THE HIGH-ROLLER ROOM. I AIN'T GONNA DISCUSS BUSINESS IN FRONT OF THE PIGEONS.
UNLESS YOU'RE PLANNIN' TA GAMBLE.

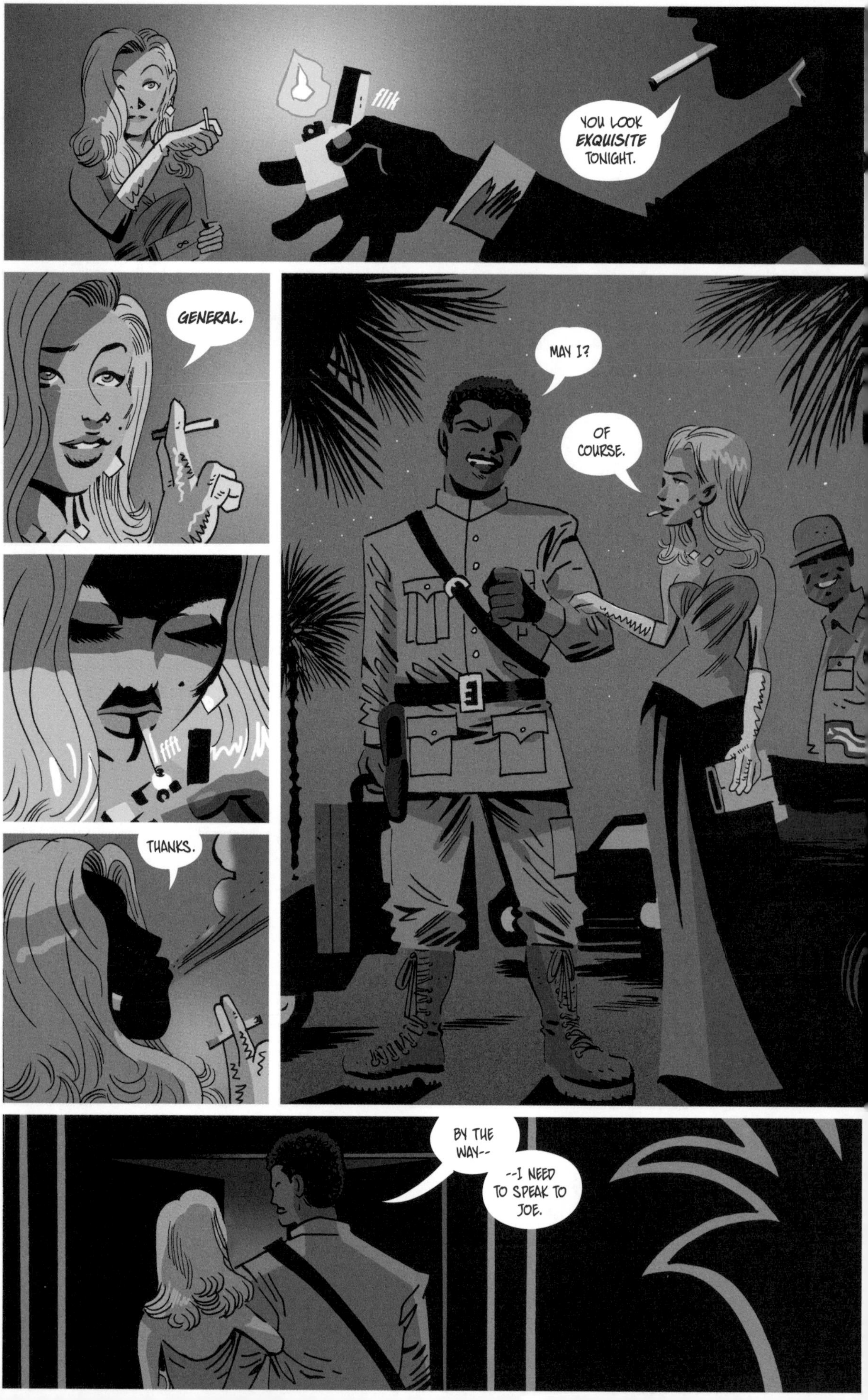
flik
YOU LOOK EXQUISITE TONIGHT.
GENERAL.
ffft
THANKS.
MAY I?
OF COURSE.
BY THE WAY--
--I NEED TO SPEAK TO JOE.

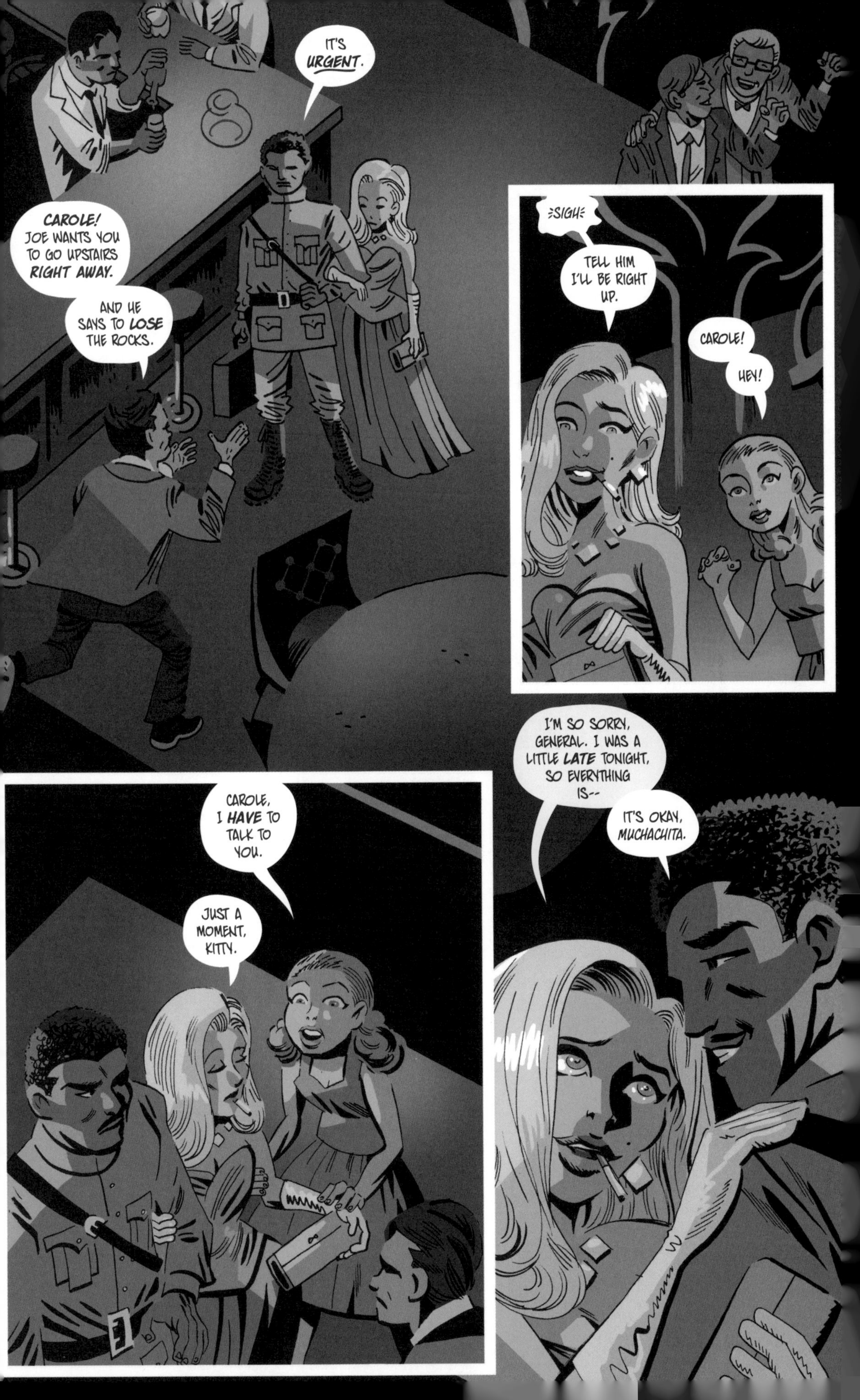
IT'S URGENT.
CAROLE! JOE WANTS YOU TO GO UPSTAIRS RIGHT AWAY.
AND HE SAYS TO LOSE THE ROCKS.
SIGH
TELL HIM I'LL BE RIGHT UP.
CAROLE!
HEY!
CAROLE, I HAVE TO TALK TO YOU.
JUST A MOMENT, KITTY.
I'M SO SORRY, GENERAL. I WAS A LITTLE LATE TONIGHT, SO EVERYTHING IS--
IT'S OKAY, MUCHACHITA.

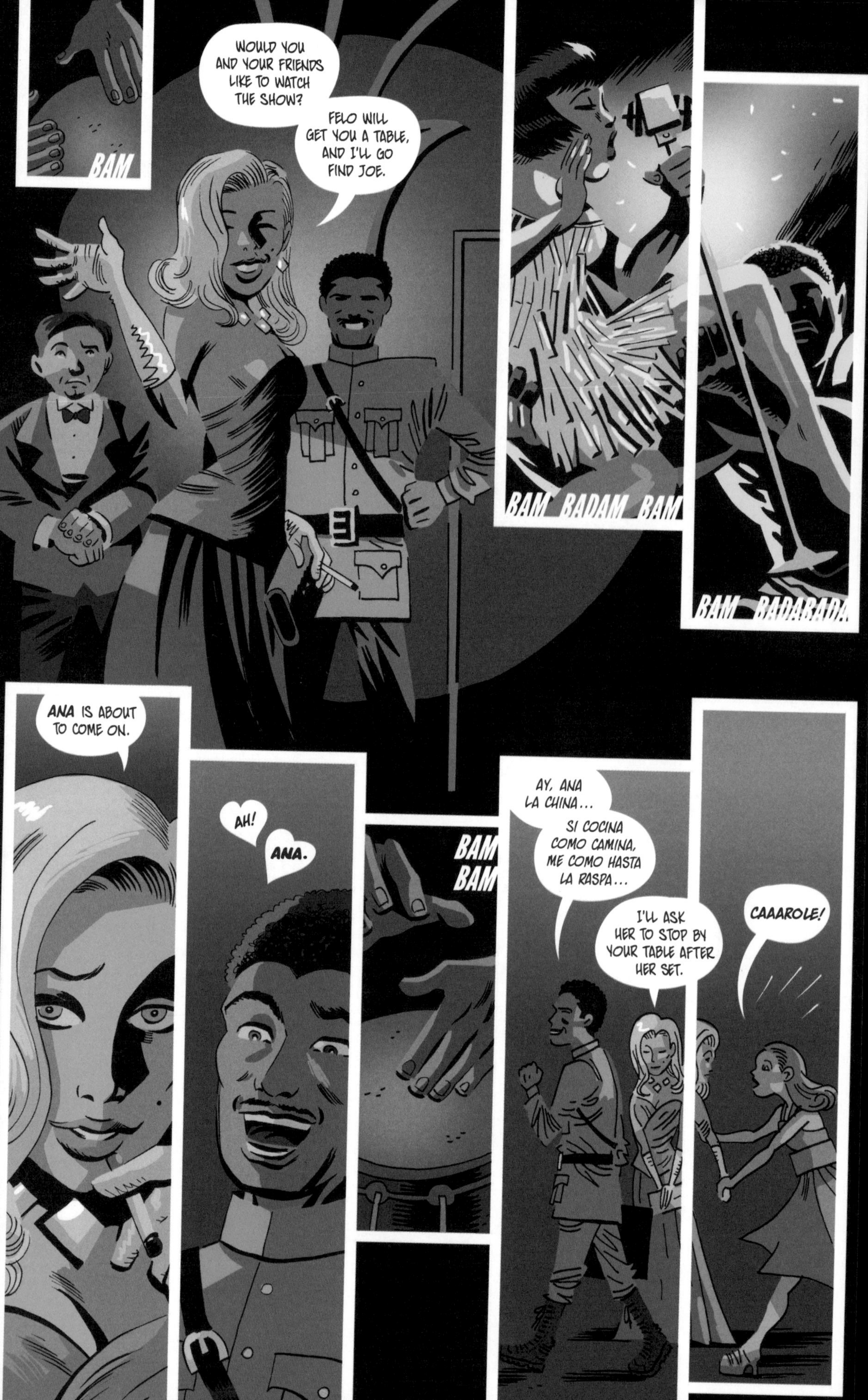
BAM
WOULD YOU AND YOUR FRIENDS LIKE TO WATCH THE SHOW?
FELO WILL GET YOU A TABLE, AND I'LL GO FIND JOE.
BAM BADAM BAM
BAM BADABADA
ANA IS ABOUT TO COME ON.
AH!
ANA.
BAM BAM
AY, ANA LA CHINA...
SI COCINA COMO CAMINA, ME COMO HASTA LA RASPA...
I'LL ASK HER TO STOP BY YOUR TABLE AFTER HER SET.
CAAAROLE!

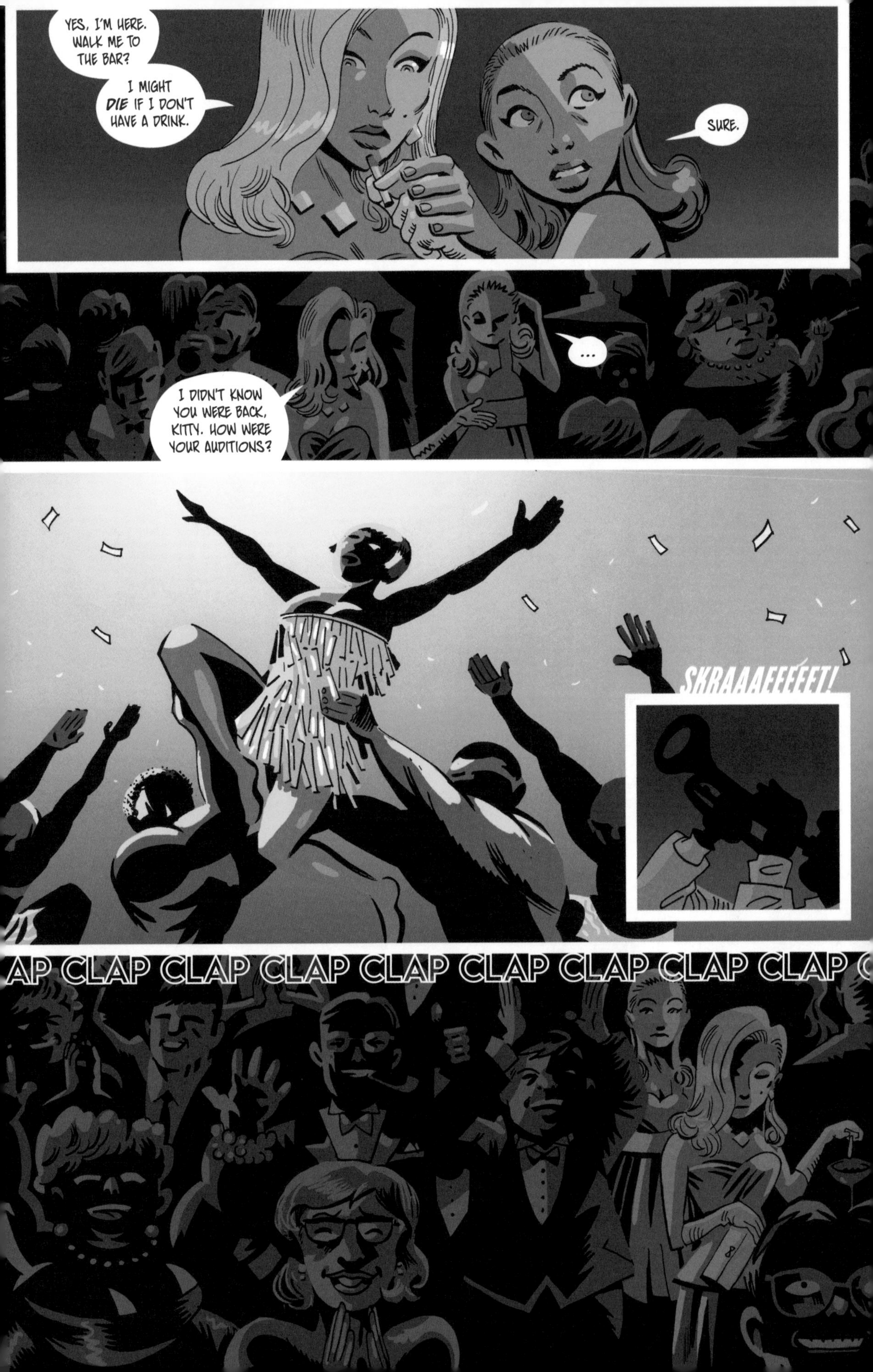
YES, I'M HERE. WALK ME TO THE BAR?
I MIGHT *DIE* IF I DON'T HAVE A DRINK.
SURE.
I DIDN'T KNOW YOU WERE BACK, KITTY. HOW WERE YOUR AUDITIONS?
...
SKRAAAAEEEEET!
AP CLAP CLAP CLAP CLAP CLAP CLAP CLAP CLAP

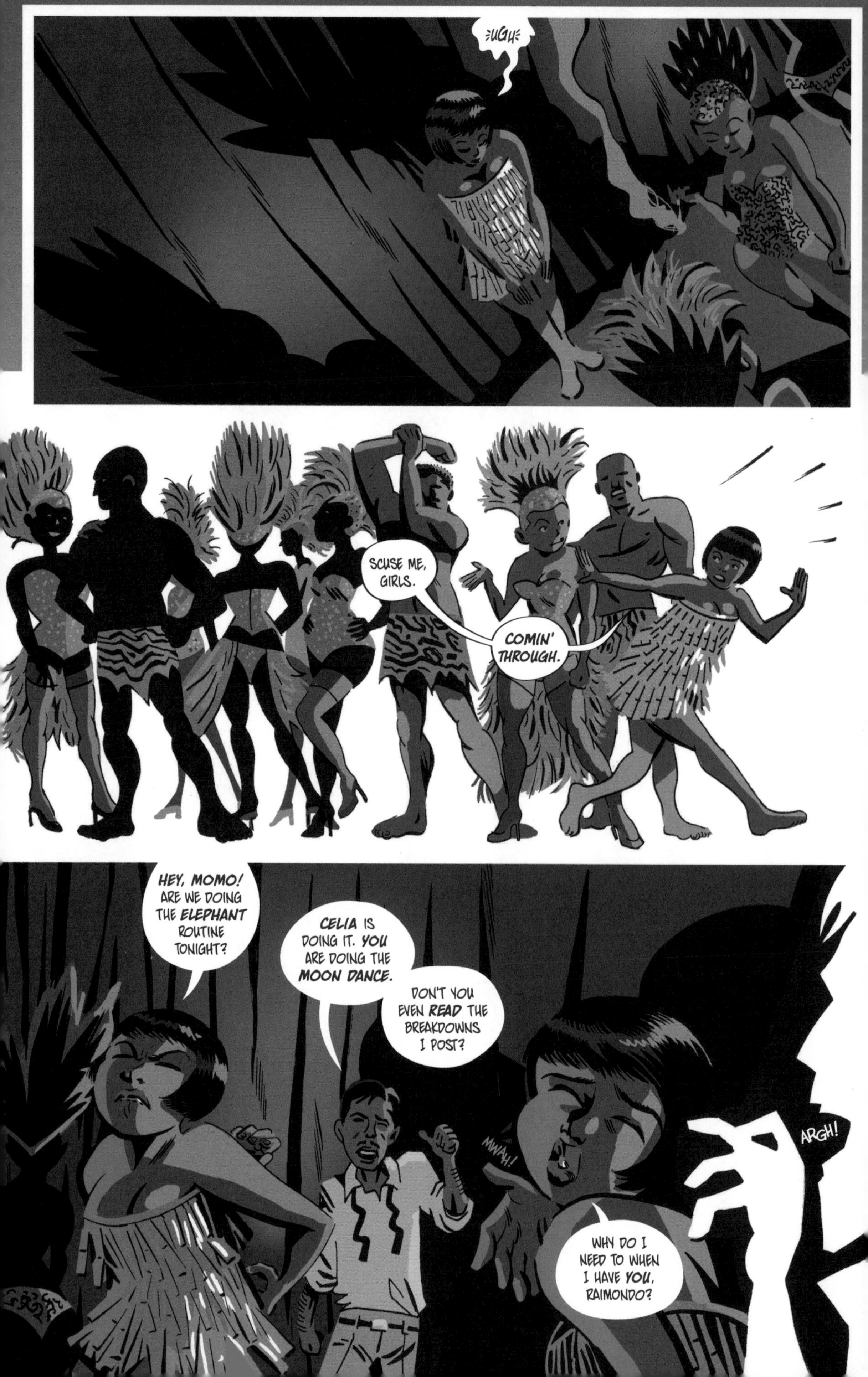
UGH
SCUSE ME, GIRLS.
COMIN' THROUGH.
HEY, MOMO! ARE WE DOING THE ELEPHANT ROUTINE TONIGHT?
CELIA IS DOING IT. YOU ARE DOING THE MOON DANCE.
DON'T YOU EVEN READ THE BREAKDOWNS I POST?
MWAH!
ARGH!
WHY DO I NEED TO WHEN I HAVE YOU, RAIMONDO?

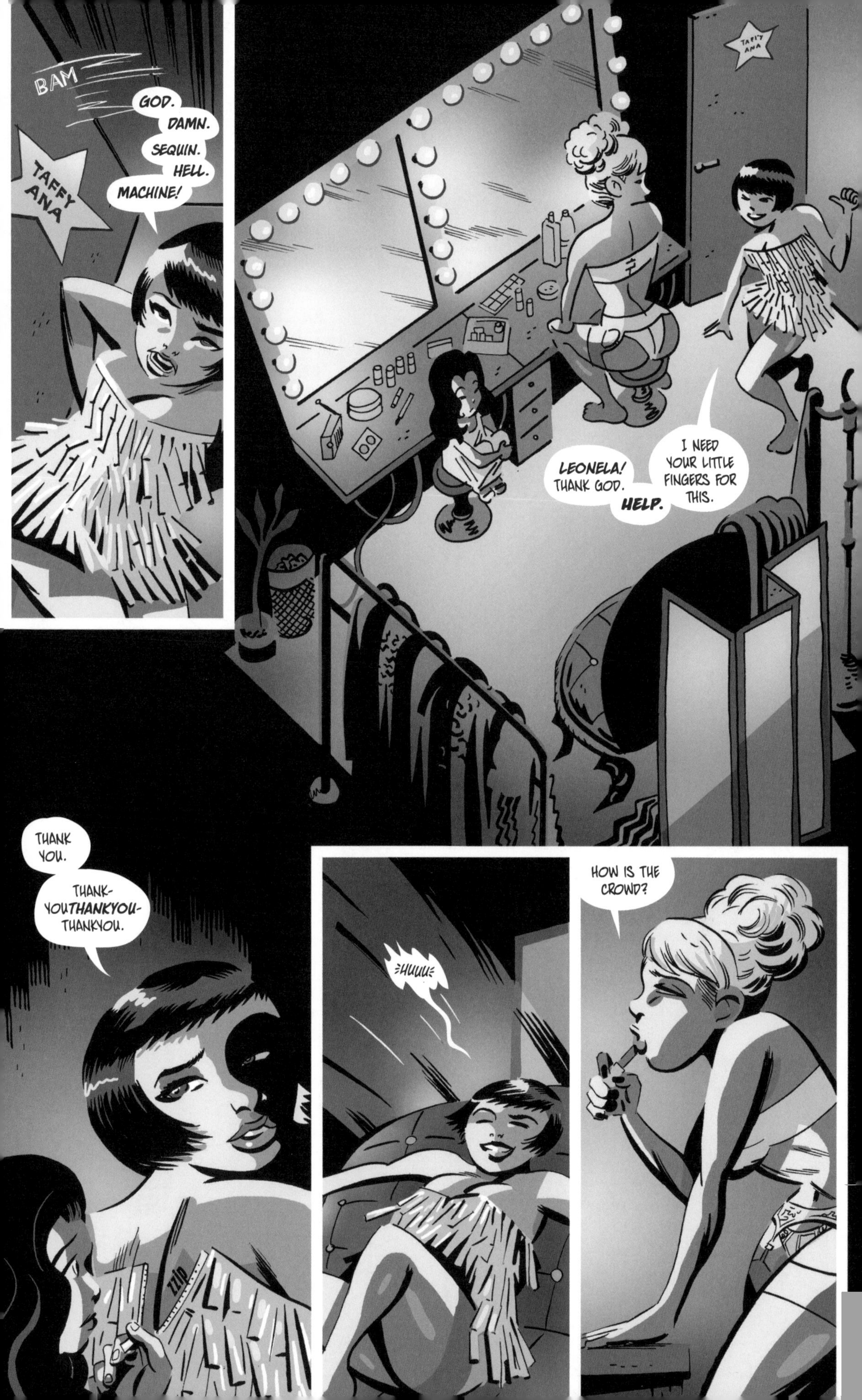
BAM
GOD.
DAMN.
SEQUIN.
HELL.
MACHINE!
TAFFY ANA
TAFFY ANA
LEONELA! THANK GOD.
HELP.
I NEED YOUR LITTLE FINGERS FOR THIS.
THANK YOU.
THANK-YOUTHANKYOU-THANKYOU.
ZZIP
HUUU
HOW IS THE CROWD?

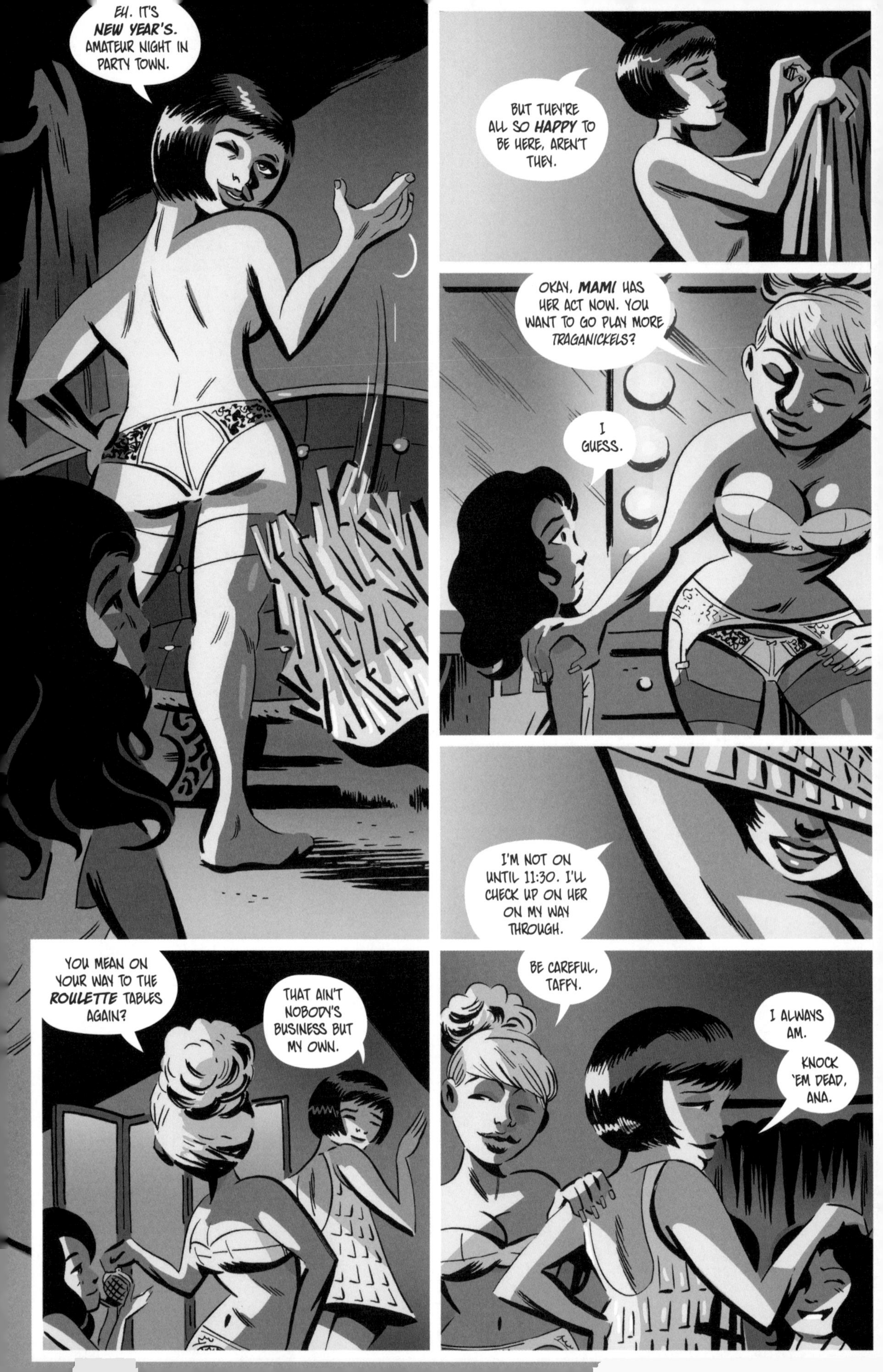

EH. IT'S NEW YEAR'S. AMATEUR NIGHT IN PARTY TOWN.
BUT THEY'RE ALL SO HAPPY TO BE HERE, AREN'T THEY.
OKAY, MAMI HAS HER ACT NOW. YOU WANT TO GO PLAY MORE TRAGANICKELS?
I GUESS.
I'M NOT ON UNTIL 11:30. I'LL CHECK UP ON HER ON MY WAY THROUGH.
YOU MEAN ON YOUR WAY TO THE ROULETTE TABLES AGAIN?
THAT AIN'T NOBODY'S BUSINESS BUT MY OWN.
BE CAREFUL, TAFFY.
I ALWAYS AM.
KNOCK 'EM DEAD, ANA.

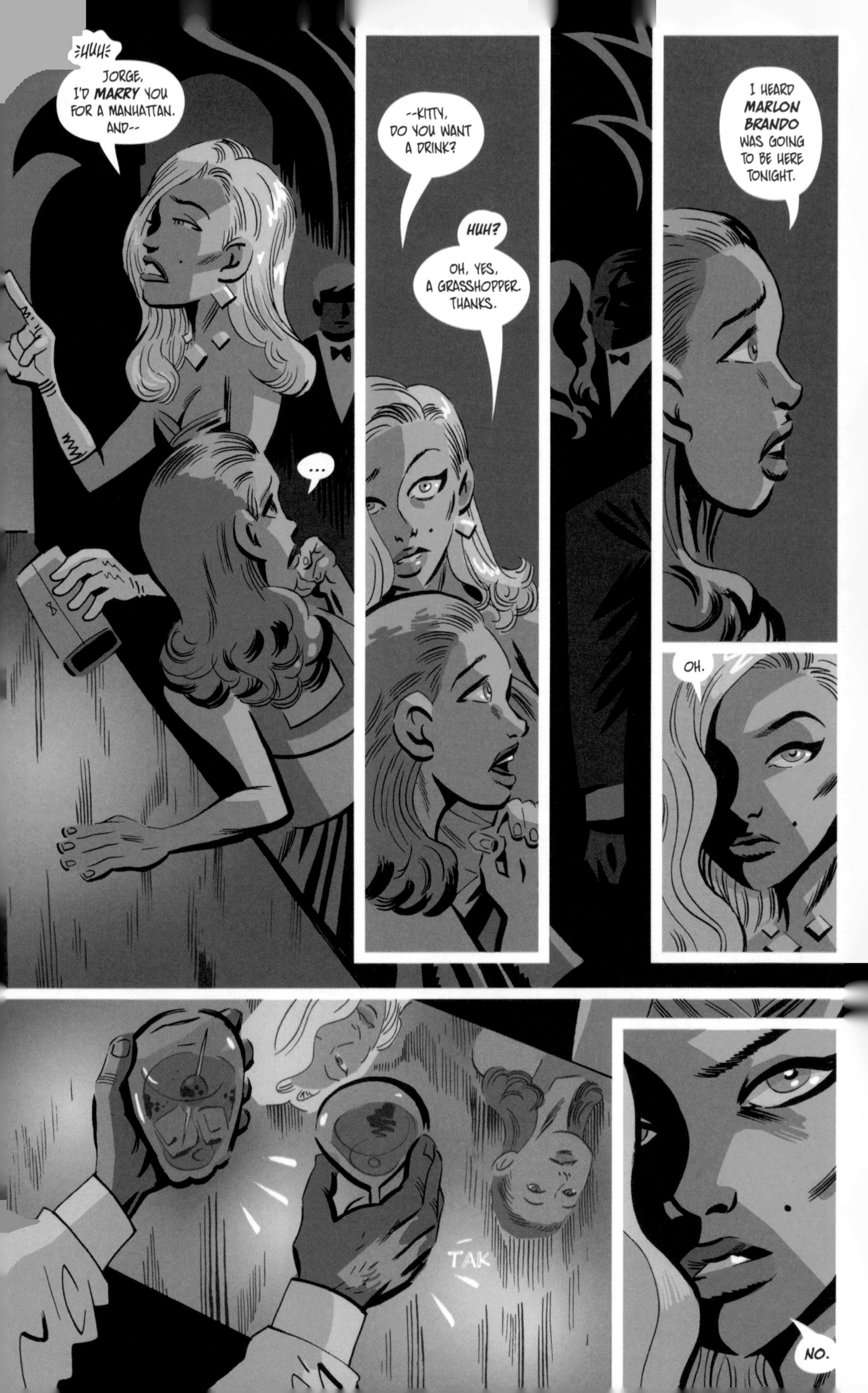
HUH
JORGE, I'D MARRY YOU FOR A MANHATTAN. AND--
...
--KITTY, DO YOU WANT A DRINK?
HUH?
OH, YES, A GRASSHOPPER. THANKS.
I HEARD MARLON BRANDO WAS GOING TO BE HERE TONIGHT.
OH.
TAK
NO.

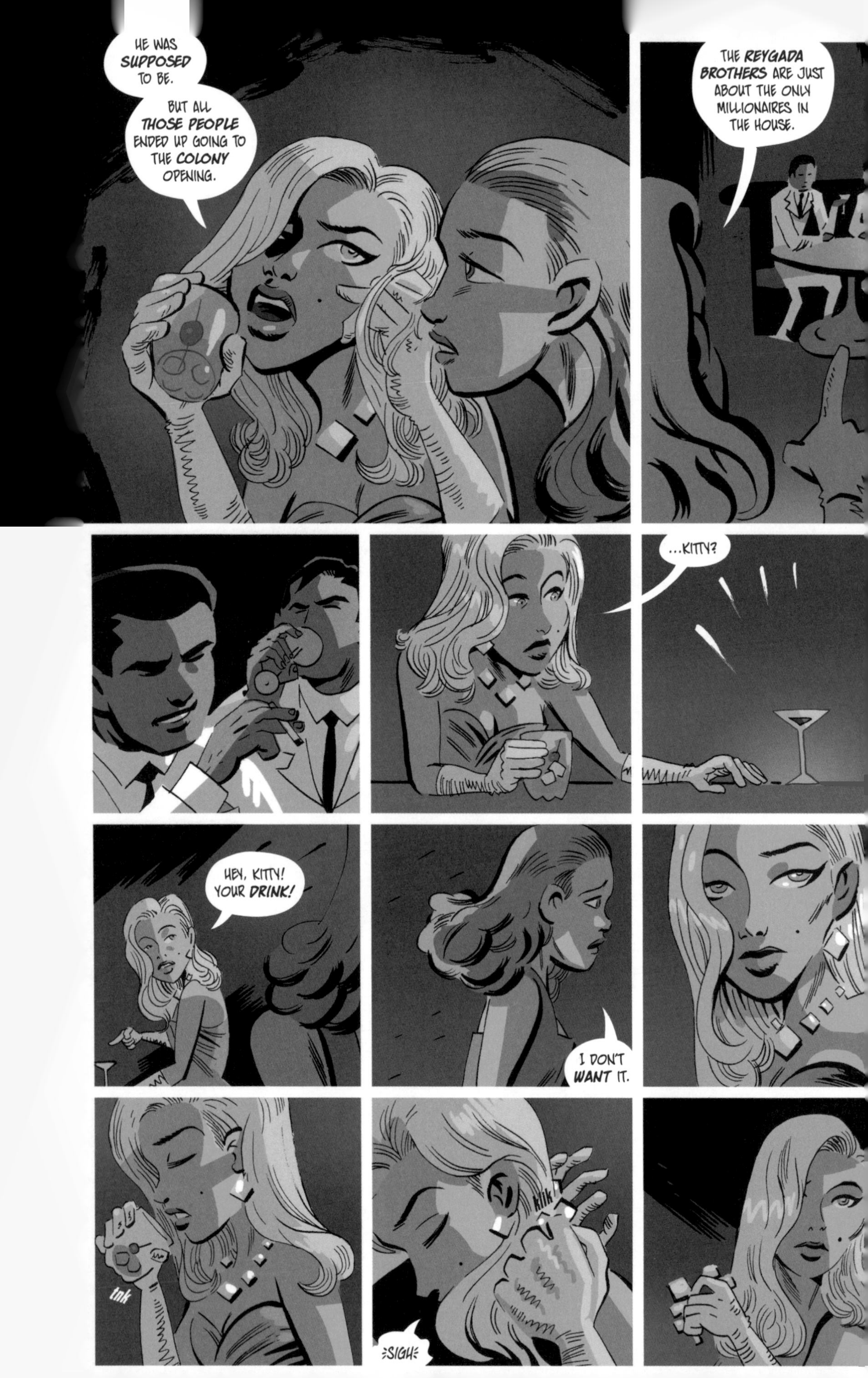
HE WAS SUPPOSED TO BE.
BUT ALL THOSE PEOPLE ENDED UP GOING TO THE COLONY OPENING.
THE REYGADA BROTHERS ARE JUST ABOUT THE ONLY MILLIONAIRES IN THE HOUSE.
...KITTY?
HEY, KITTY! YOUR DRINK!
I DON'T WANT IT.
klik
SIGH
tnk

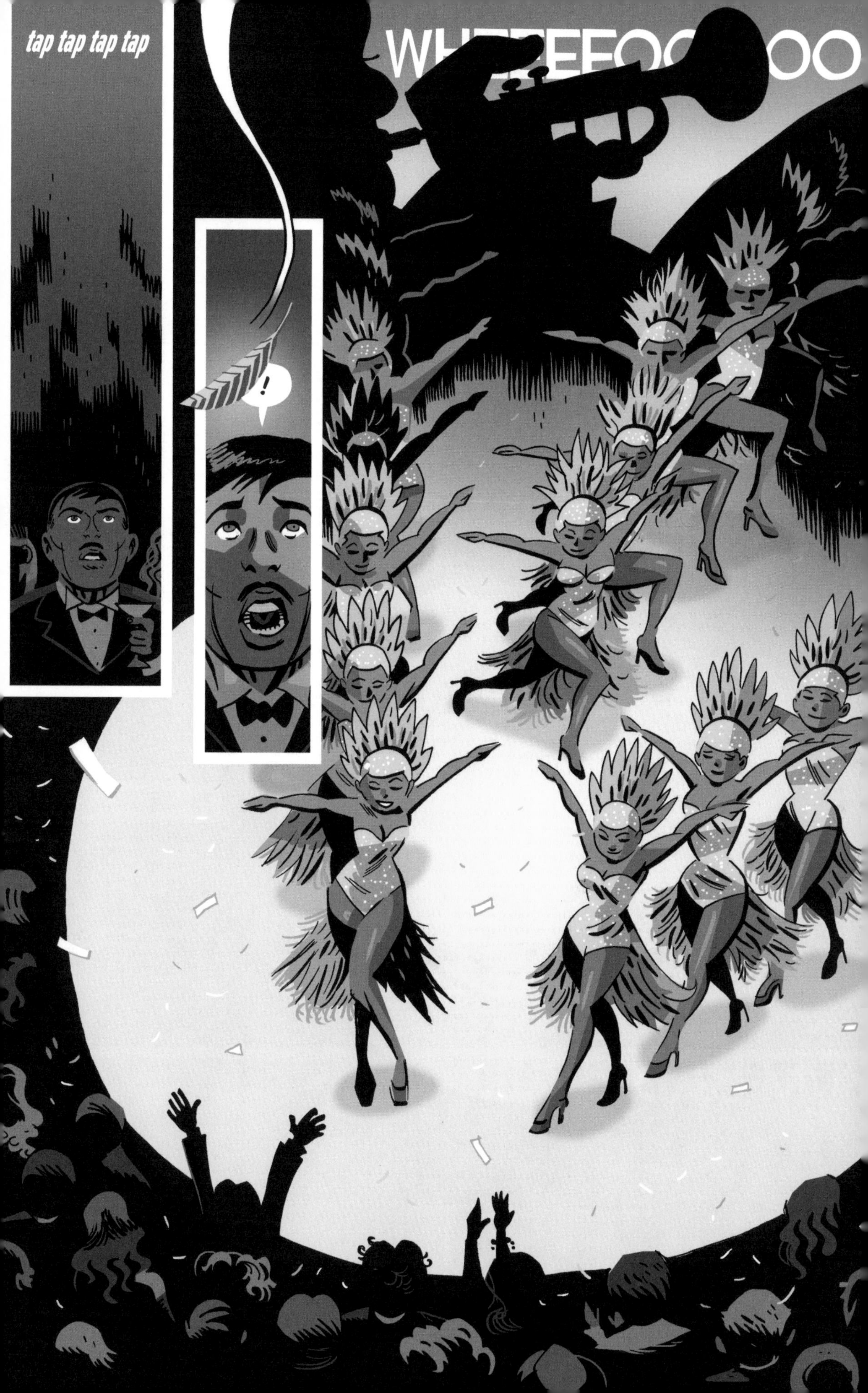

tap tap tap tap
!

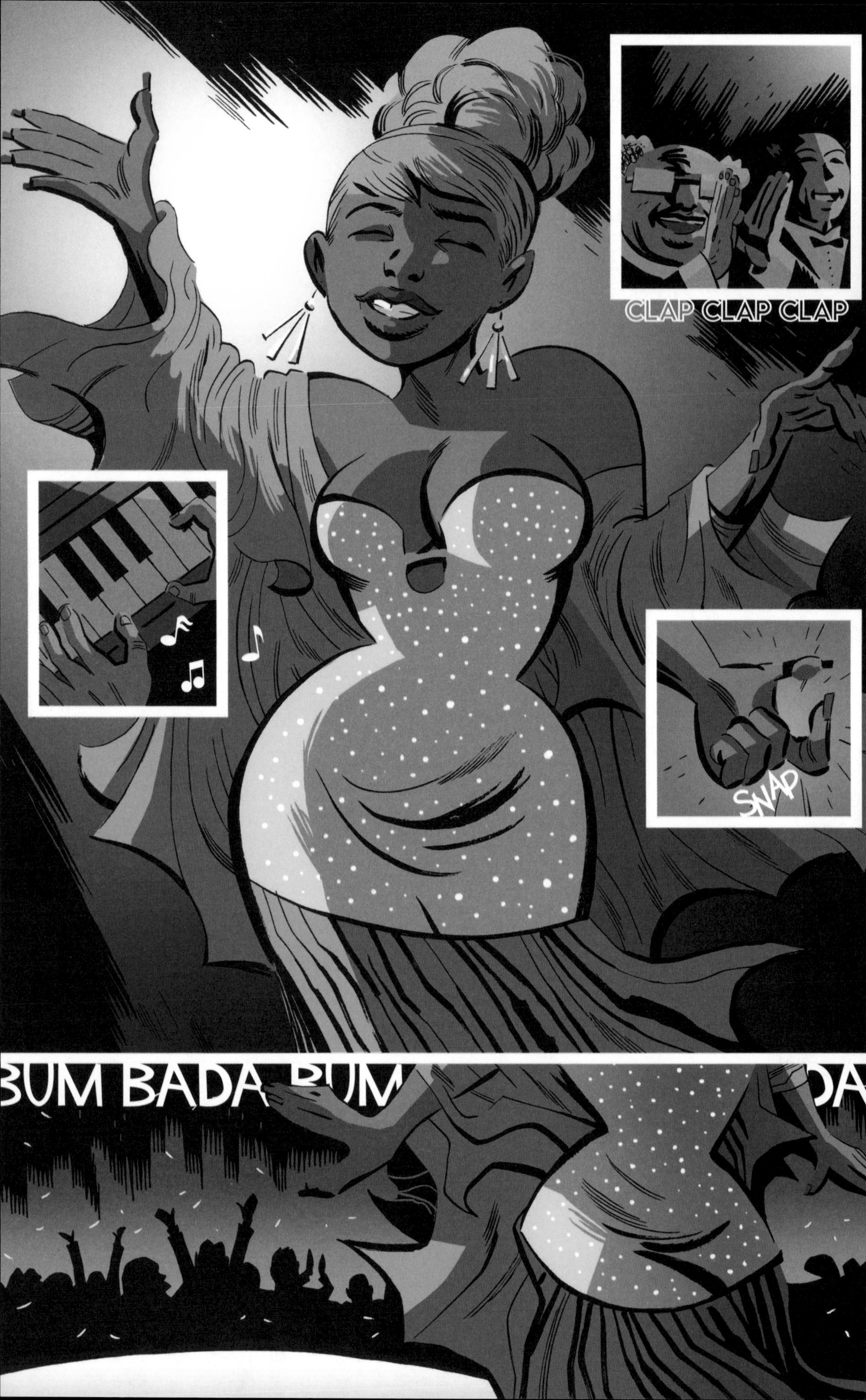
CLAP CLAP CLAP
SNAP
BUM BADA BUM
DA

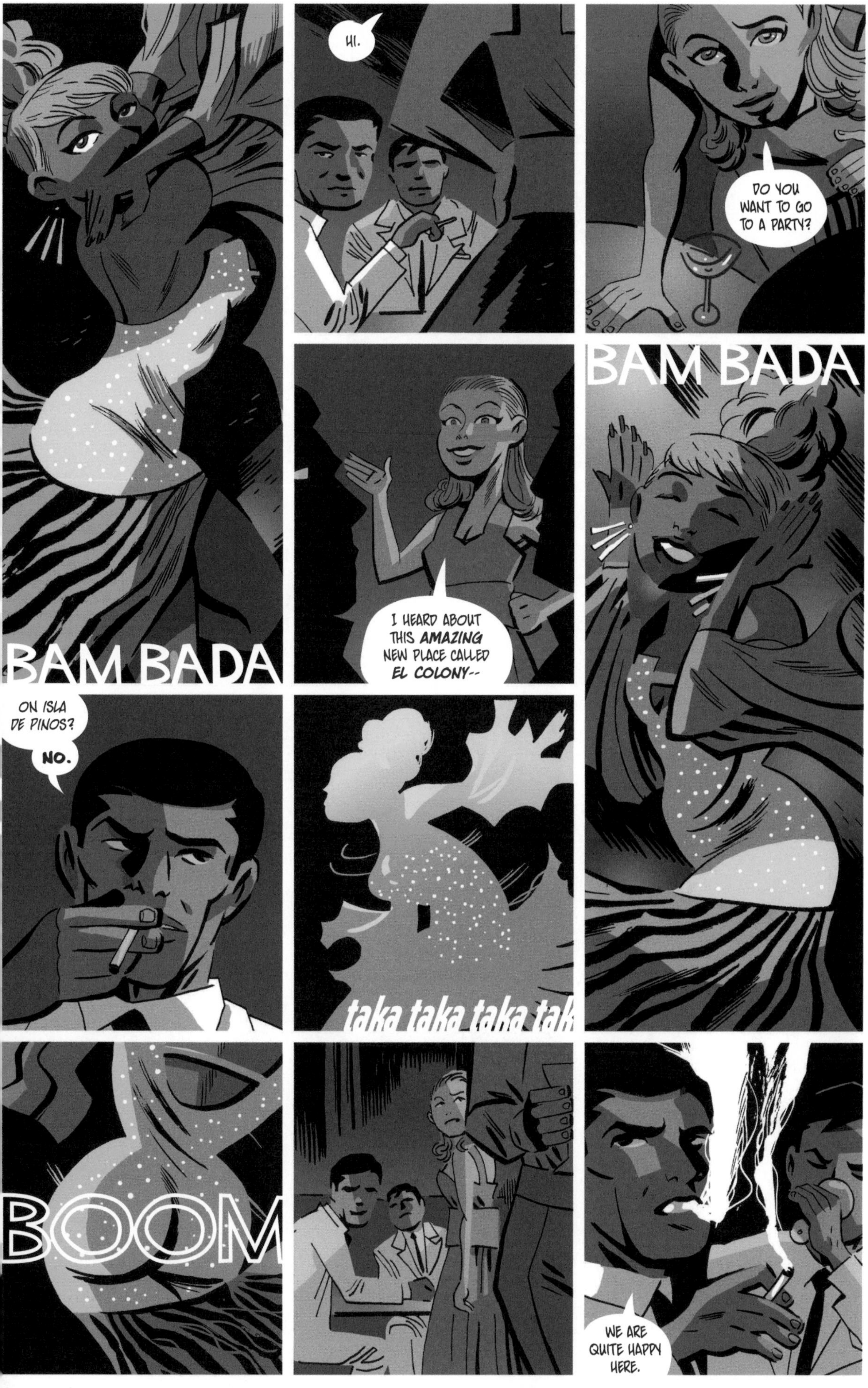
BAM BADA
HI.
DO YOU WANT TO GO TO A PARTY?
I HEARD ABOUT THIS **AMAZING** NEW PLACE CALLED ***EL COLONY***--
BAM BADA
ON ISLA DE PINOS?
NO.
taka taka taka tak
BOOM
WE ARE QUITE HAPPY HERE.

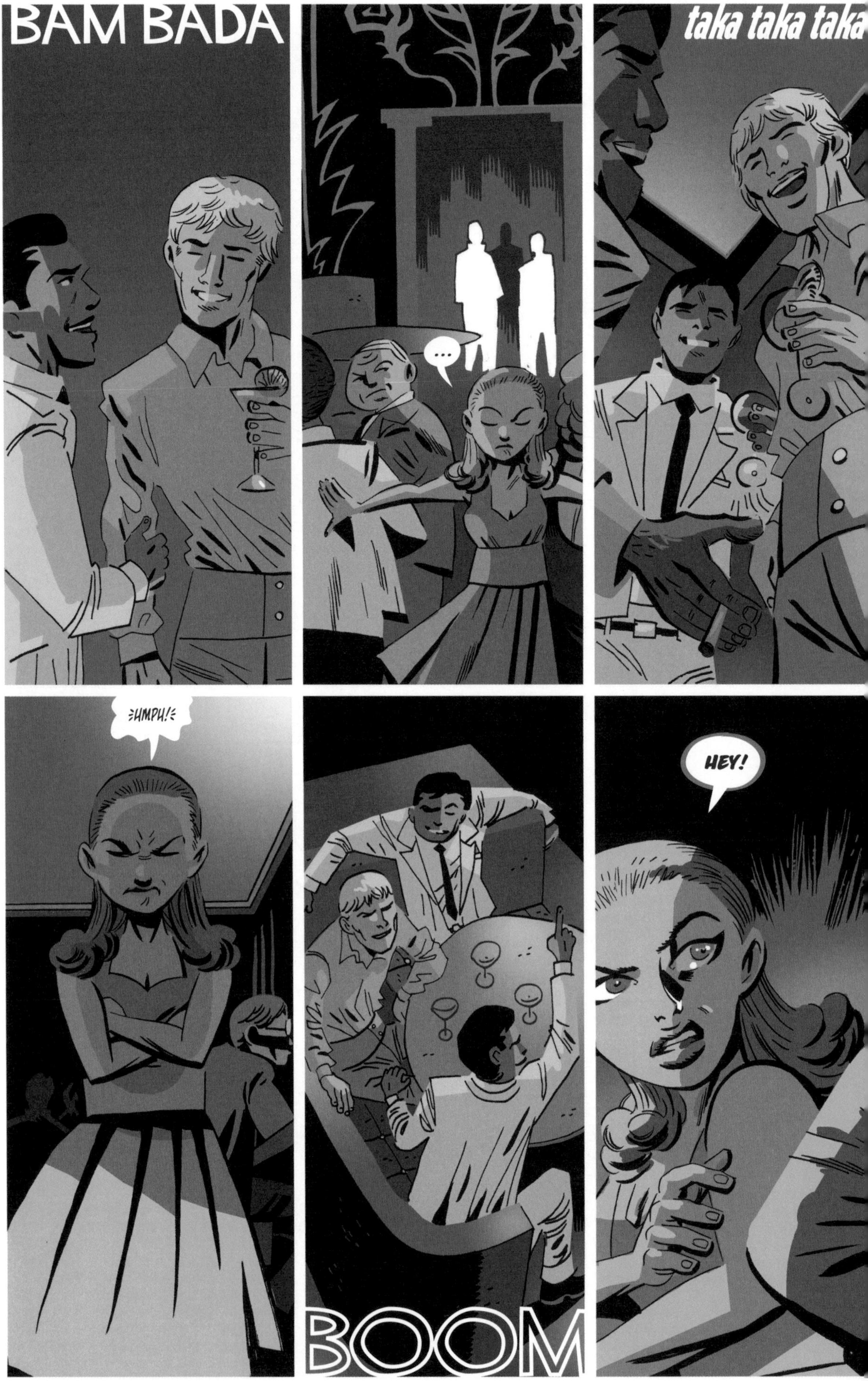
BAM BADA
...
taka taka taka
HUMPH!
BOOM
HEY!

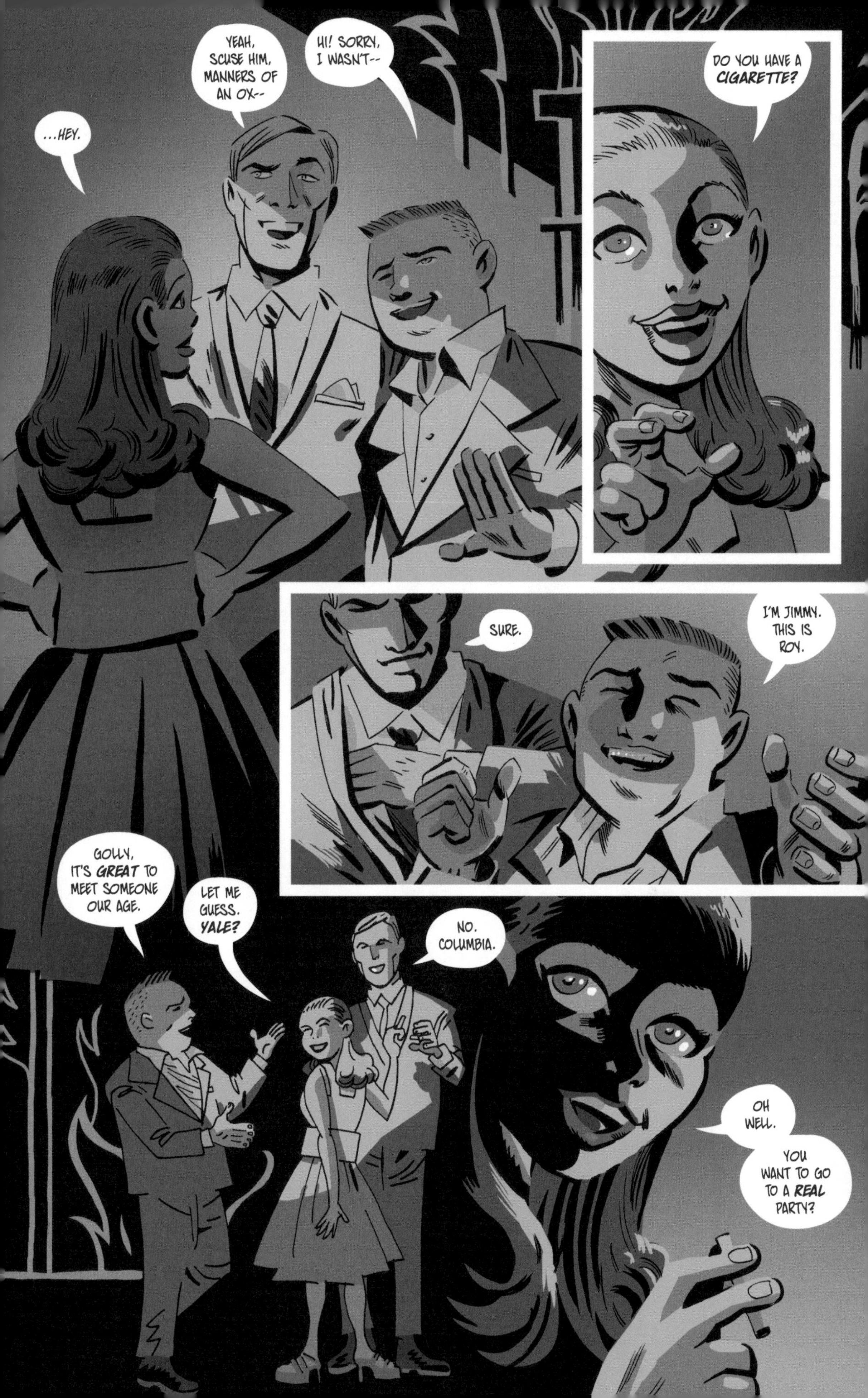
...HEY.
YEAH, SCUSE HIM, MANNERS OF AN OX--
HI! SORRY, I WASN'T--
DO YOU HAVE A CIGARETTE?
SURE.
I'M JIMMY. THIS IS ROY.
GOLLY, IT'S GREAT TO MEET SOMEONE OUR AGE.
LET ME GUESS. YALE?
NO. COLUMBIA.
OH WELL.
YOU WANT TO GO TO A REAL PARTY?

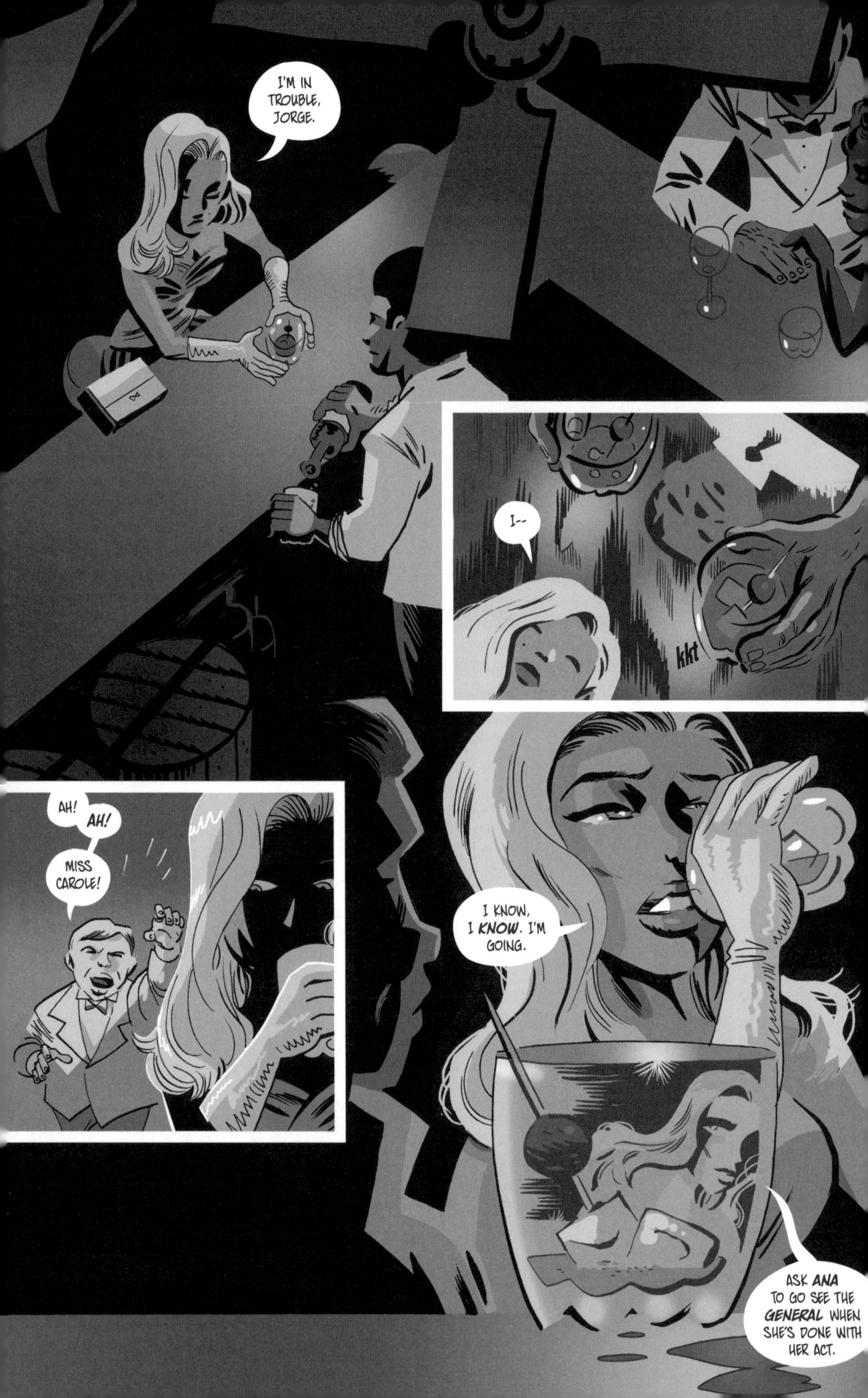
I'M IN TROUBLE, JORGE.
I--
kkt
AH! AH!
MISS CAROLE!
I KNOW, I KNOW. I'M GOING.
ASK ANA TO GO SEE THE GENERAL WHEN SHE'S DONE WITH HER ACT.

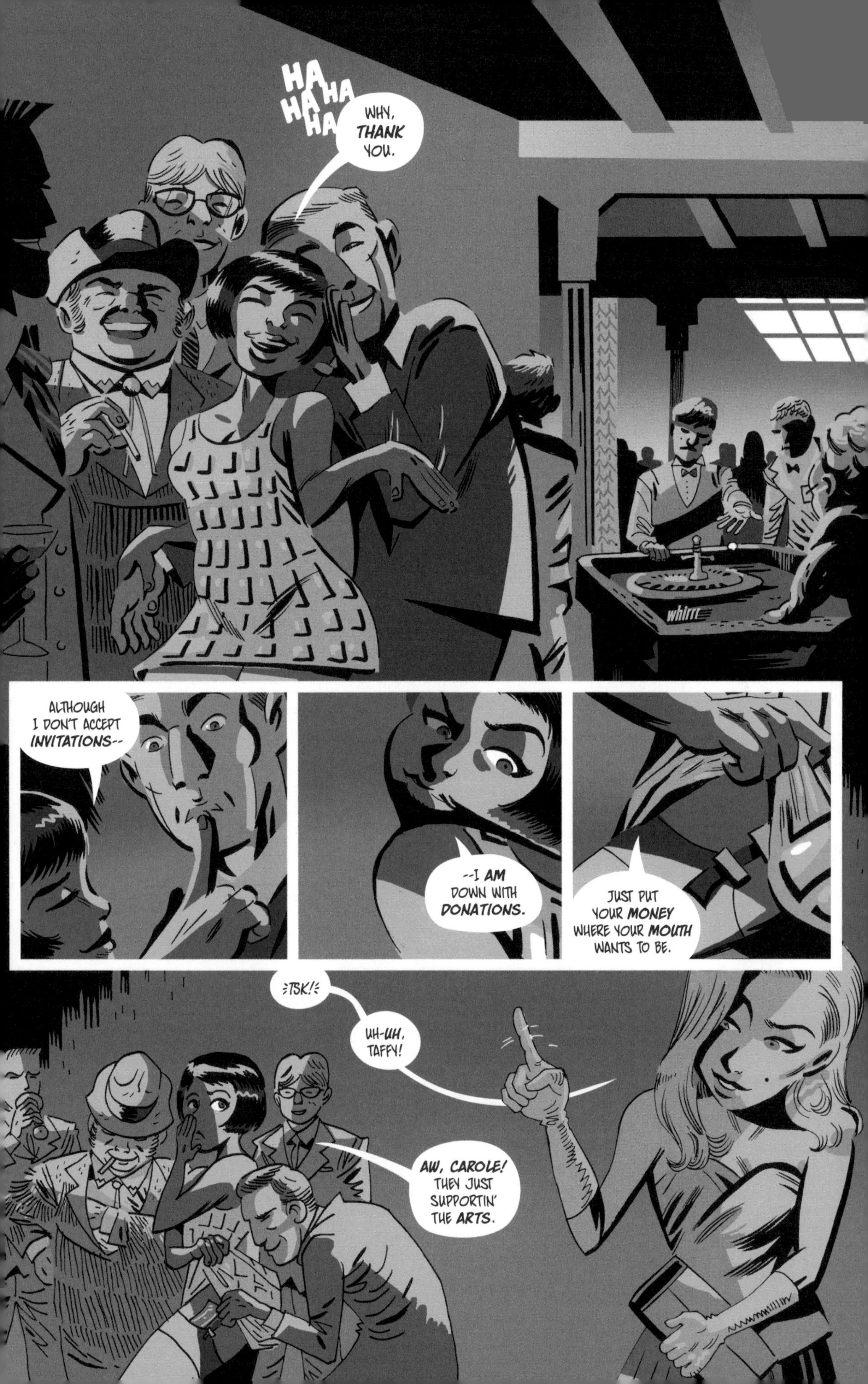
HA HA HA HA
WHY, THANK YOU.
whirr
ALTHOUGH I DON'T ACCEPT INVITATIONS--
--I AM DOWN WITH DONATIONS.
JUST PUT YOUR MONEY WHERE YOUR MOUTH WANTS TO BE.
TSK!
UH-UH, TAFFY!
AW, CAROLE! THEY JUST SUPPORTIN' THE ARTS.

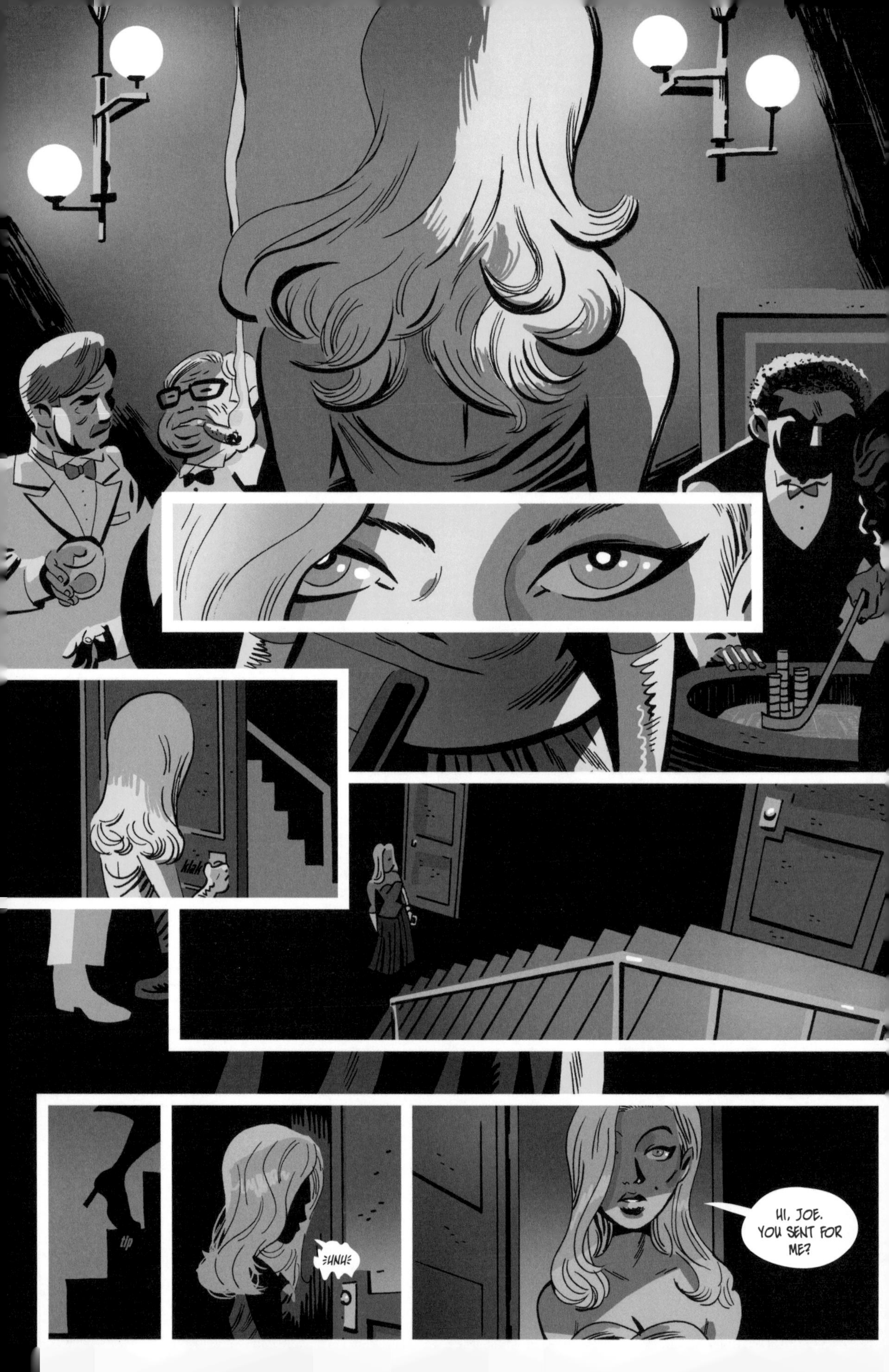
klak
tip
=HNH=
HI, JOE. YOU SENT FOR ME?

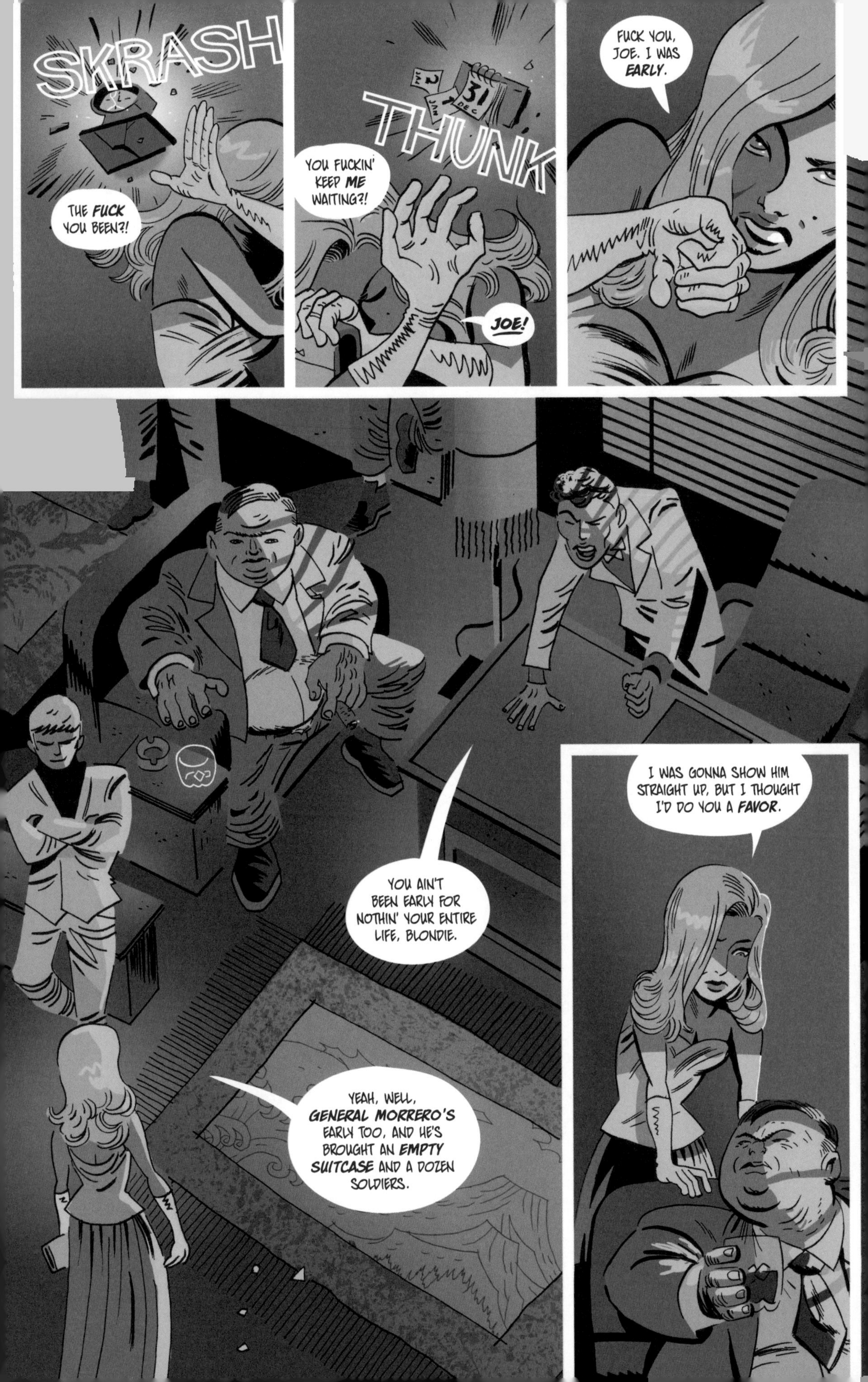
SKRASH
THE FUCK YOU BEEN?!
THUNK
YOU FUCKIN' KEEP ME WAITING?!
JOE!
FUCK YOU, JOE. I WAS EARLY.
YOU AIN'T BEEN EARLY FOR NOTHIN' YOUR ENTIRE LIFE, BLONDIE.
YEAH, WELL, GENERAL MORRERO'S EARLY TOO, AND HE'S BROUGHT AN EMPTY SUITCASE AND A DOZEN SOLDIERS.
I WAS GONNA SHOW HIM STRAIGHT UP, BUT I THOUGHT I'D DO YOU A FAVOR.

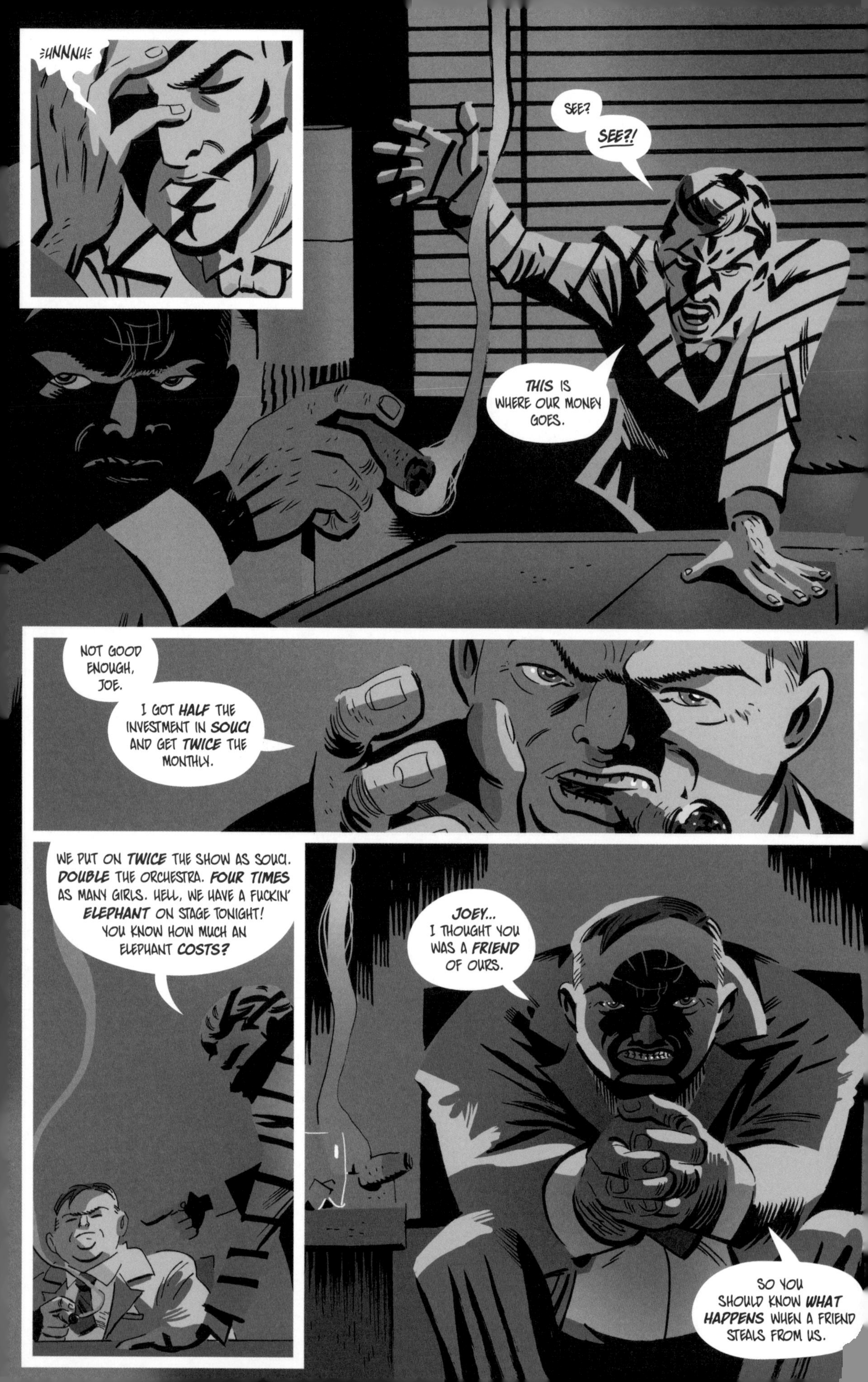
UHNNNH
SEE?
SEE?!
THIS IS WHERE OUR MONEY GOES.
NOT GOOD ENOUGH, JOE.
I GOT HALF THE INVESTMENT IN SOUCI AND GET TWICE THE MONTHLY.
WE PUT ON TWICE THE SHOW AS SOUCI. DOUBLE THE ORCHESTRA. FOUR TIMES AS MANY GIRLS. HELL, WE HAVE A FUCKIN' ELEPHANT ON STAGE TONIGHT! YOU KNOW HOW MUCH AN ELEPHANT COSTS?
JOEY... I THOUGHT YOU WAS A FRIEND OF OURS.
SO YOU SHOULD KNOW WHAT HAPPENS WHEN A FRIEND STEALS FROM US.

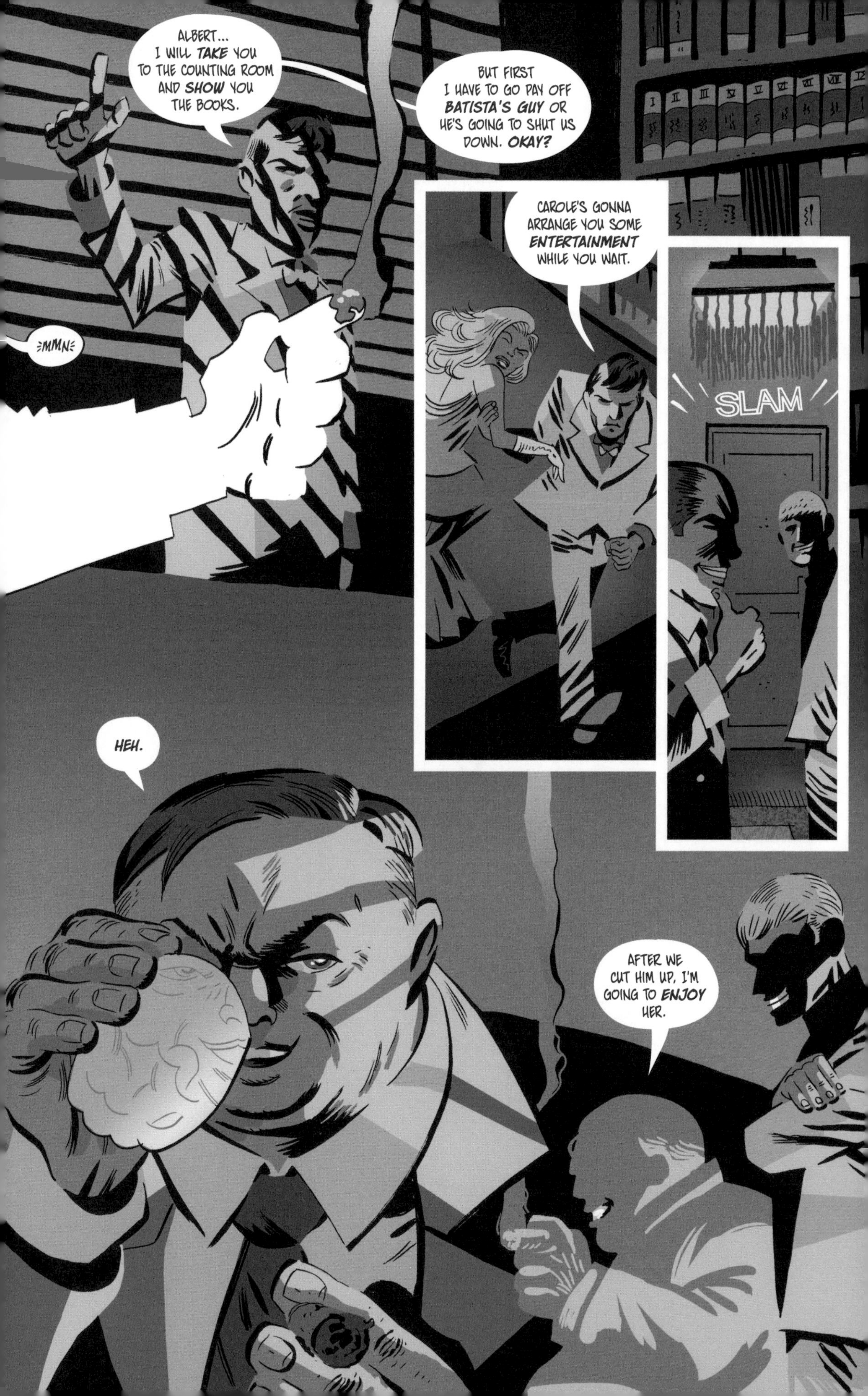
ALBERT... I WILL TAKE YOU TO THE COUNTING ROOM AND SHOW YOU THE BOOKS.
BUT FIRST I HAVE TO GO PAY OFF BATISTA'S GUY OR HE'S GOING TO SHUT US DOWN. OKAY?
MMN
CAROLE'S GONNA ARRANGE YOU SOME ENTERTAINMENT WHILE YOU WAIT.
SLAM
HEH.
AFTER WE CUT HIM UP, I'M GOING TO ENJOY HER.

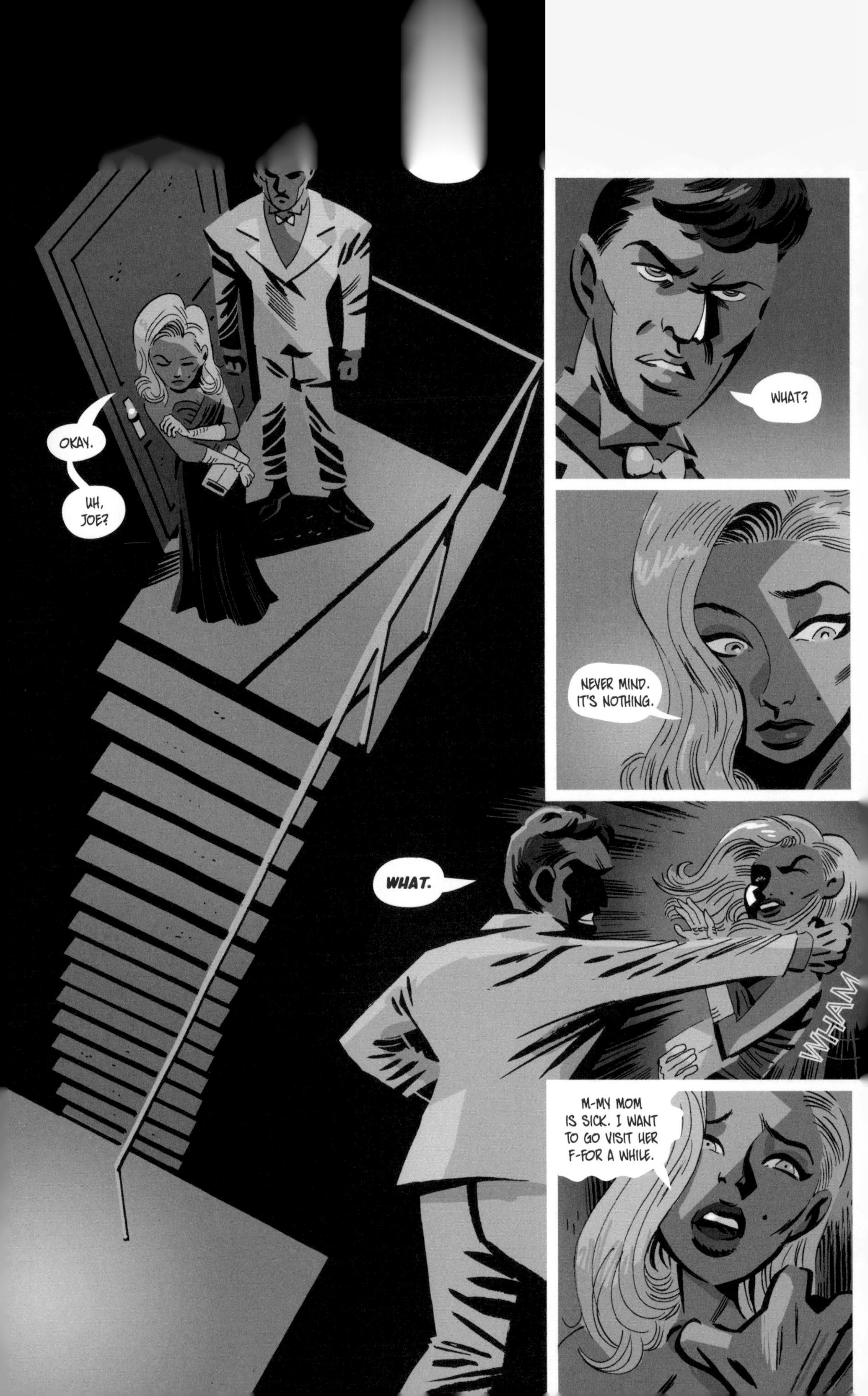
OKAY.
UH, JOE?
WHAT?
NEVER MIND. IT'S NOTHING.
WHAT.
WHAM
M-MY MOM IS SICK. I WANT TO GO VISIT HER F-FOR A WHILE.

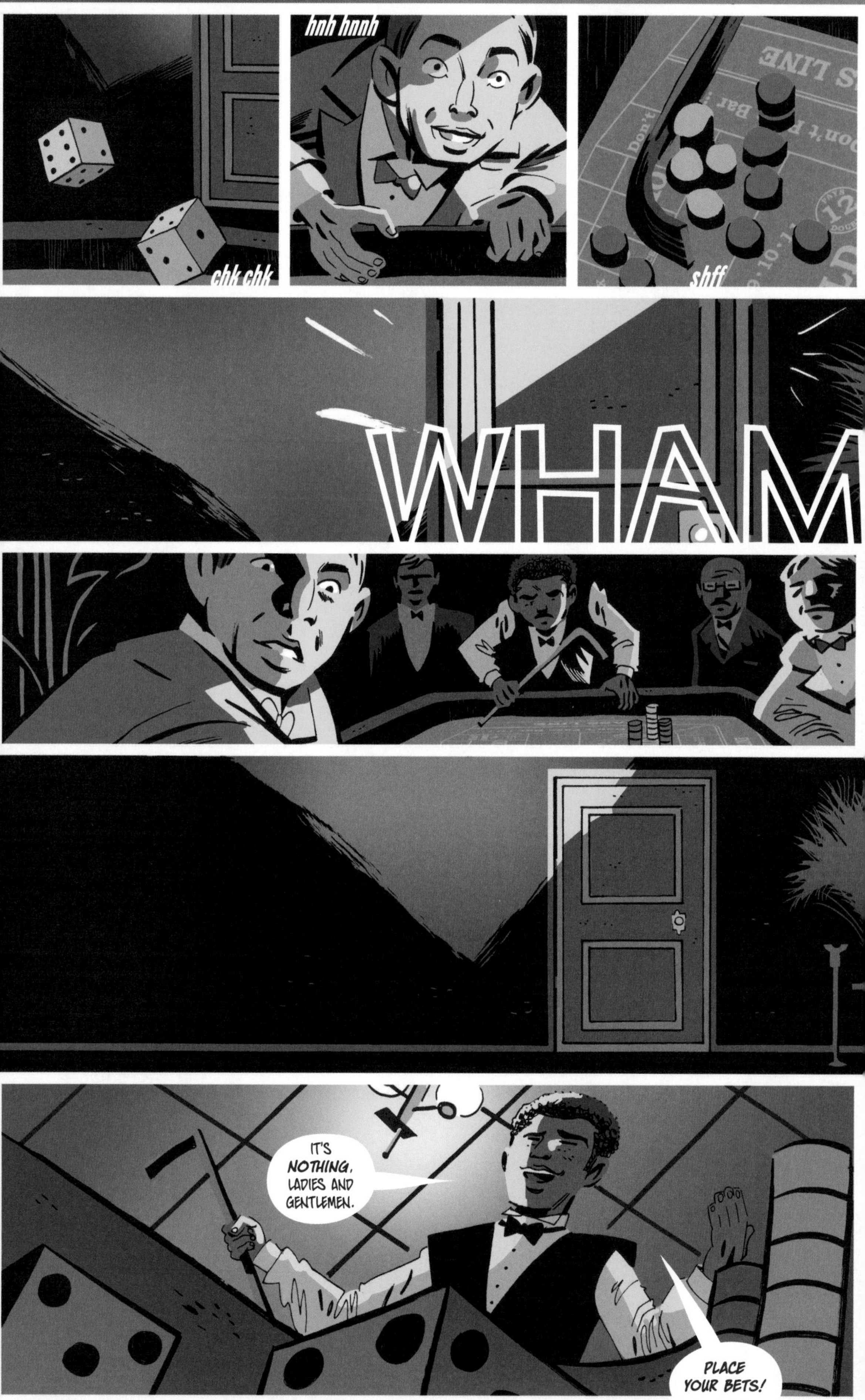
chk chk
hnh hnnh
shff
WHAM
IT'S NOTHING, LADIES AND GENTLEMEN.
PLACE YOUR BETS!

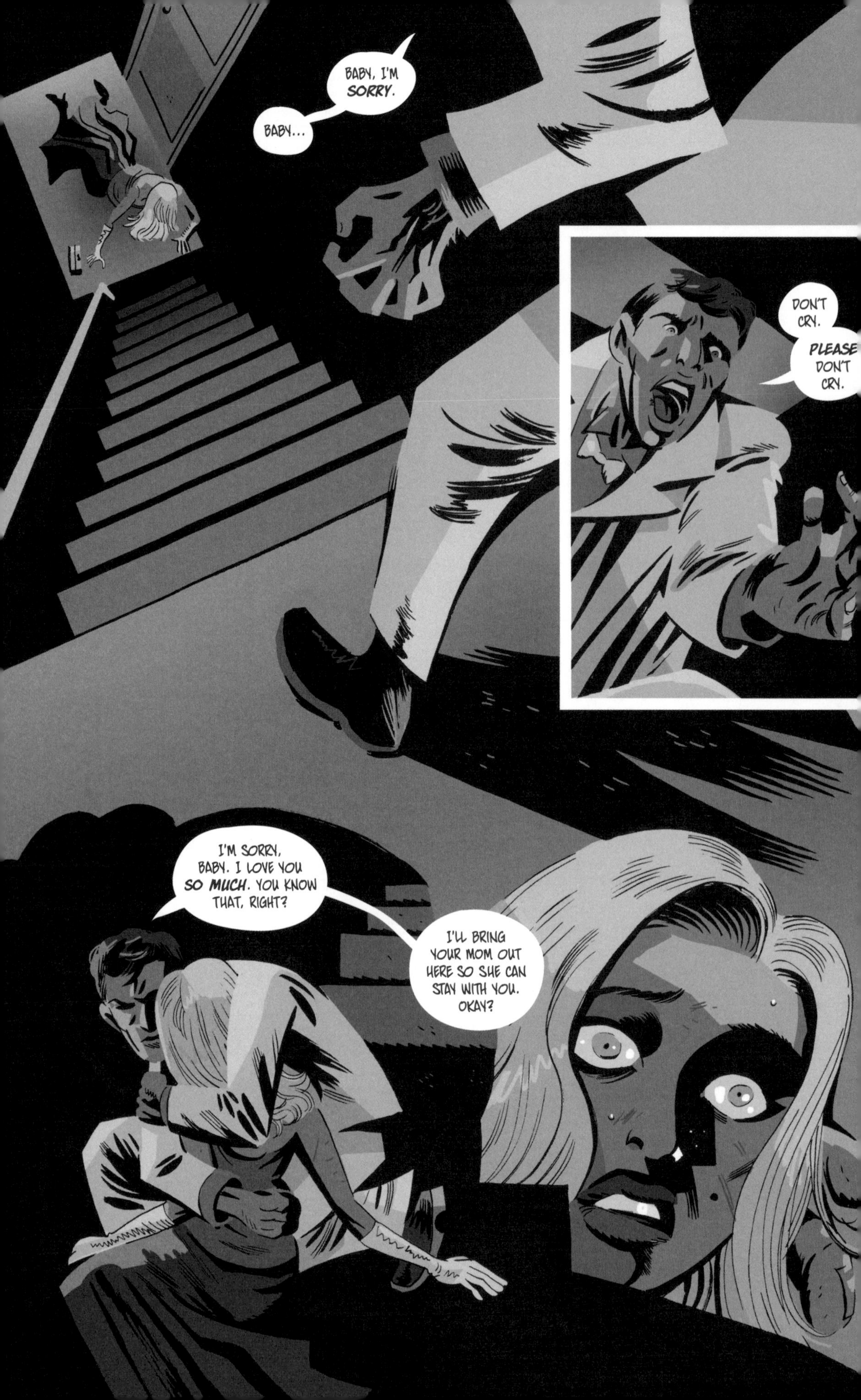
BABY, I'M SORRY.
BABY...
DON'T CRY.
PLEASE DON'T CRY.
I'M SORRY, BABY. I LOVE YOU SO MUCH. YOU KNOW THAT, RIGHT?
I'LL BRING YOUR MOM OUT HERE SO SHE CAN STAY WITH YOU. OKAY?

9:00 P.M.

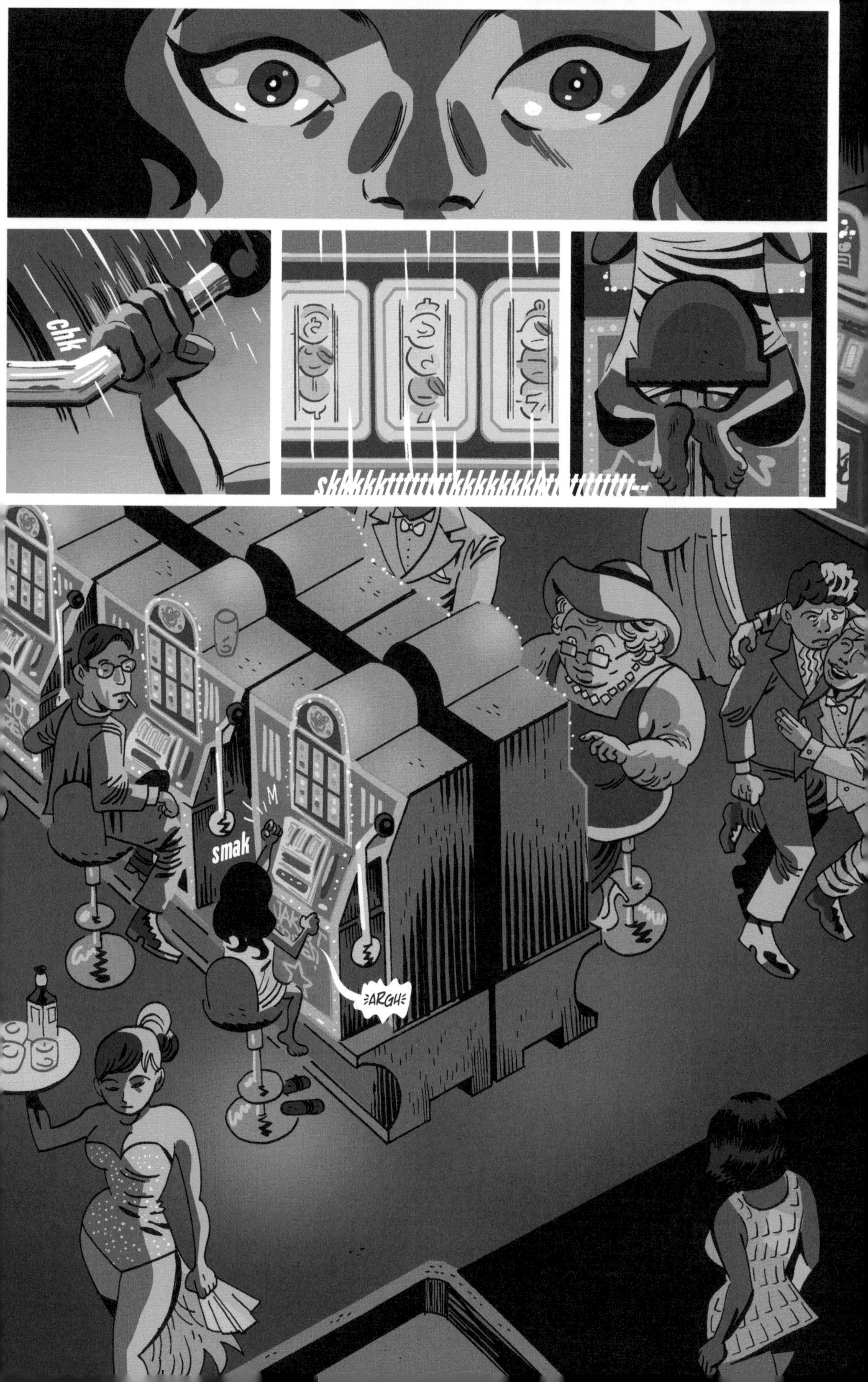
chk
skkkkttttttttkkkkkkkkttttttttt--
smak
ARGH

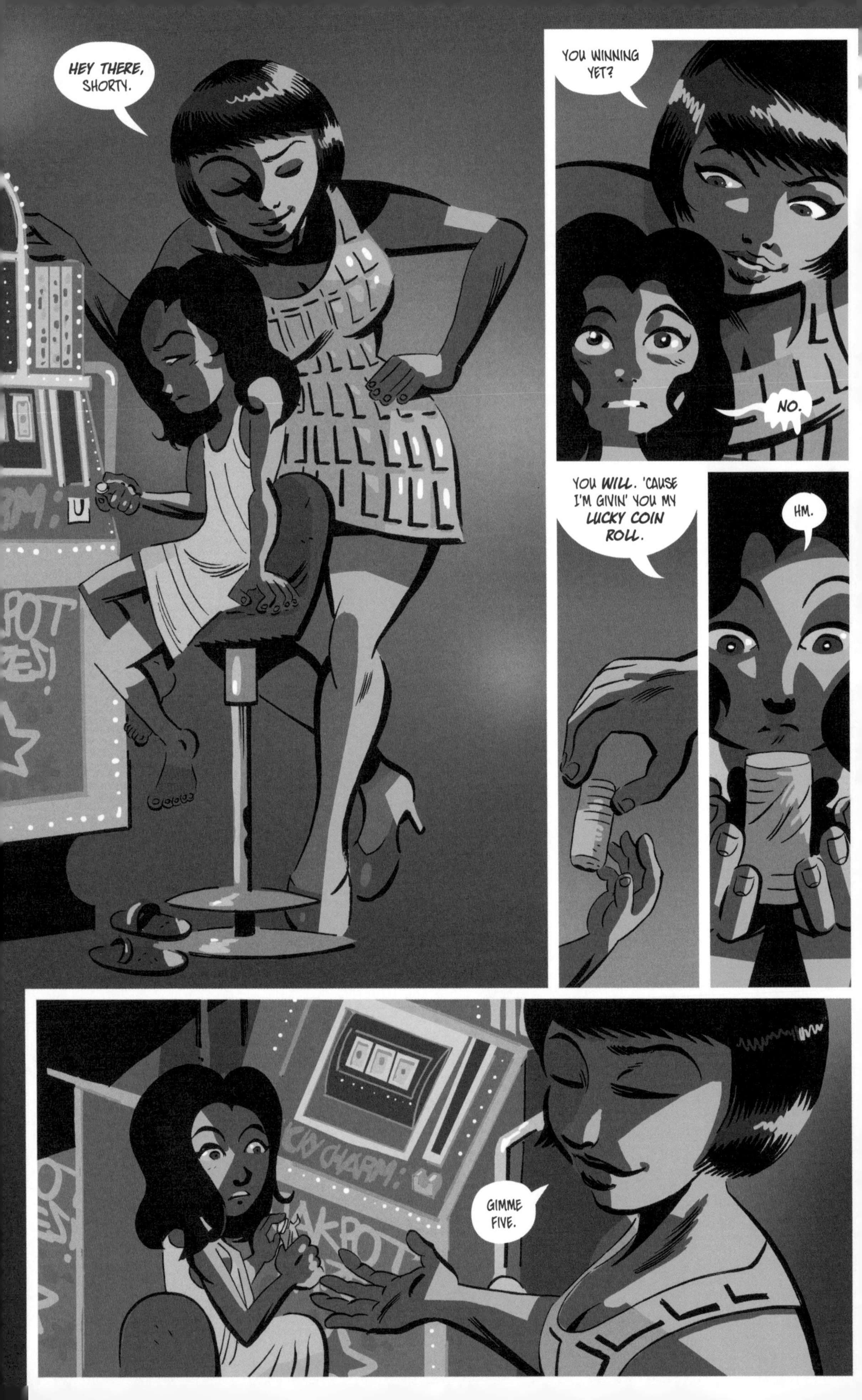
HEY THERE, SHORTY.
YOU WINNING YET?
NO.
YOU WILL. 'CAUSE I'M GIVIN' YOU MY LUCKY COIN ROLL.
HM.
GIMME FIVE.

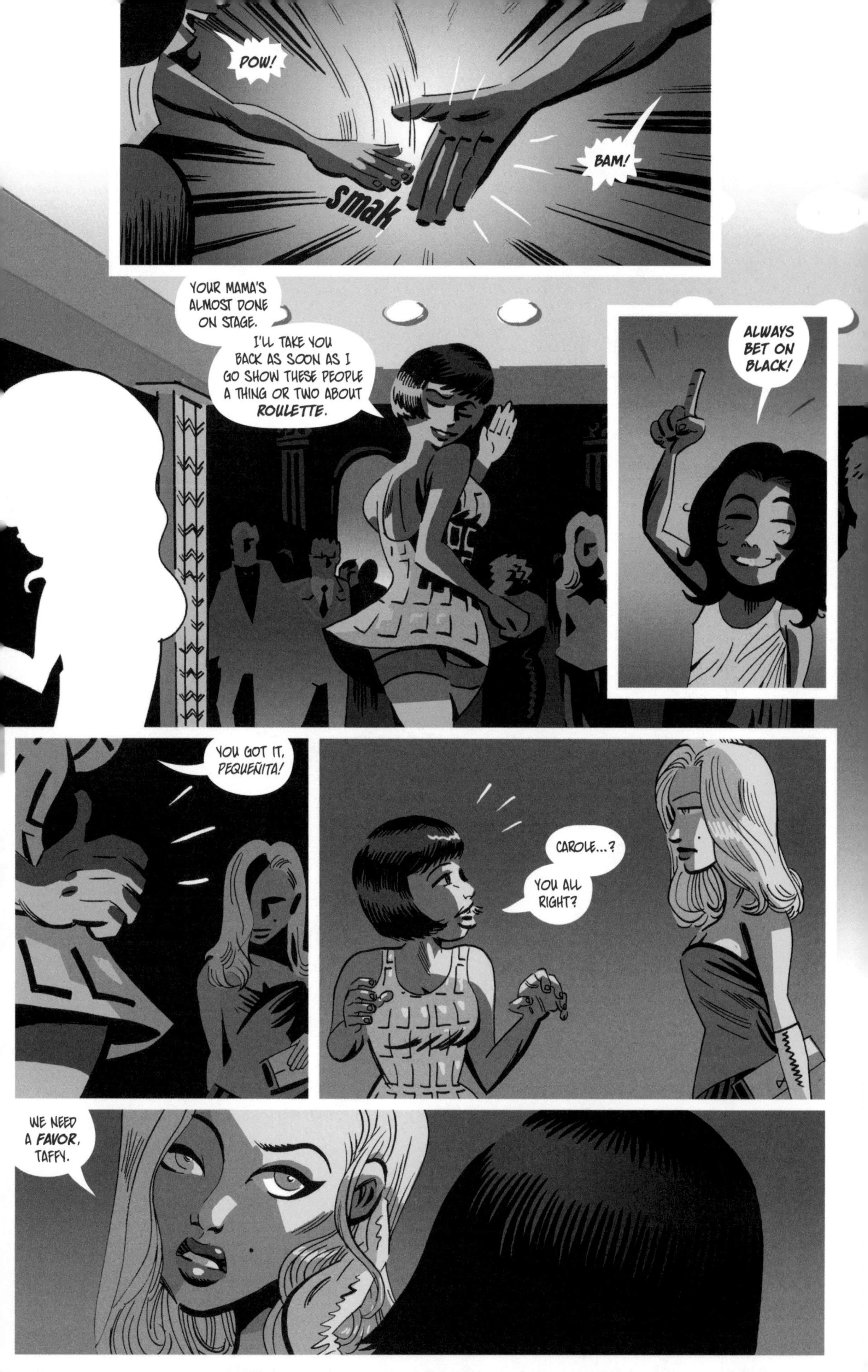
POW!
SMAK
BAM!
YOUR MAMA'S ALMOST DONE ON STAGE.
I'LL TAKE YOU BACK AS SOON AS I GO SHOW THESE PEOPLE A THING OR TWO ABOUT ROULETTE.
ALWAYS BET ON BLACK!
YOU GOT IT, PEQUEÑITA!
CAROLE...?
YOU ALL RIGHT?
WE NEED A FAVOR, TAFFY.

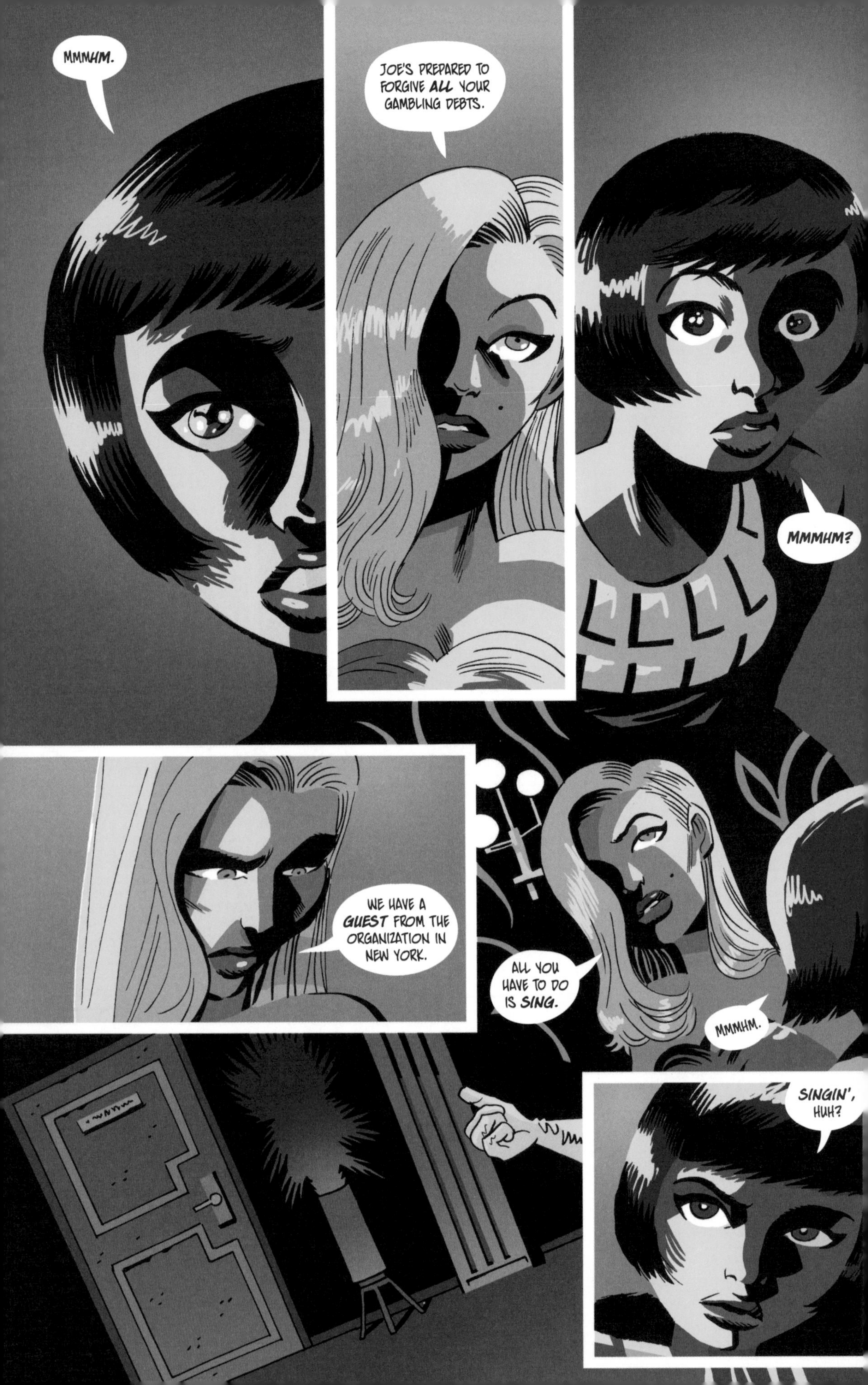
MMMHM.
JOE'S PREPARED TO FORGIVE ALL YOUR GAMBLING DEBTS.
MMMHM?
WE HAVE A GUEST FROM THE ORGANIZATION IN NEW YORK.
ALL YOU HAVE TO DO IS SING.
MMMHM.
SINGIN', HUH?

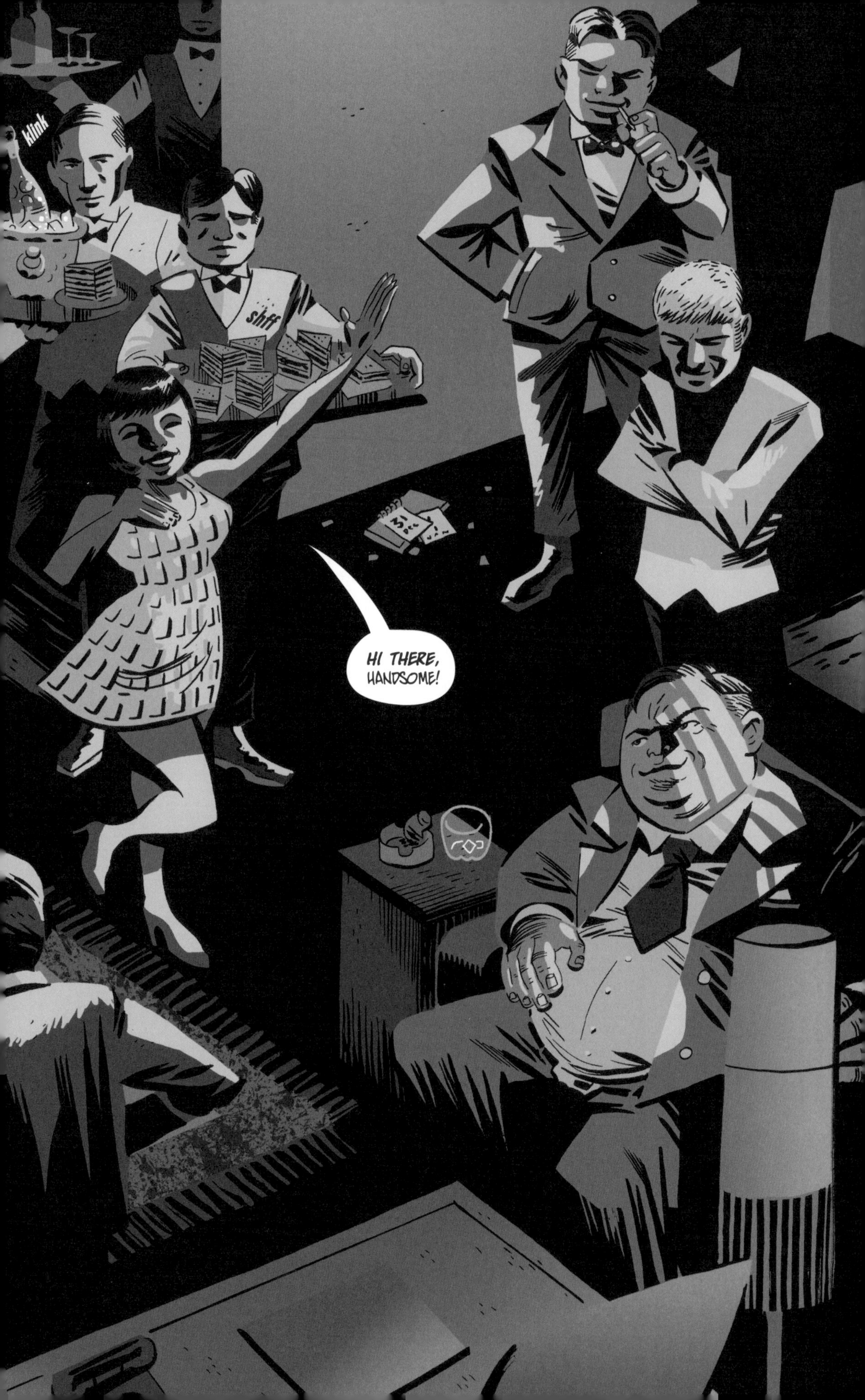
klink
shff
HI THERE, HANDSOME!

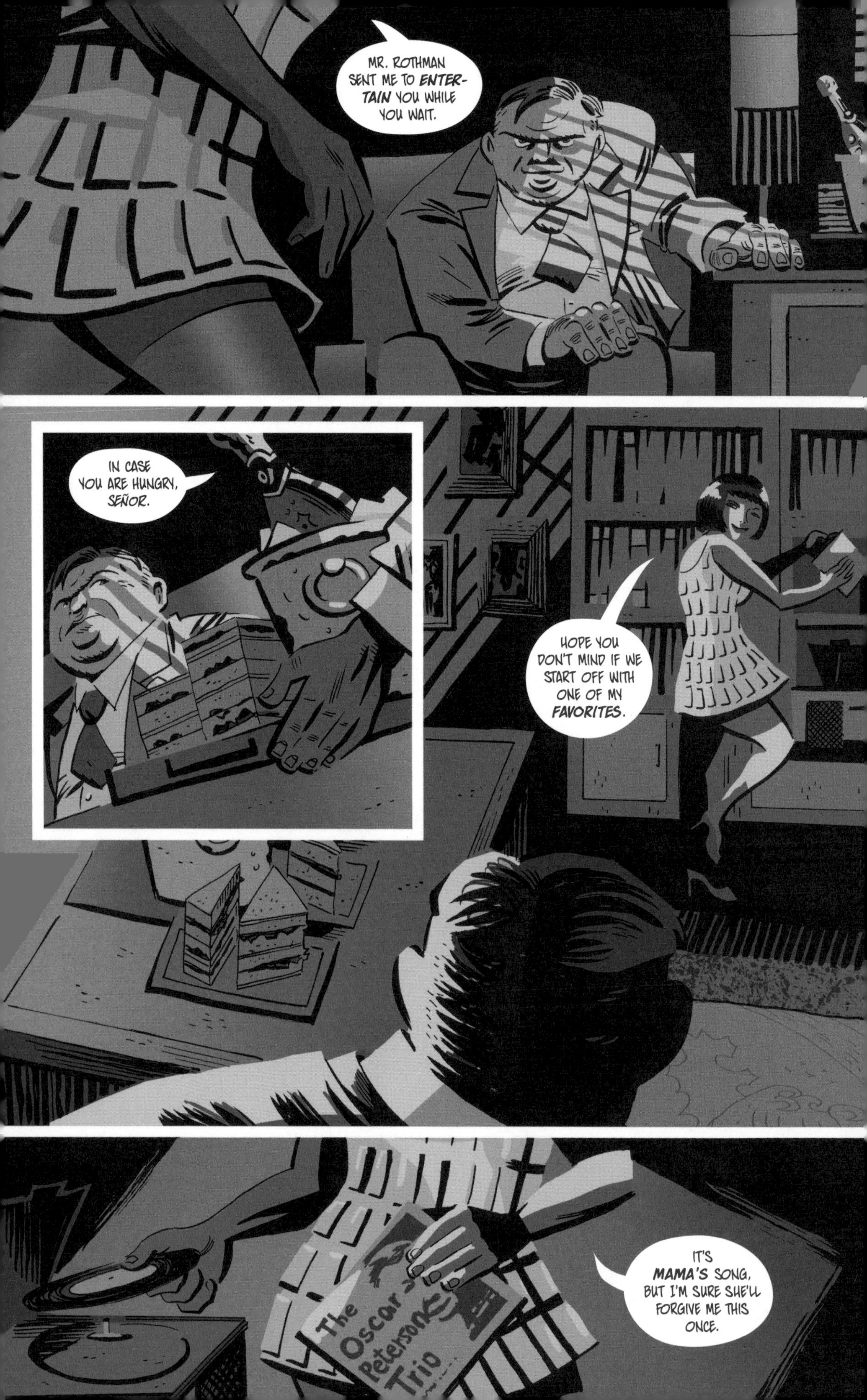
MR. ROTHMAN SENT ME TO ENTERTAIN YOU WHILE YOU WAIT.
IN CASE YOU ARE HUNGRY, SEÑOR.
HOPE YOU DON'T MIND IF WE START OFF WITH ONE OF MY FAVORITES.
The Oscar Peterson Trio
IT'S MAMA'S SONG, BUT I'M SURE SHE'LL FORGIVE ME THIS ONCE.

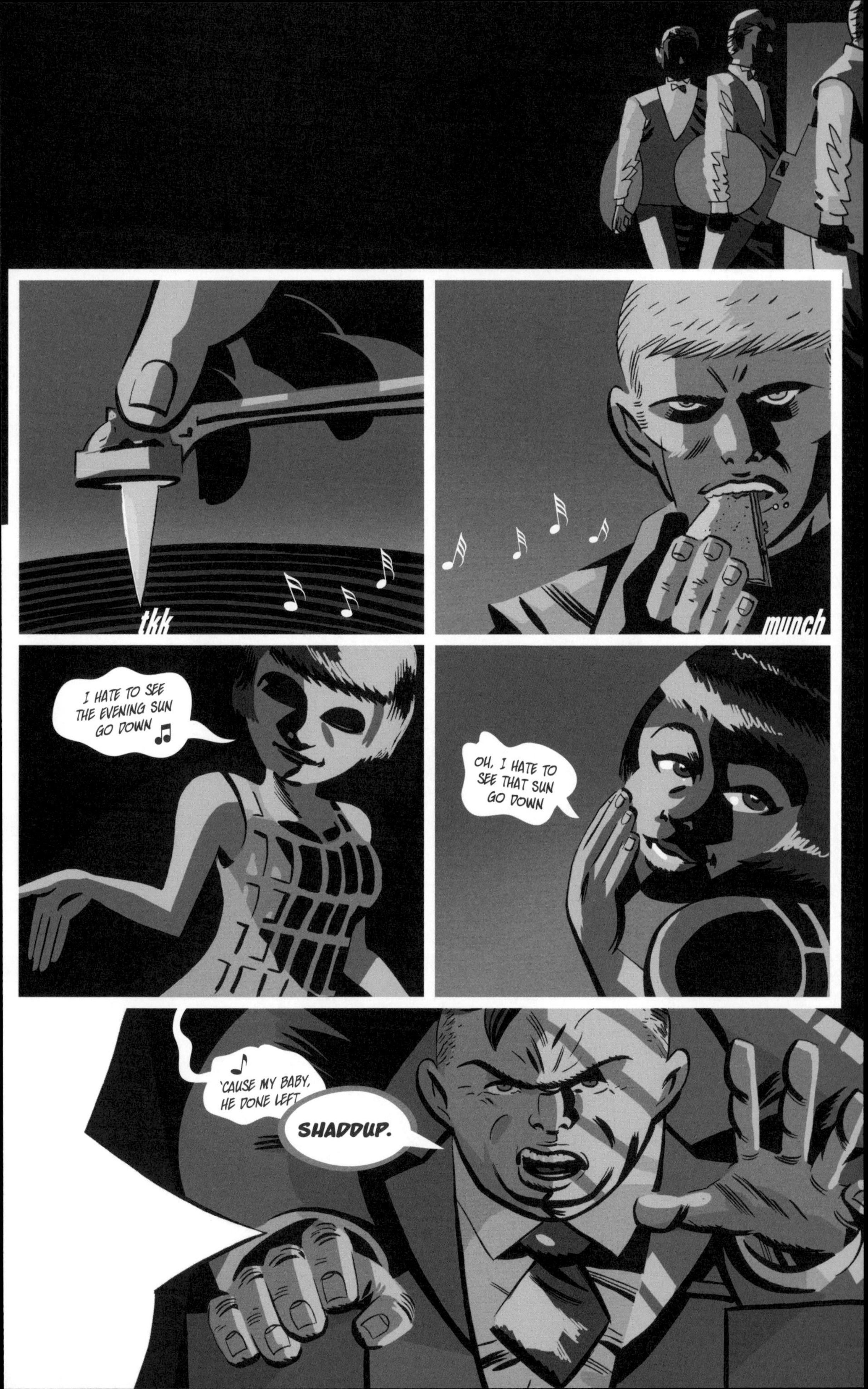
tkk
munch
I HATE TO SEE THE EVENING SUN GO DOWN ♫
OH, I HATE TO SEE THAT SUN GO DOWN
♪ 'CAUSE MY BABY, HE DONE LEFT
SHADDUP.

≈FUH≈

gulp

SING SOMETHIN' **ITALIAN**.

SICILY

rrrt

I...

≈UH≈

≈UM≈

LET...

LET ME SEE WHAT MR. ROTHMAN HAS.

IS THIS ONE OKAY?

ROSEMARY CLOONE

Mambo Italiano

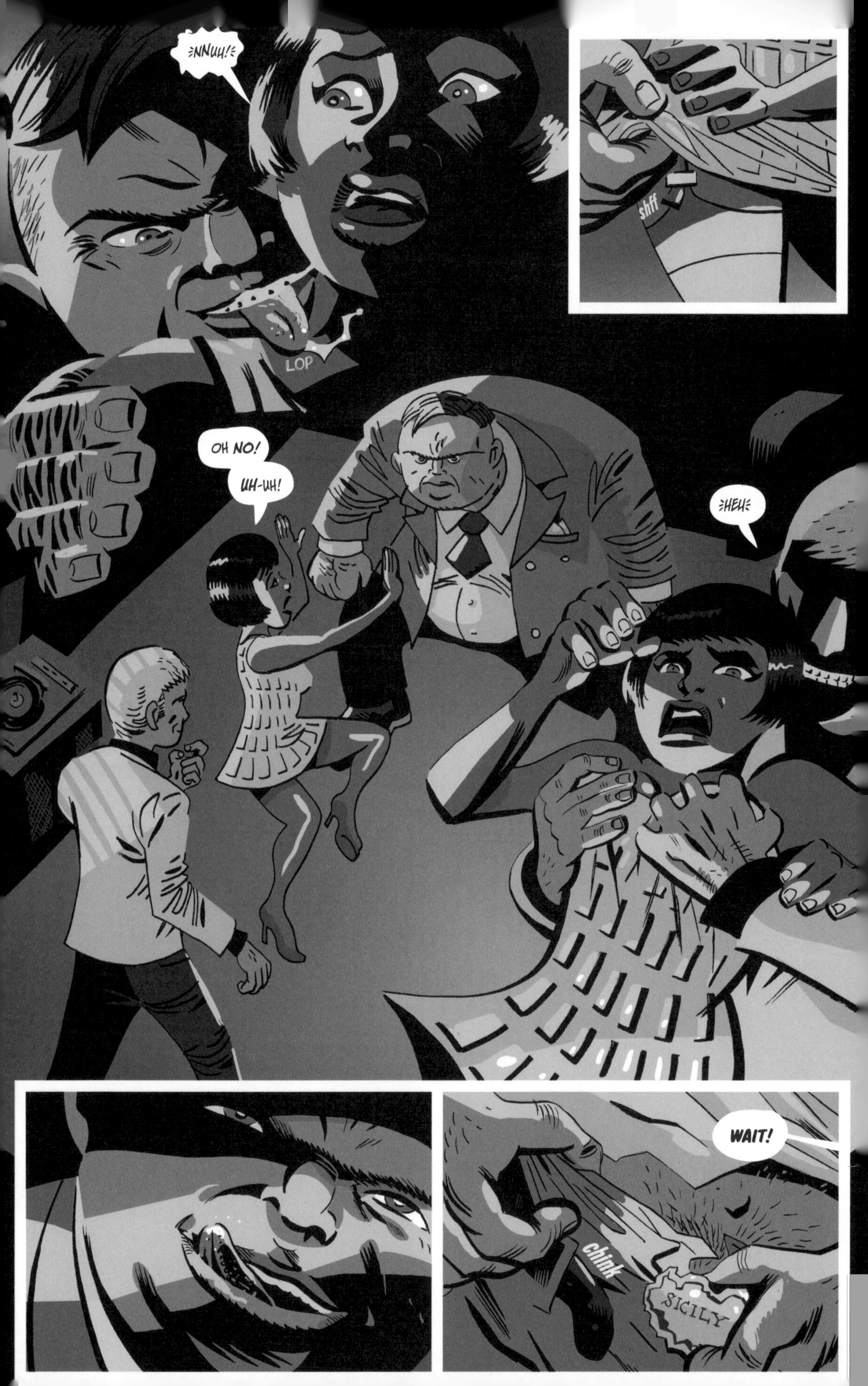
NNUH!
LOP
shff
OH NO!
UH-UH!
HEH
WAIT!
chink
SICILY

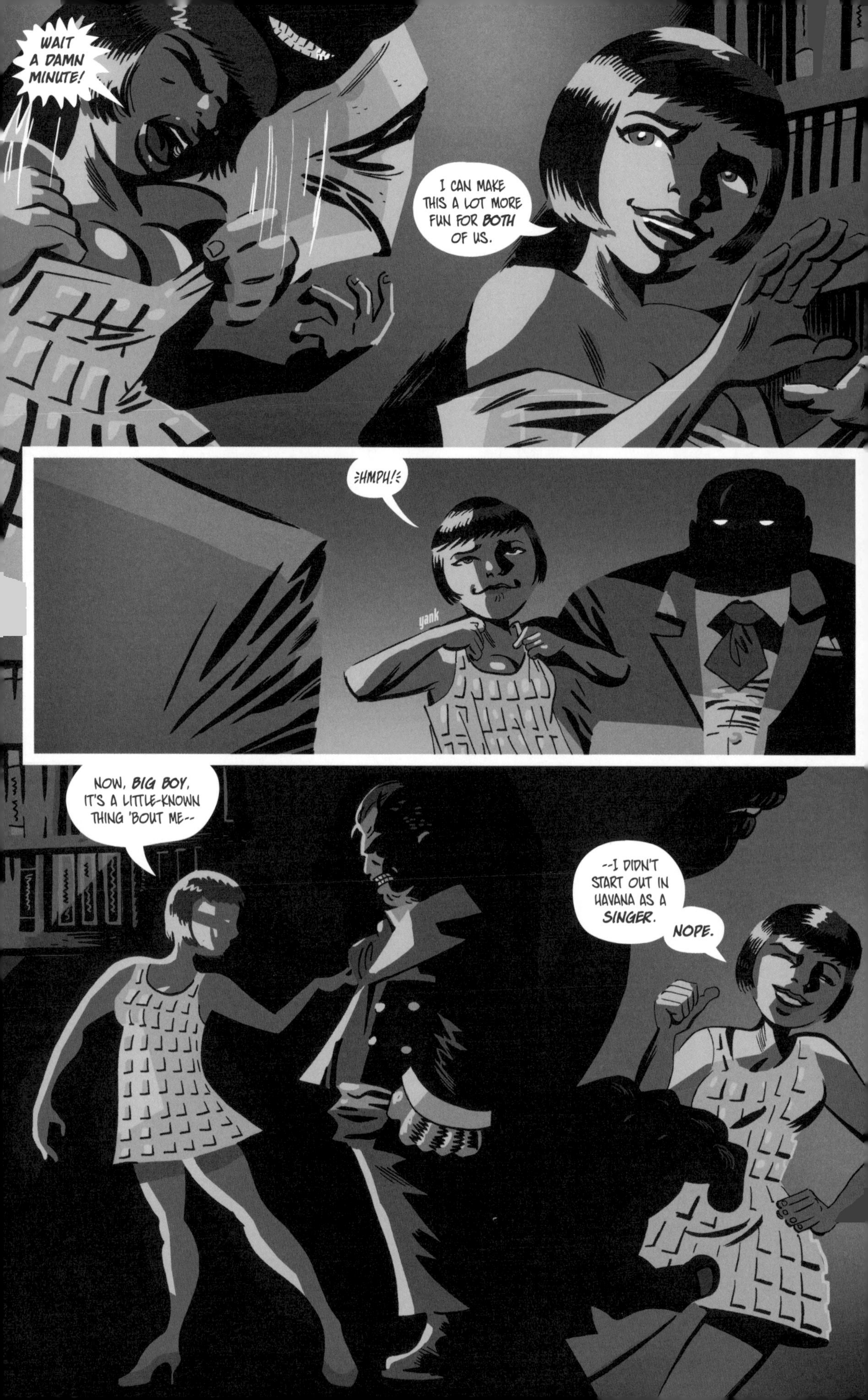
WAIT A DAMN MINUTE!
I CAN MAKE THIS A LOT MORE FUN FOR BOTH OF US.
HMPH!
yank
NOW, BIG BOY, IT'S A LITTLE-KNOWN THING 'BOUT ME--
--I DIDN'T START OUT IN HAVANA AS A SINGER.
NOPE.

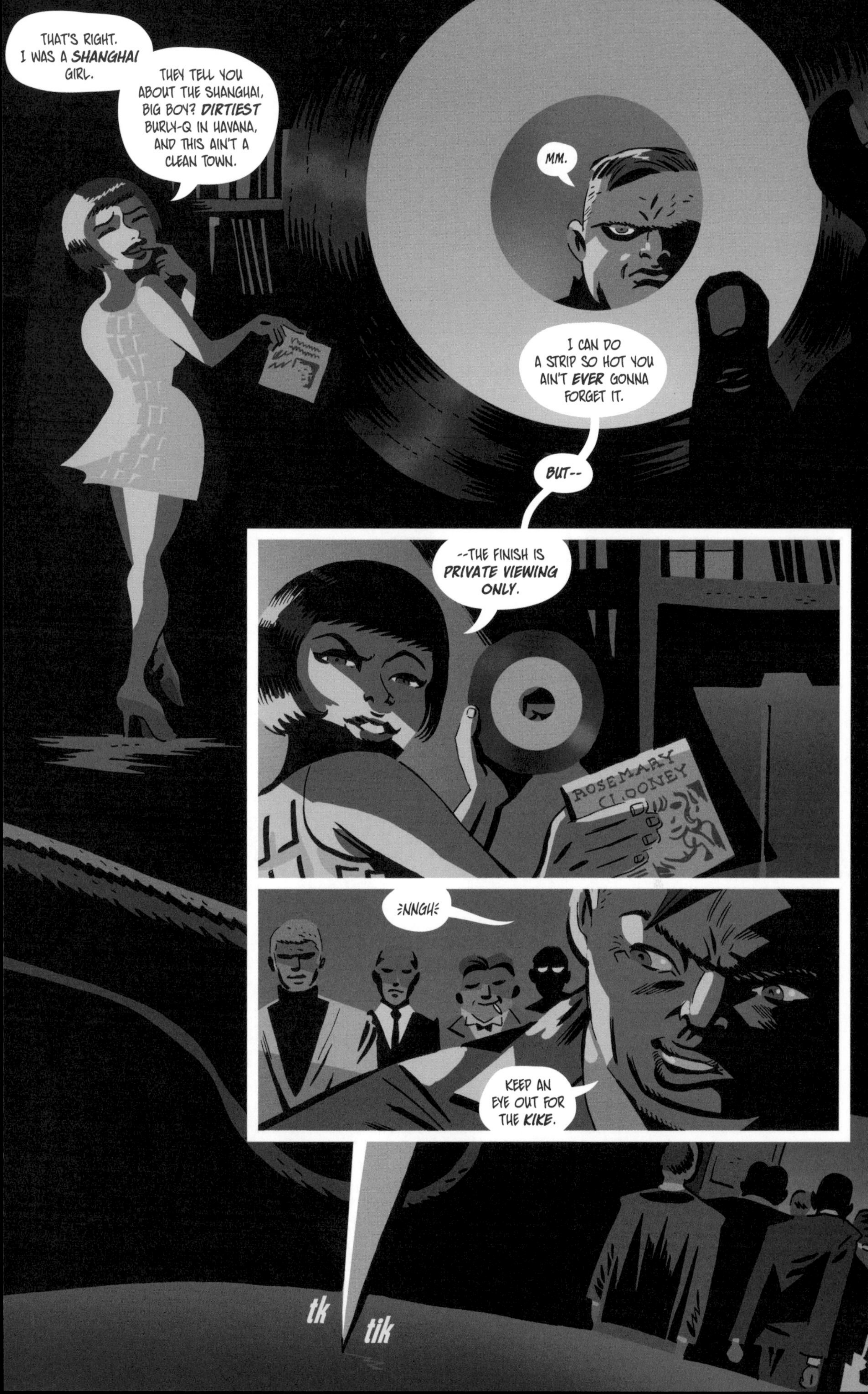
THAT'S RIGHT. I WAS A SHANGHAI GIRL.
THEY TELL YOU ABOUT THE SHANGHAI, BIG BOY? DIRTIEST BURLY-Q IN HAVANA, AND THIS AIN'T A CLEAN TOWN.
MM.
I CAN DO A STRIP SO HOT YOU AIN'T EVER GONNA FORGET IT.
BUT--
--THE FINISH IS PRIVATE VIEWING ONLY.
ROSEMARY CLOONEY
NNGH
KEEP AN EYE OUT FOR THE KIKE.
tk
tik

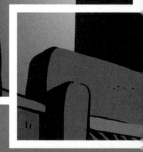

WHY DON'T YOU SIT DOWN AND MAKE YOURSELF COMFORTABLE, BIG BOY?

A girl went back to Napoli
Because she missed the scenery

≥MMN≤

zip

The native dances and the charming songs

shff

slip

But wait a minute, something's wrong--

flik

Hey, mambo!
Mambo Italiano
Hey, mambo!

YEAH.

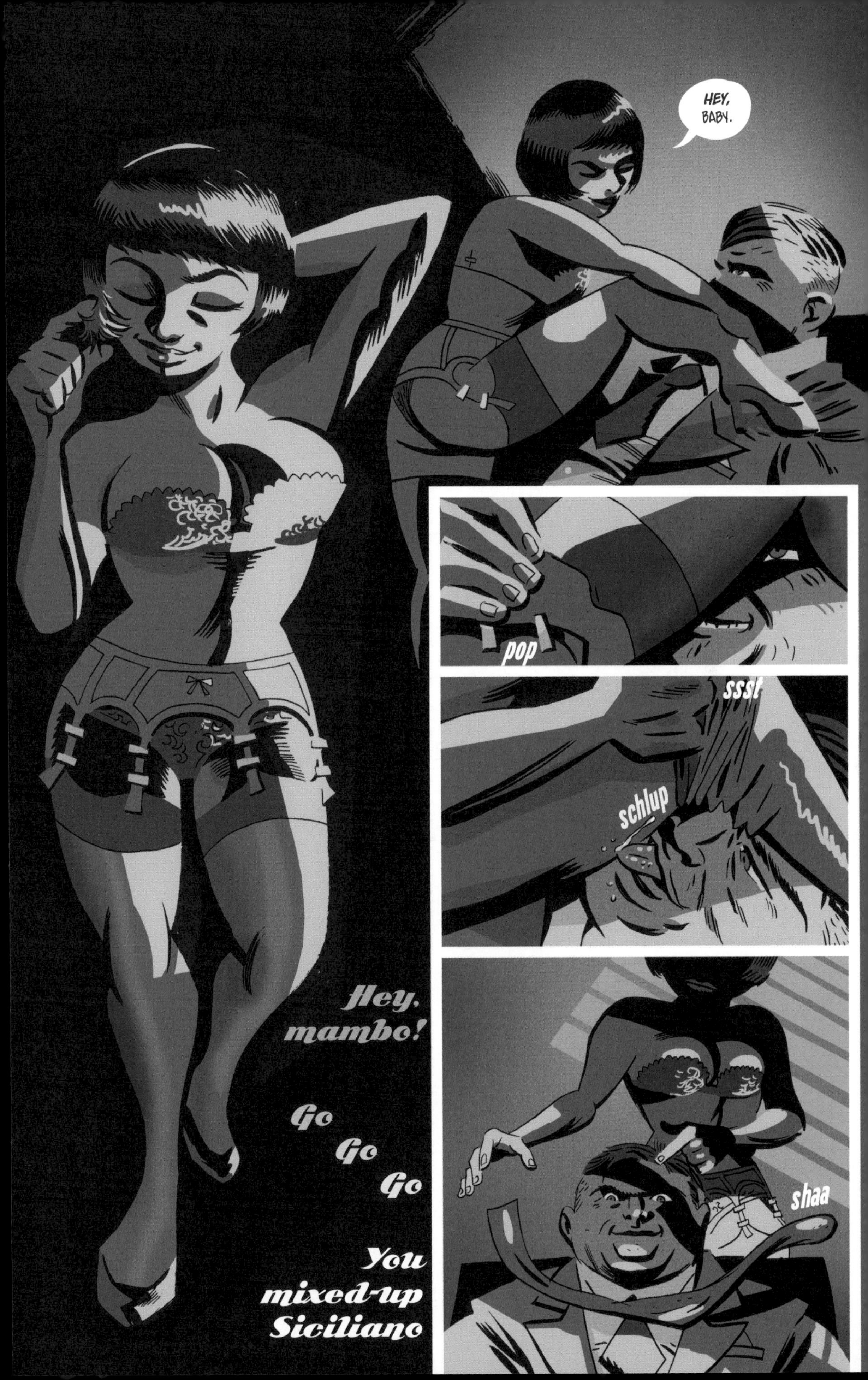
HEY, BABY.
pop
ssst
schlup
shaa
Hey, mambo!
Go
Go
Go
You mixed-up Siciliano

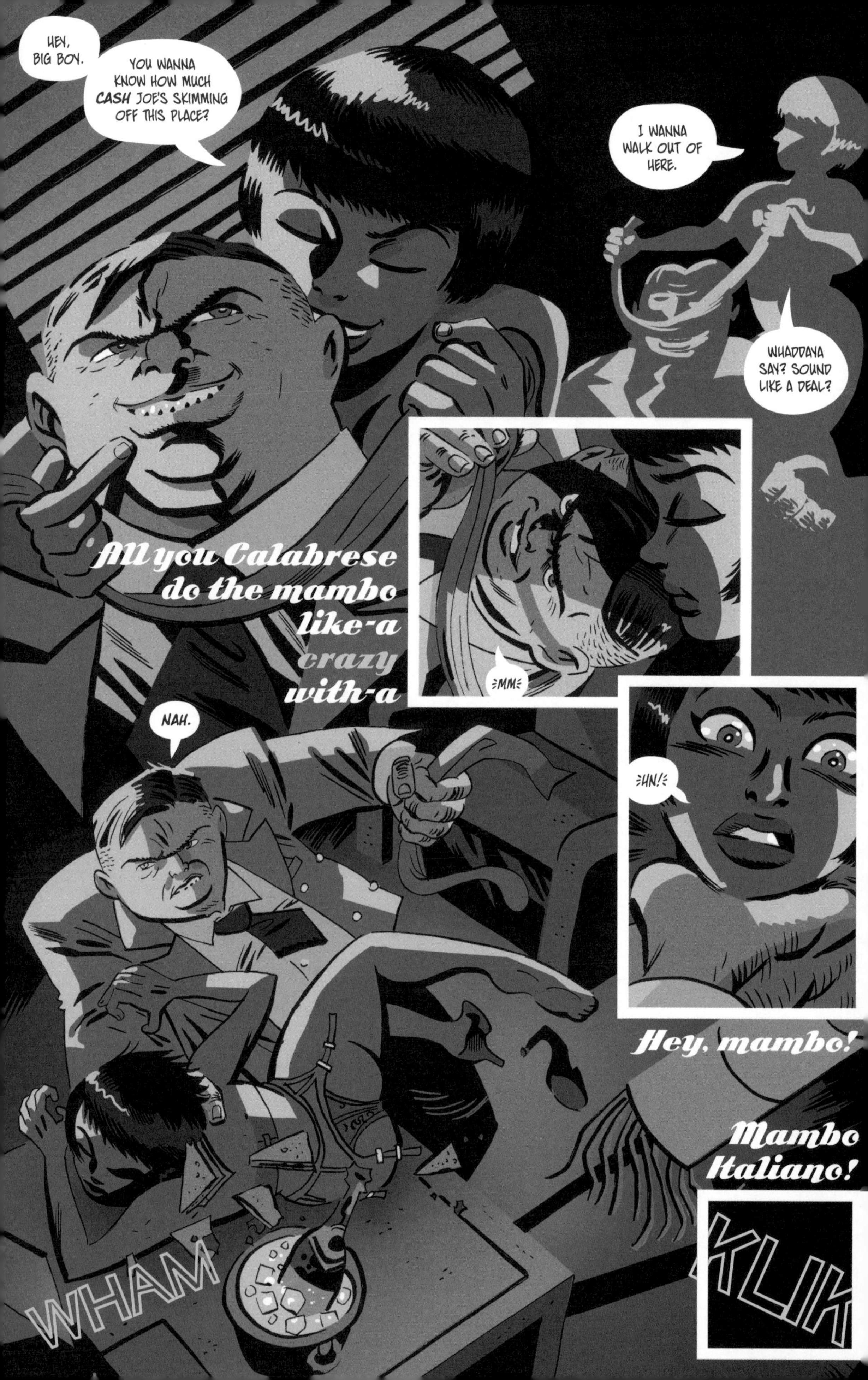
HEY, BIG BOY.
YOU WANNA KNOW HOW MUCH CASH JOE'S SKIMMING OFF THIS PLACE?
I WANNA WALK OUT OF HERE.
WHADDAYA SAY? SOUND LIKE A DEAL?
All you Calabrese do the mambo like-a crazy with-a
MM
NAH.
HN!
Hey, mambo!
Mambo Italiano!
WHAM
KLIK

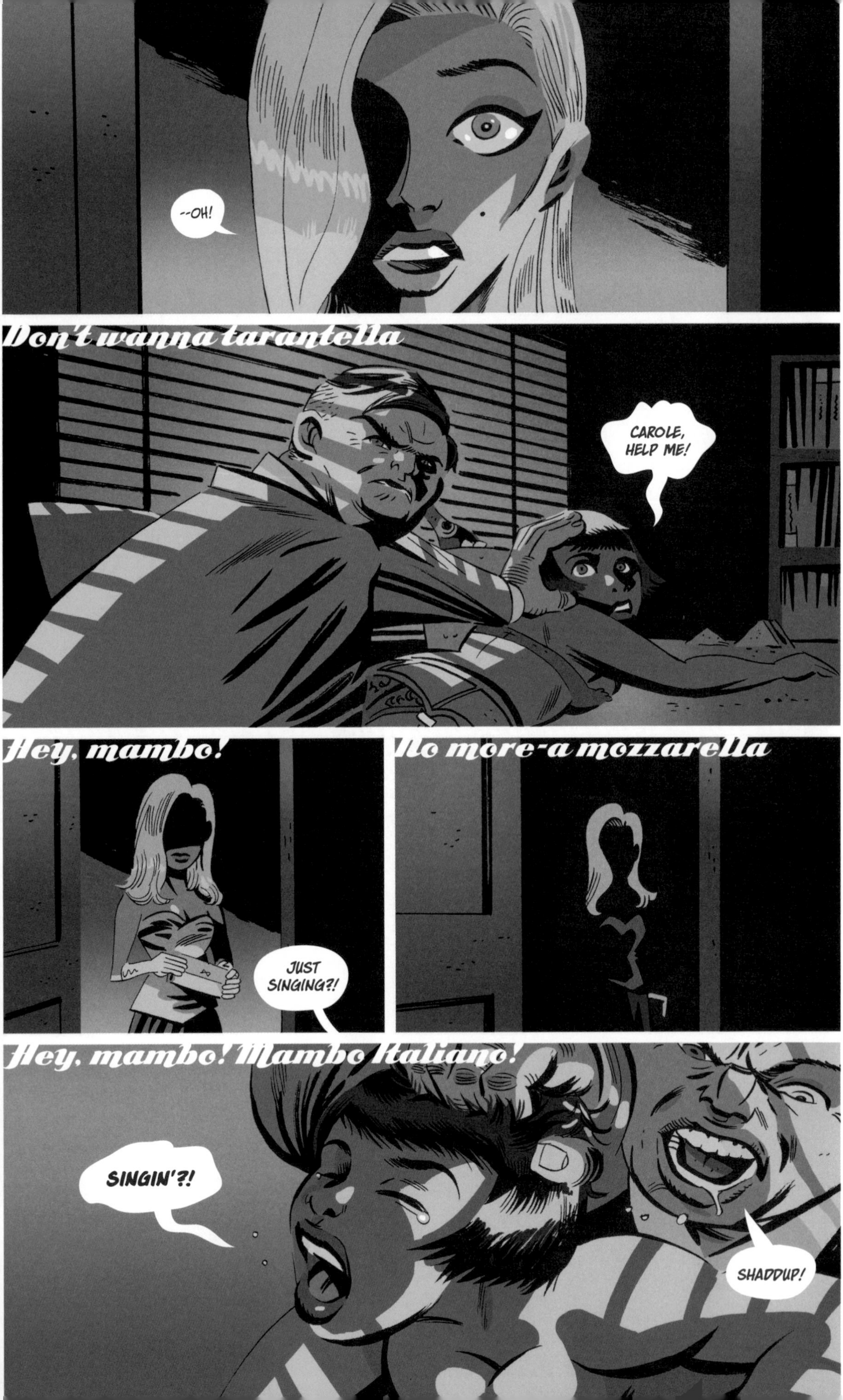
--OH!
Don't wanna tarantella
CAROLE, HELP ME!
Hey, mambo!
JUST SINGING?!
No more-a mozzarella
Hey, mambo! Mambo Italiano!
SINGIN'?!
SHADDUP!

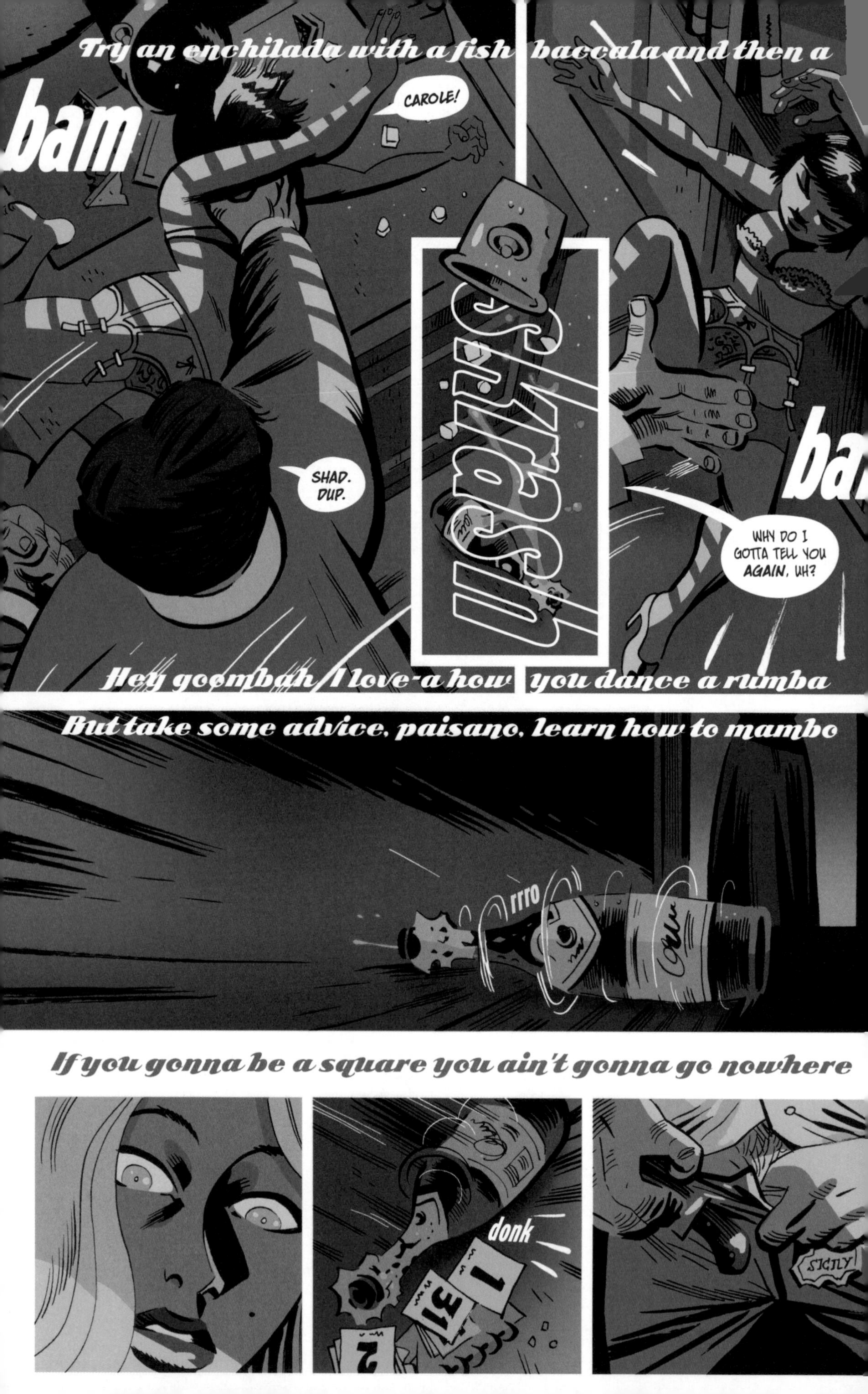
Try an enchilada with a fish baccala and then a
bam
CAROLE!
SHAD. DUP.
Shhhash
WHY DO I GOTTA TELL YOU AGAIN, UH?
bam
Hey goombah I love-a how you dance a rumba
But take some advice, paisano, learn how to mambo
rrro
If you gonna be a square you ain't gonna go nowhere
donk
SICILY

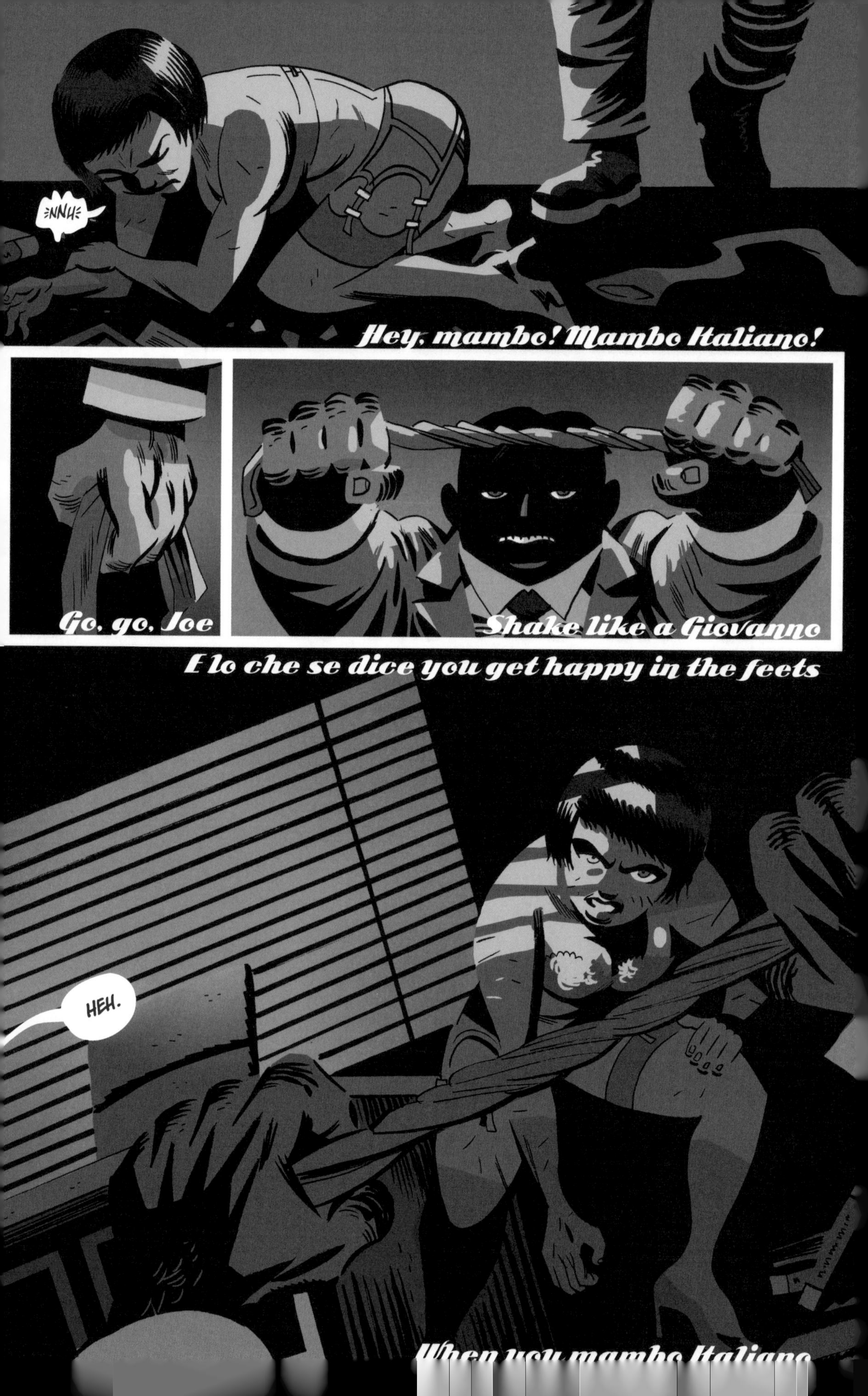
NNH
Hey, mambo! Mambo Italiano!
Go, go, Joe
Shake like a Giovanno
E lo che se dice you get happy in the feets
HEH.
When you mambo Italiano

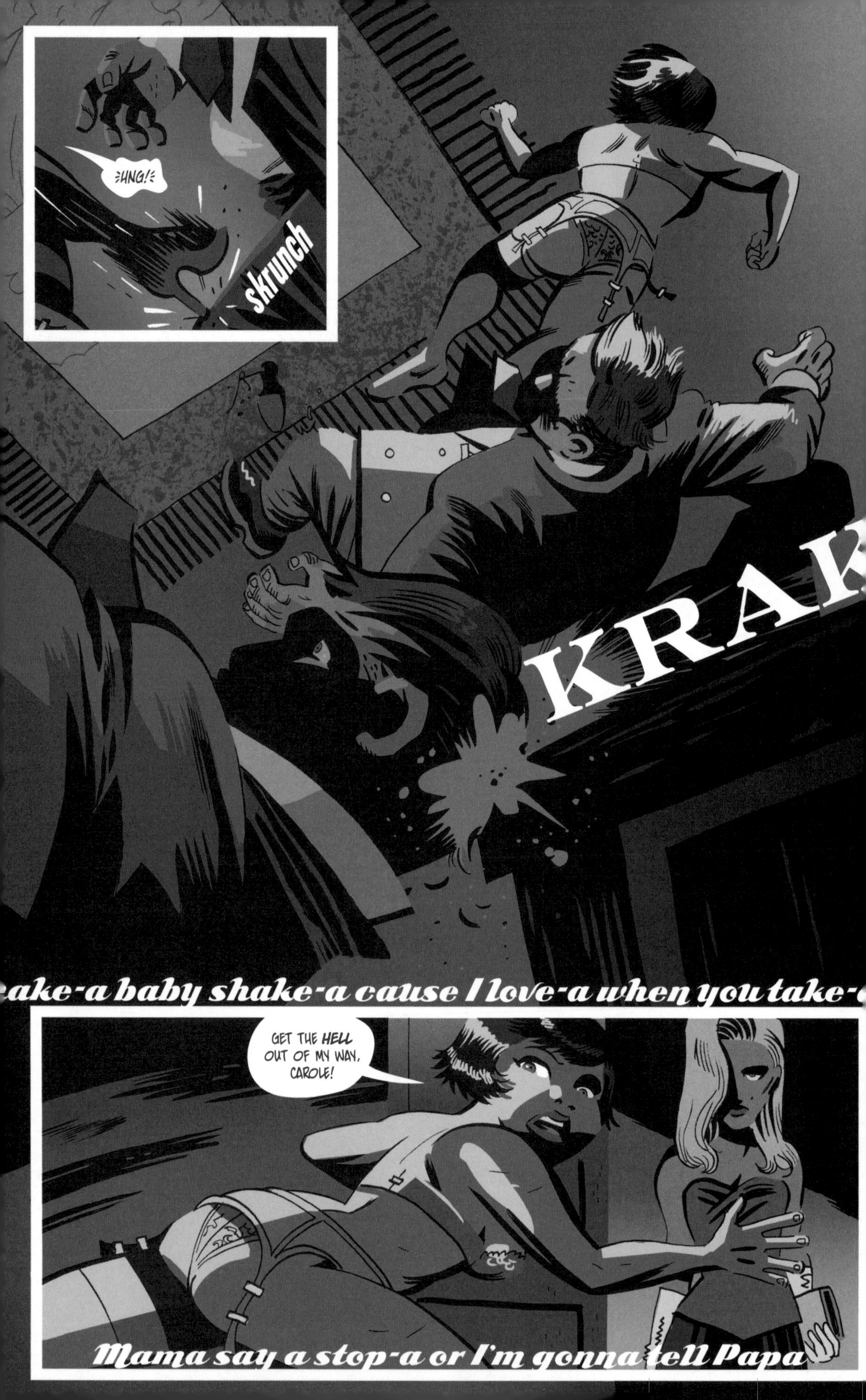
UNG!
skrunch
KRAK
ake-a baby shake-a cause I love-a when you take-
GET THE HELL OUT OF MY WAY, CAROLE!
Mama say a stop-a or I'm gonna tell Papa

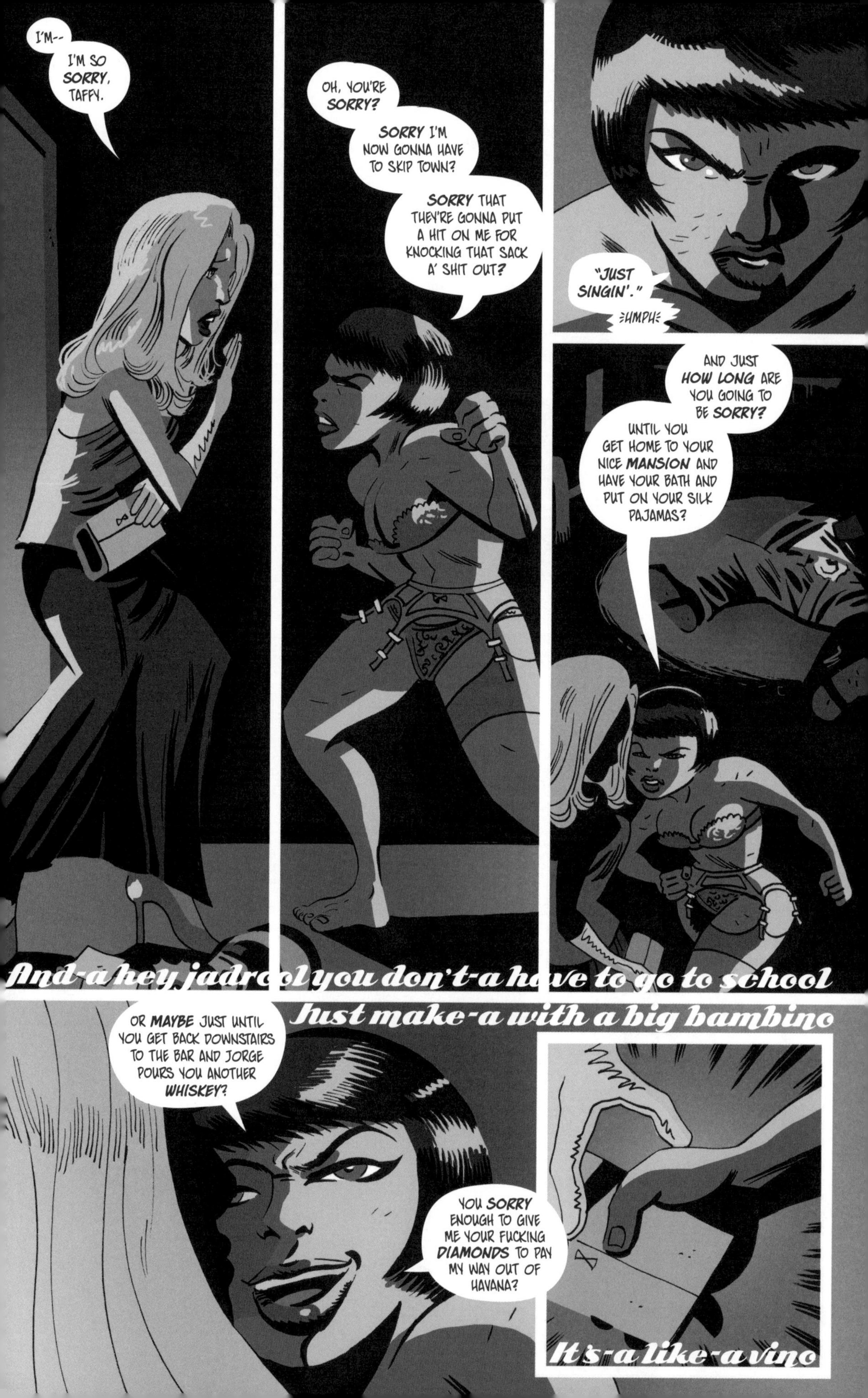

I'M--
I'M SO SORRY, TAFFY.
OH, YOU'RE SORRY?
SORRY I'M NOW GONNA HAVE TO SKIP TOWN?
SORRY THAT THEY'RE GONNA PUT A HIT ON ME FOR KNOCKING THAT SACK A' SHIT OUT?
"JUST SINGIN'."
HMPH
AND JUST HOW LONG ARE YOU GOING TO BE SORRY?
UNTIL YOU GET HOME TO YOUR NICE MANSION AND HAVE YOUR BATH AND PUT ON YOUR SILK PAJAMAS?
And-a hey jadrool you don't-a have to go to school
Just make-a with a big bambino
OR MAYBE JUST UNTIL YOU GET BACK DOWNSTAIRS TO THE BAR AND JORGE POURS YOU ANOTHER WHISKEY?
YOU SORRY ENOUGH TO GIVE ME YOUR FUCKING DIAMONDS TO PAY MY WAY OUT OF HAVANA?
It's-a like-a vino

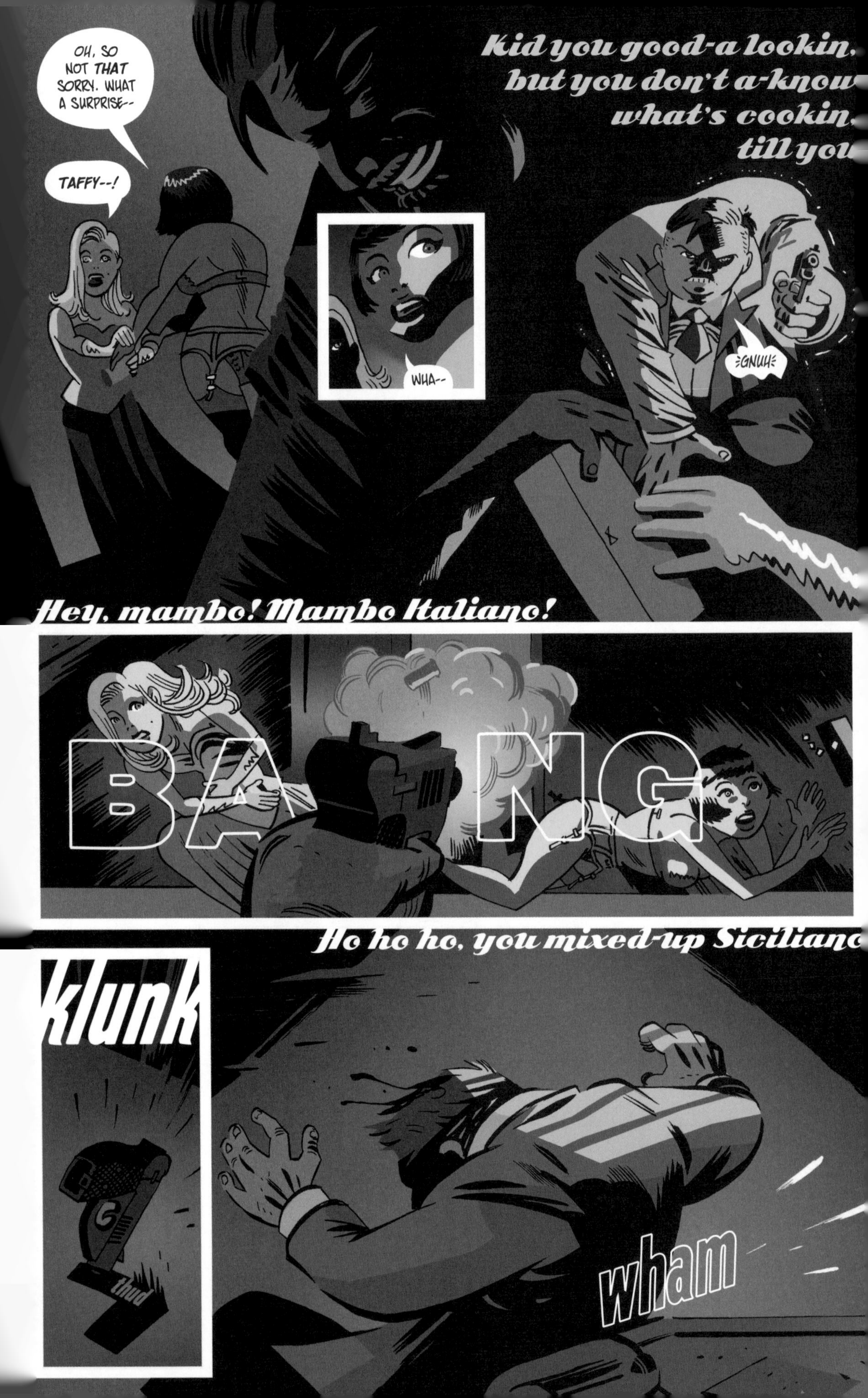
OH, SO NOT THAT SORRY. WHAT A SURPRISE--
TAFFY--!
Kid you good-a lookin, but you don't a-know what's cookin till you
WHA--
GNUH
Hey, mambo! Mambo Italiano!
BANG
Ho ho ho, you mixed-up Siciliano
klunk
thud
wham

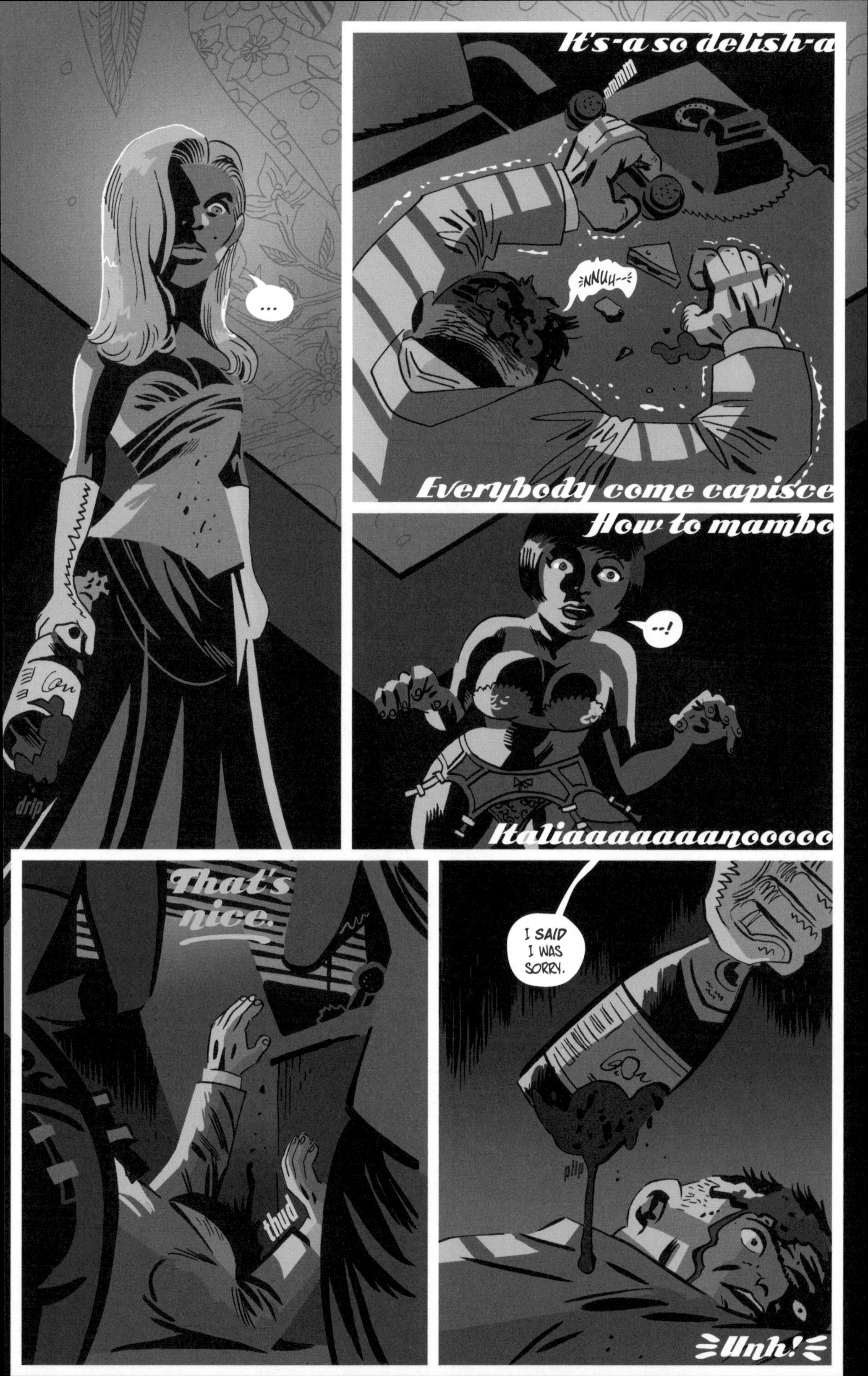

...
It's-a so delish-a
mmmm
NNUH--
Everybody come capisce
How to mambo
--!
Italiaaaaaaanooooo
drip
That's nice.
thud
I SAID I WAS SORRY.
plip
Unh!

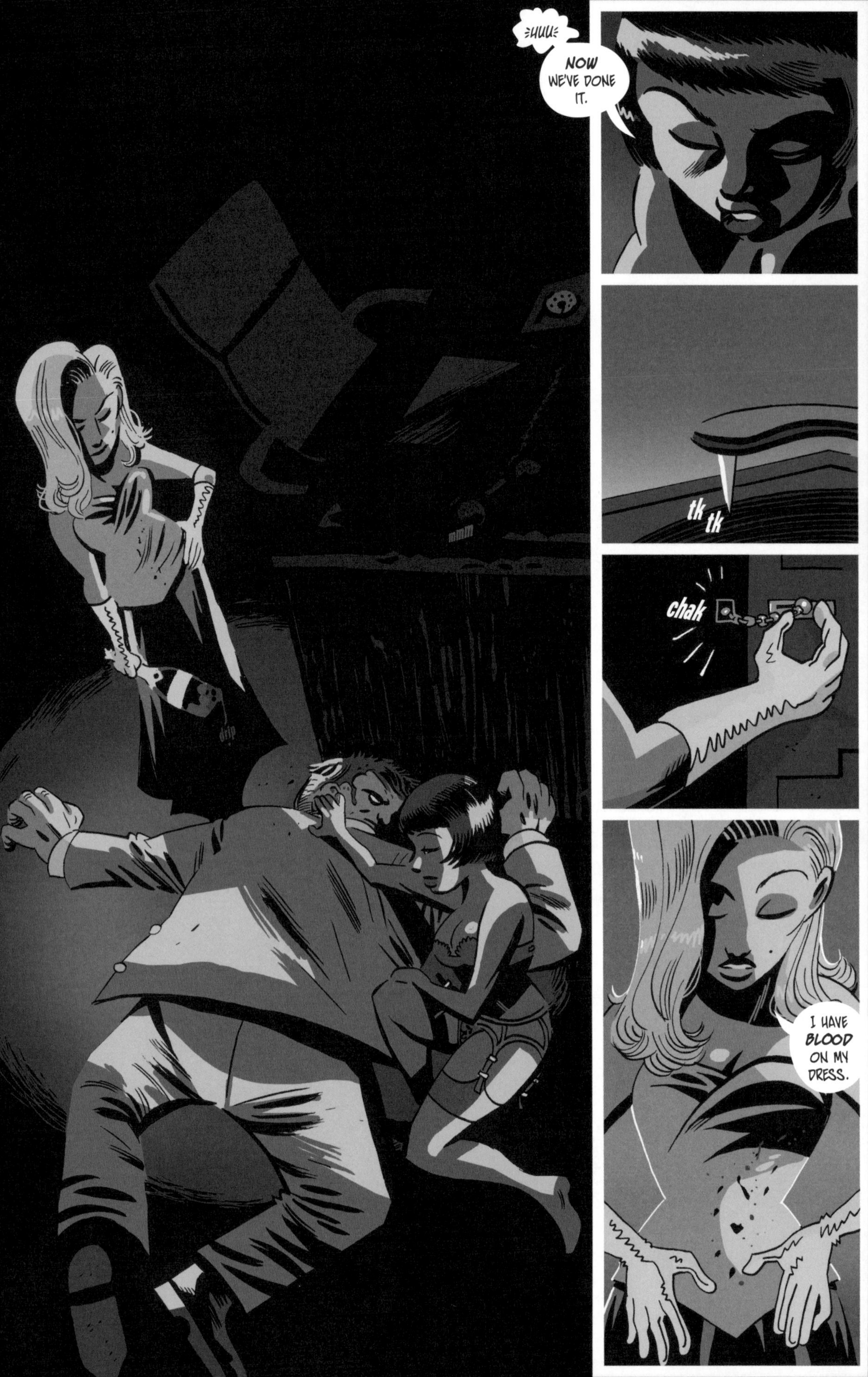
HUU
NOW WE'VE DONE IT.
drip
tk tk
chak
I HAVE BLOOD ON MY DRESS.

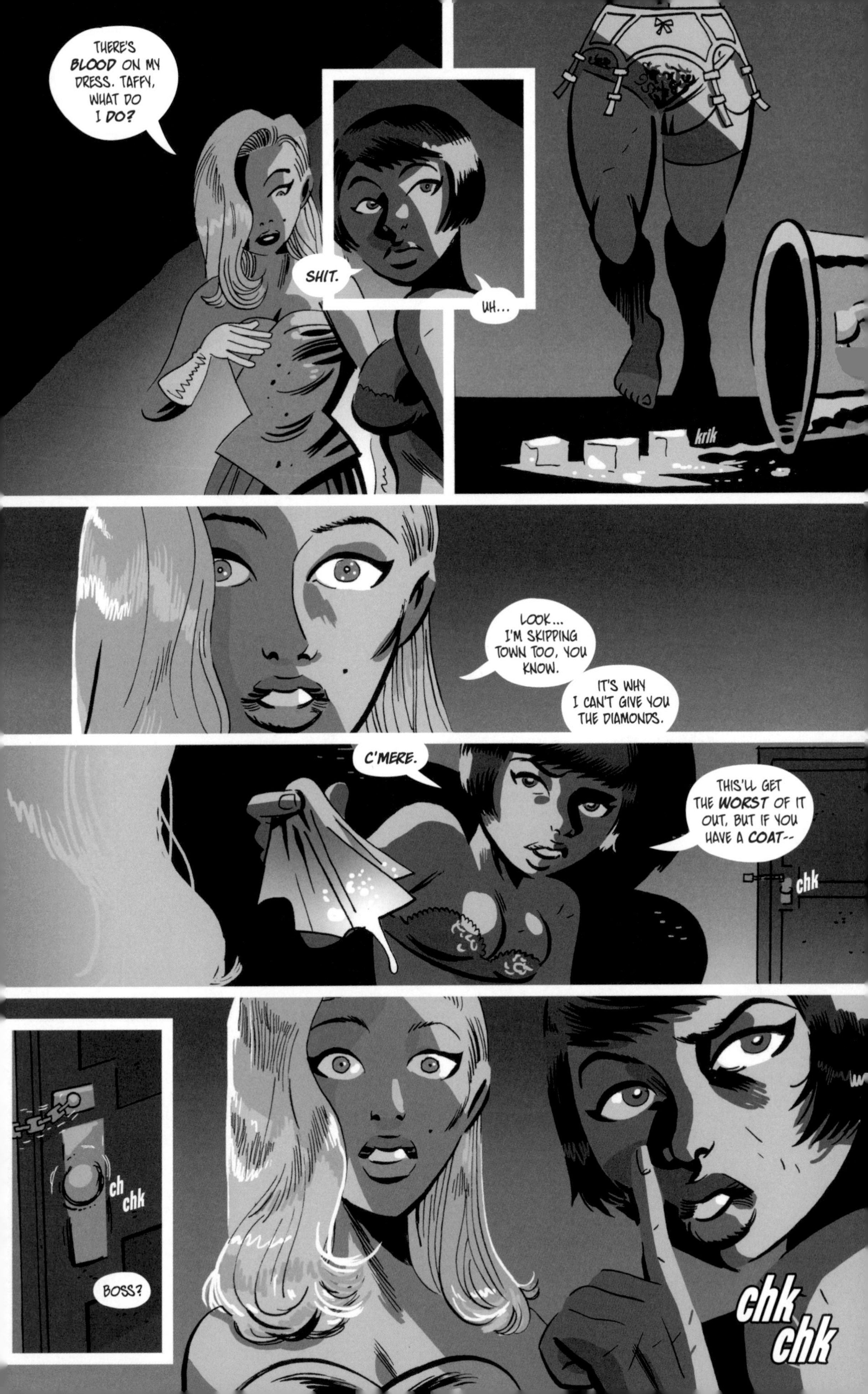
THERE'S BLOOD ON MY DRESS. TAFFY, WHAT DO I DO?
SHIT.
UH...
krik
LOOK... I'M SKIPPING TOWN TOO, YOU KNOW.
IT'S WHY I CAN'T GIVE YOU THE DIAMONDS.
C'MERE.
THIS'LL GET THE WORST OF IT OUT, BUT IF YOU HAVE A COAT--
chk
ch chk
BOSS?
chk chk

10:00 P.M.

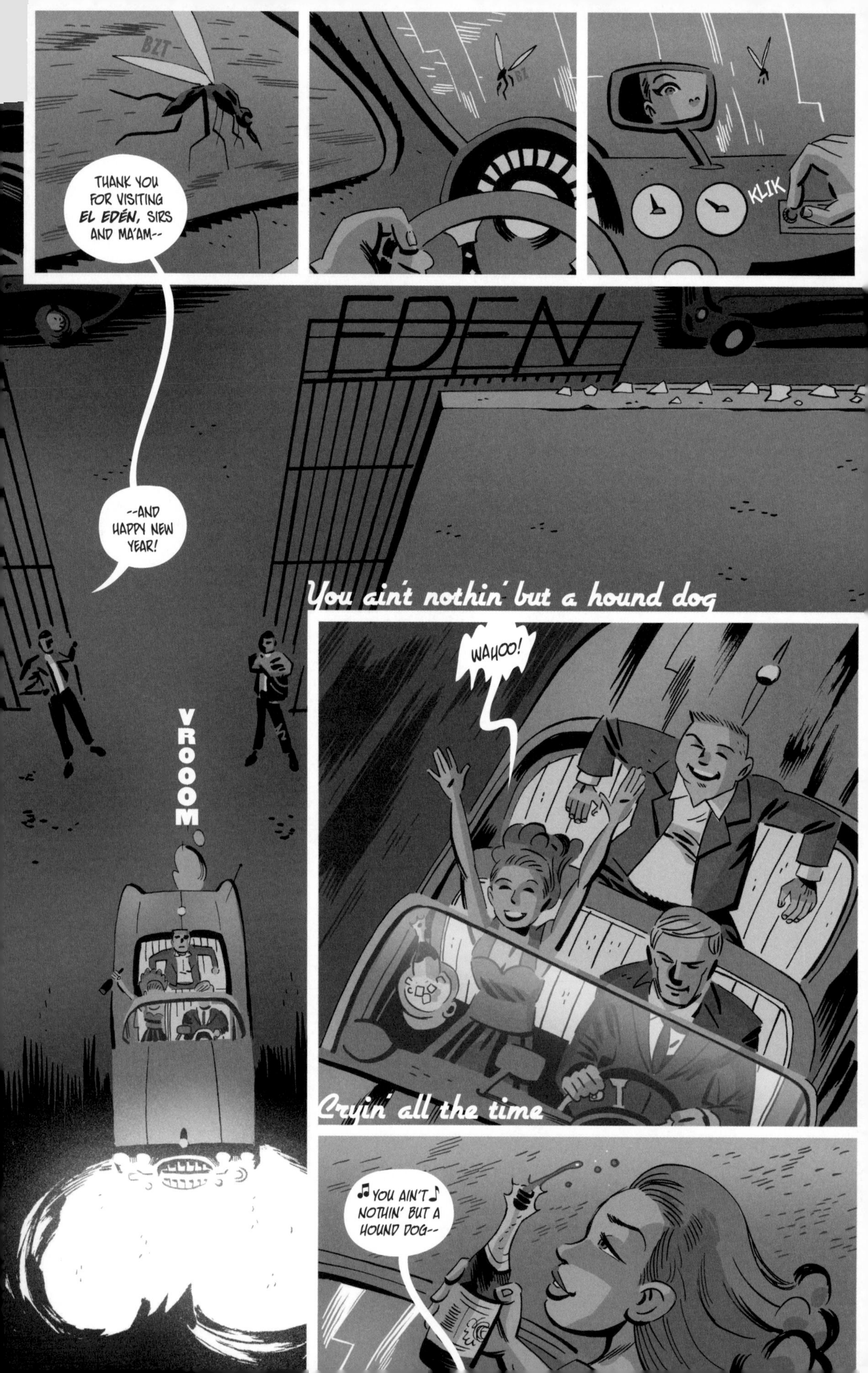
BZT
BZ
KLIK
THANK YOU FOR VISITING EL EDÉN, SIRS AND MA'AM--
EDEN
--AND HAPPY NEW YEAR!
VROOOM
You ain't nothin' but a hound dog
WAHOO!
Cryin' all the time
♫YOU AIN'T♪ NOTHIN' BUT A HOUND DOG--

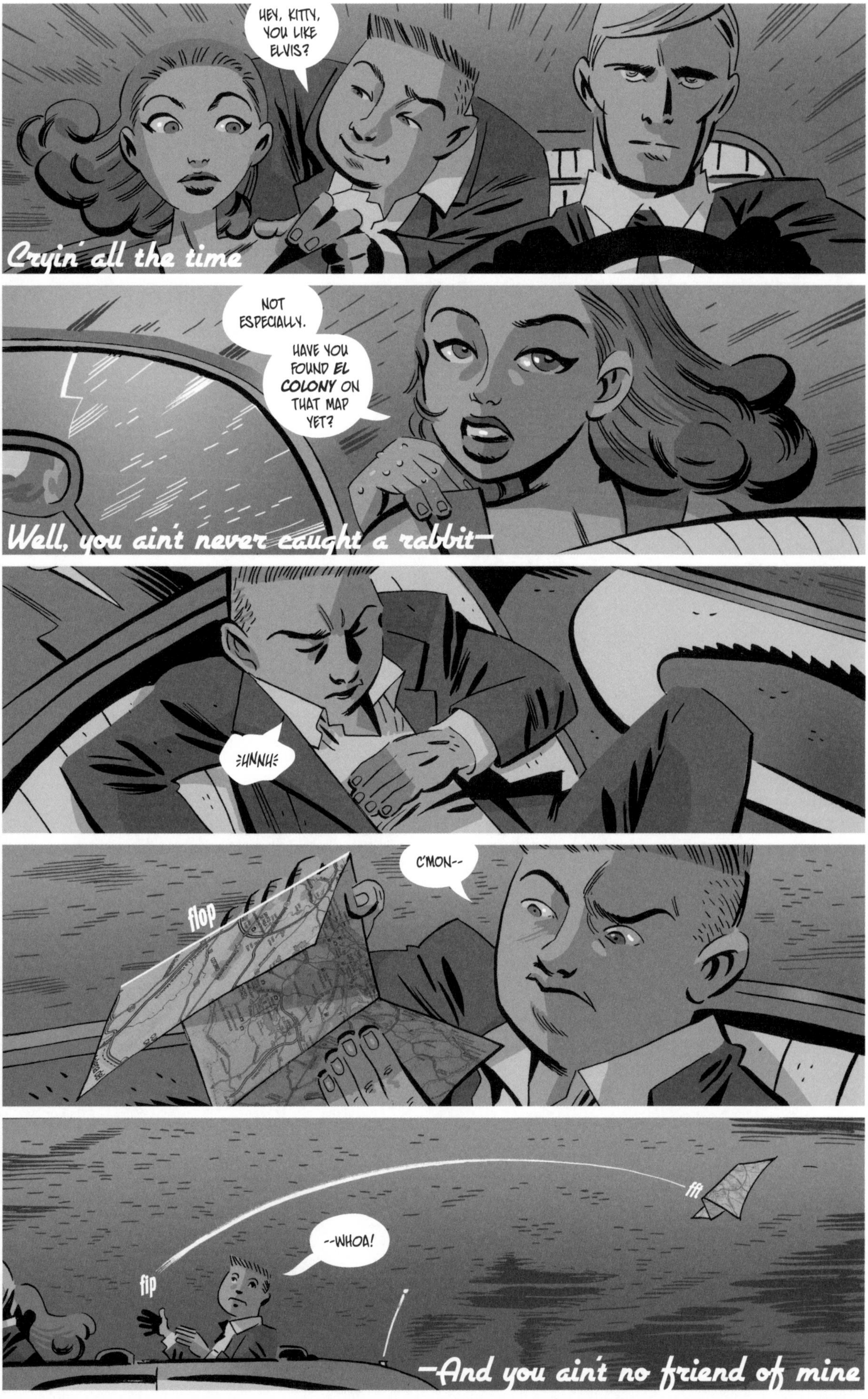
HEY, KITTY, YOU LIKE ELVIS?
Cryin' all the time
NOT ESPECIALLY.
HAVE YOU FOUND EL COLONY ON THAT MAP YET?
Well, you ain't never caught a rabbit—
UNNH
flop
C'MON--
fft
fip
--WHOA!
—And you ain't no friend of mine

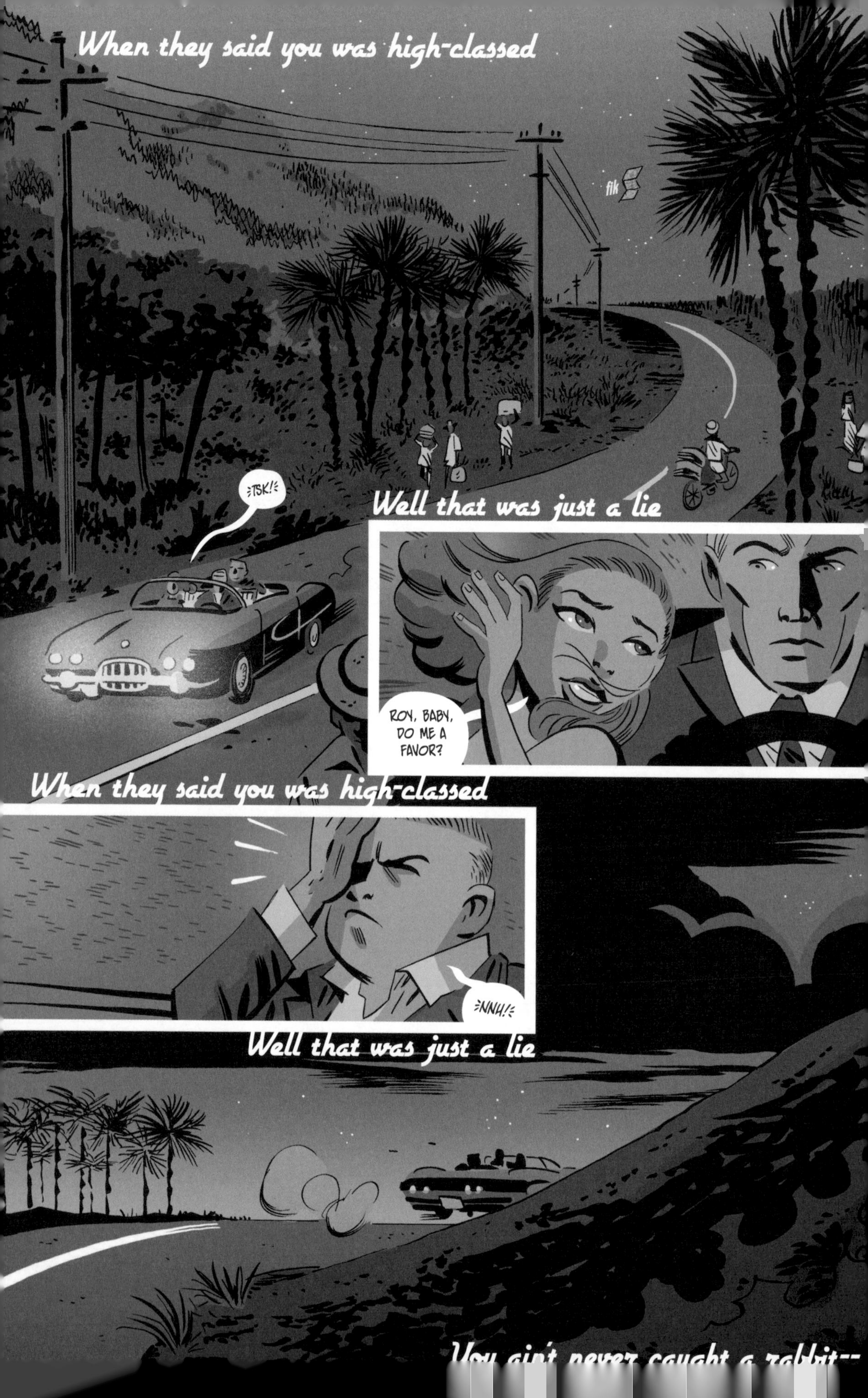
When they said you was high-classed
fik
TSK!
Well that was just a lie
ROY, BABY, DO ME A FAVOR?
When they said you was high-classed
NNH!
Well that was just a lie
You ain't never caught a rabbit--

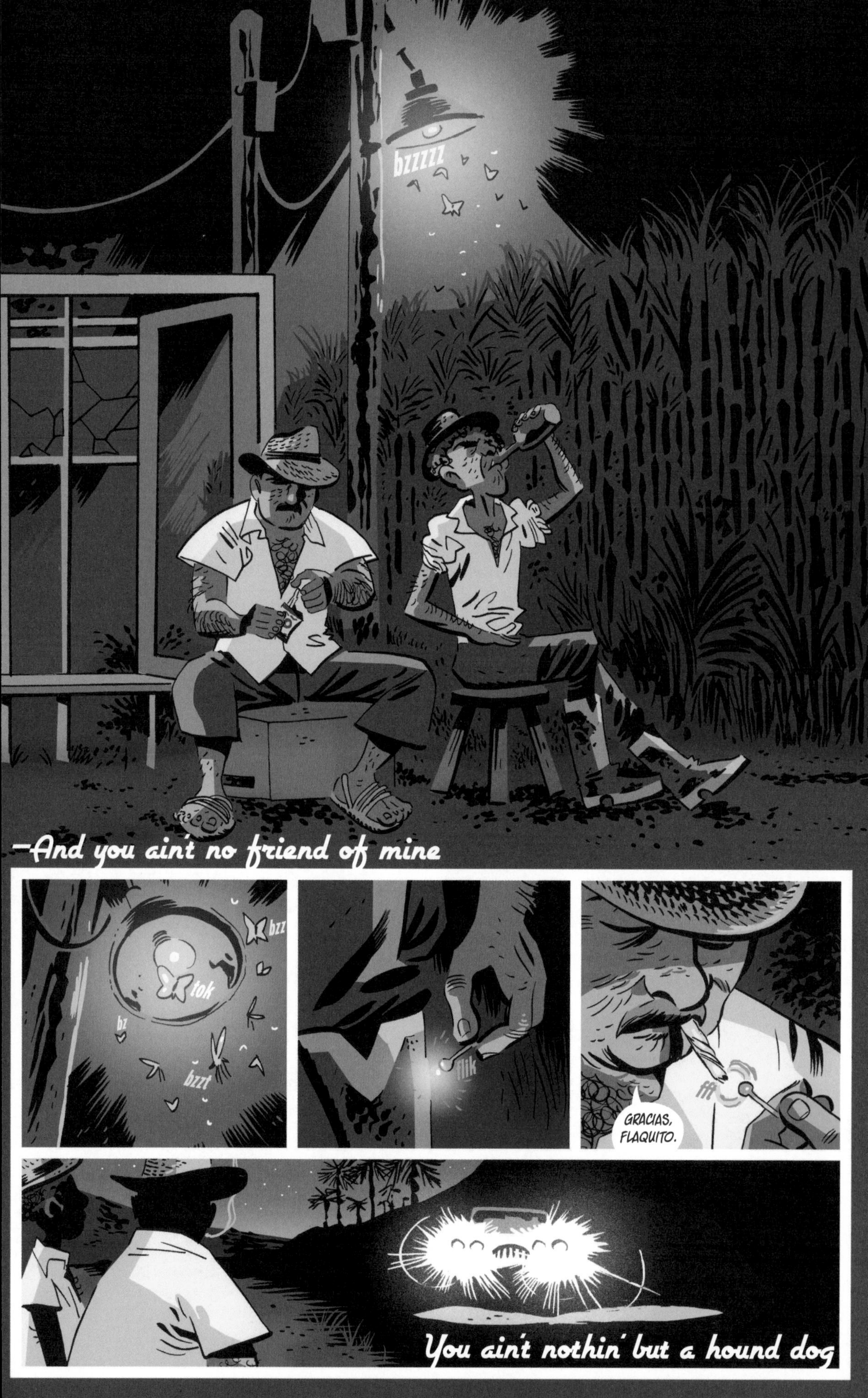
bzzzzz
—And you ain't no friend of mine
bzz
tok
bz
bzzt
flik
fft
GRACIAS, FLAQUITO.
You ain't nothin' but a hound dog

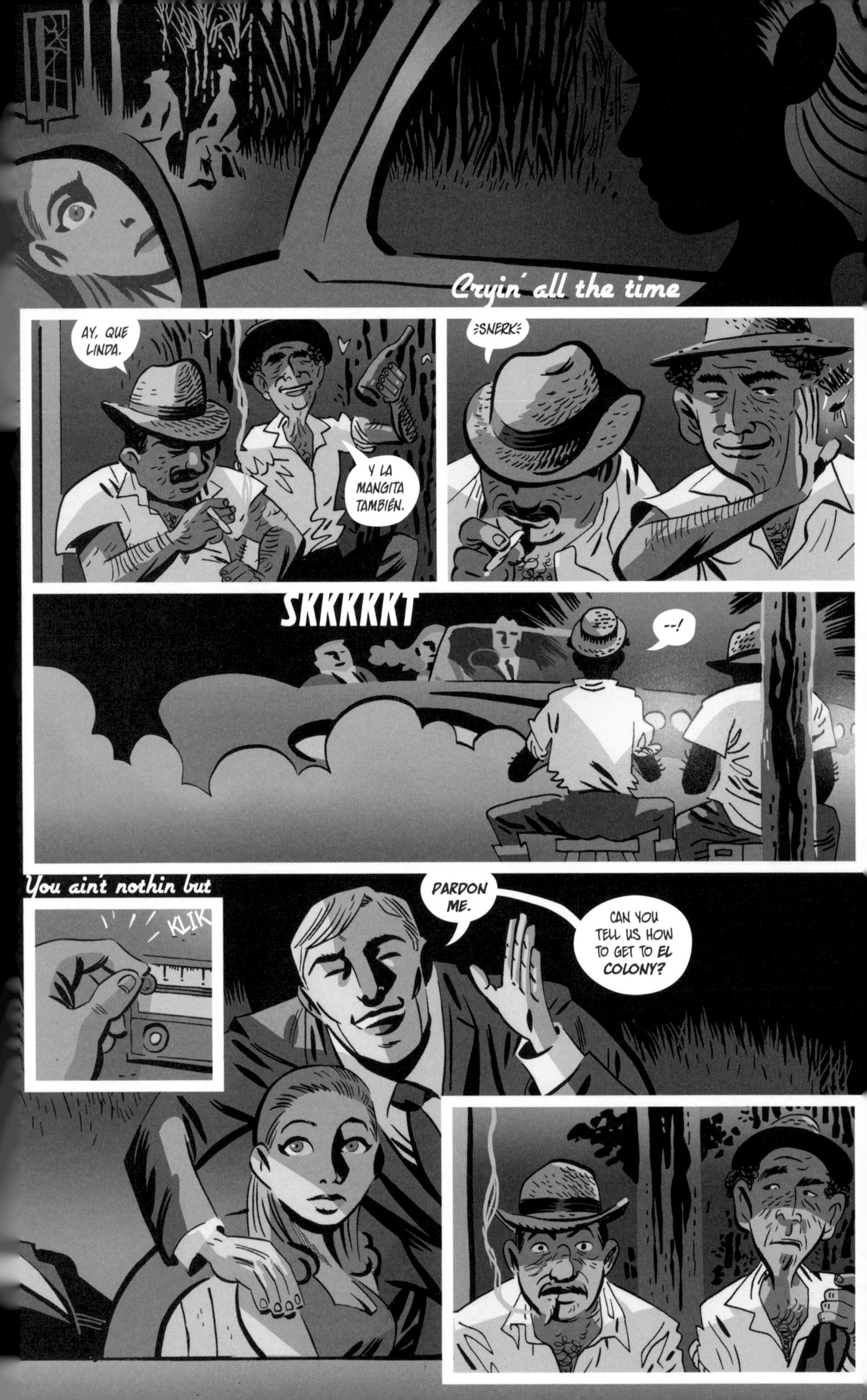
Cryin' all the time
AY, QUE LINDA.
Y LA MANGITA TAMBIÉN.
SNERK
SMAK
SKKKKKT
--!
You ain't nothin but
KLIK
PARDON ME.
CAN YOU TELL US HOW TO GET TO EL COLONY?

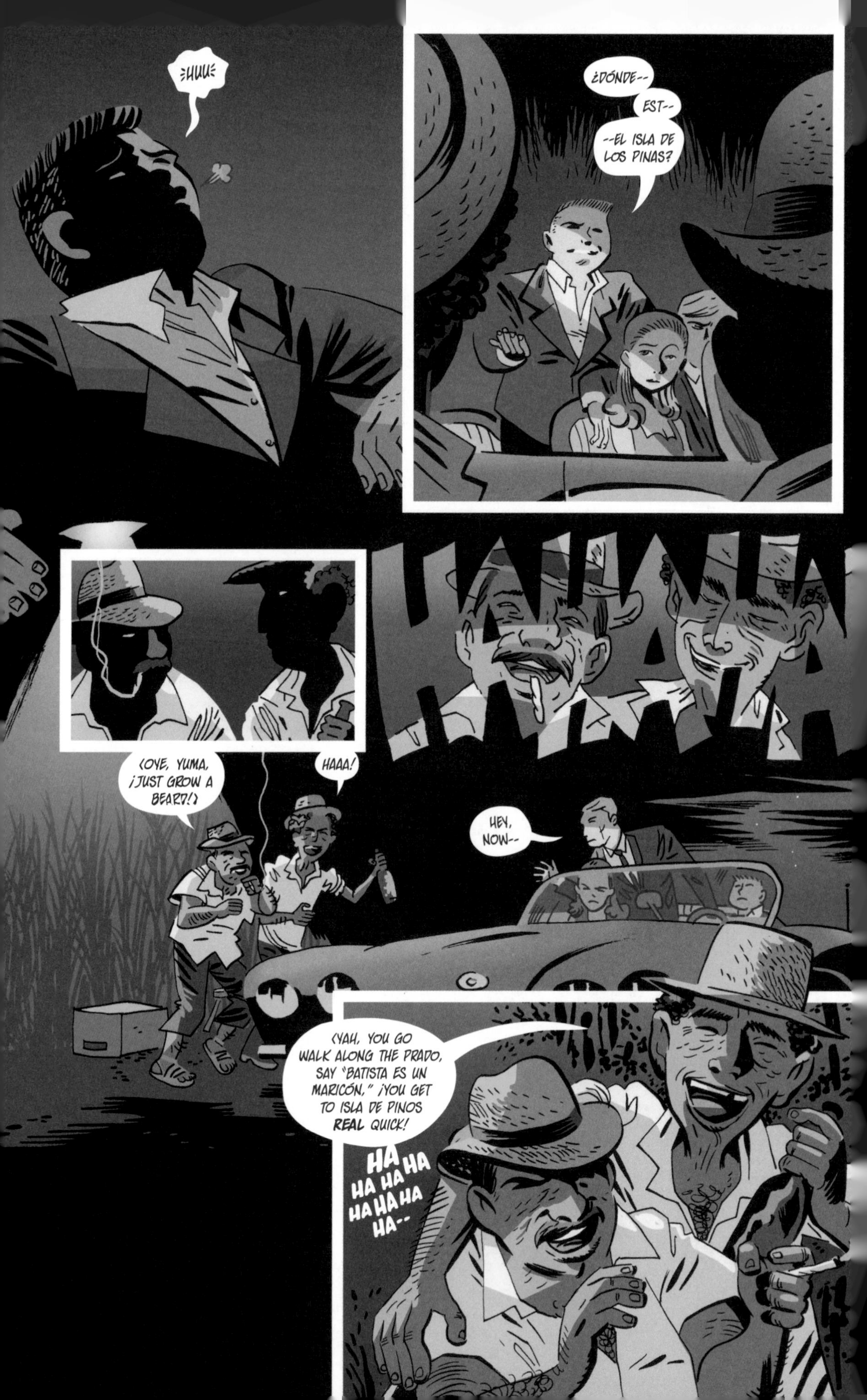
¡HUU!
¿DÓNDE--
EST--
--EL ISLA DE LOS PINAS?
HA HA HA
‹OYE, YUMA, ¡JUST GROW A BEARD!›
HAAA!
HEY, NOW--
‹YAH, YOU GO WALK ALONG THE PRADO, SAY "BATISTA ES UN MARICÓN," ¡YOU GET TO ISLA DE PINOS **REAL** QUICK!
HA HA HA HA HA HA HA HA HA--

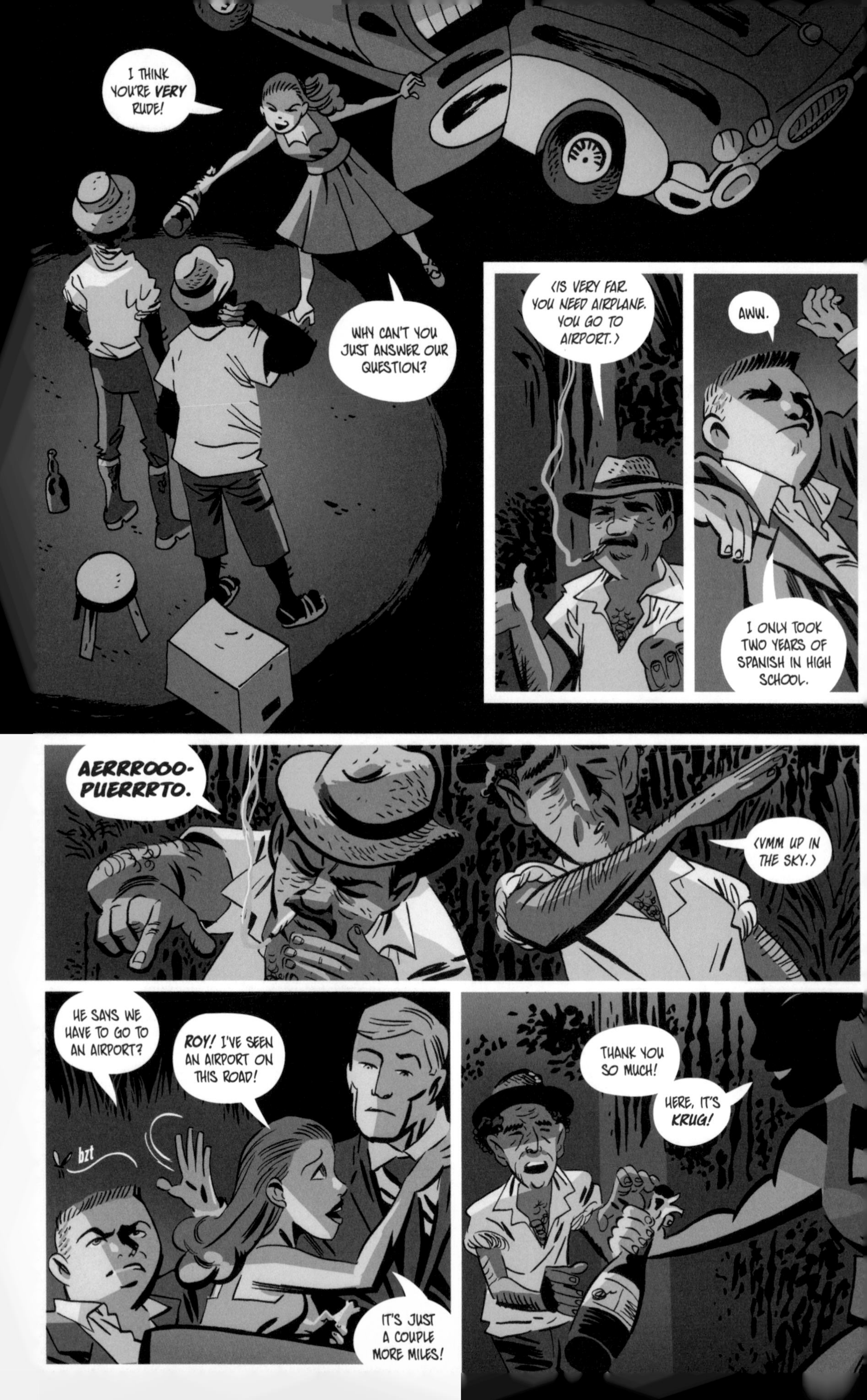
I THINK YOU'RE VERY RUDE!
WHY CAN'T YOU JUST ANSWER OUR QUESTION?
‹IS VERY FAR. YOU NEED AIRPLANE. YOU GO TO AIRPORT.›
AWW.
I ONLY TOOK TWO YEARS OF SPANISH IN HIGH SCHOOL.
AERRROOO-PUERRRTO.
‹VMM UP IN THE SKY.›
HE SAYS WE HAVE TO GO TO AN AIRPORT?
ROY! I'VE SEEN AN AIRPORT ON THIS ROAD!
bzt
IT'S JUST A COUPLE MORE MILES!
THANK YOU SO MUCH!
HERE, IT'S KRUG!

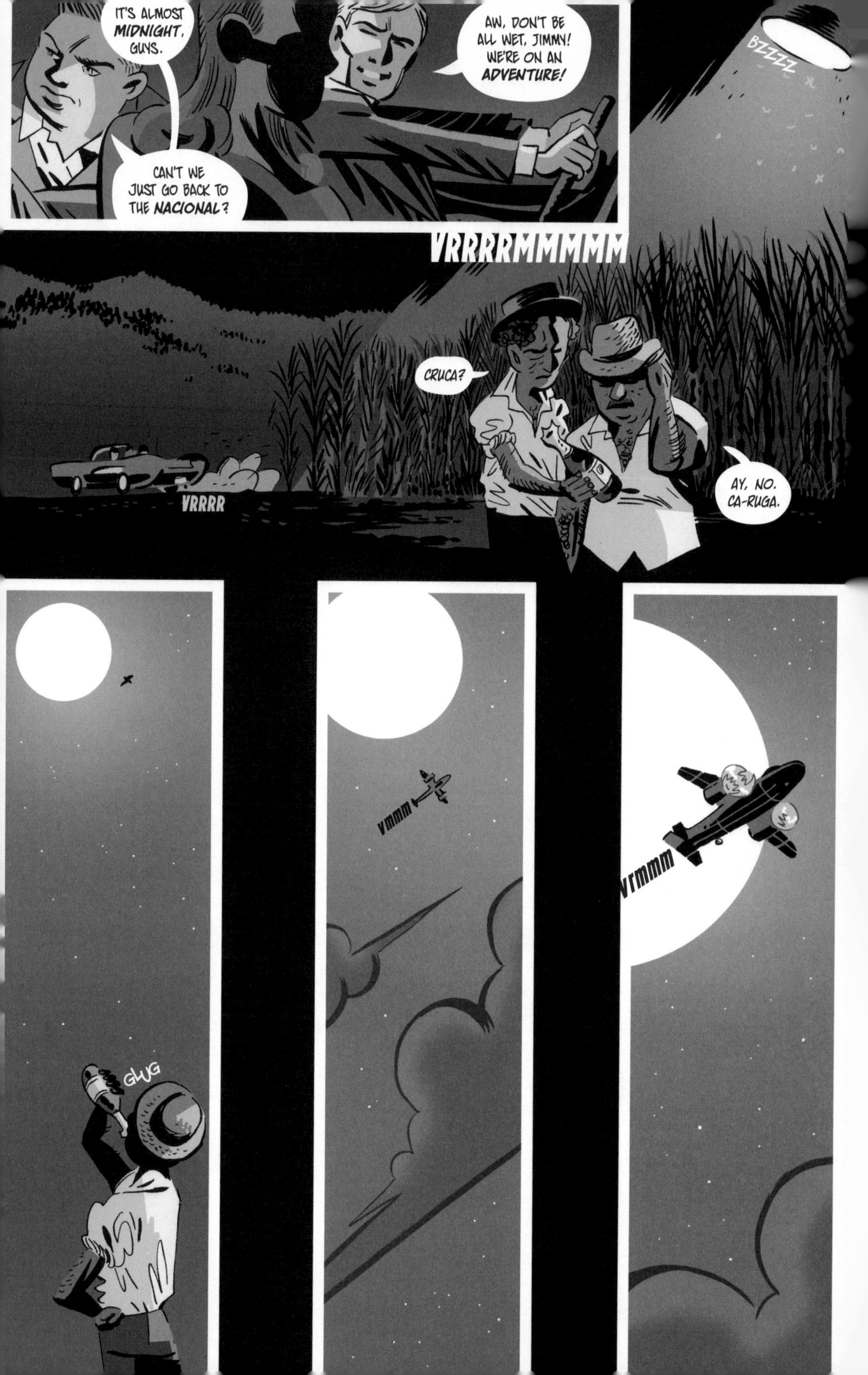
IT'S ALMOST MIDNIGHT, GUYS.
AW, DON'T BE ALL WET, JIMMY! WE'RE ON AN ADVENTURE!
CAN'T WE JUST GO BACK TO THE NACIONAL?
BZZZZ
VRRRRMMMMMM
CRUCA?
VRRRR
AY, NO. CA-RUGA.
GLUG
vmmm
vrmmm

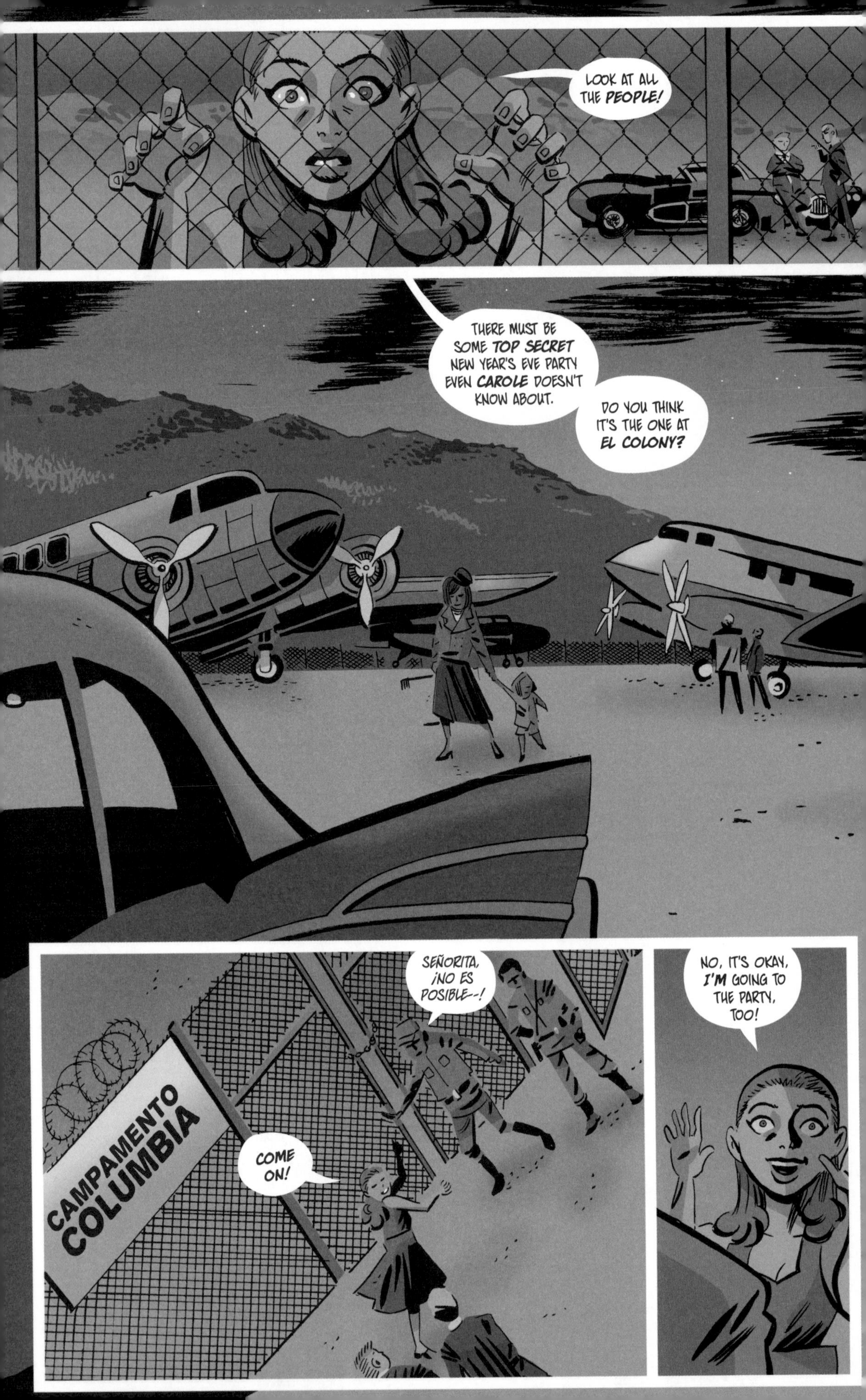
LOOK AT ALL THE PEOPLE!
THERE MUST BE SOME TOP SECRET NEW YEAR'S EVE PARTY EVEN CAROLE DOESN'T KNOW ABOUT.
DO YOU THINK IT'S THE ONE AT EL COLONY?
SEÑORITA, ¡NO ES POSIBLE--!
CAMPAMENTO COLUMBIA
COME ON!
NO, IT'S OKAY, I'M GOING TO THE PARTY, TOO!

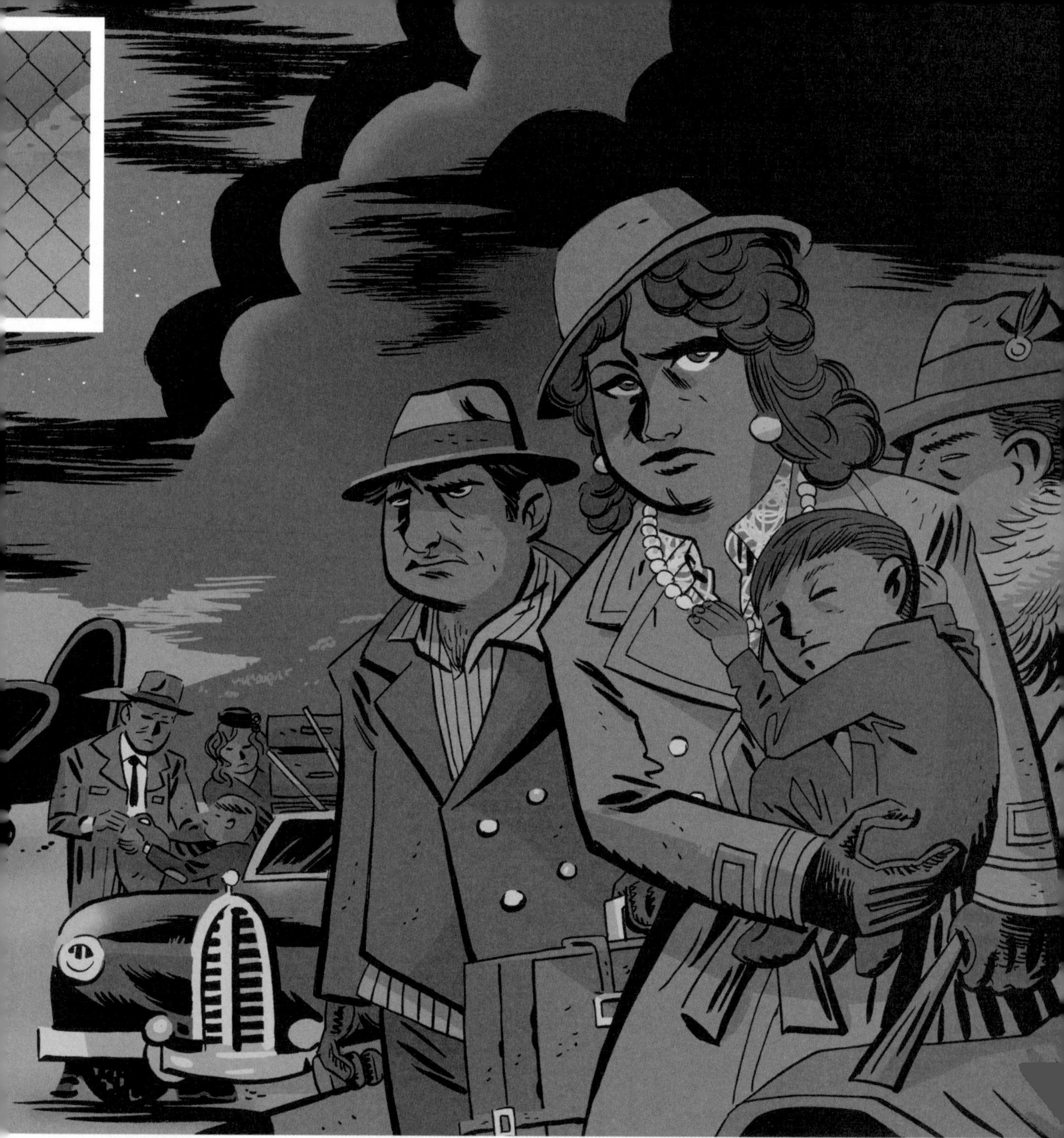

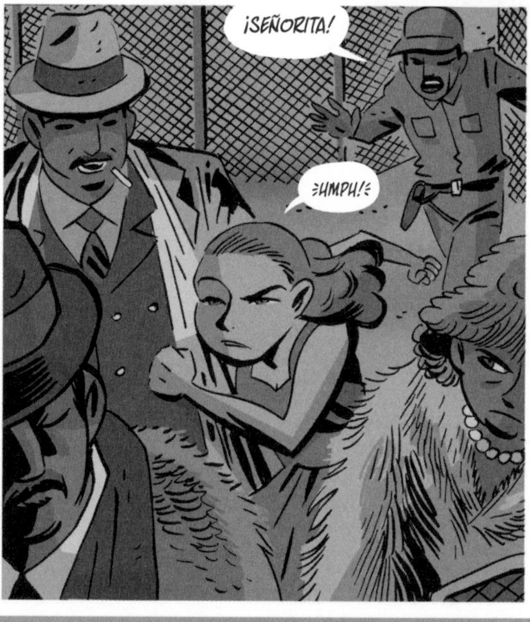
¡SEÑORITA!
HMPH!

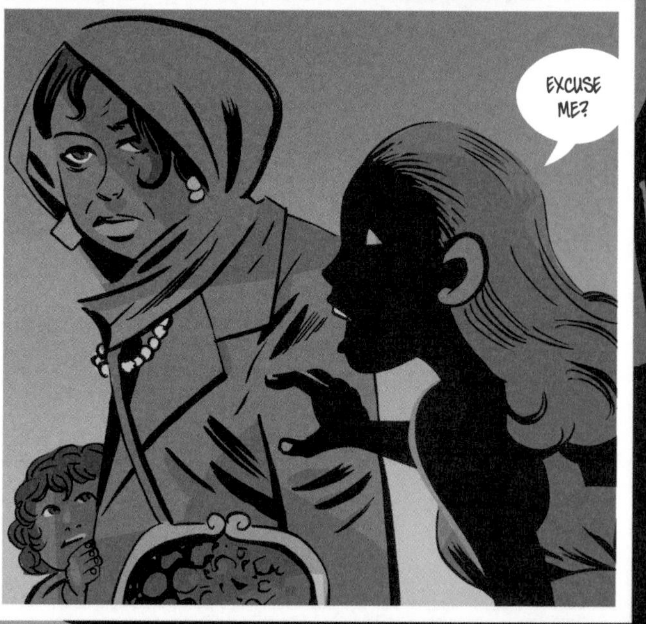
EXCUSE ME?

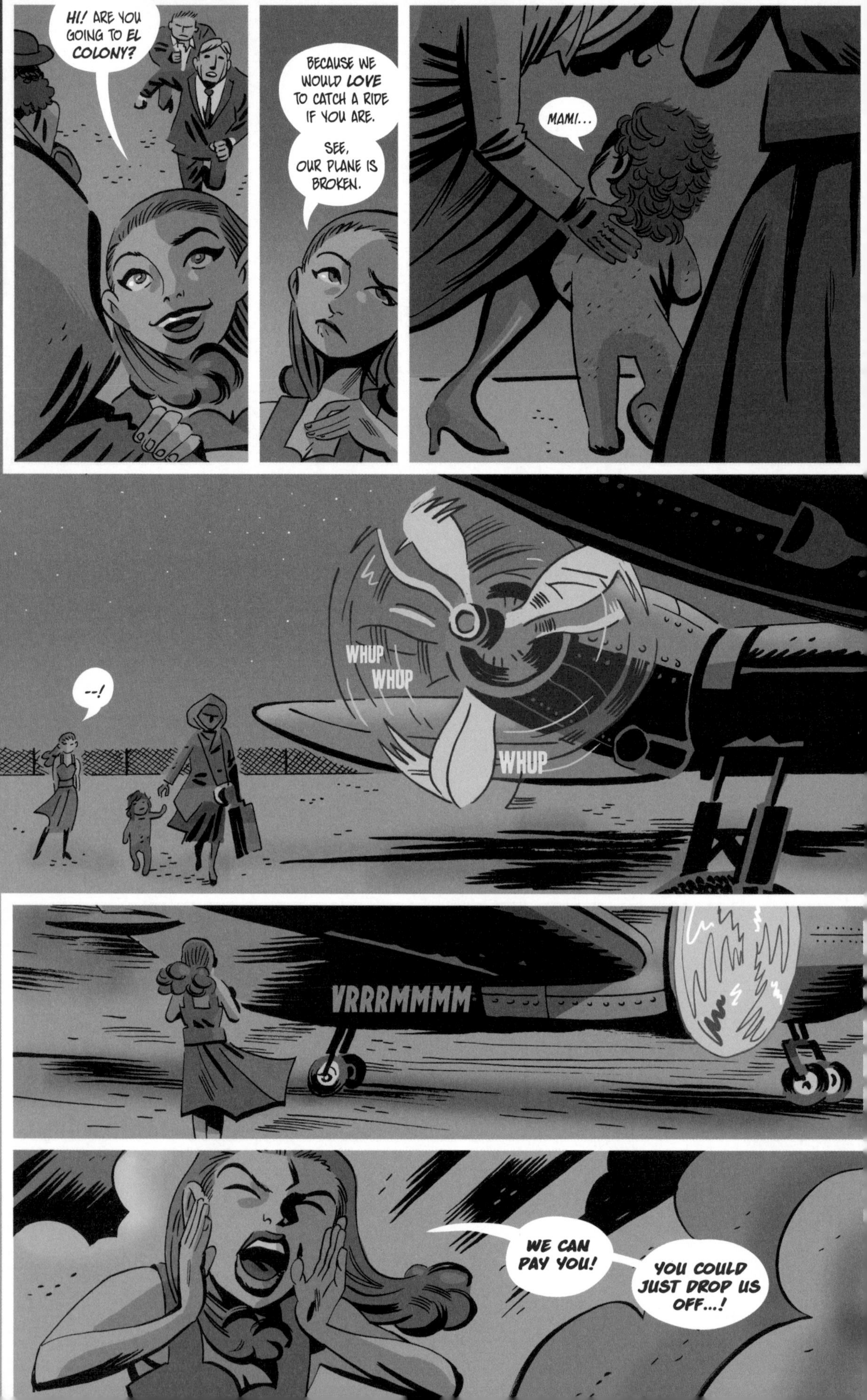
HI! ARE YOU GOING TO EL COLONY?
BECAUSE WE WOULD LOVE TO CATCH A RIDE IF YOU ARE.
SEE, OUR PLANE IS BROKEN.
MAMI...
--!
WHUP
WHUP
WHUP
VRRRMMMM
WE CAN PAY YOU!
YOU COULD JUST DROP US OFF...!

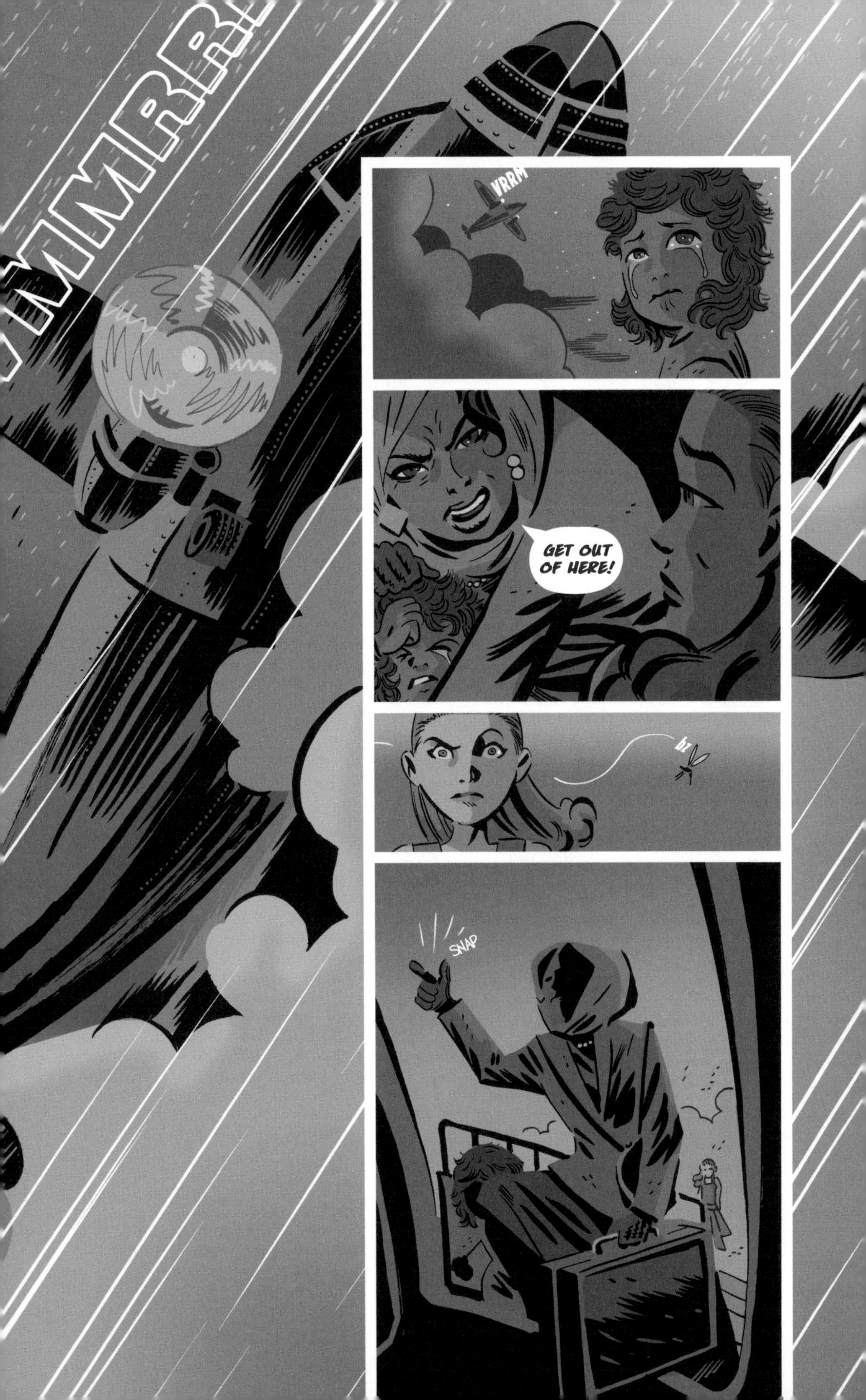
VRRM
GET OUT OF HERE!
bz
SNAP

bzz

VAMONOS, CELIA.

bzzt

¡NO PUEDE PASAR!

¡NGCUN TU OTE PEREMITO!

=NGH!=

SMAK

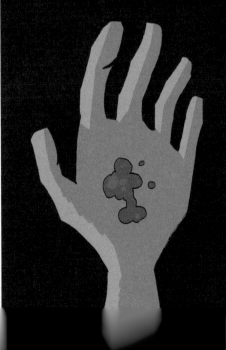

UGH. EW.

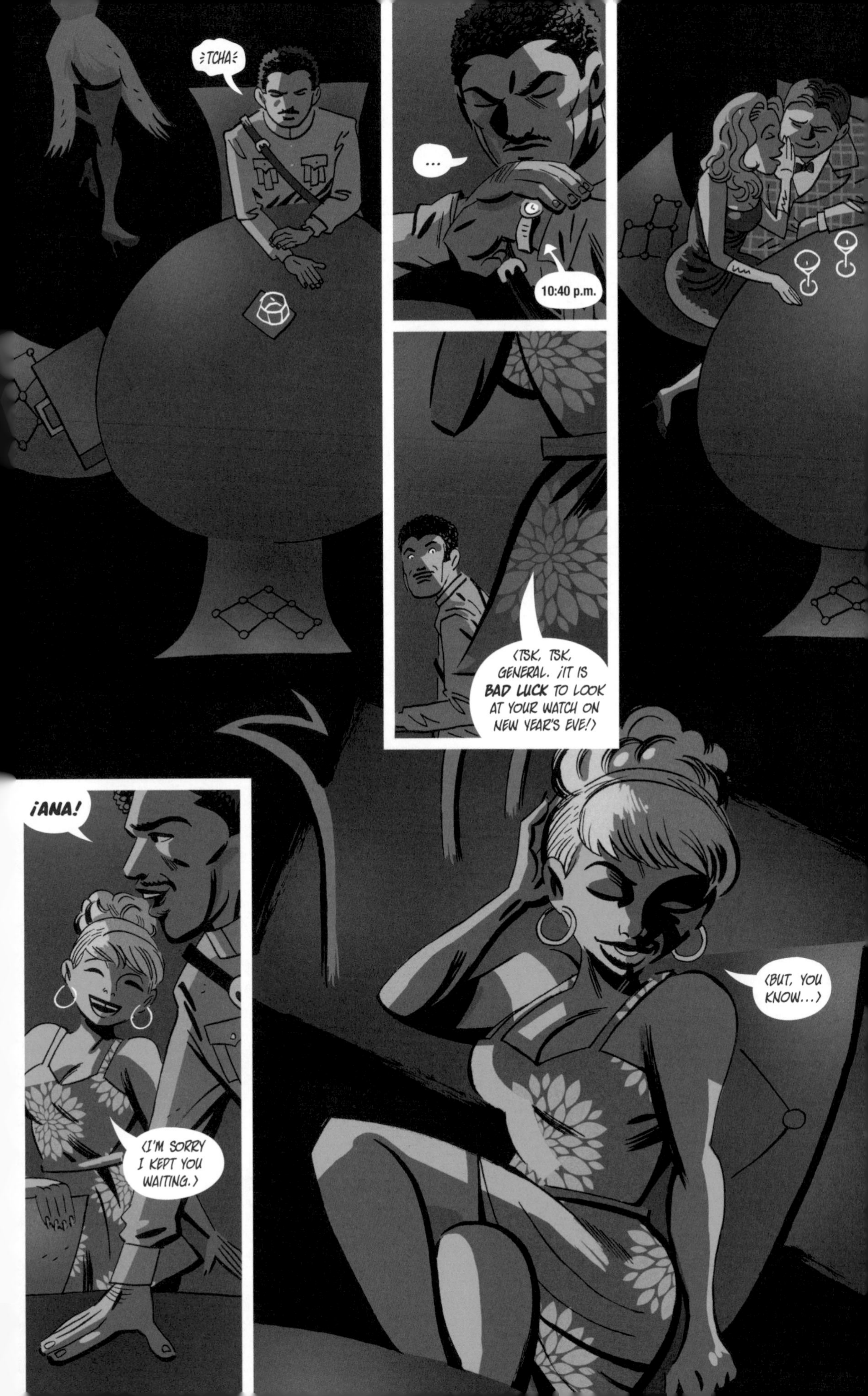
TCHA
...
10:40 p.m.
⟨TSK, TSK, GENERAL. ¡IT IS **BAD LUCK** TO LOOK AT YOUR WATCH ON NEW YEAR'S EVE!⟩
⟨BUT, YOU KNOW...⟩
¡ANA!
⟨I'M SORRY I KEPT YOU WAITING.⟩

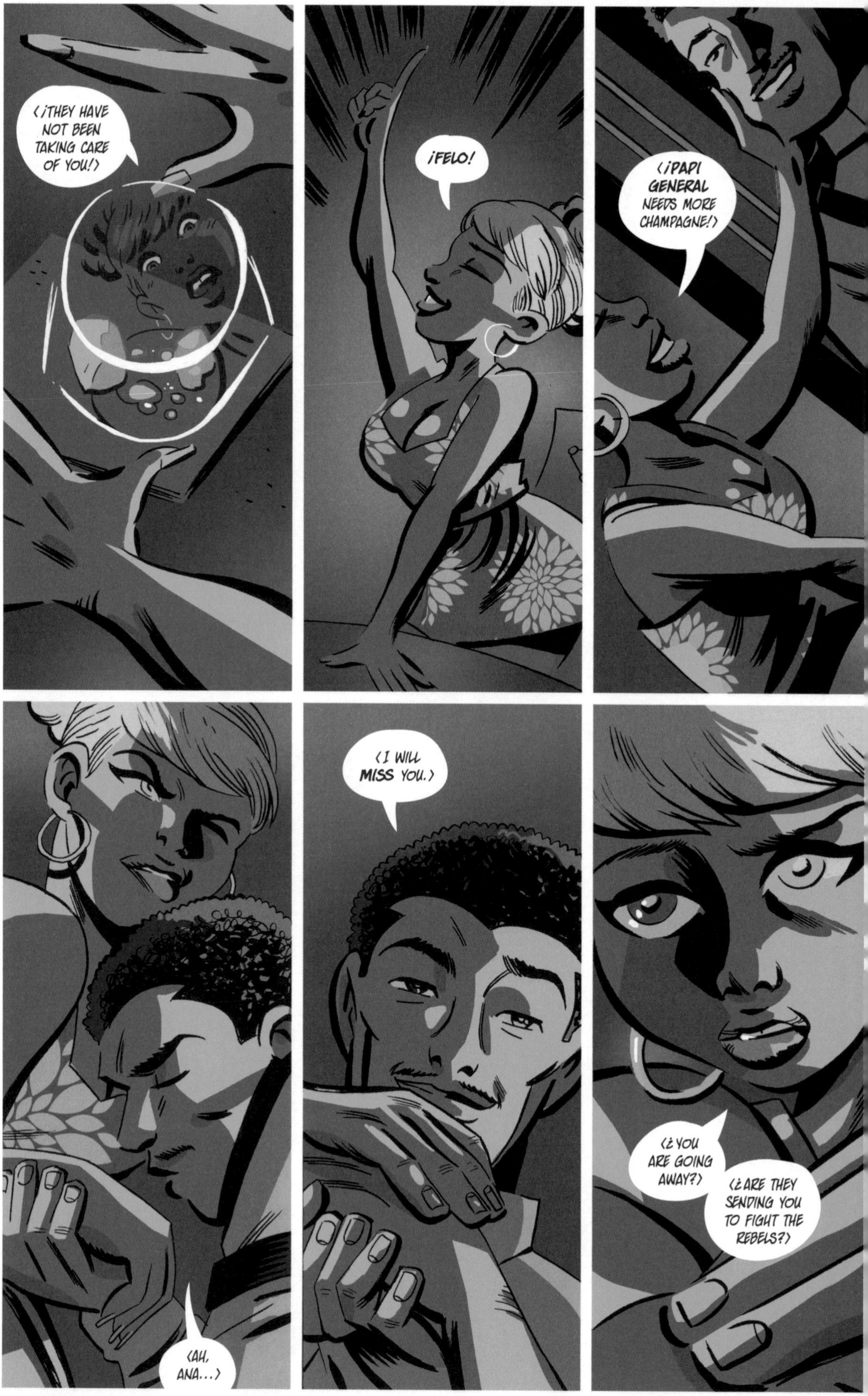
‹¡THEY HAVE NOT BEEN TAKING CARE OF YOU!›
¡FELO!
‹¡PAPI GENERAL NEEDS MORE CHAMPAGNE!›
‹AH, ANA...›
‹I WILL MISS YOU.›
‹¿YOU ARE GOING AWAY?›
‹¿ARE THEY SENDING YOU TO FIGHT THE REBELS?›

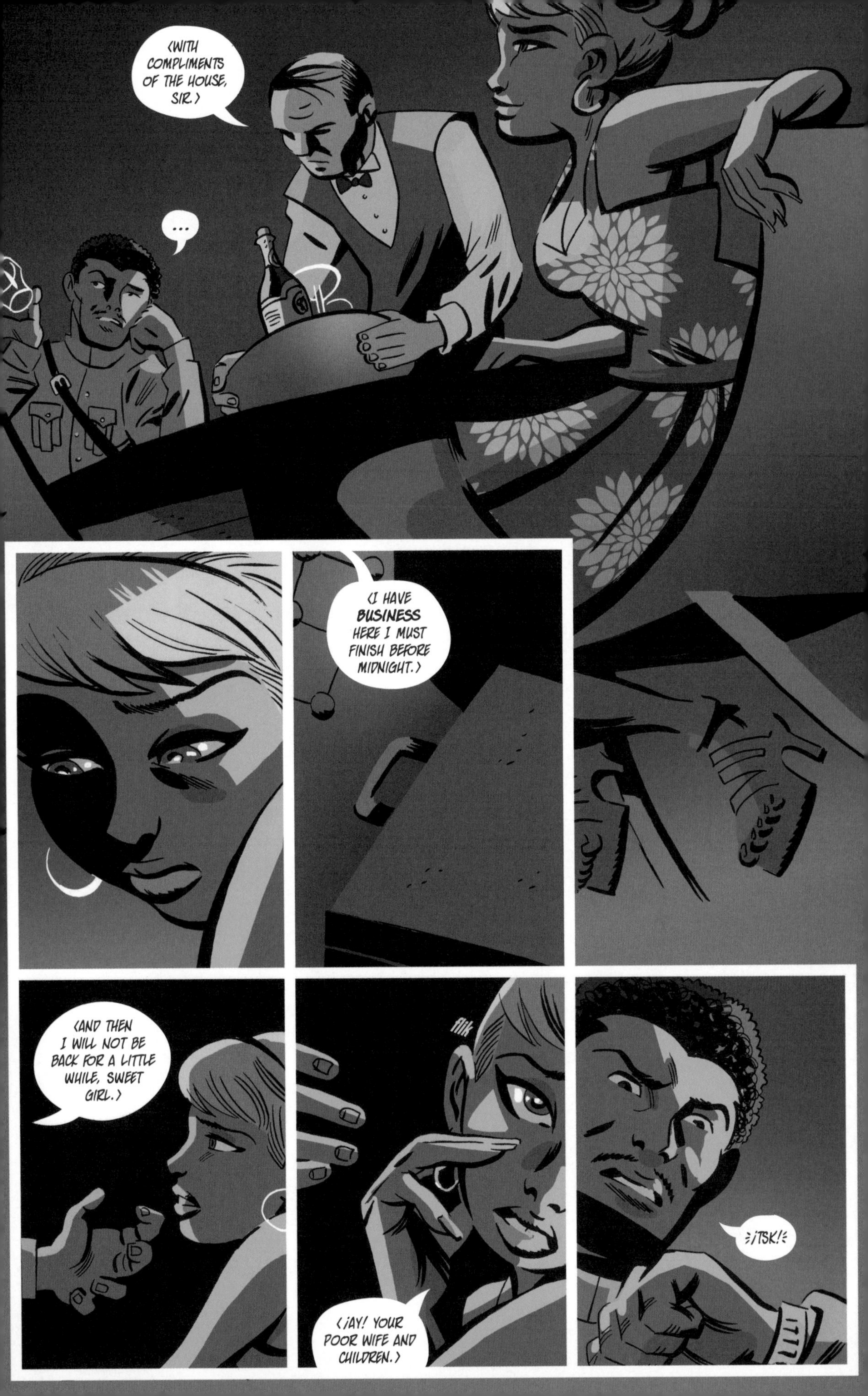
‹WITH COMPLIMENTS OF THE HOUSE, SIR.›
...
‹I HAVE BUSINESS HERE I MUST FINISH BEFORE MIDNIGHT.›
‹AND THEN I WILL NOT BE BACK FOR A LITTLE WHILE, SWEET GIRL.›
flik
‹¡AY! YOUR POOR WIFE AND CHILDREN.›
¡TSK!

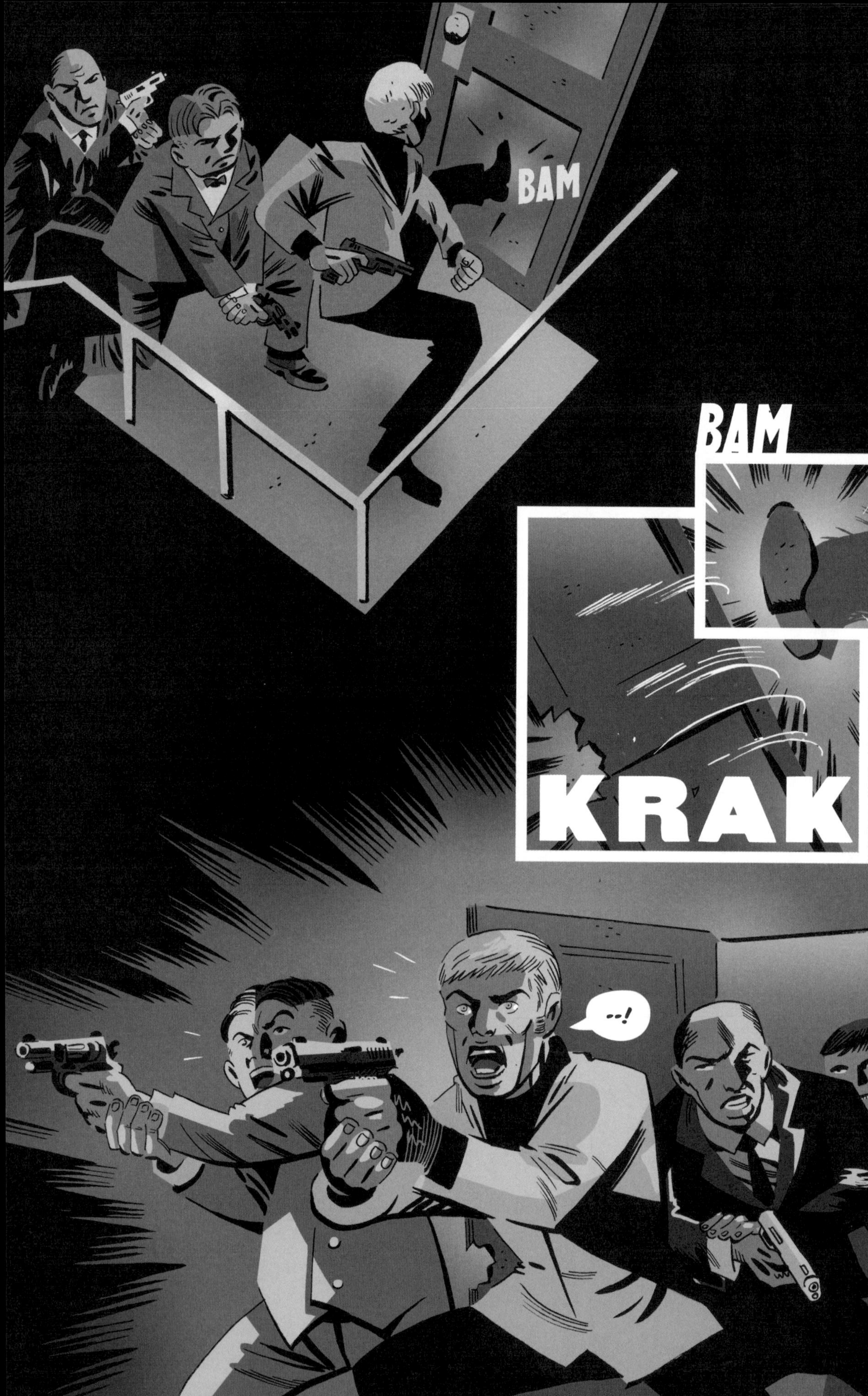
BAM
BAM
KRAK
--!

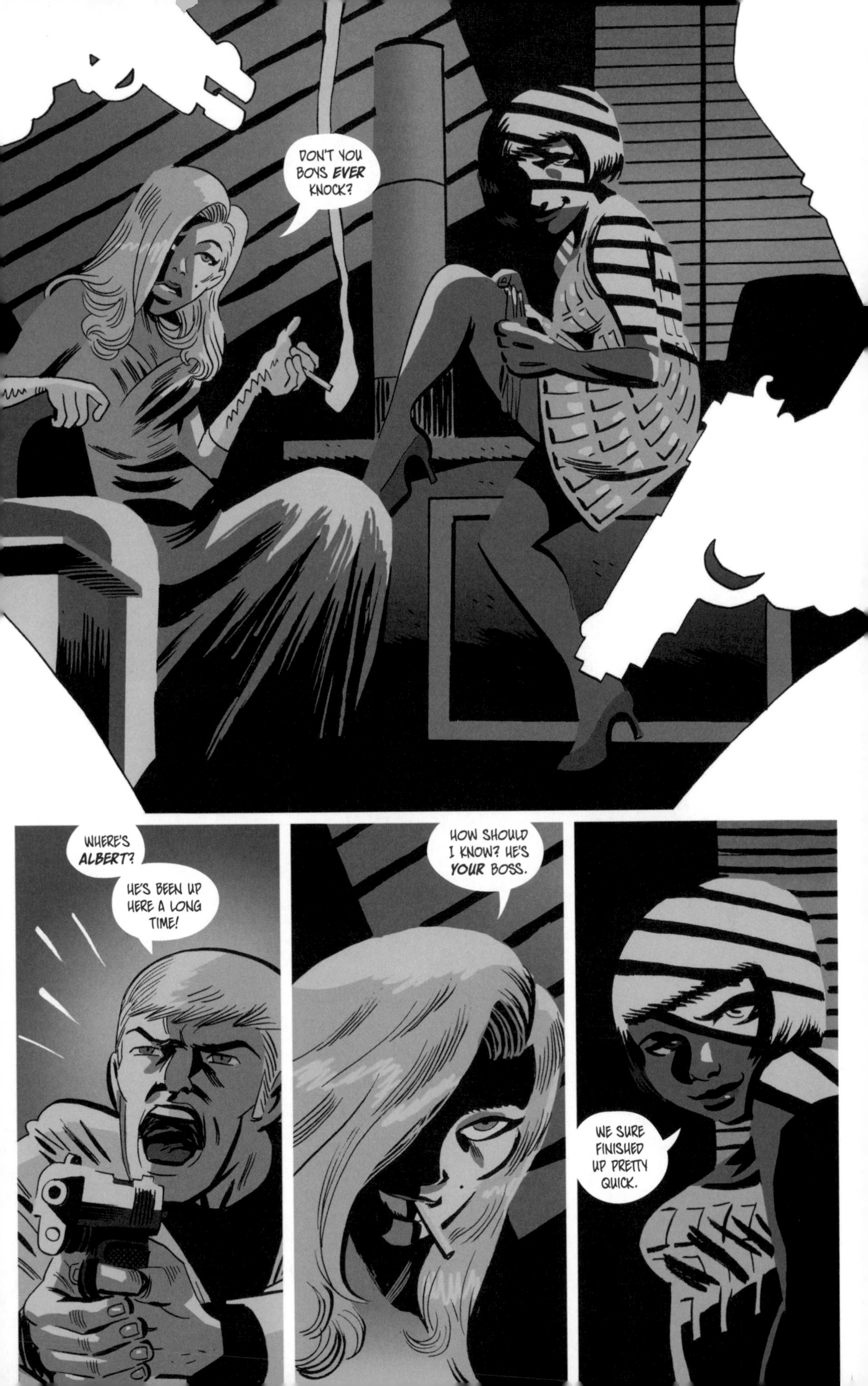
DON'T YOU BOYS EVER KNOCK?
WHERE'S ALBERT?
HE'S BEEN UP HERE A LONG TIME!
HOW SHOULD I KNOW? HE'S YOUR BOSS.
WE SURE FINISHED UP PRETTY QUICK.

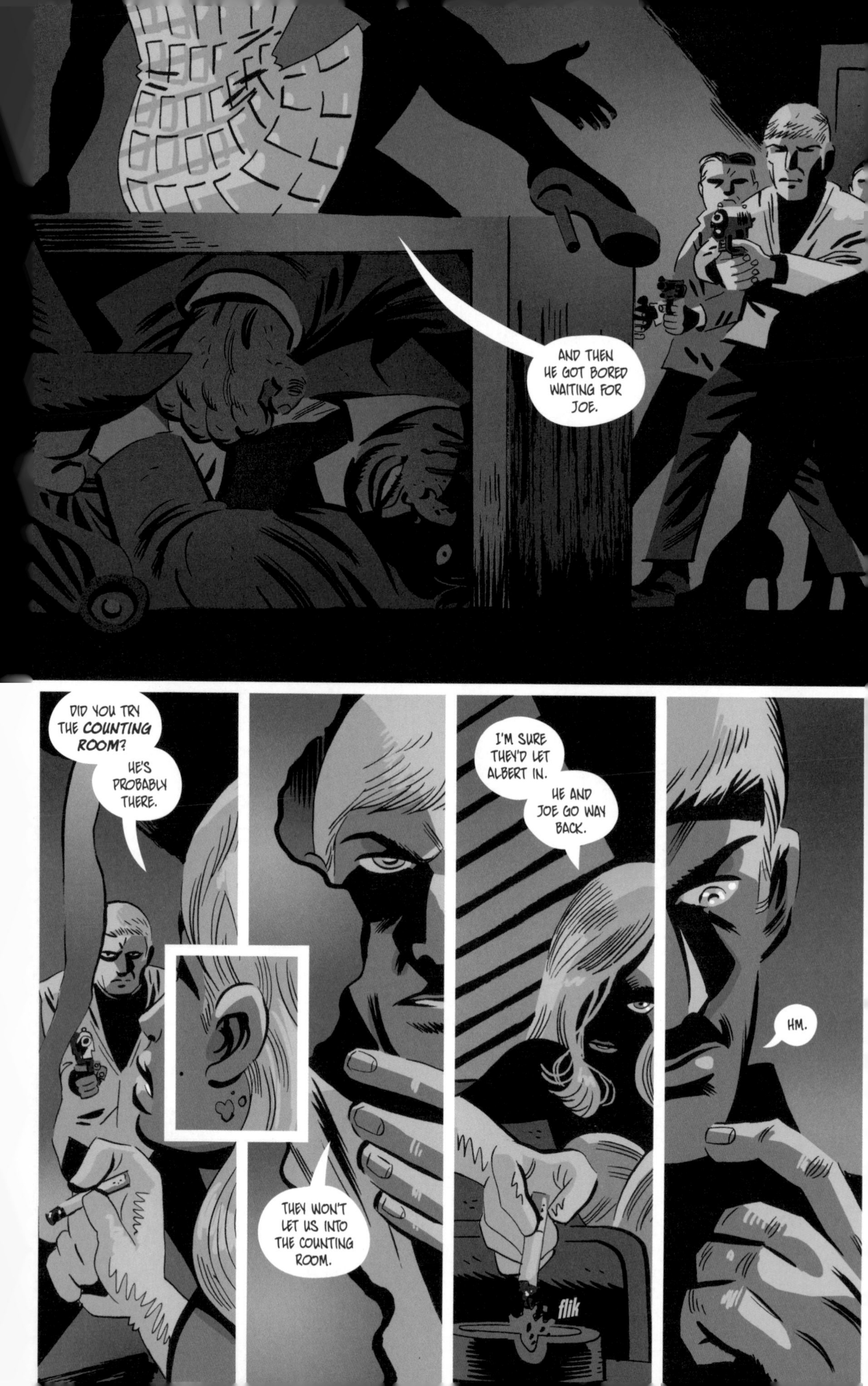
AND THEN HE GOT BORED WAITING FOR JOE.
DID YOU TRY THE COUNTING ROOM?
HE'S PROBABLY THERE.
THEY WON'T LET US INTO THE COUNTING ROOM.
I'M SURE THEY'D LET ALBERT IN.
HE AND JOE GO WAY BACK.
flik
HM.

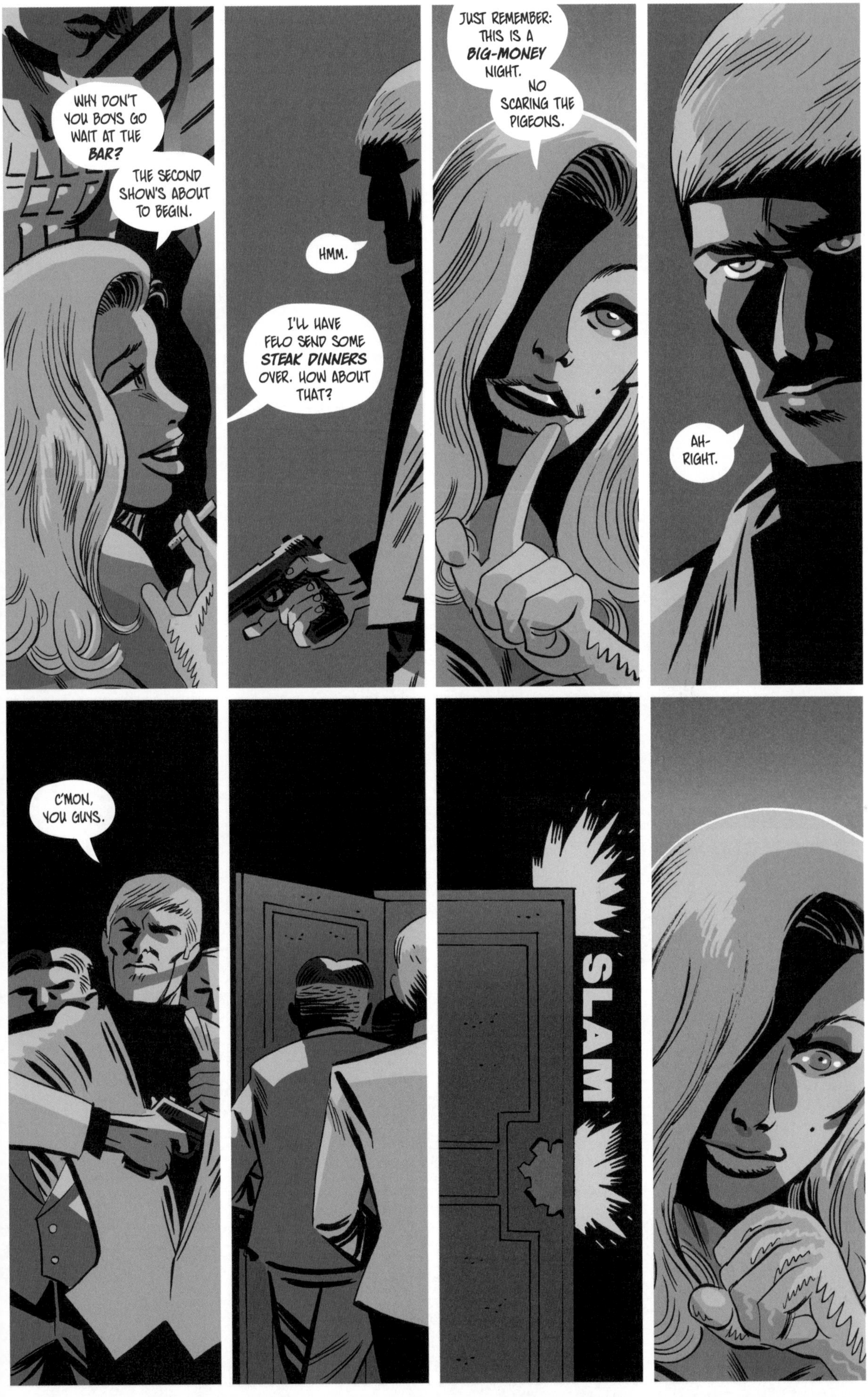
WHY DON'T YOU BOYS GO WAIT AT THE BAR?
THE SECOND SHOW'S ABOUT TO BEGIN.
HMM.
I'LL HAVE FELO SEND SOME STEAK DINNERS OVER. HOW ABOUT THAT?
JUST REMEMBER: THIS IS A BIG-MONEY NIGHT.
NO SCARING THE PIGEONS.
AH-RIGHT.
C'MON, YOU GUYS.
SLAM

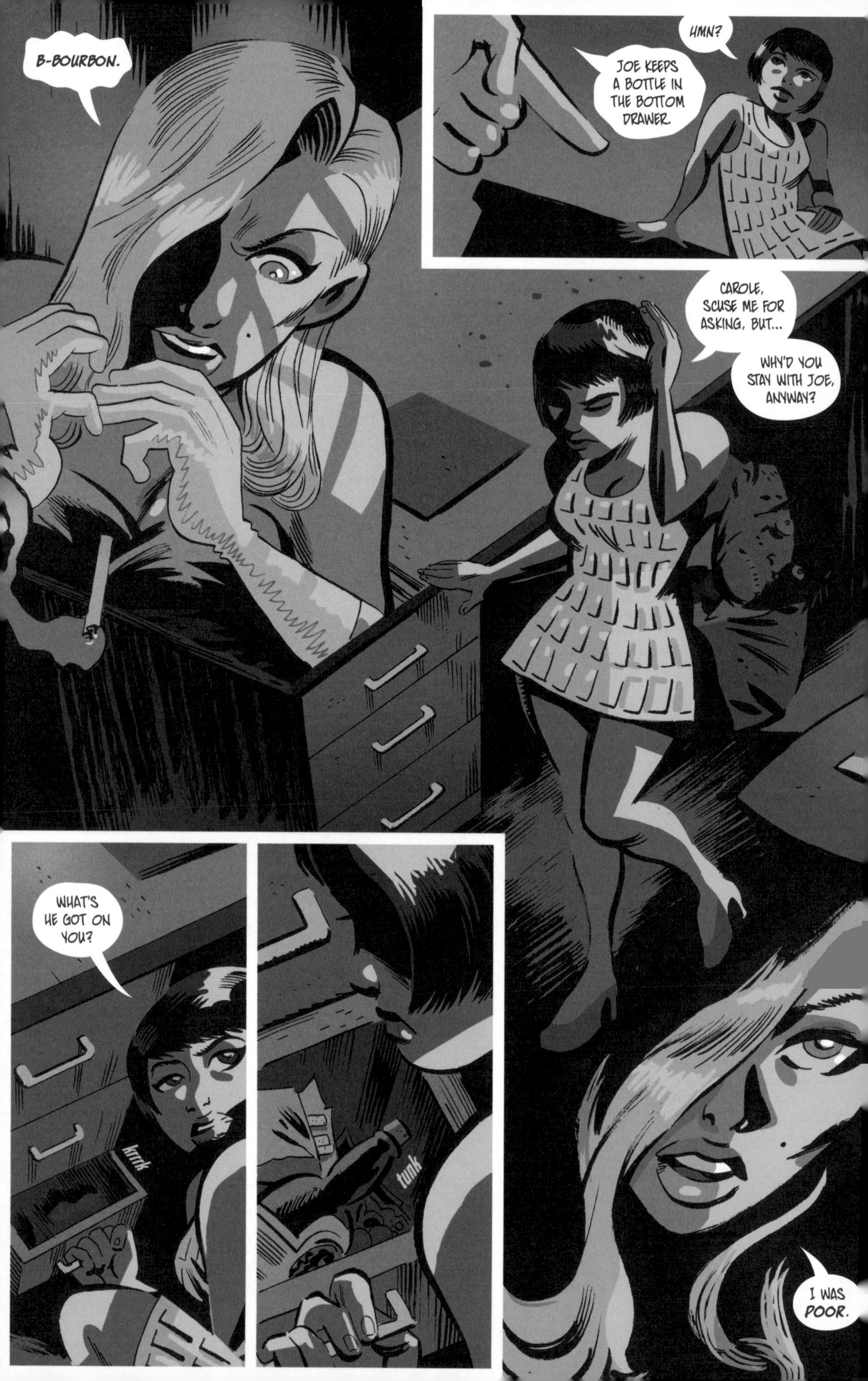
B-BOURBON.
HMN?
JOE KEEPS A BOTTLE IN THE BOTTOM DRAWER.
CAROLE, SCUSE ME FOR ASKING, BUT...
WHY'D YOU STAY WITH JOE, ANYWAY?
WHAT'S HE GOT ON YOU?
krrrk
tunk
I WAS POOR.

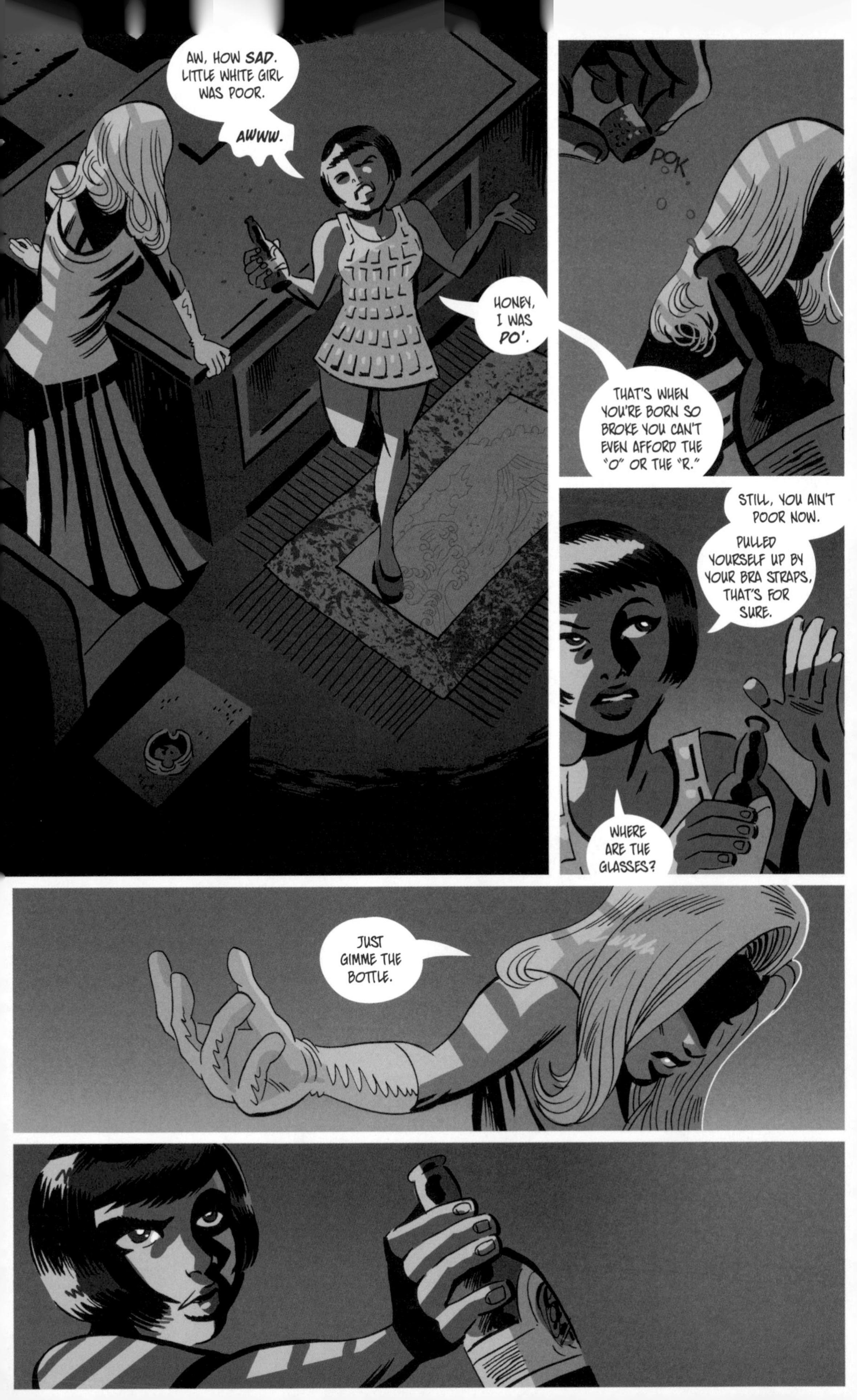
AW, HOW SAD. LITTLE WHITE GIRL WAS POOR.
AWWW.
HONEY, I WAS PO'.
THAT'S WHEN YOU'RE BORN SO BROKE YOU CAN'T EVEN AFFORD THE "O" OR THE "R."
POK
STILL, YOU AIN'T POOR NOW.
PULLED YOURSELF UP BY YOUR BRA STRAPS, THAT'S FOR SURE.
WHERE ARE THE GLASSES?
JUST GIMME THE BOTTLE.

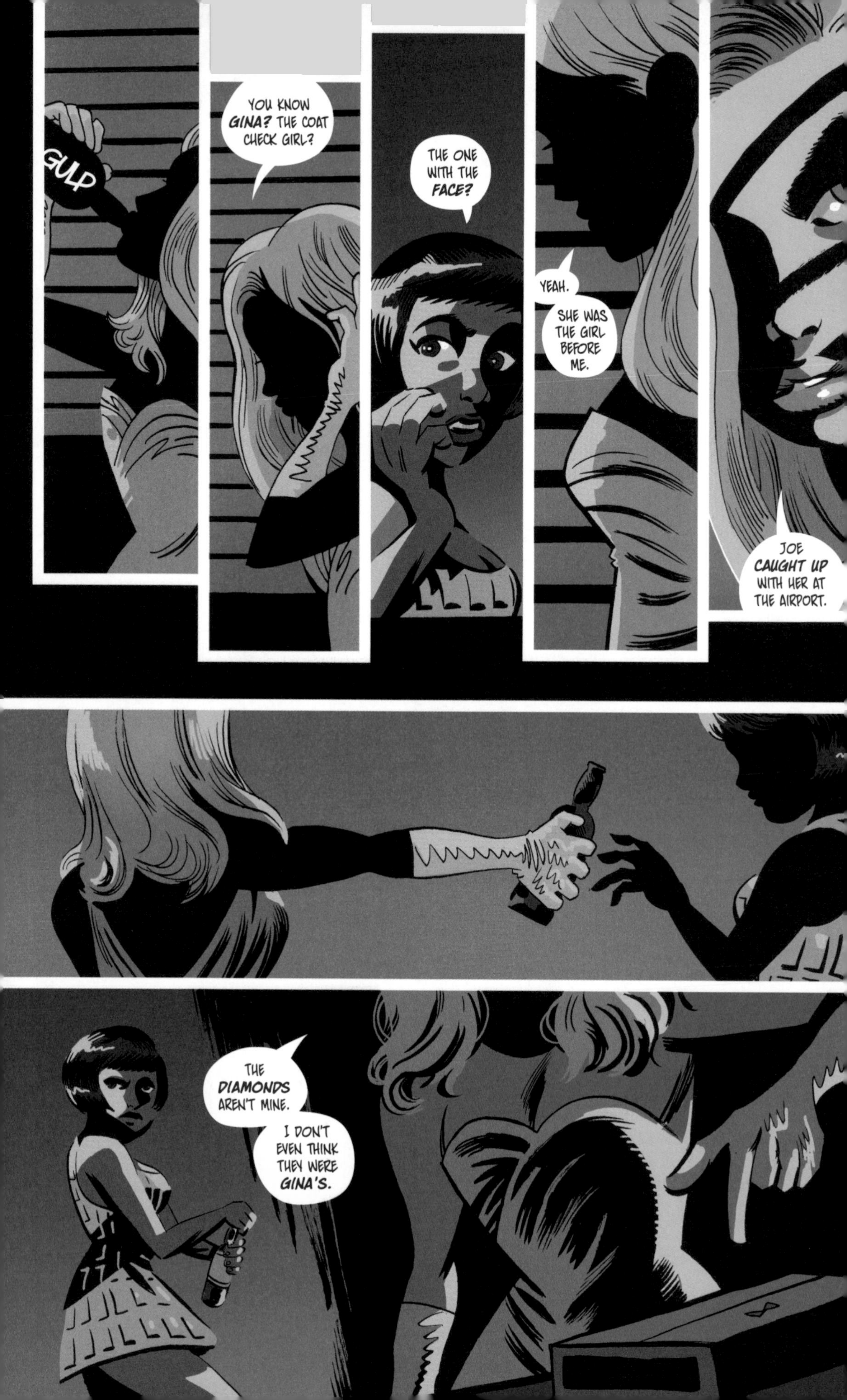
GULP
YOU KNOW GINA? THE COAT CHECK GIRL?
THE ONE WITH THE FACE?
YEAH.
SHE WAS THE GIRL BEFORE ME.
JOE CAUGHT UP WITH HER AT THE AIRPORT.
THE DIAMONDS AREN'T MINE.
I DON'T EVEN THINK THEY WERE GINA'S.

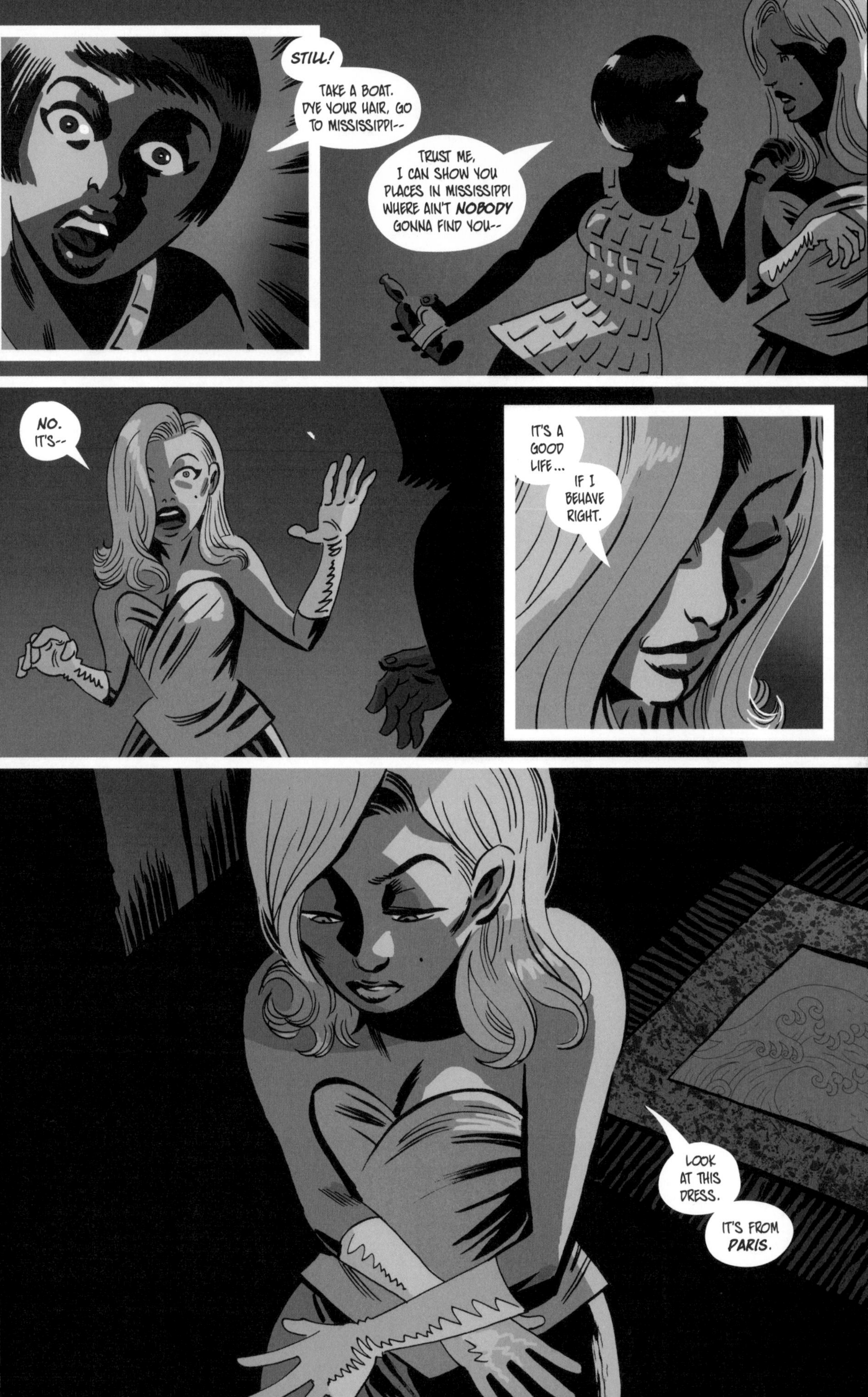
STILL!
TAKE A BOAT. DYE YOUR HAIR, GO TO MISSISSIPPI--
TRUST ME, I CAN SHOW YOU PLACES IN MISSISSIPPI WHERE AIN'T **NOBODY** GONNA FIND YOU--
NO. IT'S--
IT'S A GOOD LIFE...
IF I BEHAVE RIGHT.
LOOK AT THIS DRESS.
IT'S FROM **PARIS**.

11:00 P.M.

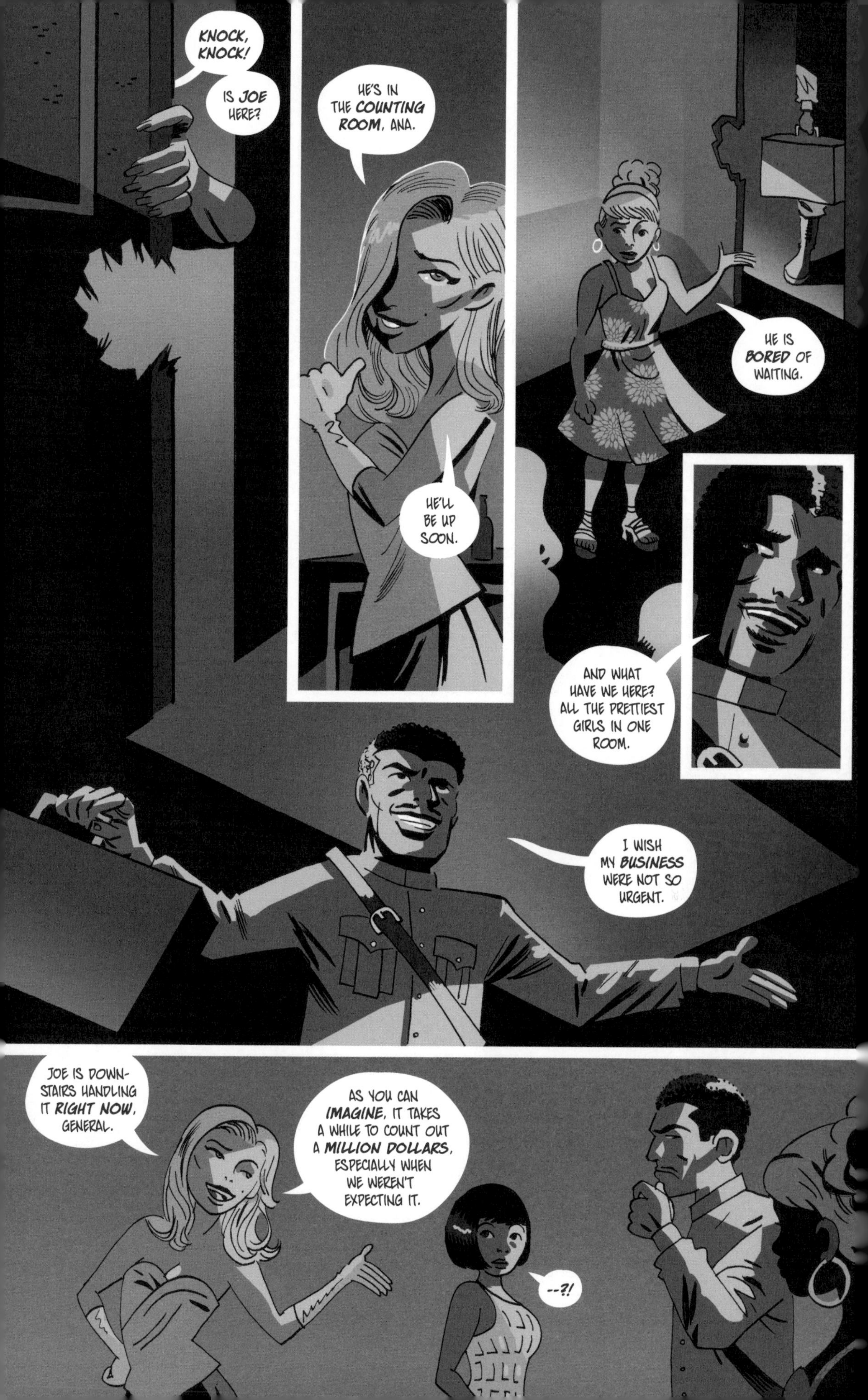
KNOCK, KNOCK!
IS JOE HERE?
HE'S IN THE COUNTING ROOM, ANA.
HE'LL BE UP SOON.
HE IS BORED OF WAITING.
AND WHAT HAVE WE HERE? ALL THE PRETTIEST GIRLS IN ONE ROOM.
I WISH MY BUSINESS WERE NOT SO URGENT.
JOE IS DOWN-STAIRS HANDLING IT RIGHT NOW, GENERAL.
AS YOU CAN IMAGINE, IT TAKES A WHILE TO COUNT OUT A MILLION DOLLARS, ESPECIALLY WHEN WE WEREN'T EXPECTING IT.
--?!

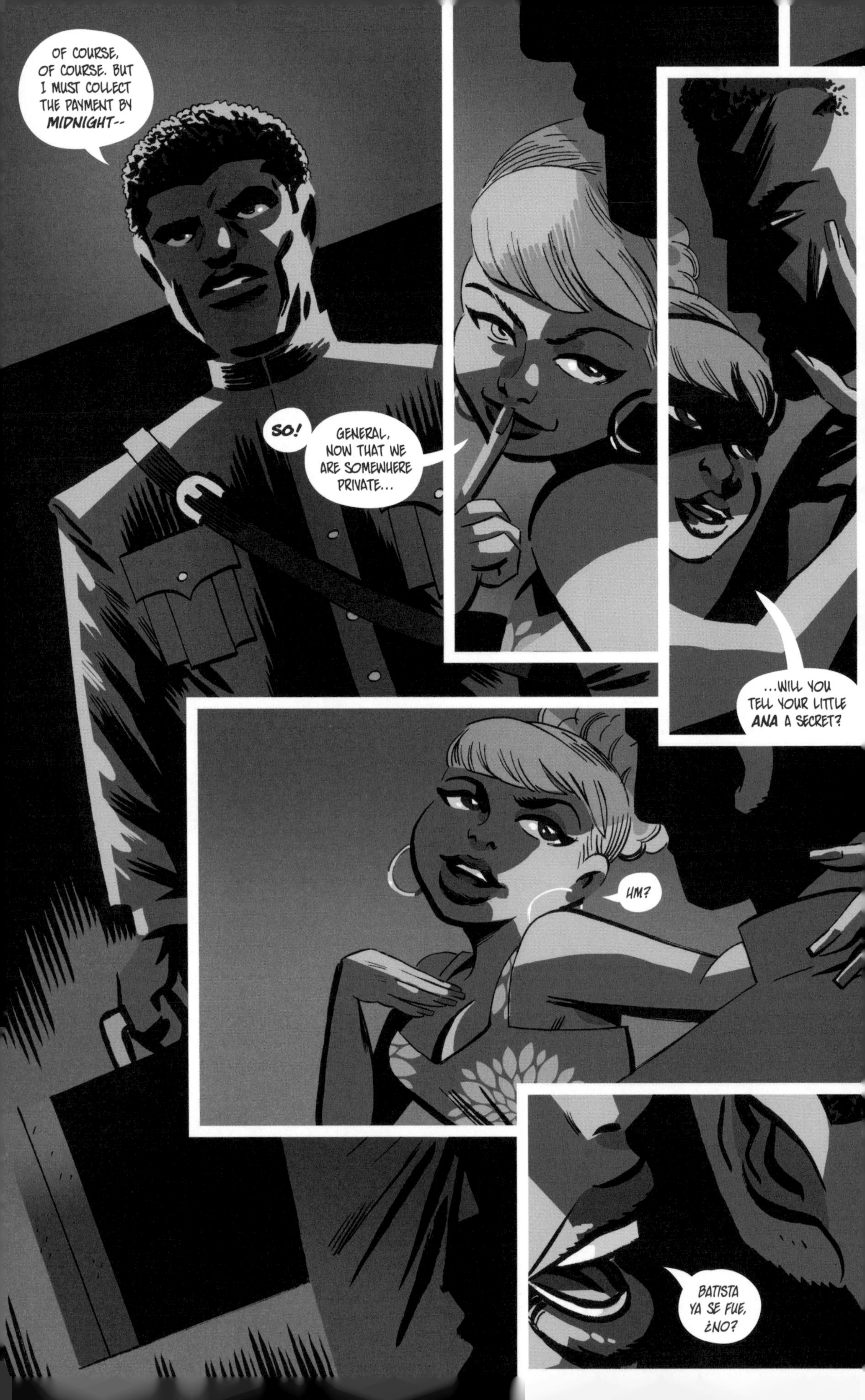
OF COURSE, OF COURSE. BUT I MUST COLLECT THE PAYMENT BY MIDNIGHT--
SO!
GENERAL, NOW THAT WE ARE SOMEWHERE PRIVATE...
...WILL YOU TELL YOUR LITTLE ANA A SECRET?
HM?
BATISTA YA SE FUE, ¿NO?

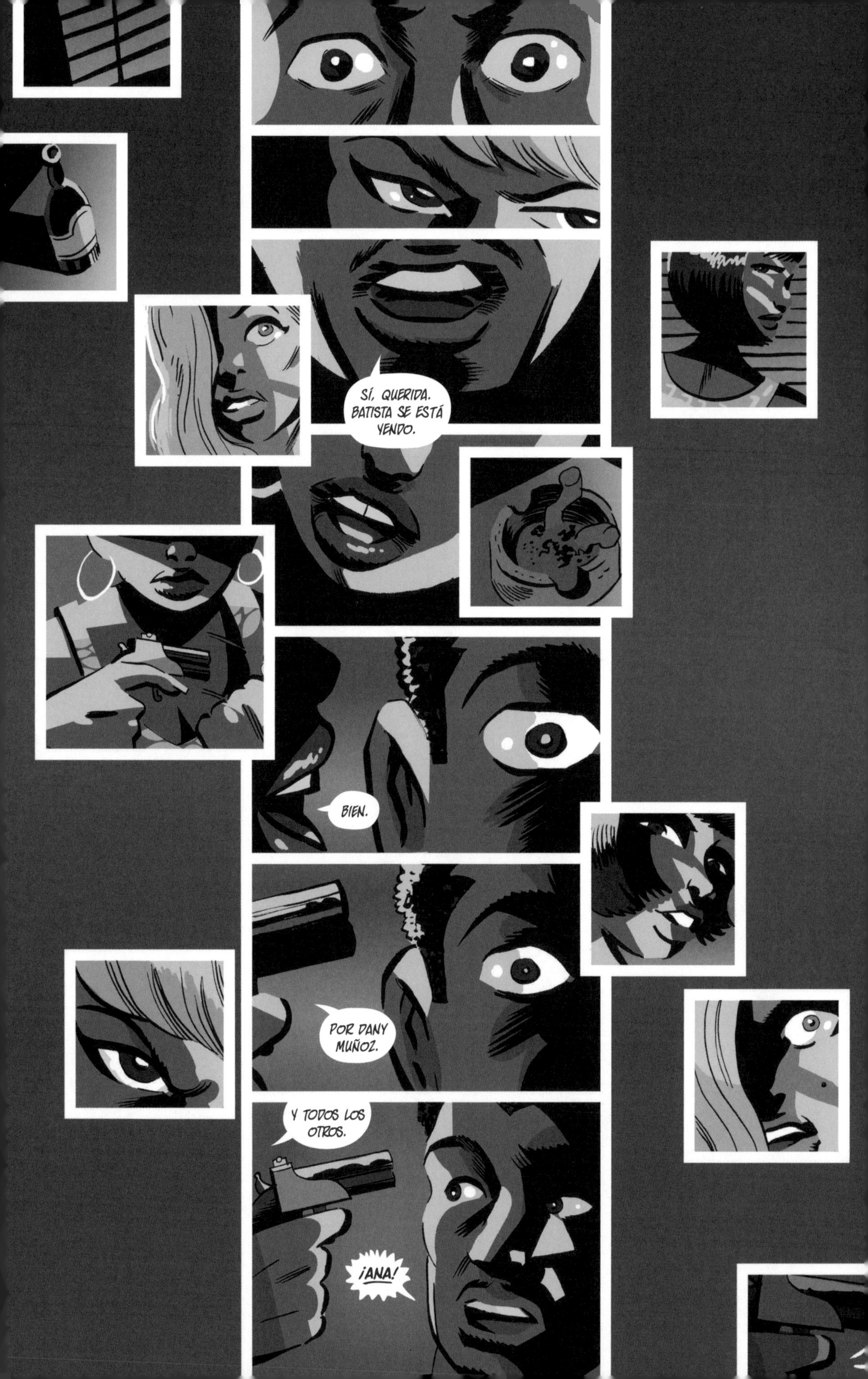
SÍ, QUERIDA. BATISTA SE ESTÁ YENDO.
BIEN.
POR DANY MUÑOZ.
Y TODOS LOS OTROS.
¡ANA!

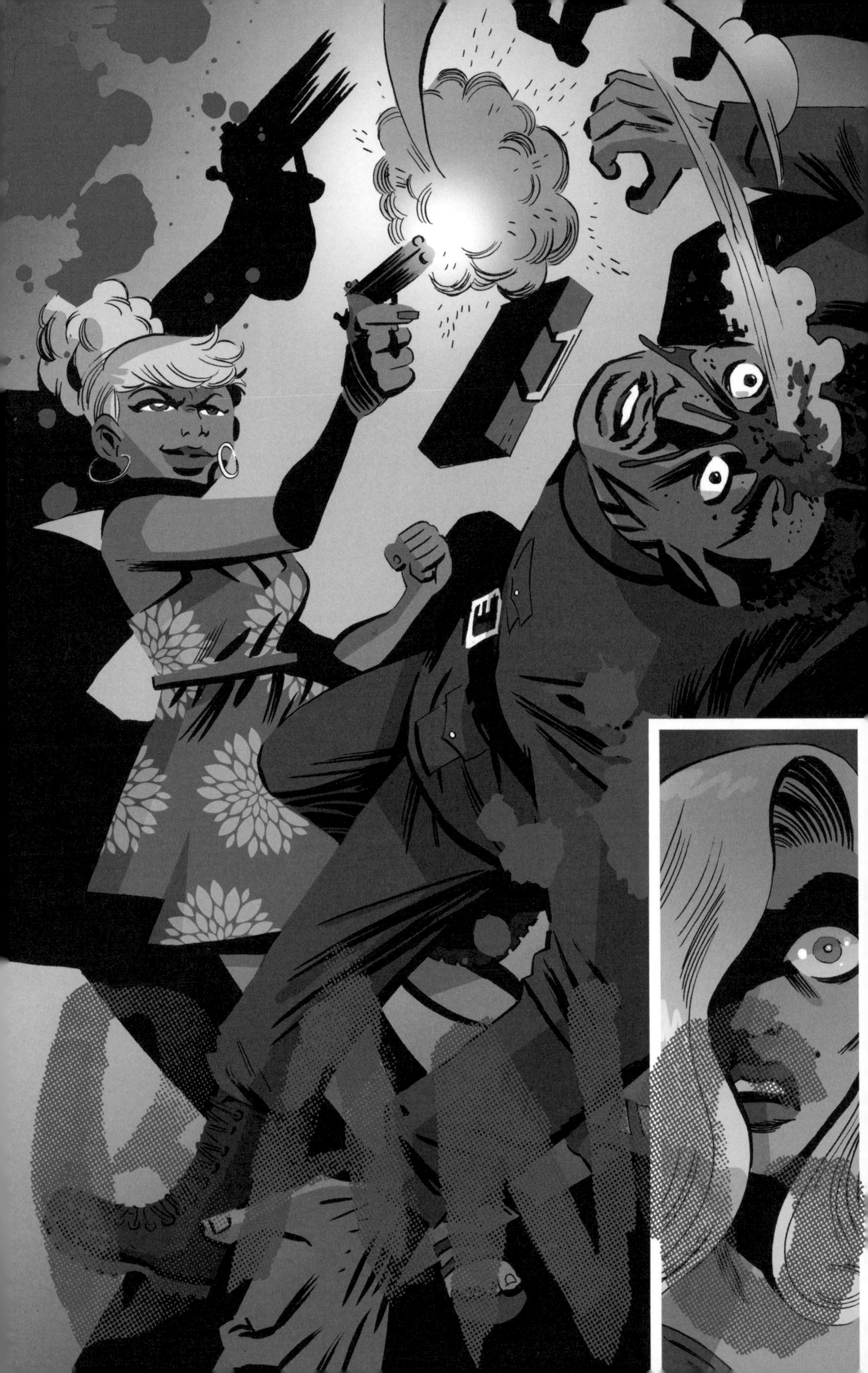

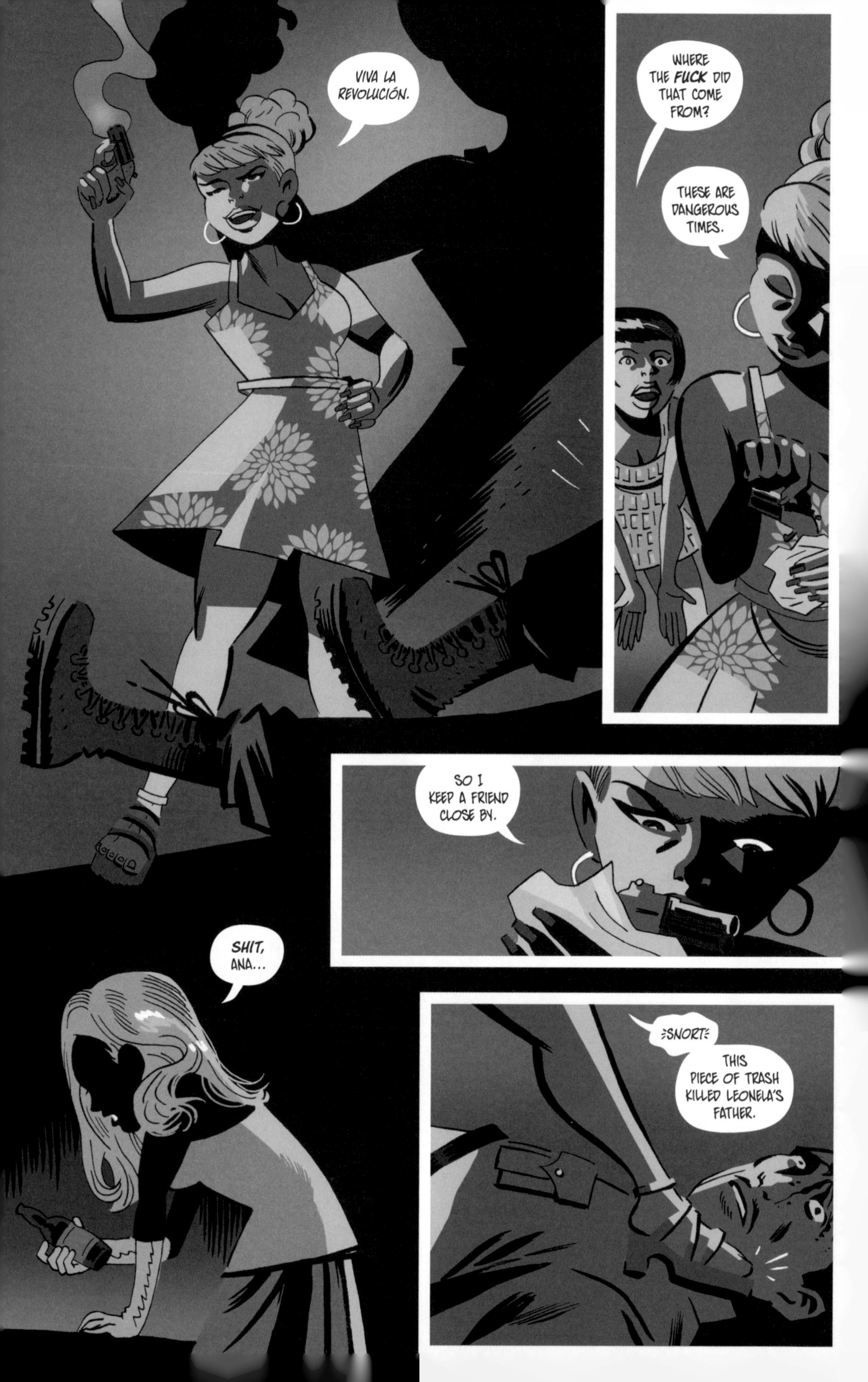
VIVA LA REVOLUCIÓN.
WHERE THE FUCK DID THAT COME FROM?
THESE ARE DANGEROUS TIMES.
SO I KEEP A FRIEND CLOSE BY.
SHIT, ANA...
≶SNORT≶
THIS PIECE OF TRASH KILLED LEONELA'S FATHER.

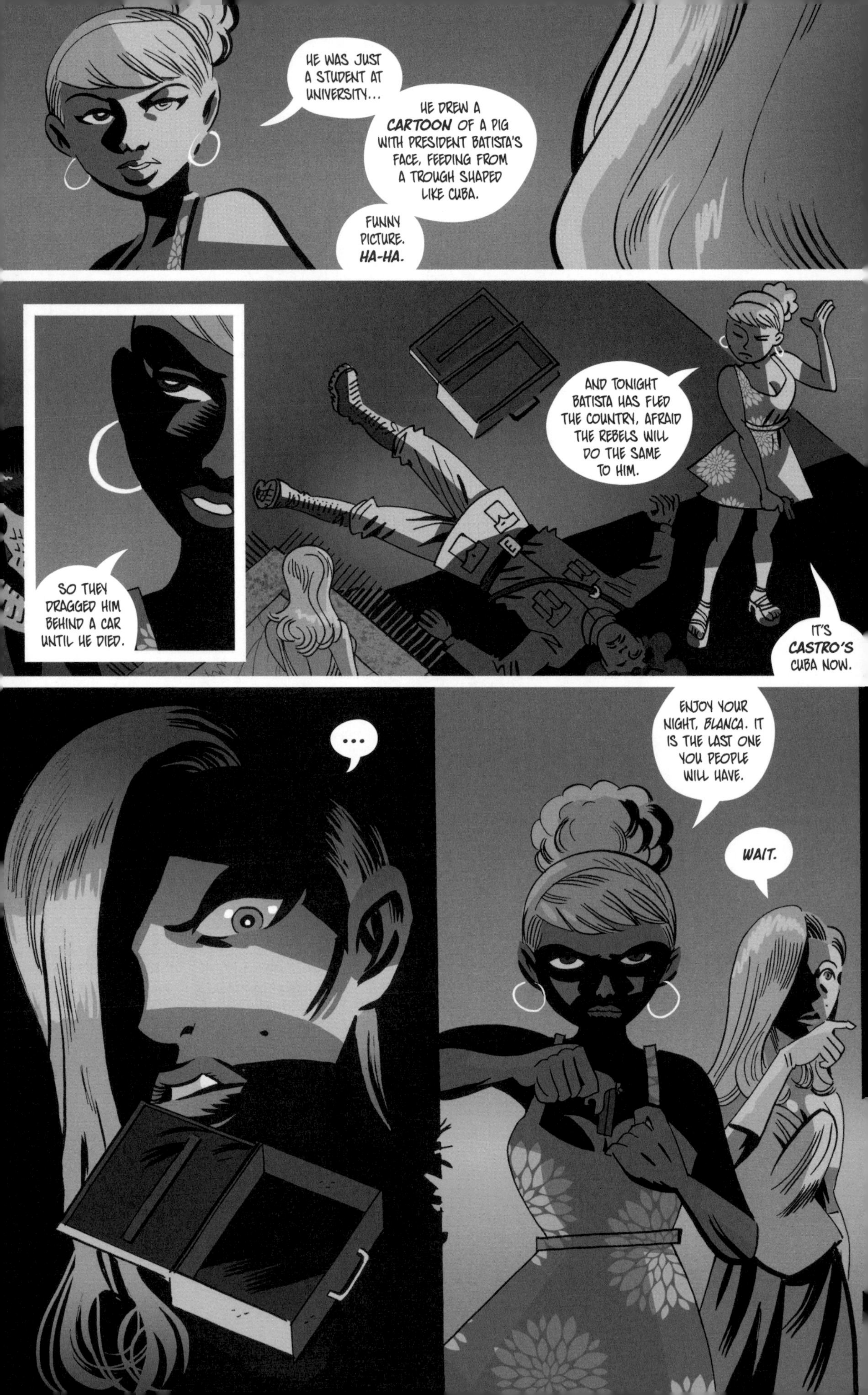
HE WAS JUST A STUDENT AT UNIVERSITY...
HE DREW A CARTOON OF A PIG WITH PRESIDENT BATISTA'S FACE, FEEDING FROM A TROUGH SHAPED LIKE CUBA.
FUNNY PICTURE. HA-HA.
SO THEY DRAGGED HIM BEHIND A CAR UNTIL HE DIED.
AND TONIGHT BATISTA HAS FLED THE COUNTRY, AFRAID THE REBELS WILL DO THE SAME TO HIM.
IT'S CASTRO'S CUBA NOW.
...
ENJOY YOUR NIGHT, BLANCA. IT IS THE LAST ONE YOU PEOPLE WILL HAVE.
WAIT.

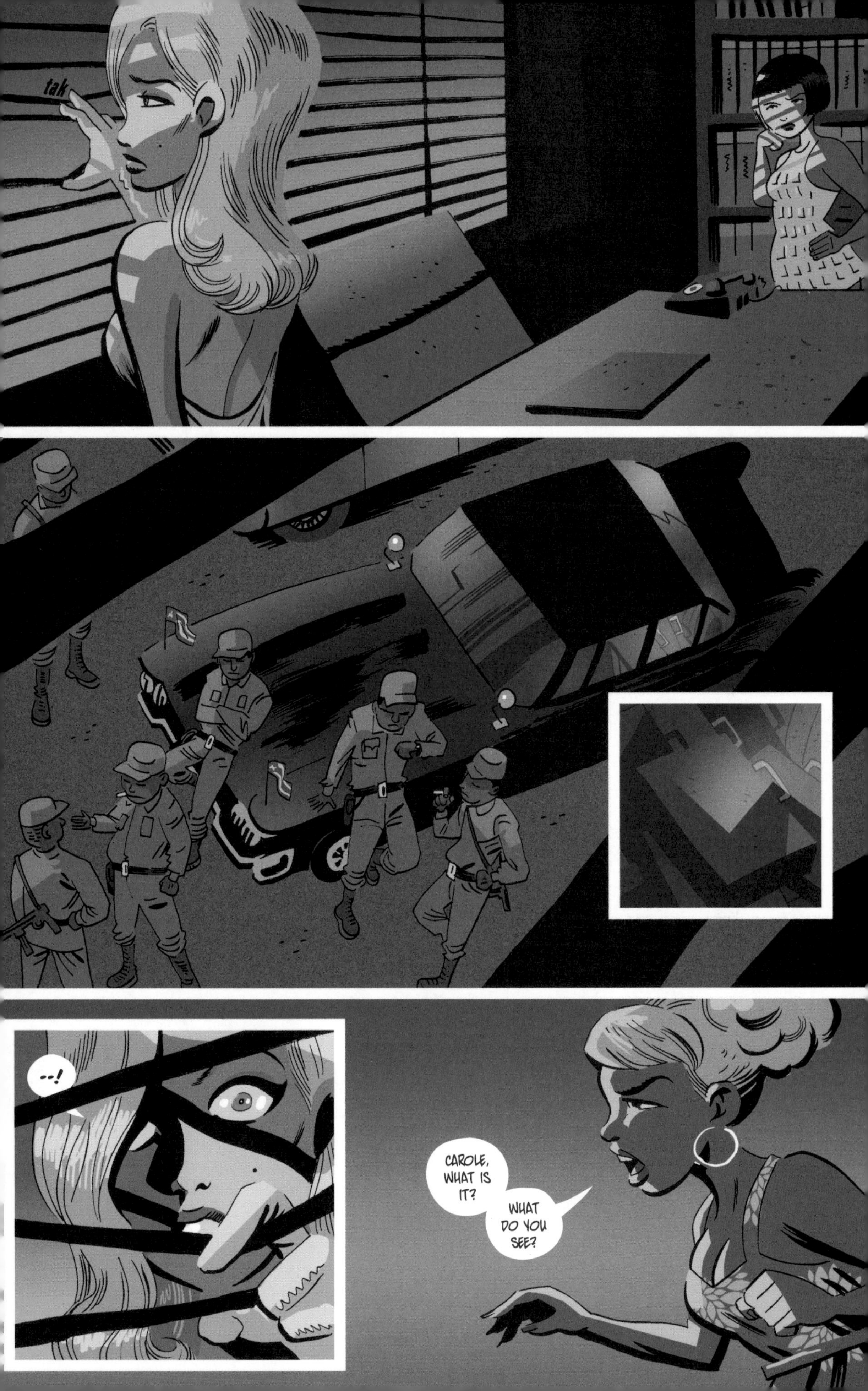
tak
--!
CAROLE, WHAT IS IT?
WHAT DO YOU SEE?

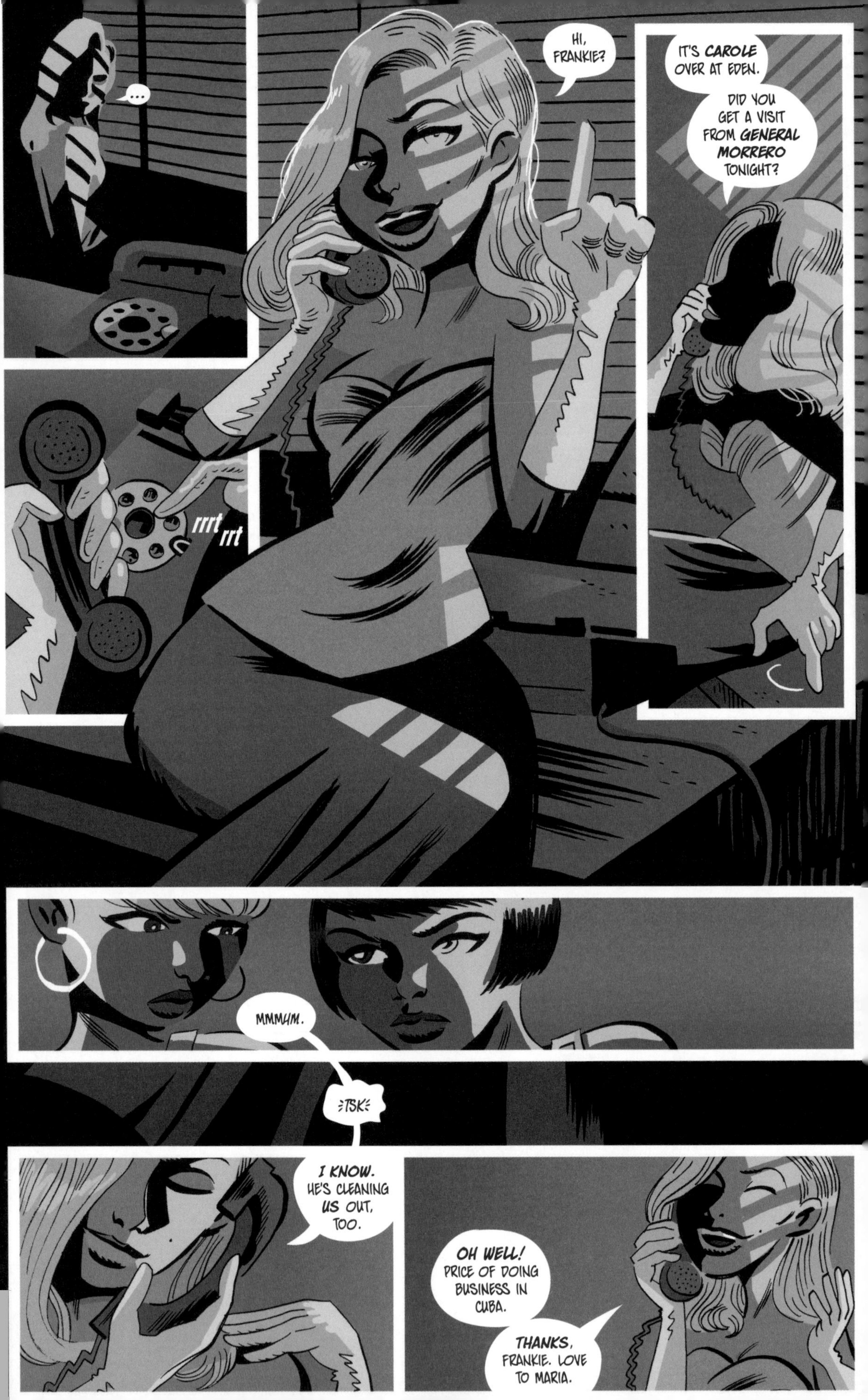
...
rrrt rrt
HI, FRANKIE?
IT'S **CAROLE** OVER AT EDEN.
DID YOU GET A VISIT FROM **GENERAL MORRERO** TONIGHT?
MMMHM.
TSK
I KNOW. HE'S CLEANING **US** OUT, TOO.
OH WELL! PRICE OF DOING BUSINESS IN CUBA.
THANKS, FRANKIE. LOVE TO MARIA.

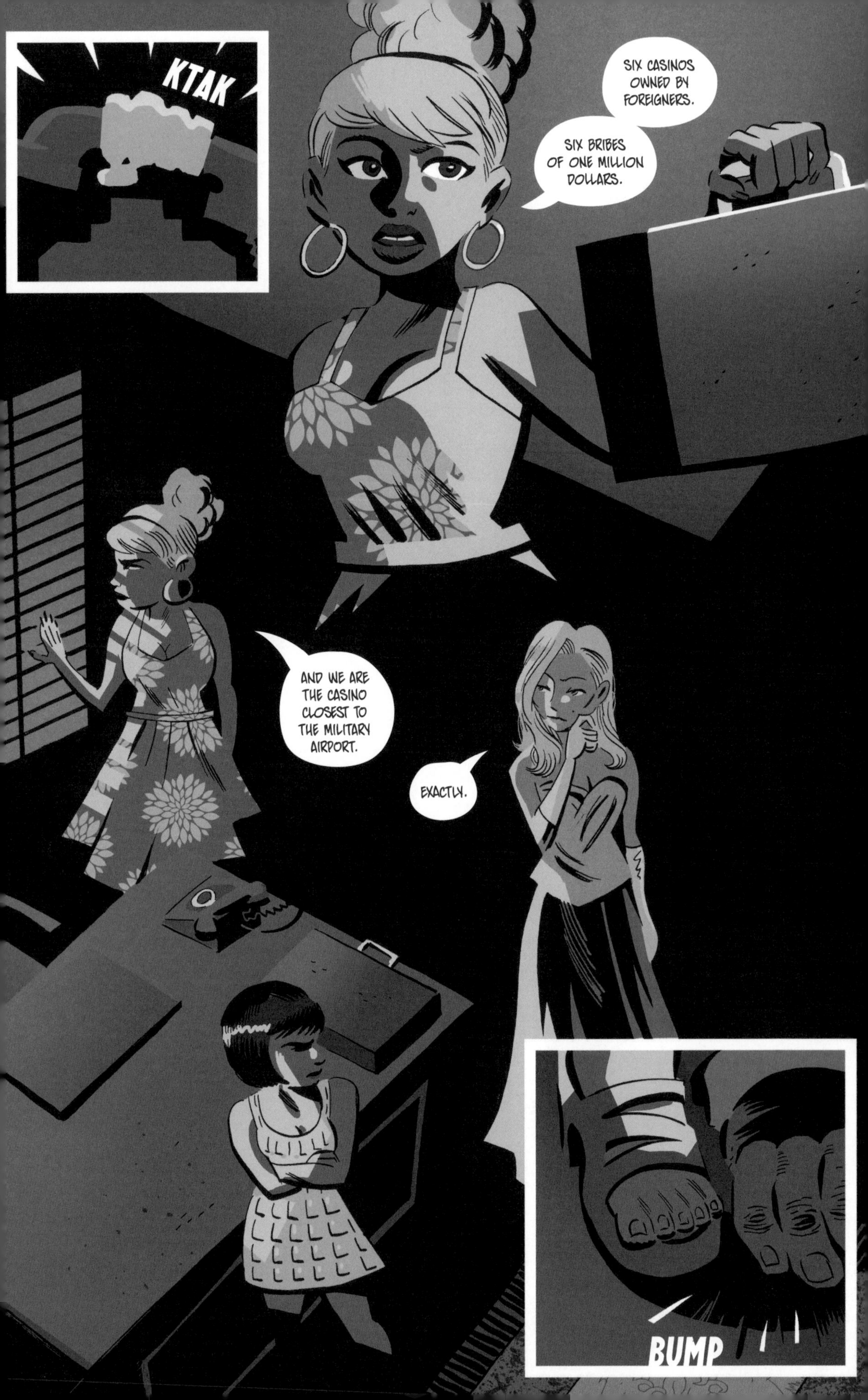
KTAK
SIX CASINOS OWNED BY FOREIGNERS.
SIX BRIBES OF ONE MILLION DOLLARS.
AND WE ARE THE CASINO CLOSEST TO THE MILITARY AIRPORT.
EXACTLY.
BUMP

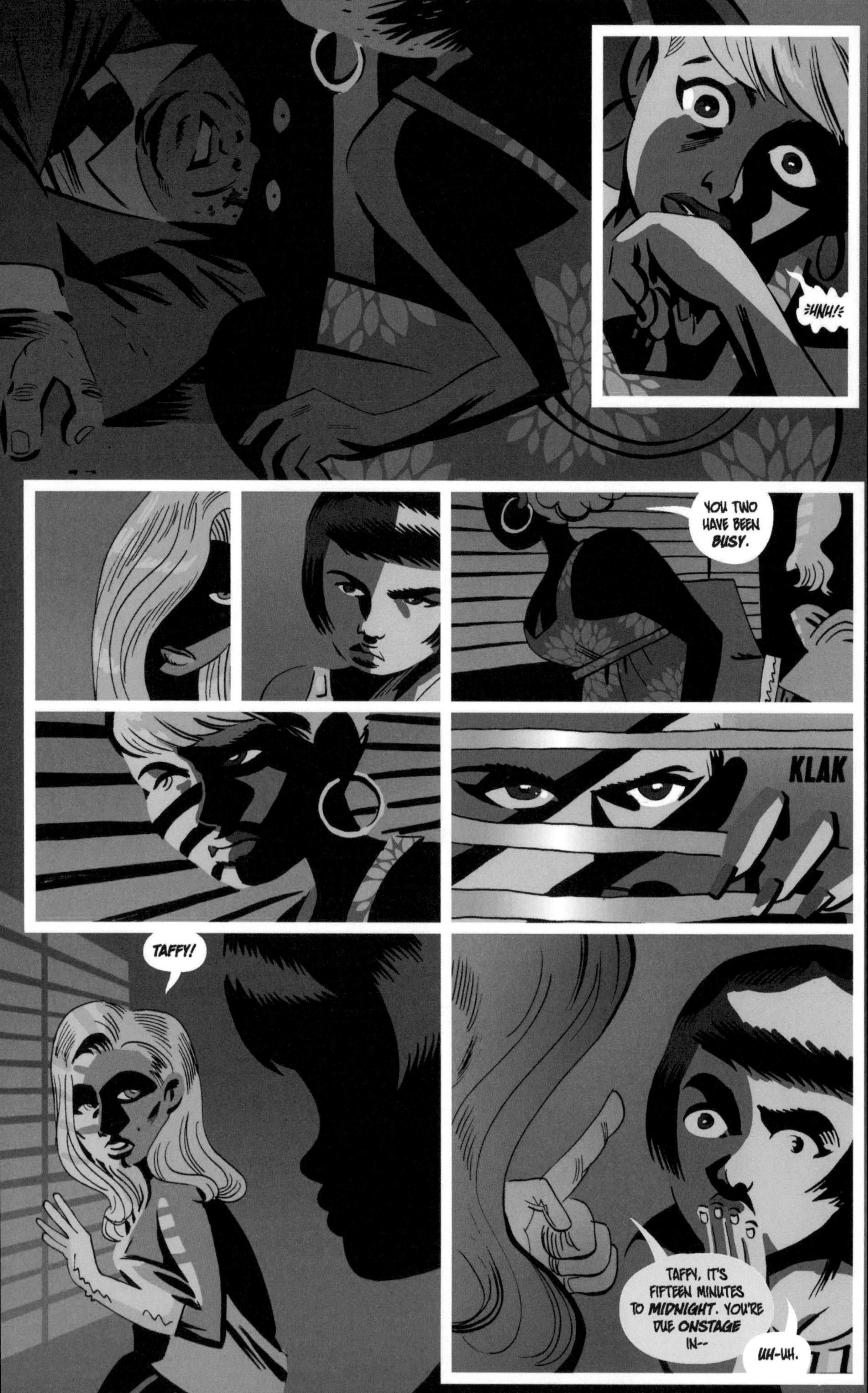
UNH!
YOU TWO HAVE BEEN BUSY.
KLAK
TAFFY!
TAFFY, IT'S FIFTEEN MINUTES TO MIDNIGHT. YOU'RE DUE ONSTAGE IN--
UH-UH.

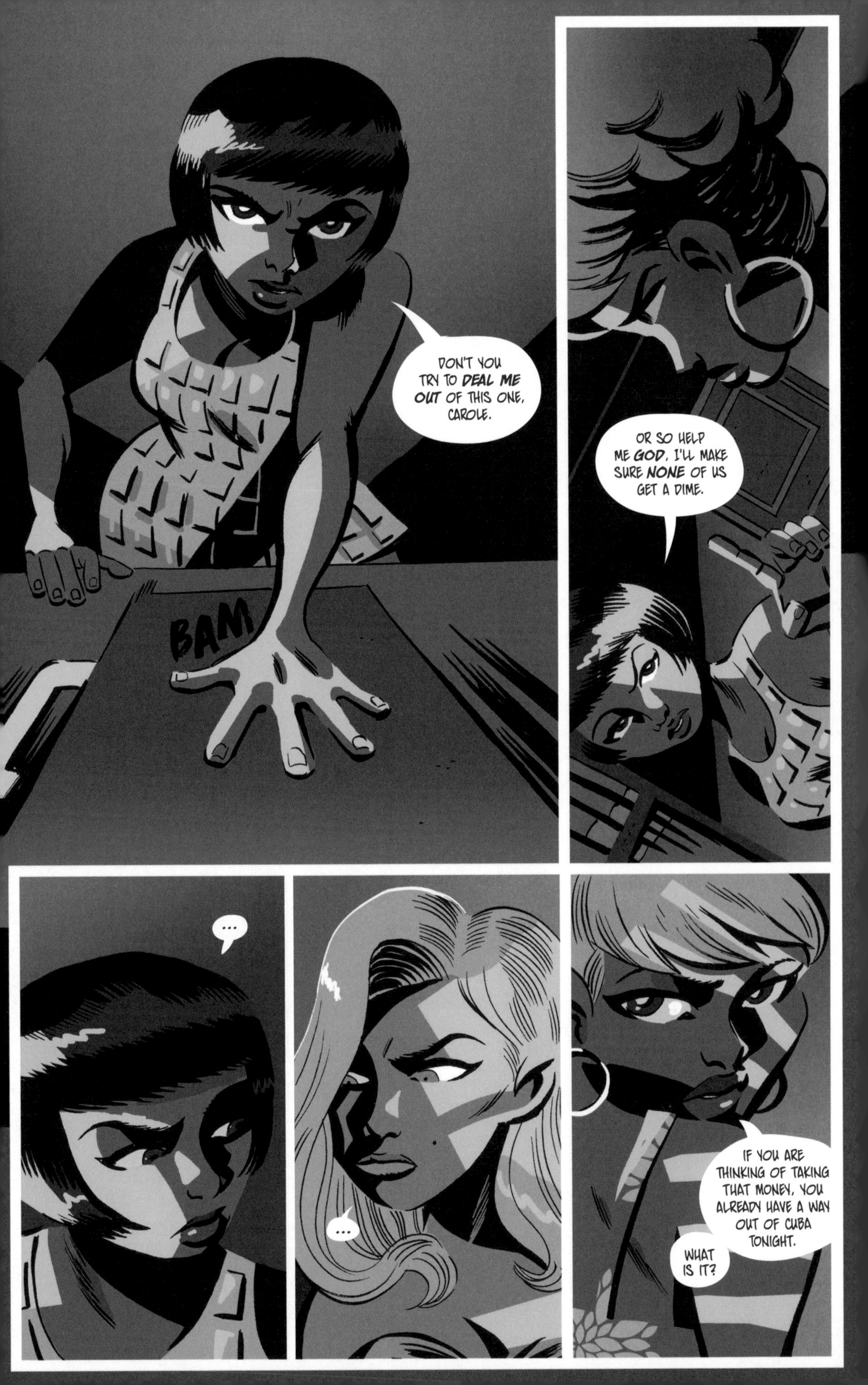
DON'T YOU TRY TO DEAL ME OUT OF THIS ONE, CAROLE.
BAM
OR SO HELP ME GOD, I'LL MAKE SURE NONE OF US GET A DIME.
...
...
IF YOU ARE THINKING OF TAKING THAT MONEY, YOU ALREADY HAVE A WAY OUT OF CUBA TONIGHT.
WHAT IS IT?

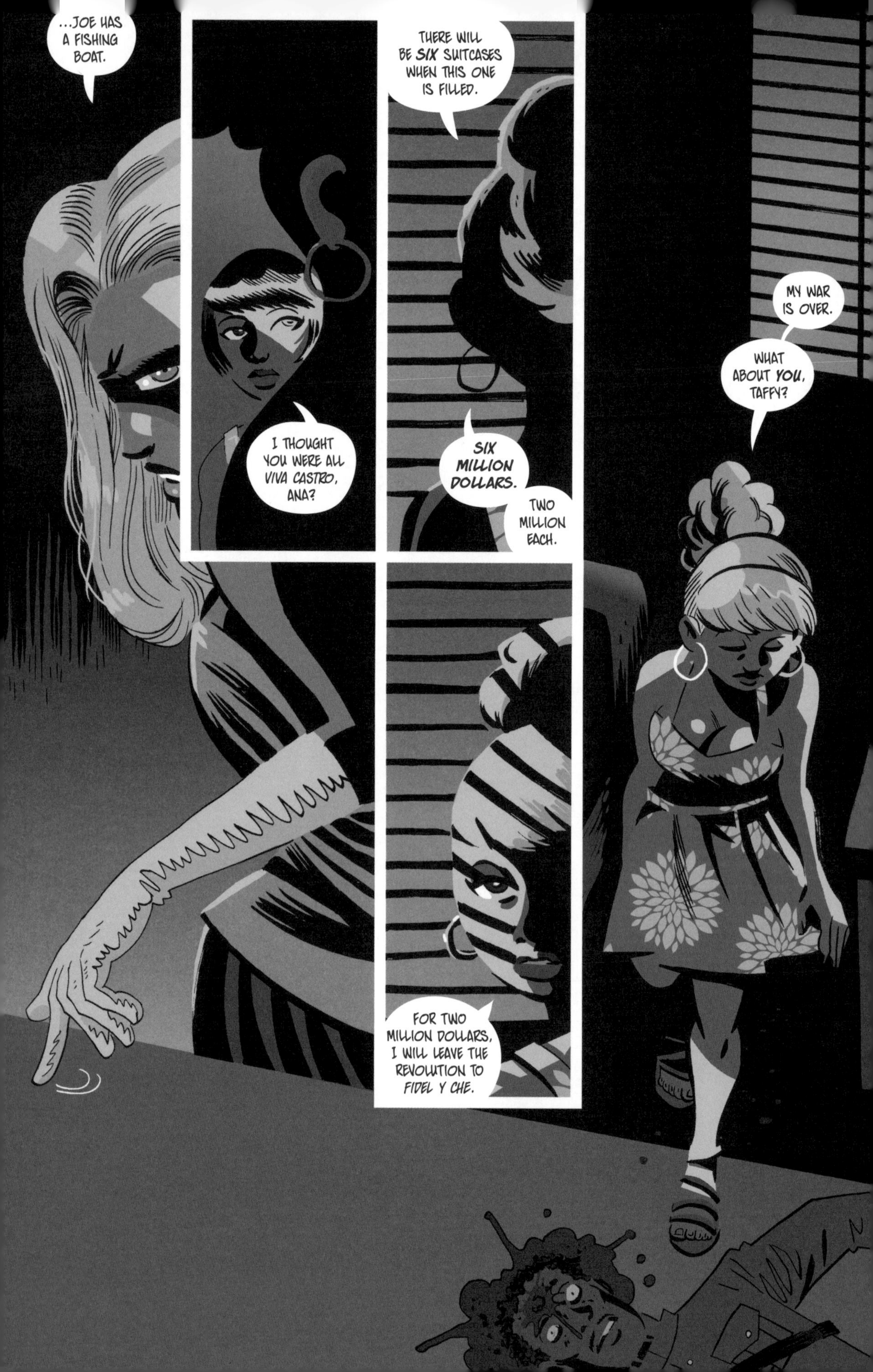
...JOE HAS A FISHING BOAT.
THERE WILL BE SIX SUITCASES WHEN THIS ONE IS FILLED.
I THOUGHT YOU WERE ALL VIVA CASTRO, ANA?
SIX MILLION DOLLARS.
TWO MILLION EACH.
FOR TWO MILLION DOLLARS, I WILL LEAVE THE REVOLUTION TO FIDEL Y CHE.
MY WAR IS OVER.
WHAT ABOUT YOU, TAFFY?

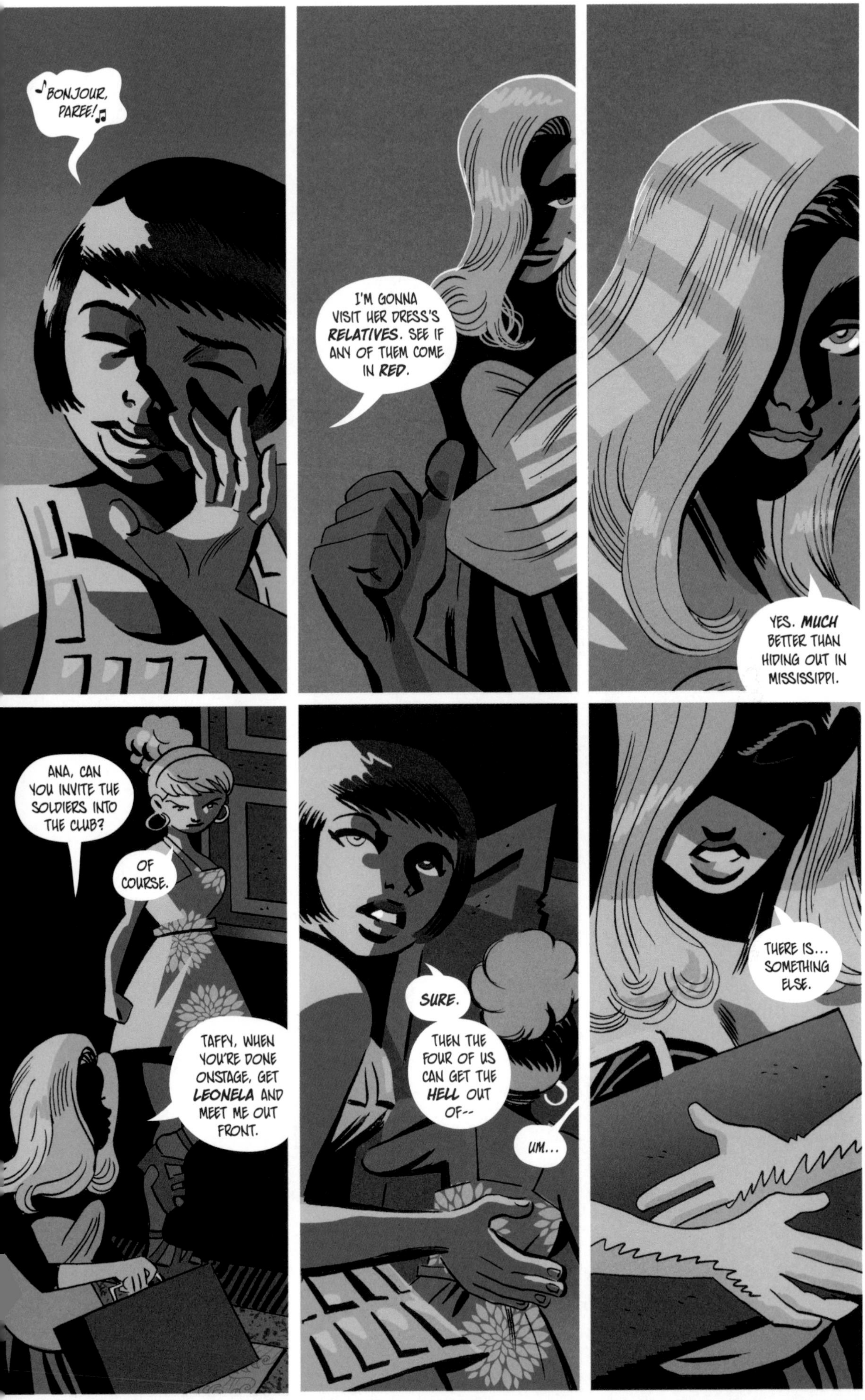
♪BONJOUR, PAREE!♫
I'M GONNA VISIT HER DRESS'S RELATIVES. SEE IF ANY OF THEM COME IN RED.
YES. MUCH BETTER THAN HIDING OUT IN MISSISSIPPI.
ANA, CAN YOU INVITE THE SOLDIERS INTO THE CLUB?
OF COURSE.
TAFFY, WHEN YOU'RE DONE ONSTAGE, GET LEONELA AND MEET ME OUT FRONT.
SURE.
THEN THE FOUR OF US CAN GET THE HELL OUT OF--
UM...
THERE IS... SOMETHING ELSE.

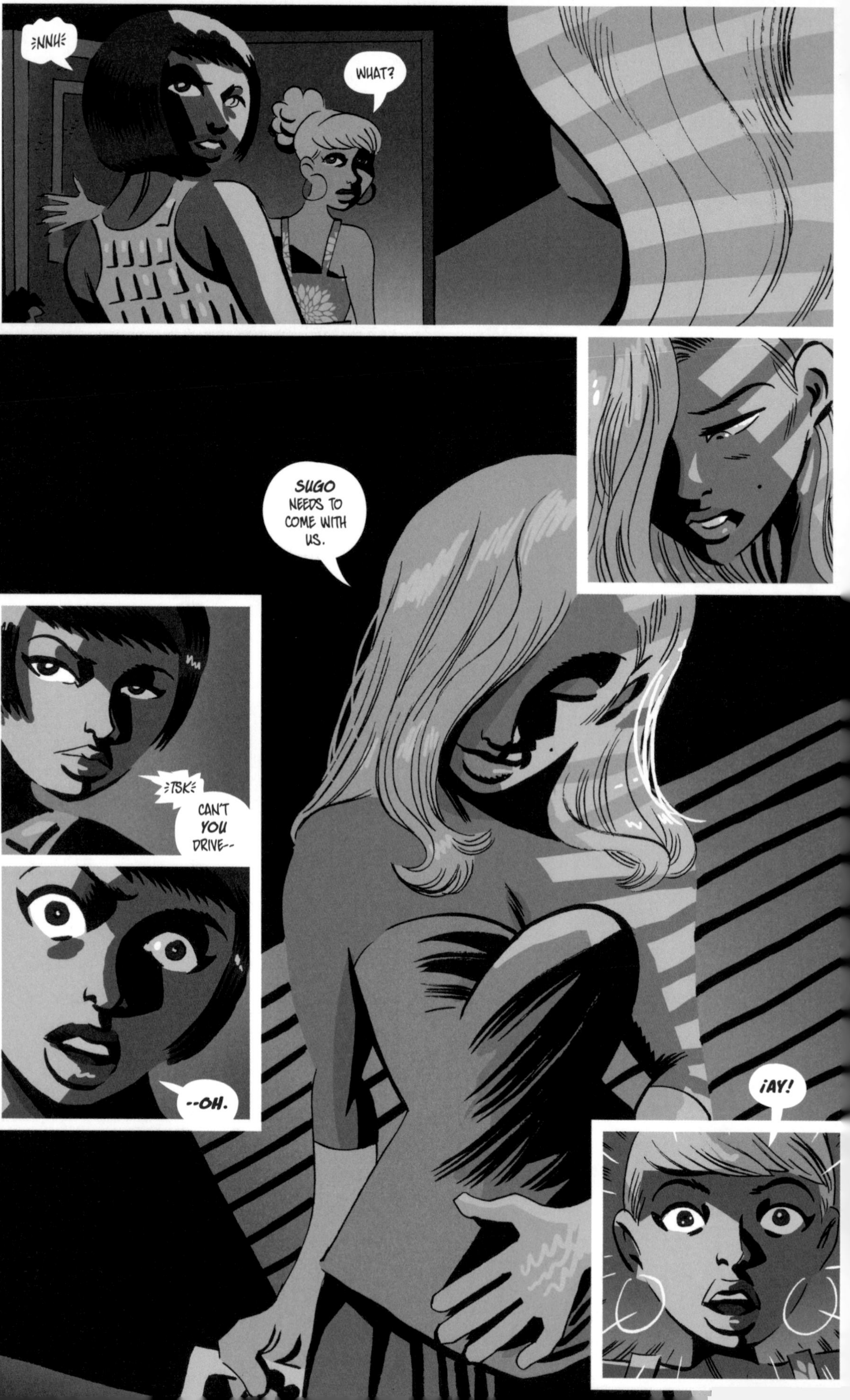
NNH
WHAT?
SUGO NEEDS TO COME WITH US.
TSK
CAN'T YOU DRIVE--
--OH.
¡AY!

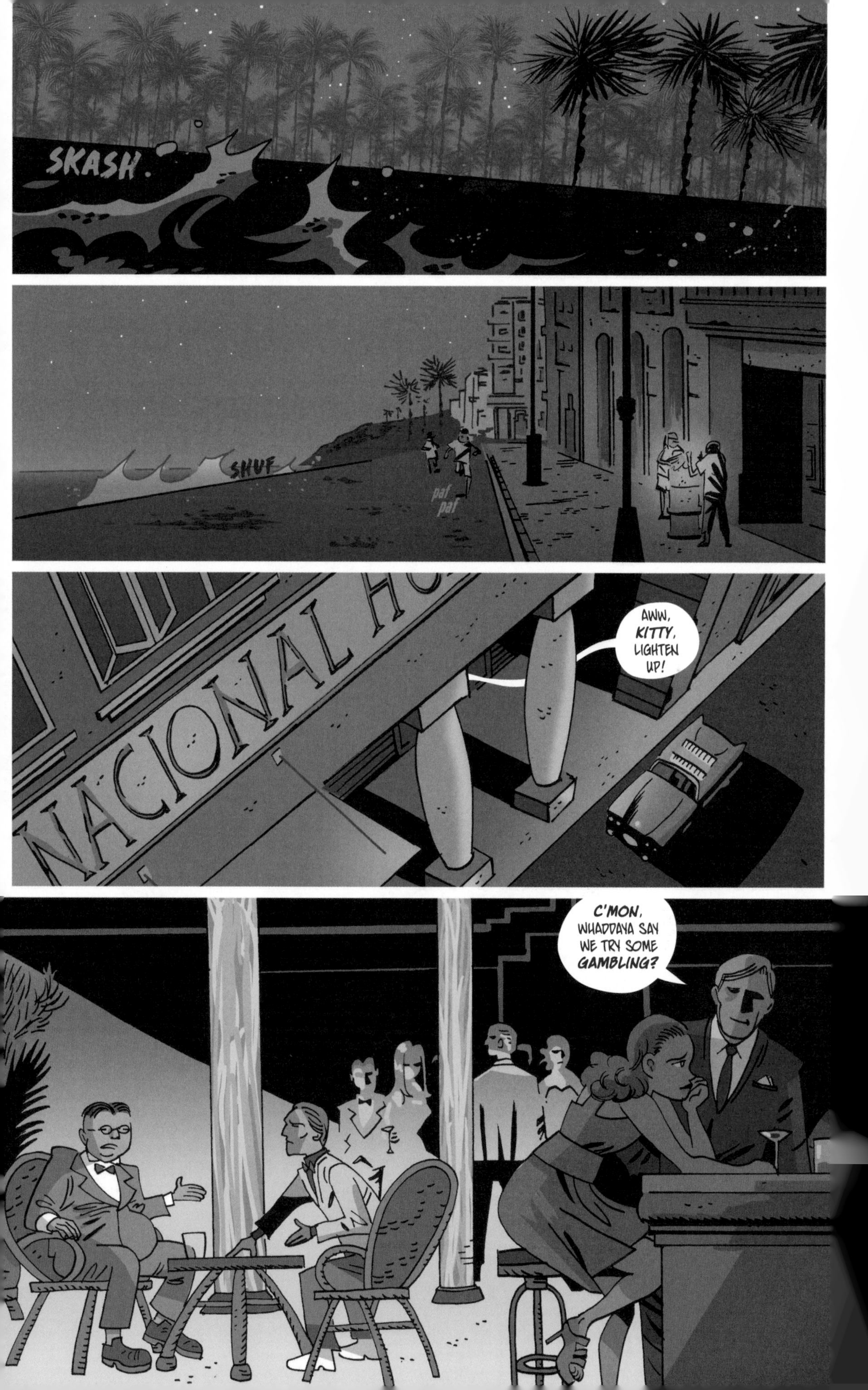
SKASH
SHUF
paf paf
NACIONAL HO
AWW, KITTY, LIGHTEN UP!
C'MON, WHADDAYA SAY WE TRY SOME GAMBLING?

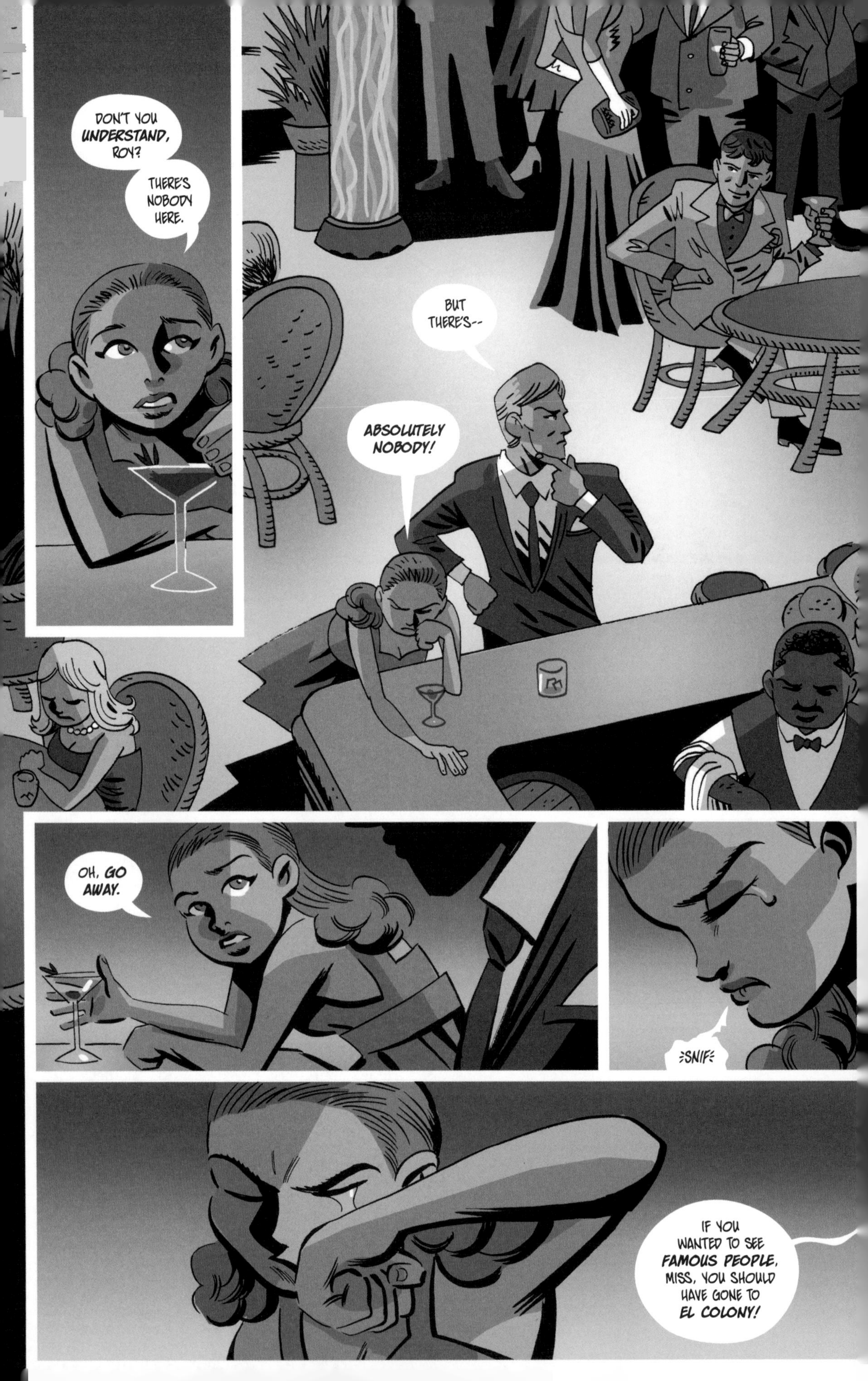
DON'T YOU **UNDERSTAND,** ROY?
THERE'S NOBODY HERE.
BUT THERE'S--
ABSOLUTELY NOBODY!
OH, **GO AWAY.**
SNIF
IF YOU WANTED TO SEE **FAMOUS PEOPLE,** MISS, YOU SHOULD HAVE GONE TO **EL COLONY!**

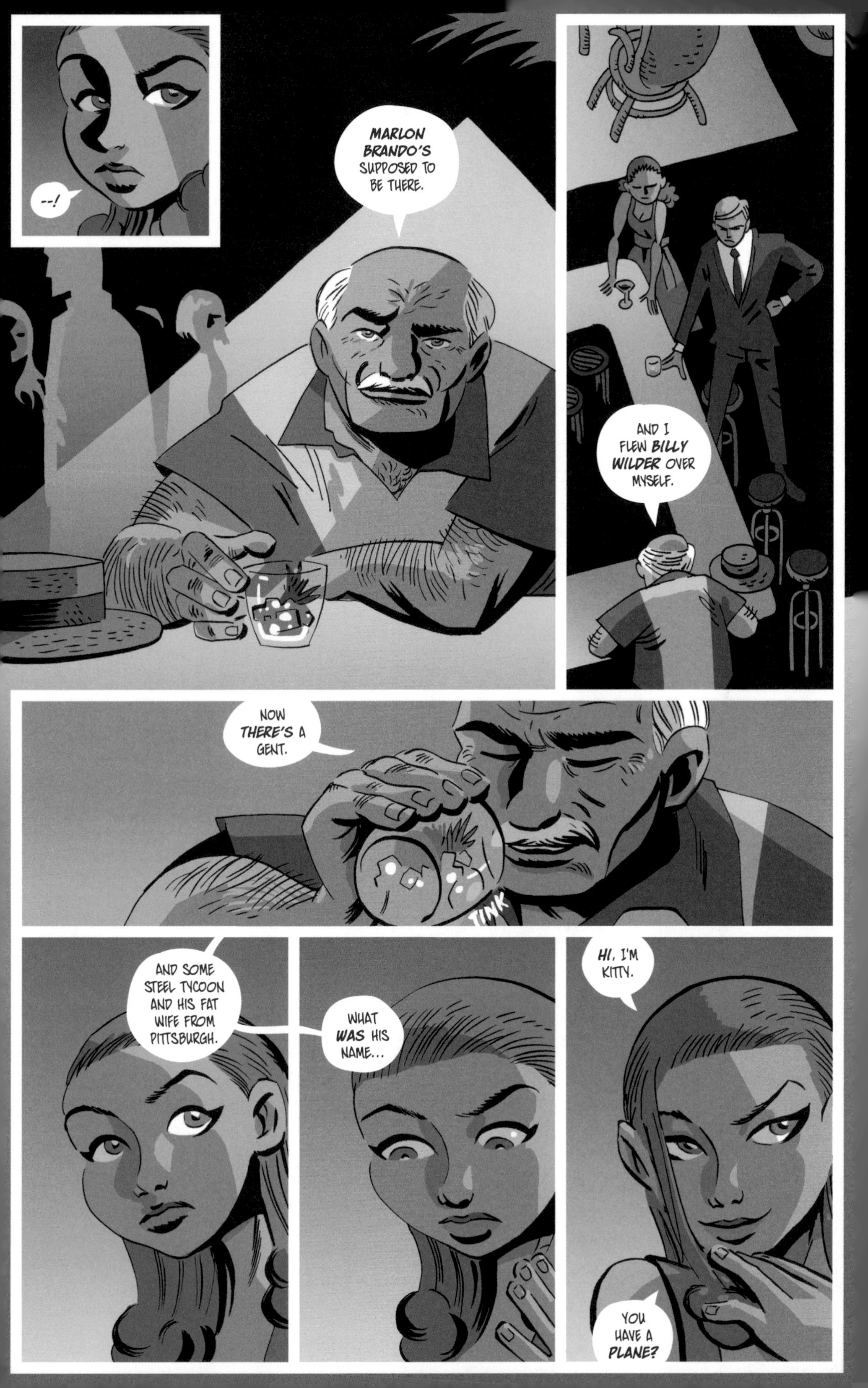
--!
MARLON BRANDO'S SUPPOSED TO BE THERE.
AND I FLEW BILLY WILDER OVER MYSELF.
NOW THERE'S A GENT.
TINK
AND SOME STEEL TYCOON AND HIS FAT WIFE FROM PITTSBURGH.
WHAT WAS HIS NAME...
HI, I'M KITTY.
YOU HAVE A PLANE?

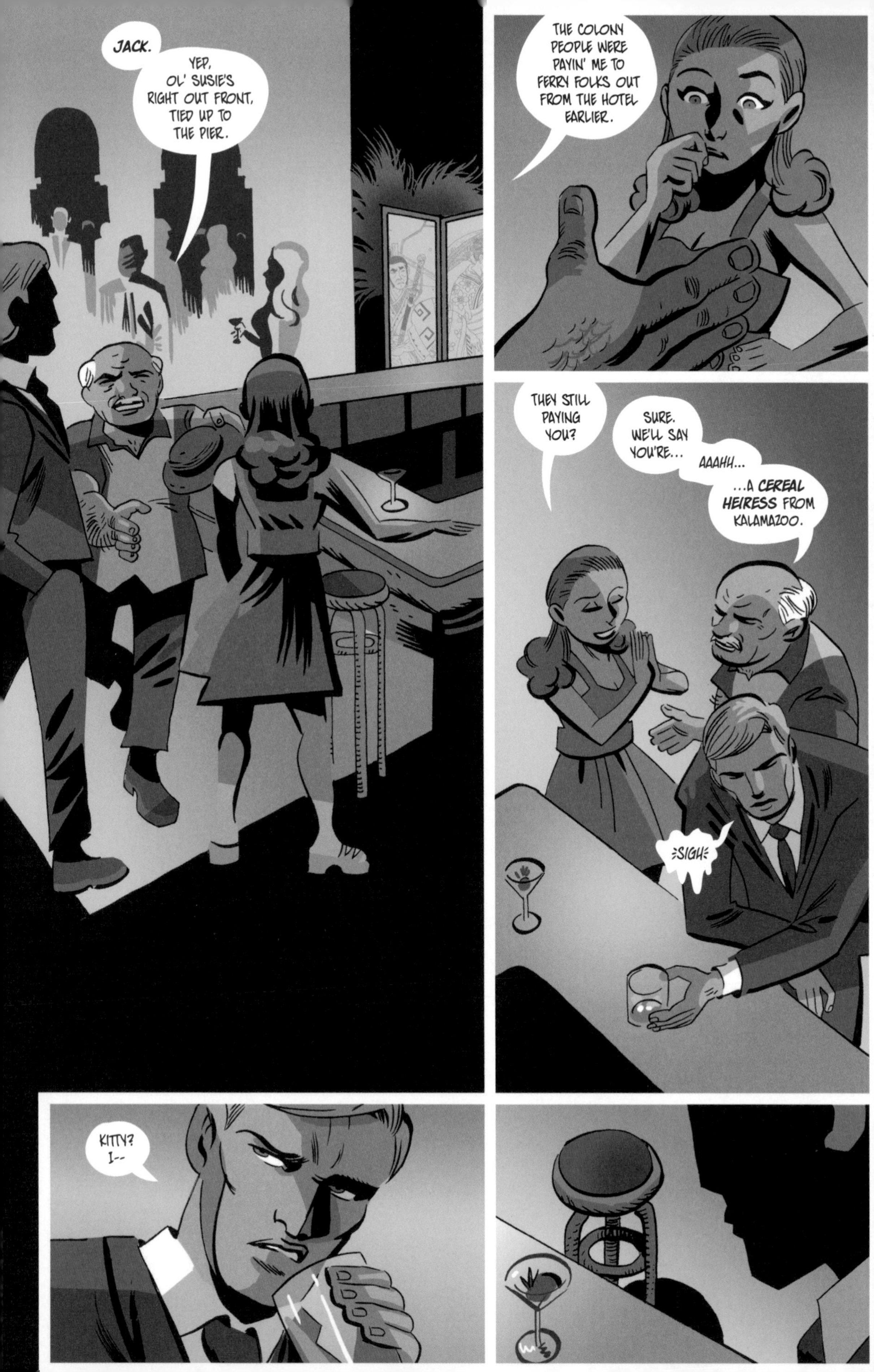
JACK.
YEP, OL' SUSIE'S RIGHT OUT FRONT, TIED UP TO THE PIER.
THE COLONY PEOPLE WERE PAYIN' ME TO FERRY FOLKS OUT FROM THE HOTEL EARLIER.
THEY STILL PAYING YOU?
SURE. WE'LL SAY YOU'RE...
AAAHH...
...A CEREAL HEIRESS FROM KALAMAZOO.
SIGH
KITTY? I--

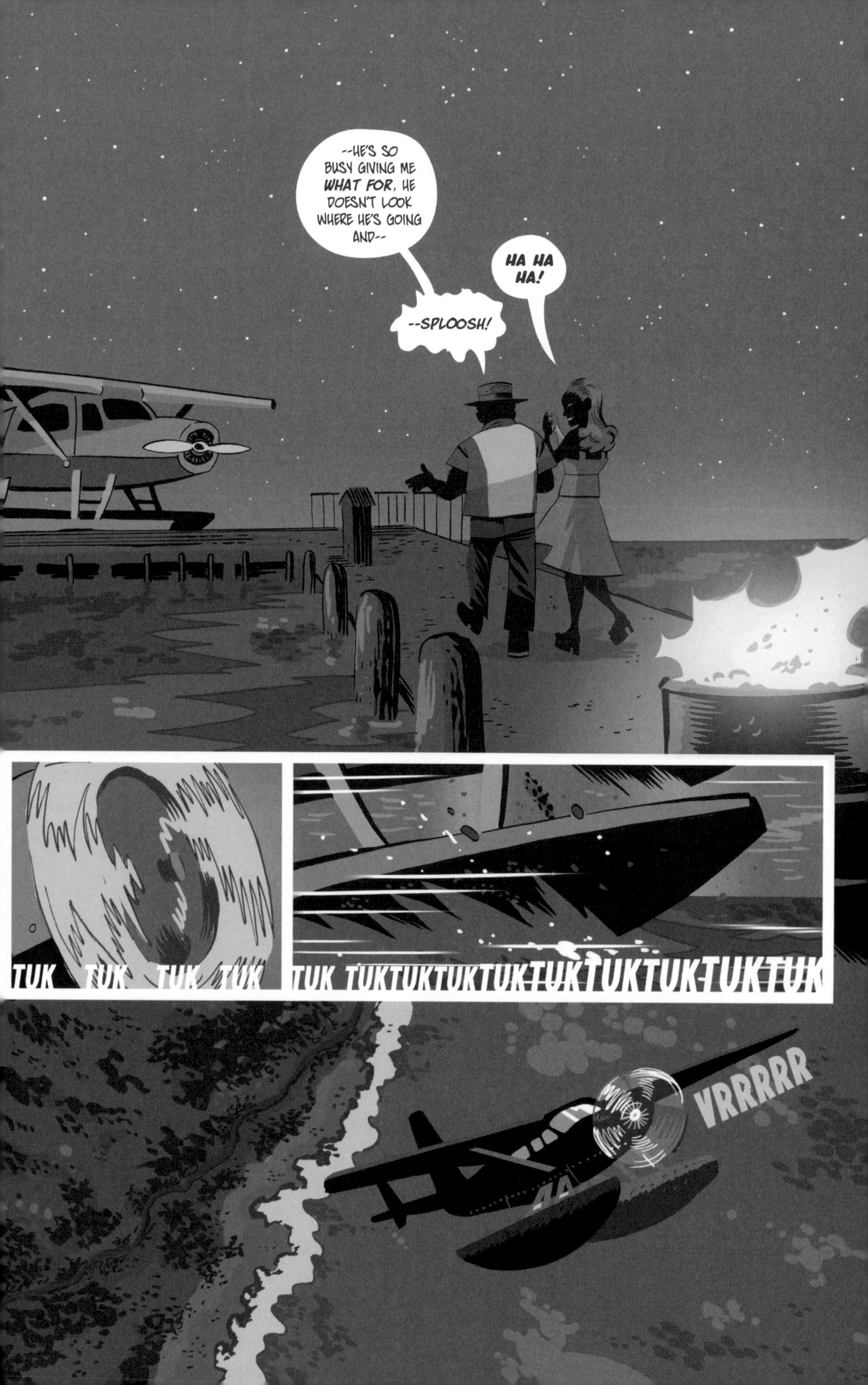
--HE'S SO BUSY GIVING ME **WHAT FOR**, HE DOESN'T LOOK WHERE HE'S GOING AND--
HA HA HA!
--SPLOOSH!
TUK TUK TUK TUK
TUK TUKTUKTUKTUKTUKTUKTUKTUKTUK
VRRRRR

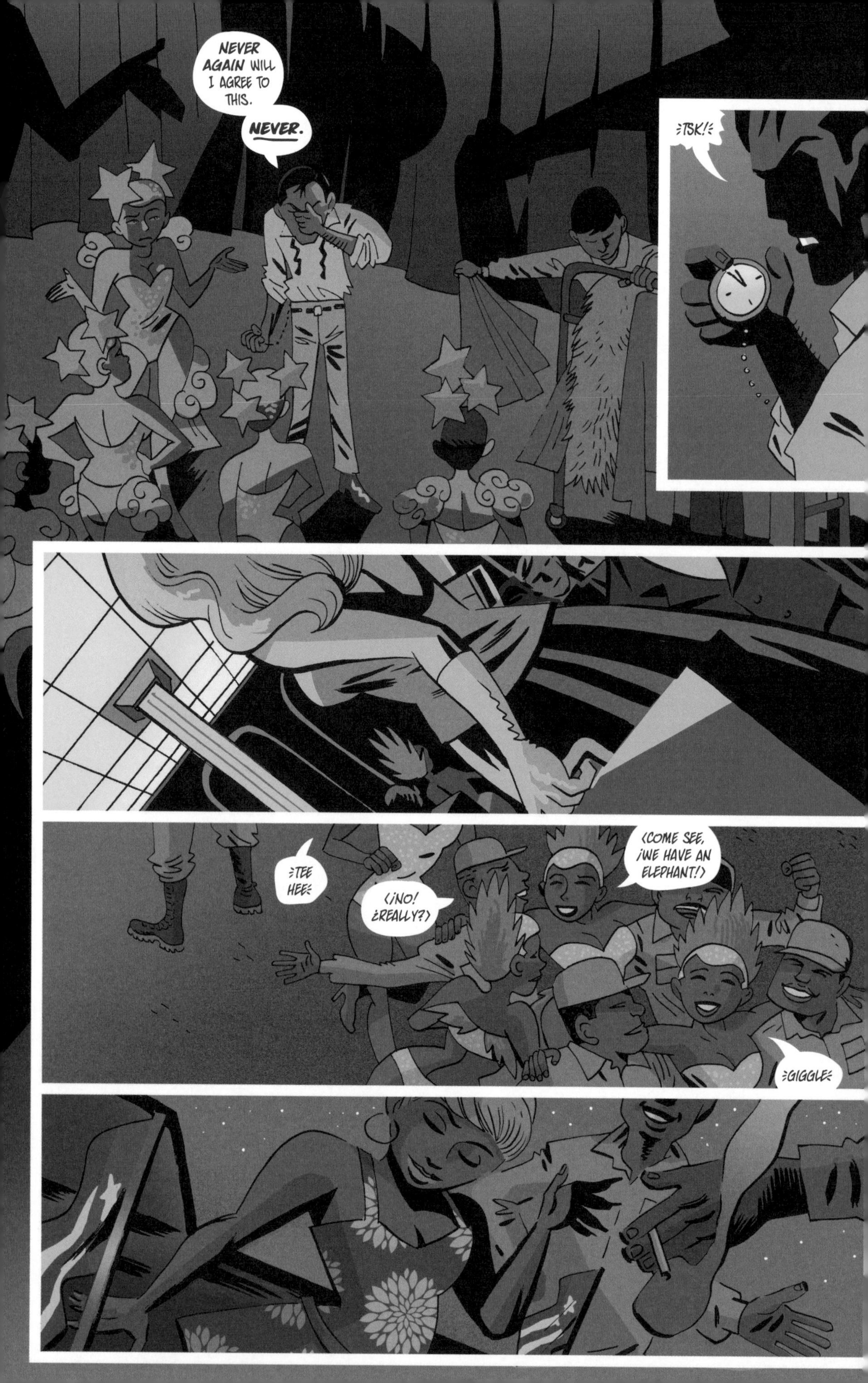
NEVER AGAIN WILL I AGREE TO THIS.
NEVER.
TSK!
TEE HEE
‹¡NO! ¿REALLY?›
‹COME SEE, ¡WE HAVE AN ELEPHANT!›
GIGGLE

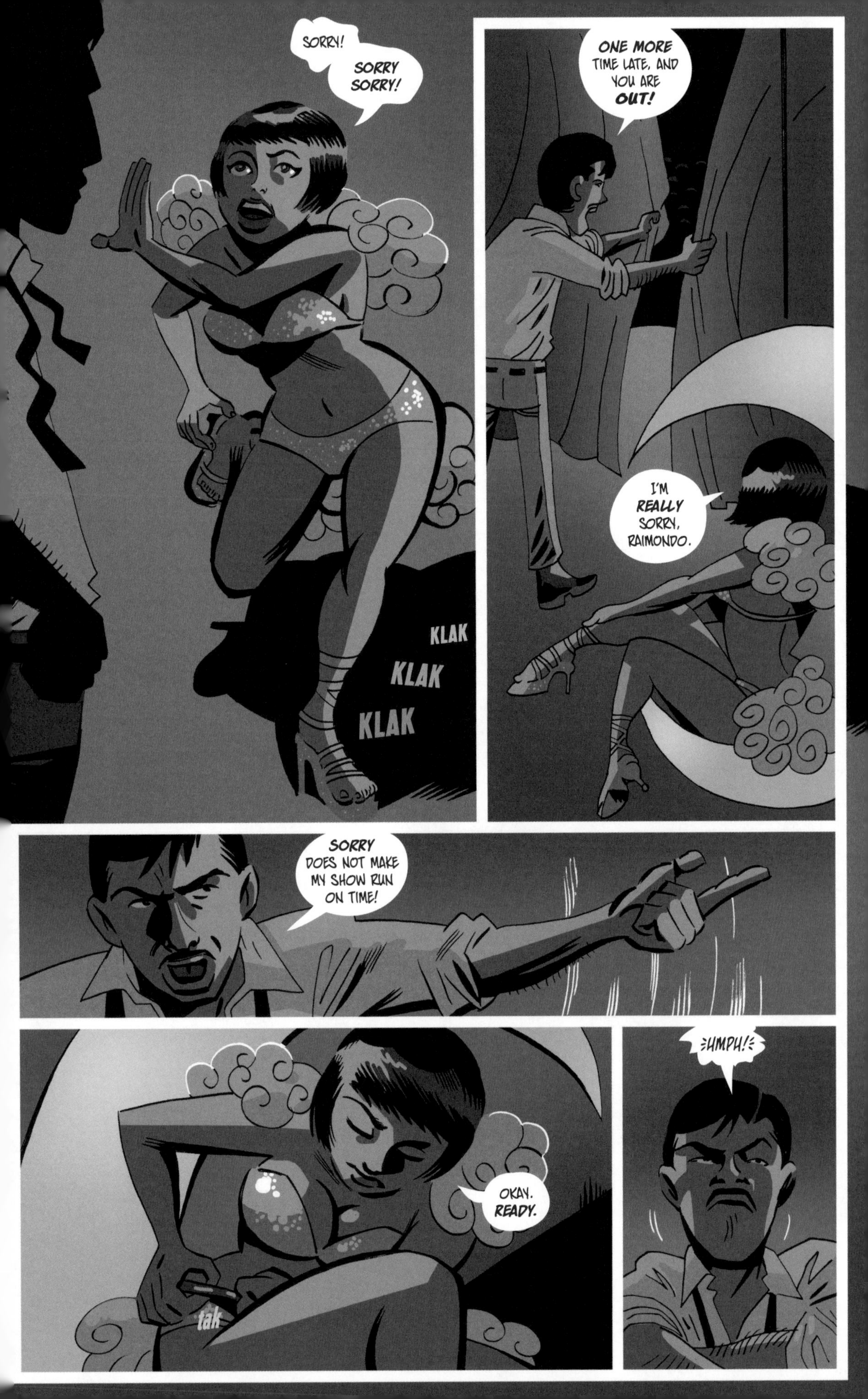
SORRY!
SORRY SORRY!
KLAK
KLAK
KLAK
ONE MORE TIME LATE, AND YOU ARE OUT!
I'M REALLY SORRY, RAIMONDO.
SORRY DOES NOT MAKE MY SHOW RUN ON TIME!
tak
OKAY. READY.
UMPH!

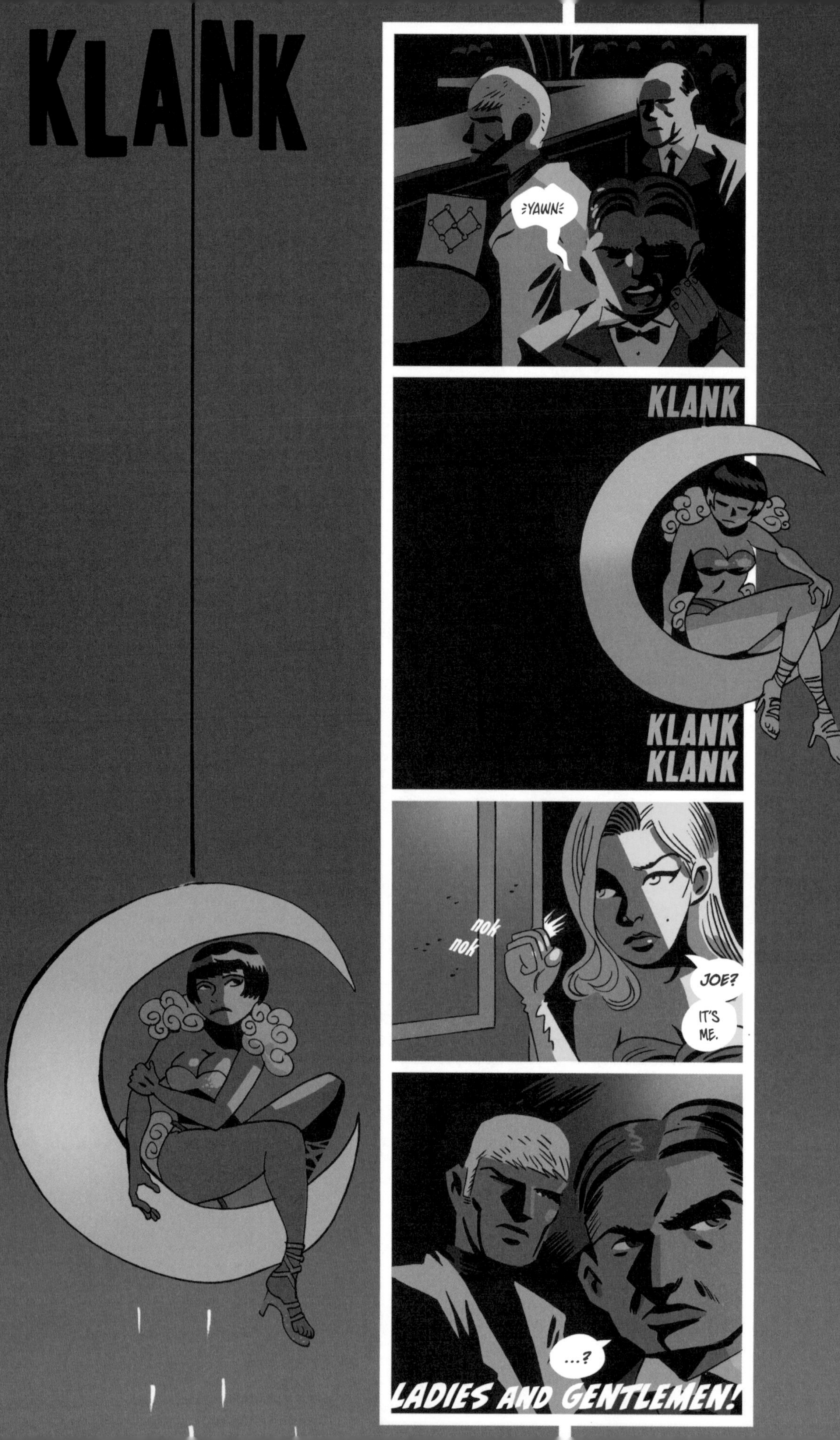
KLANK
YAWN
KLANK
KLANK
KLANK
nok nok
JOE?
IT'S ME.
...?
LADIES AND GENTLEMEN!

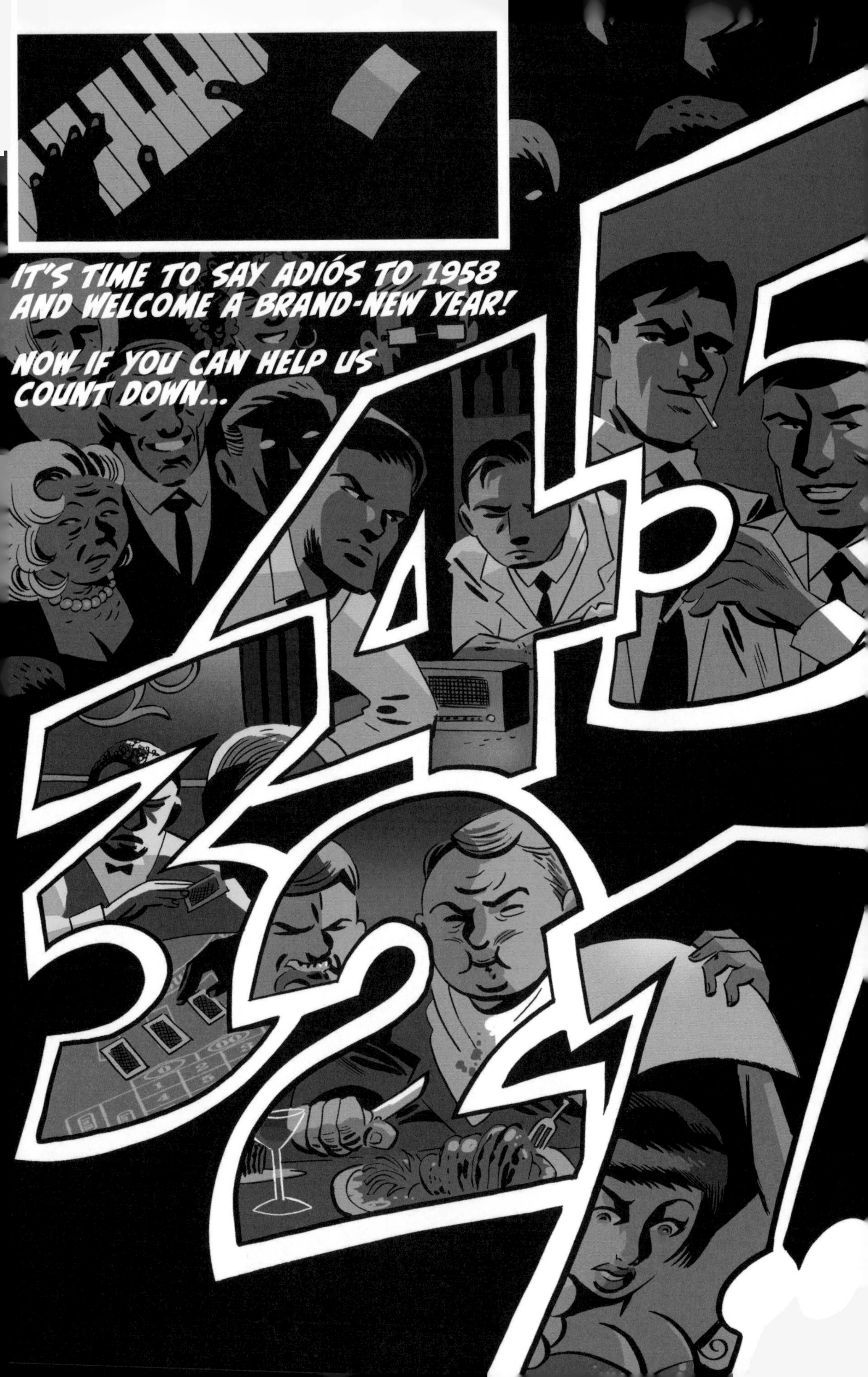
IT'S TIME TO SAY ADIÓS TO 1958 AND WELCOME A BRAND-NEW YEAR!
NOW IF YOU CAN HELP US COUNT DOWN...
5
4
3
2
1

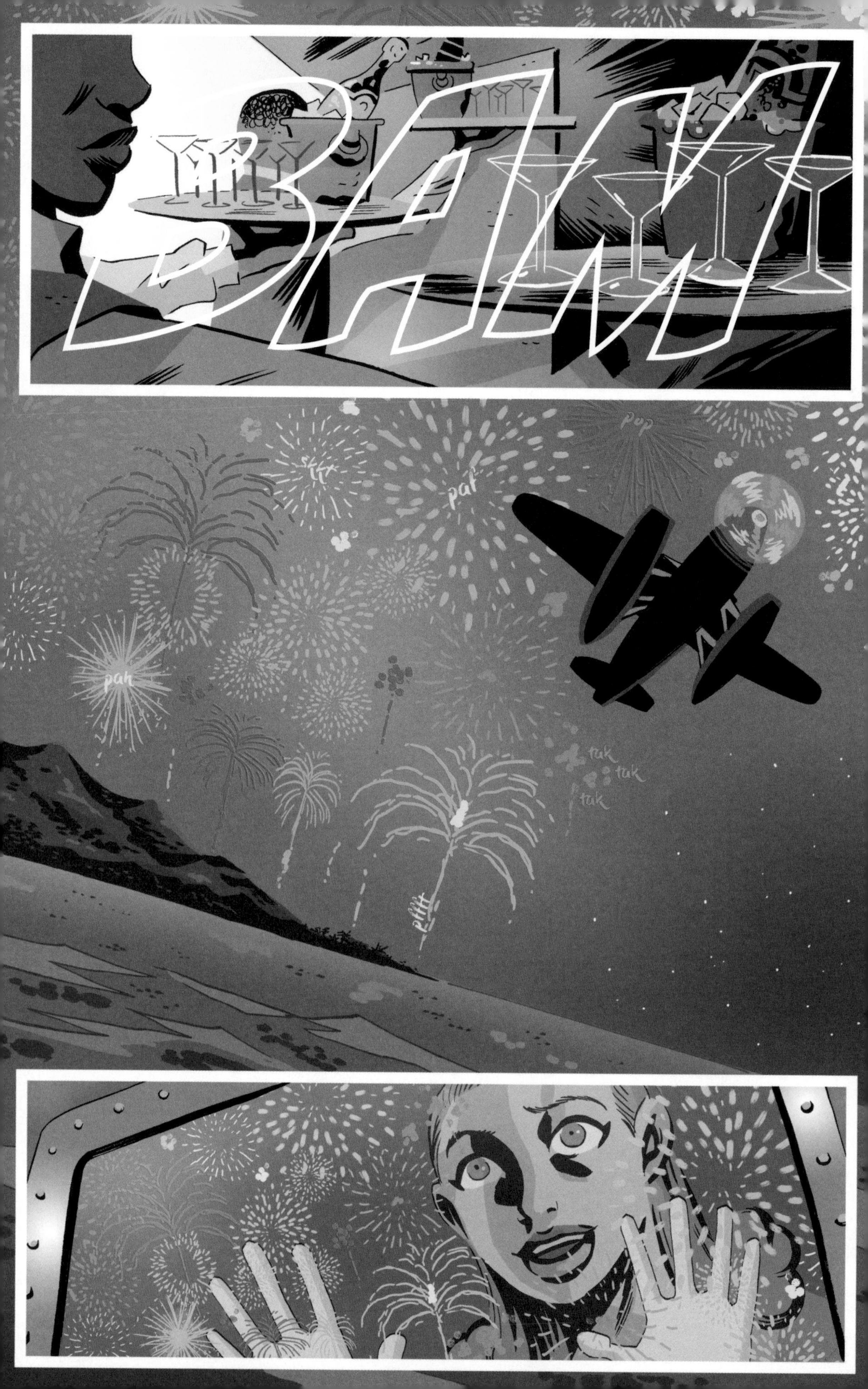
BAM
paf
pop
pah
tak
tak
tak

12:00 A.M.

THURSDAY 1 JANUARY 1959

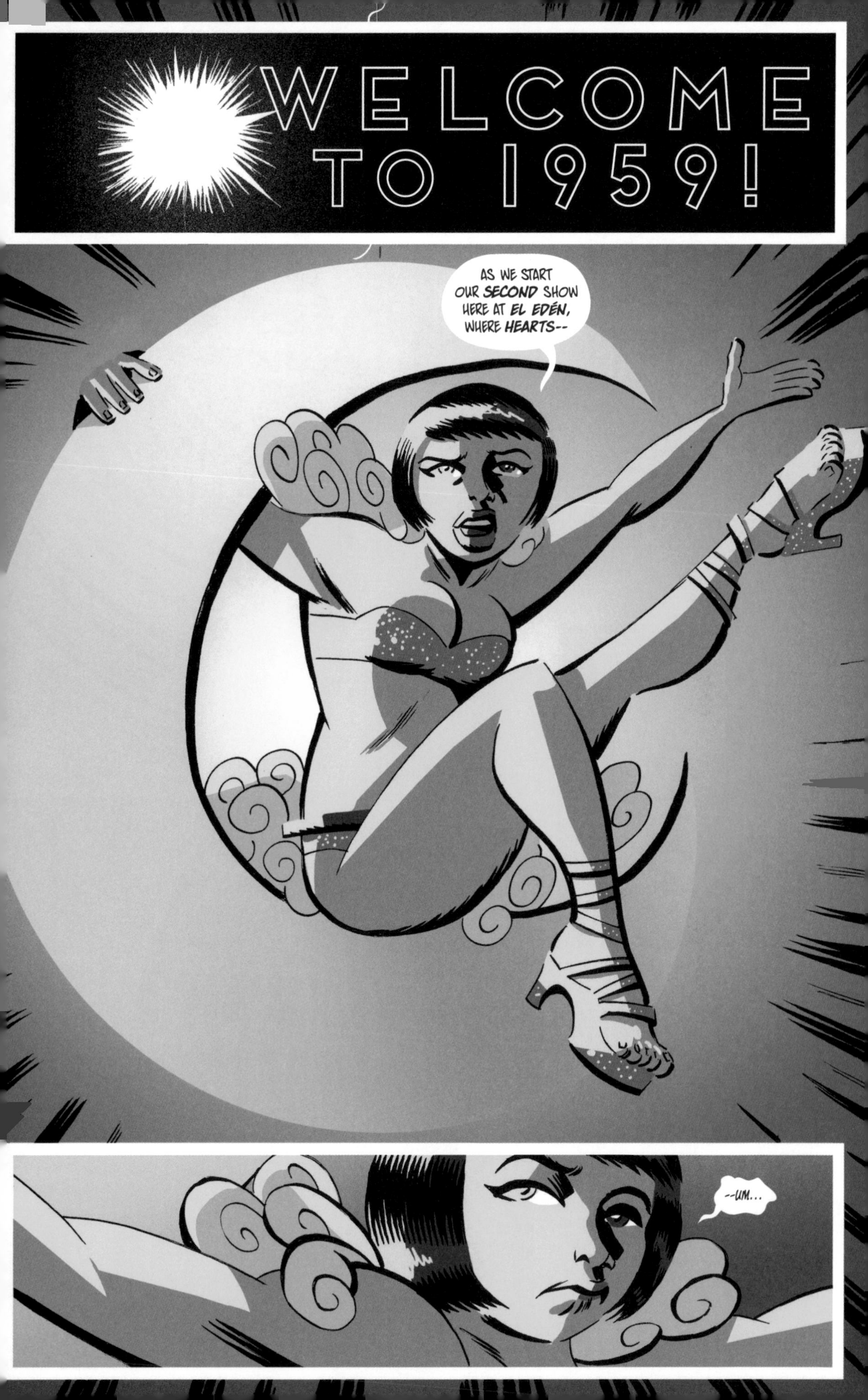
WELCOME TO 1959!
AS WE START OUR SECOND SHOW HERE AT EL EDÉN, WHERE HEARTS--
--UM...

--WHERE *FORTUNES* ARE MADE AND *HEARTS* ARE *BROKEN* EVERY SINGLE NIGHT...

...BUT NONE SO MUCH AS ON *NEW YEAR'S EVE!*

pop

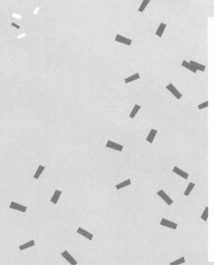

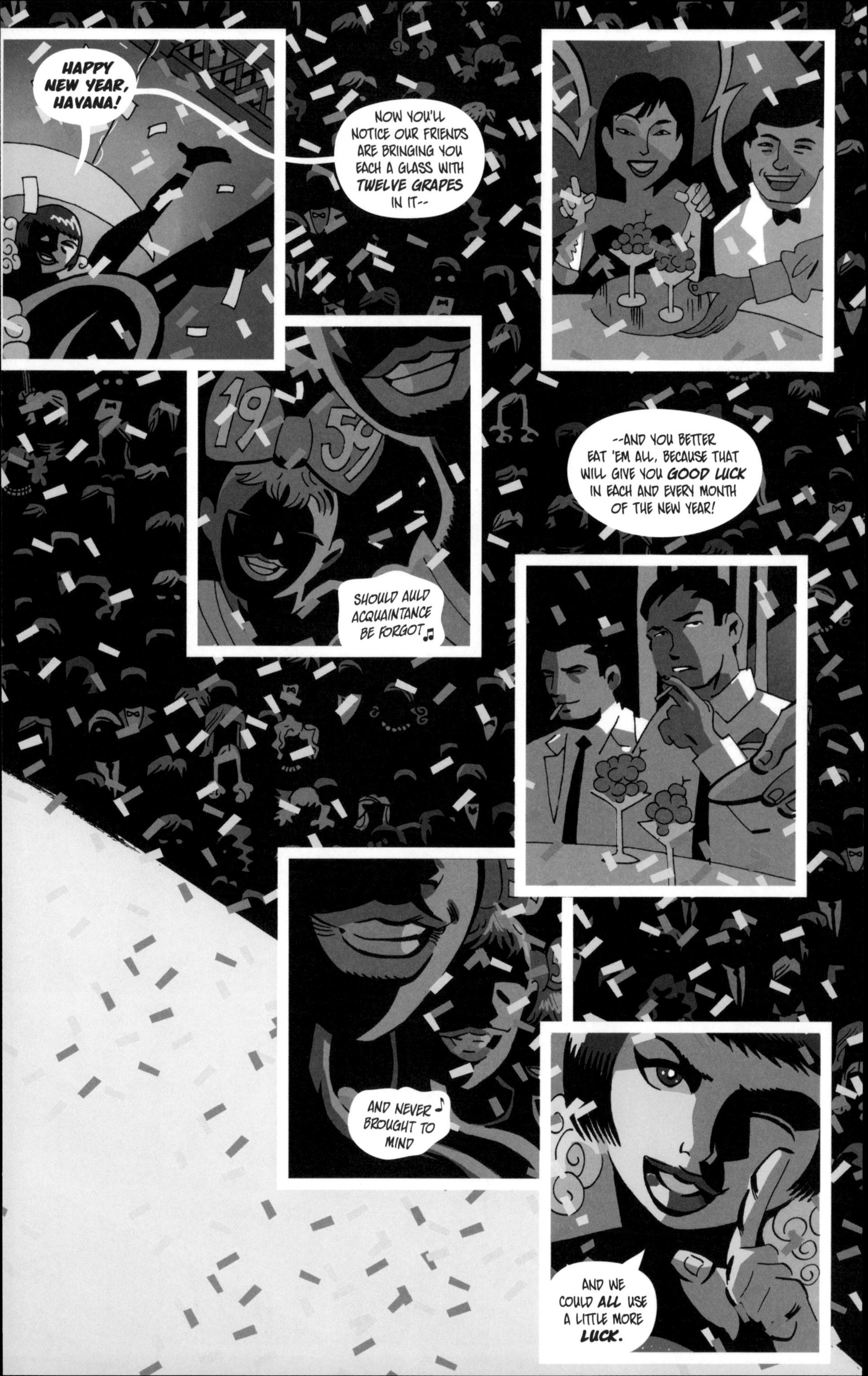
HAPPY NEW YEAR, HAVANA!
NOW YOU'LL NOTICE OUR FRIENDS ARE BRINGING YOU EACH A GLASS WITH TWELVE GRAPES IN IT--
--AND YOU BETTER EAT 'EM ALL, BECAUSE THAT WILL GIVE YOU GOOD LUCK IN EACH AND EVERY MONTH OF THE NEW YEAR!
19 59
SHOULD AULD ACQUAINTANCE BE FORGOT♫
AND NEVER♪ BROUGHT TO MIND
AND WE COULD ALL USE A LITTLE MORE LUCK.

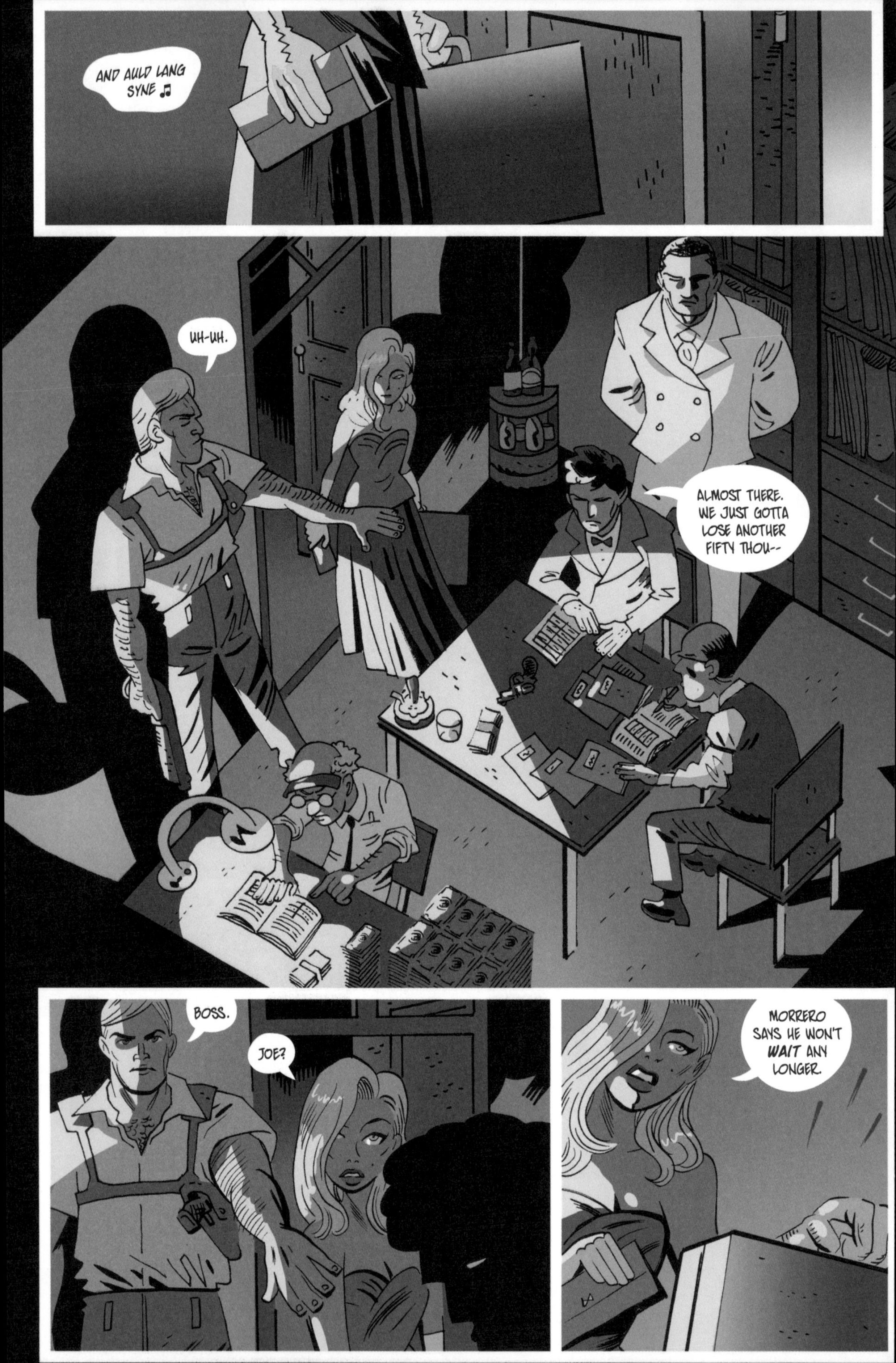
AND AULD LANG SYNE ♫
UH-UH.
ALMOST THERE. WE JUST GOTTA LOSE ANOTHER FIFTY THOU--
BOSS.
JOE?
MORRERO SAYS HE WON'T WAIT ANY LONGER.

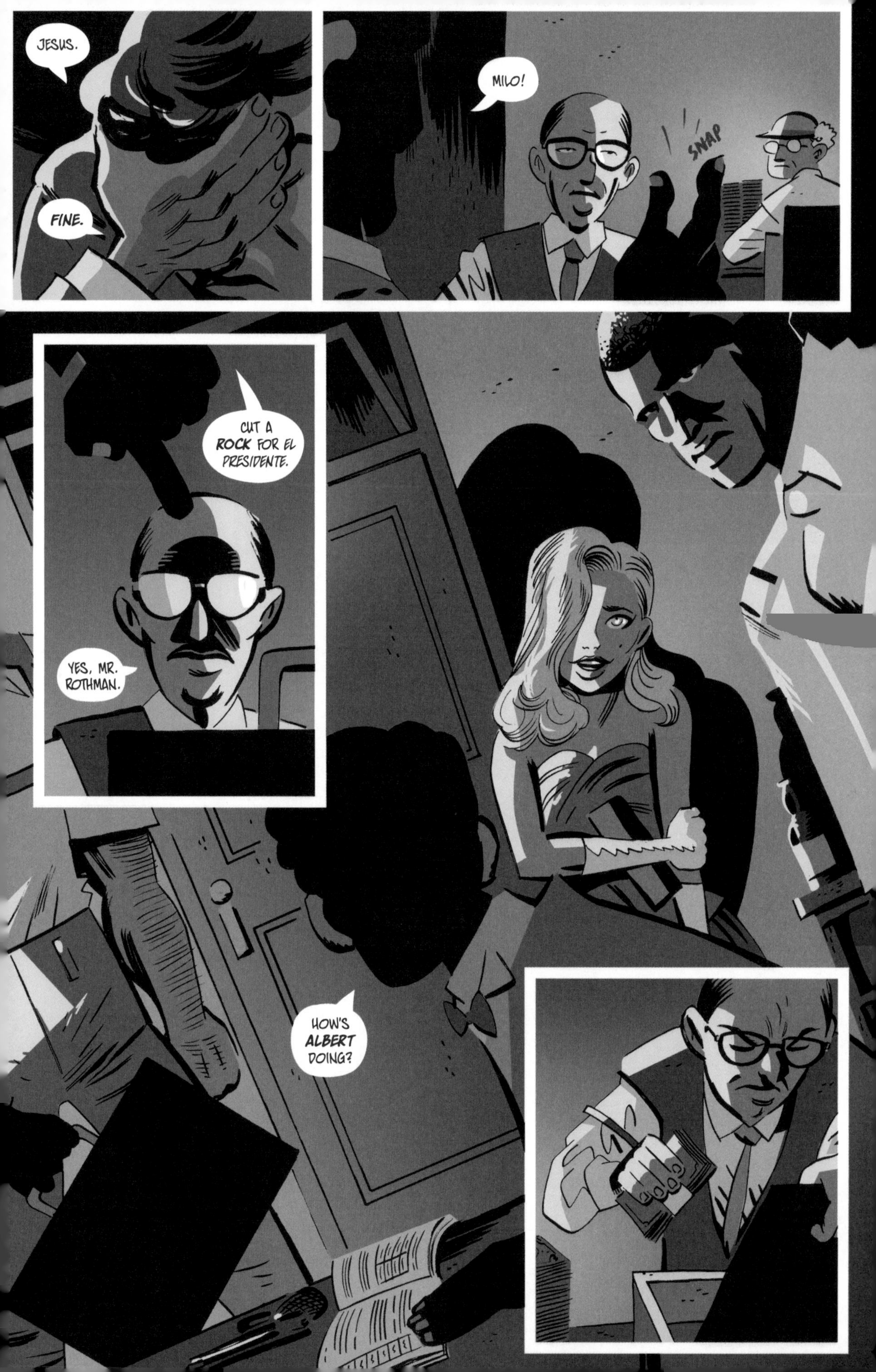
JESUS.
FINE.
MILO!
SNAP
CUT A ROCK FOR EL PRESIDENTE.
YES, MR. ROTHMAN.
HOW'S ALBERT DOING?

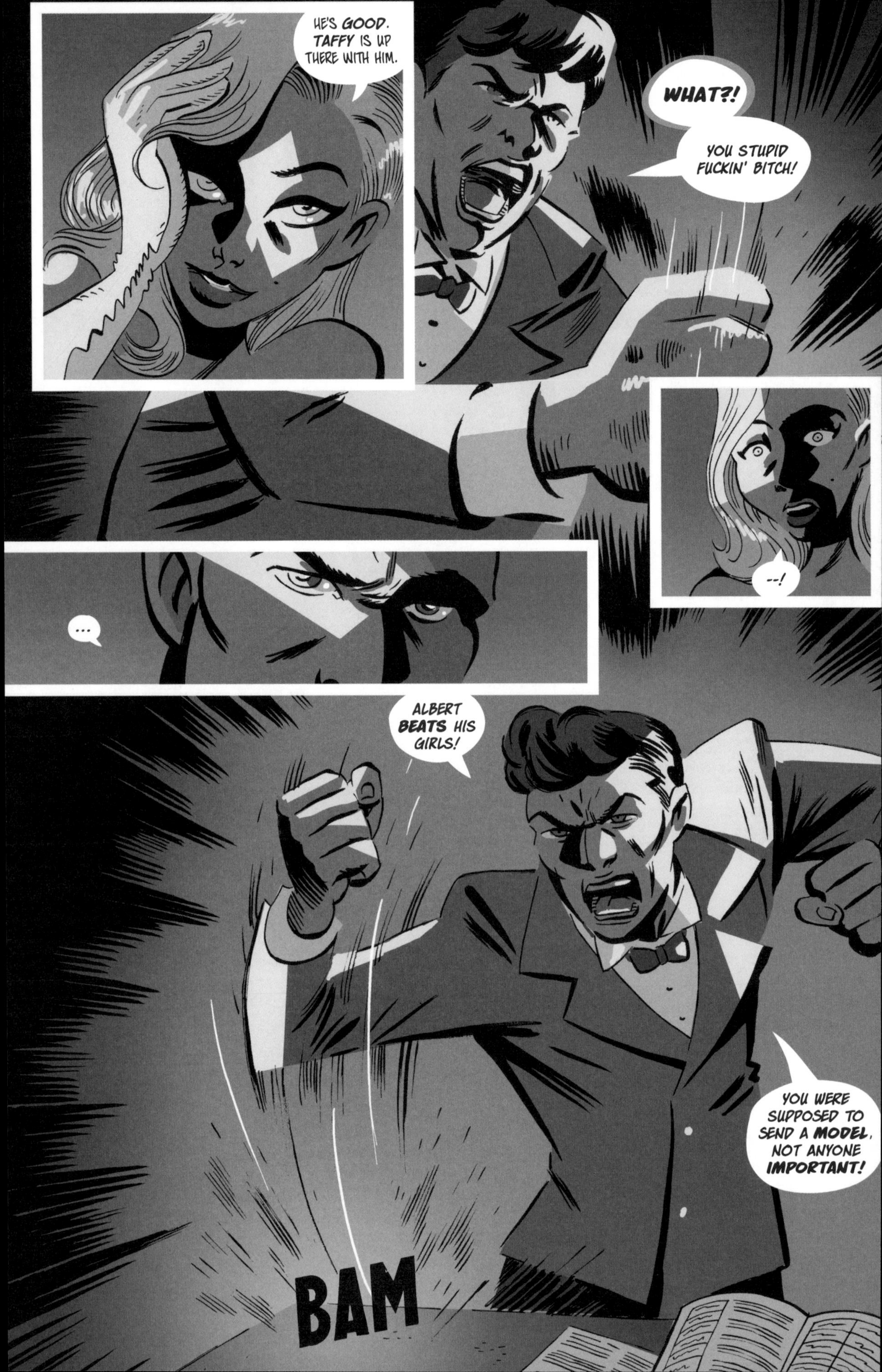
HE'S GOOD. TAFFY IS UP THERE WITH HIM.
WHAT?!
YOU STUPID FUCKIN' BITCH!
--!
...
ALBERT BEATS HIS GIRLS!
YOU WERE SUPPOSED TO SEND A MODEL, NOT ANYONE IMPORTANT!
BAM

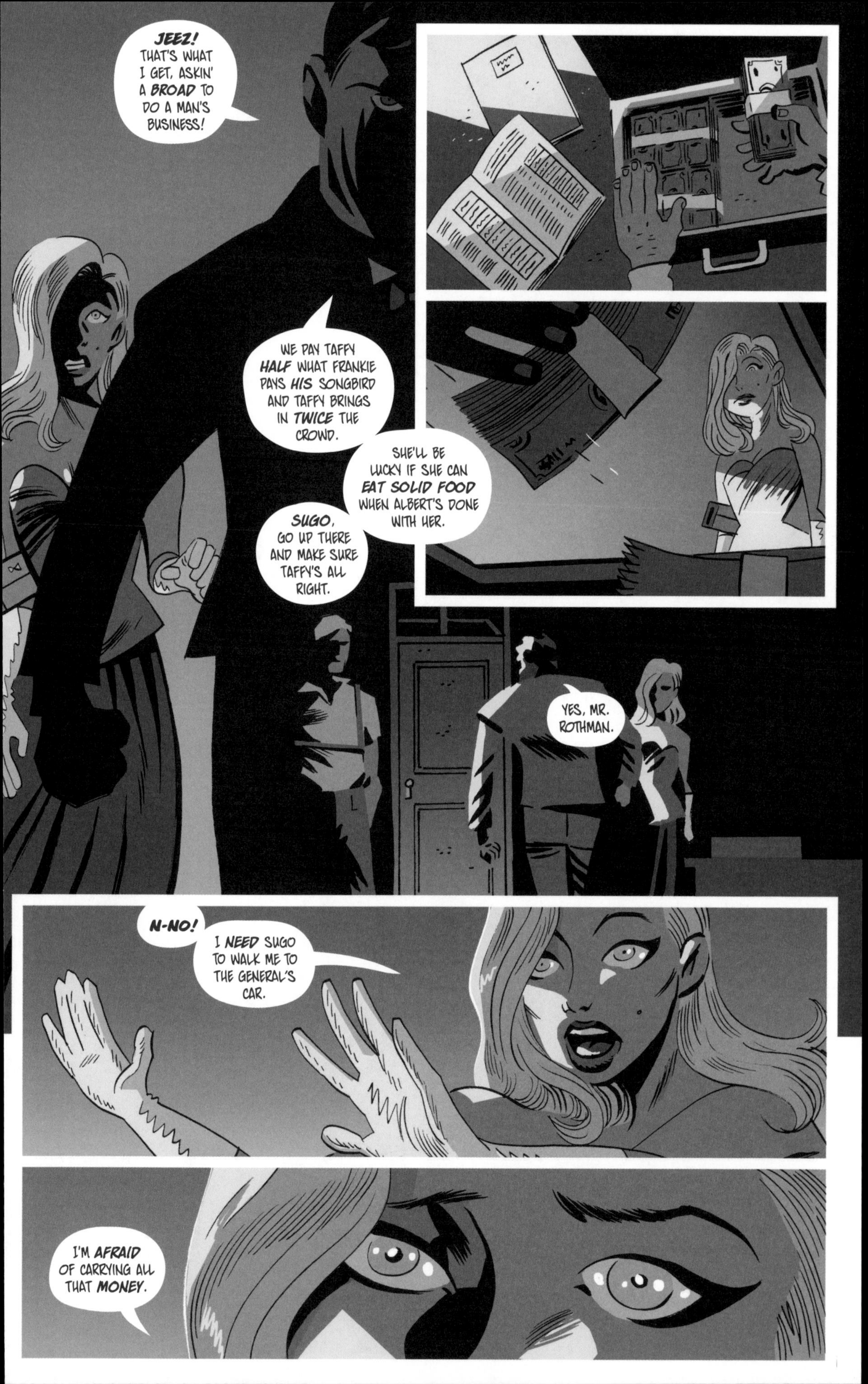
JEEZ! THAT'S WHAT I GET, ASKIN' A BROAD TO DO A MAN'S BUSINESS!
WE PAY TAFFY HALF WHAT FRANKIE PAYS HIS SONGBIRD AND TAFFY BRINGS IN TWICE THE CROWD.
SHE'LL BE LUCKY IF SHE CAN EAT SOLID FOOD WHEN ALBERT'S DONE WITH HER.
SUGO, GO UP THERE AND MAKE SURE TAFFY'S ALL RIGHT.
YES, MR. ROTHMAN.
N-NO!
I NEED SUGO TO WALK ME TO THE GENERAL'S CAR.
I'M AFRAID OF CARRYING ALL THAT MONEY.

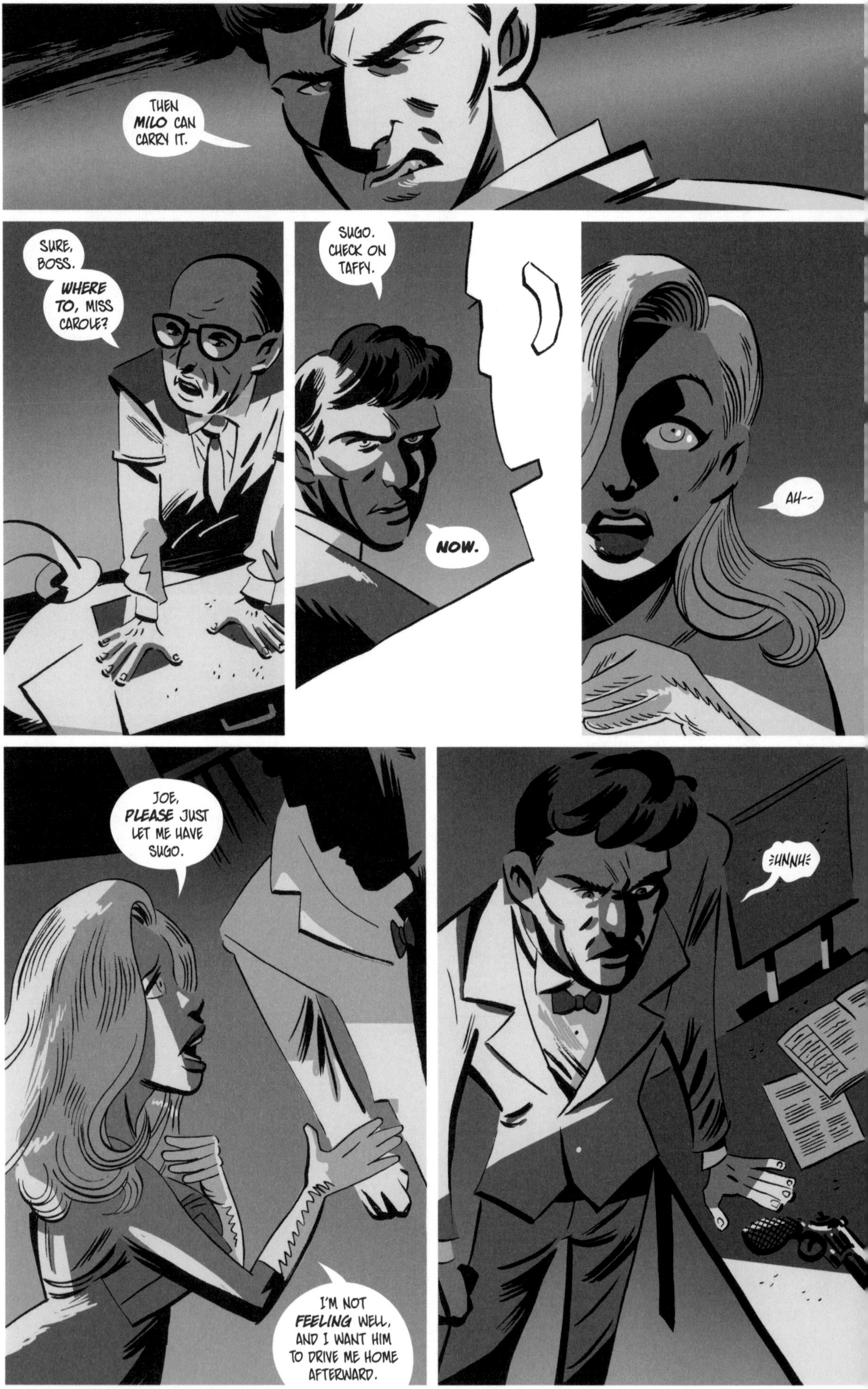
THEN MILO CAN CARRY IT.
SURE, BOSS. WHERE TO, MISS CAROLE?
SUGO. CHECK ON TAFFY.
NOW.
AH--
JOE, PLEASE JUST LET ME HAVE SUGO.
I'M NOT FEELING WELL, AND I WANT HIM TO DRIVE ME HOME AFTERWARD.
UNNH

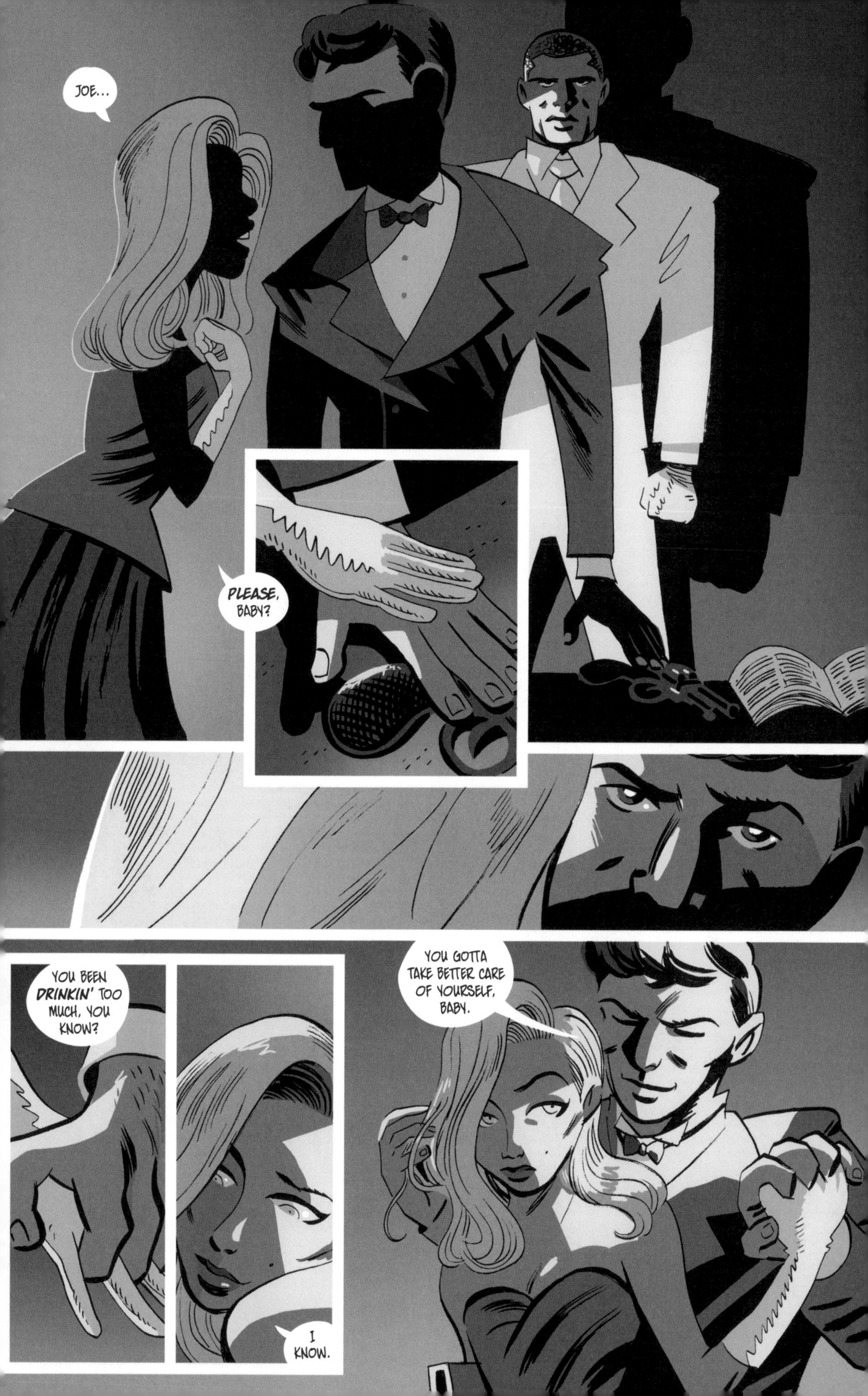
JOE...
PLEASE, BABY?
YOU BEEN DRINKIN' TOO MUCH, YOU KNOW?
I KNOW.
YOU GOTTA TAKE BETTER CARE OF YOURSELF, BABY.

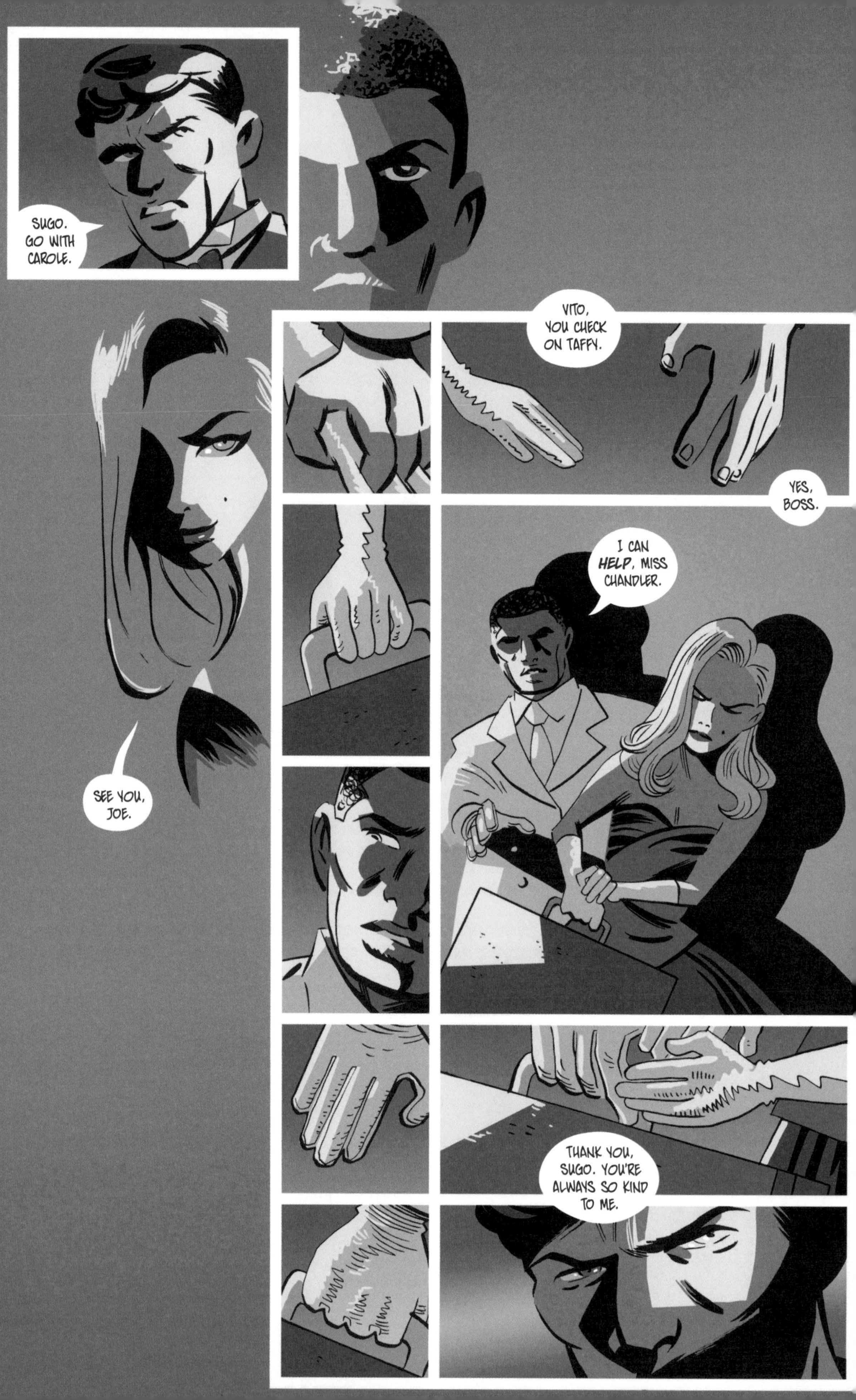
SUGO. GO WITH CAROLE.
SEE YOU, JOE.
VITO, YOU CHECK ON TAFFY.
YES, BOSS.
I CAN HELP, MISS CHANDLER.
THANK YOU, SUGO. YOU'RE ALWAYS SO KIND TO ME.

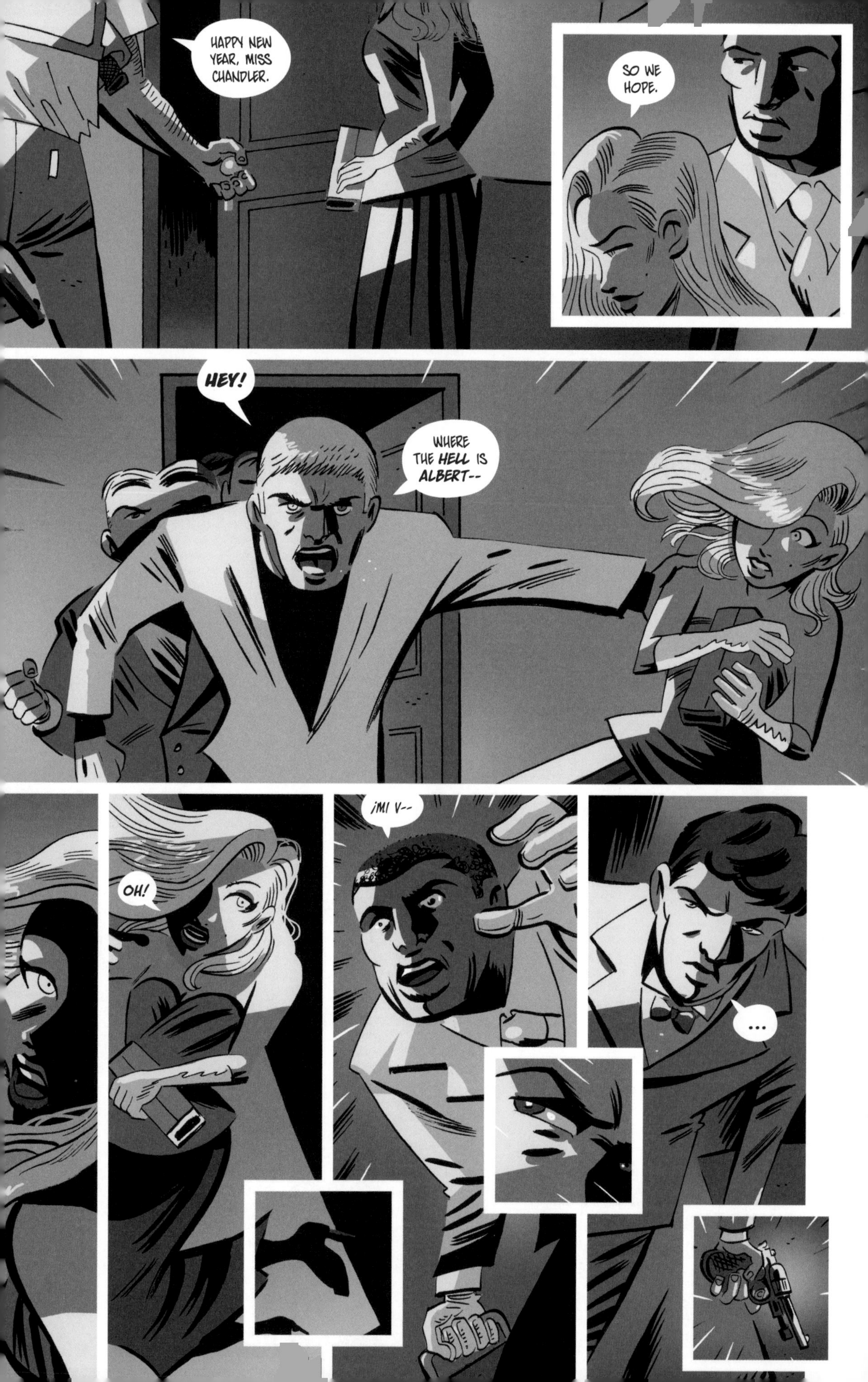
HAPPY NEW YEAR, MISS CHANDLER.
SO WE HOPE.
HEY!
WHERE THE HELL IS ALBERT--
OH!
¡MI V--
...

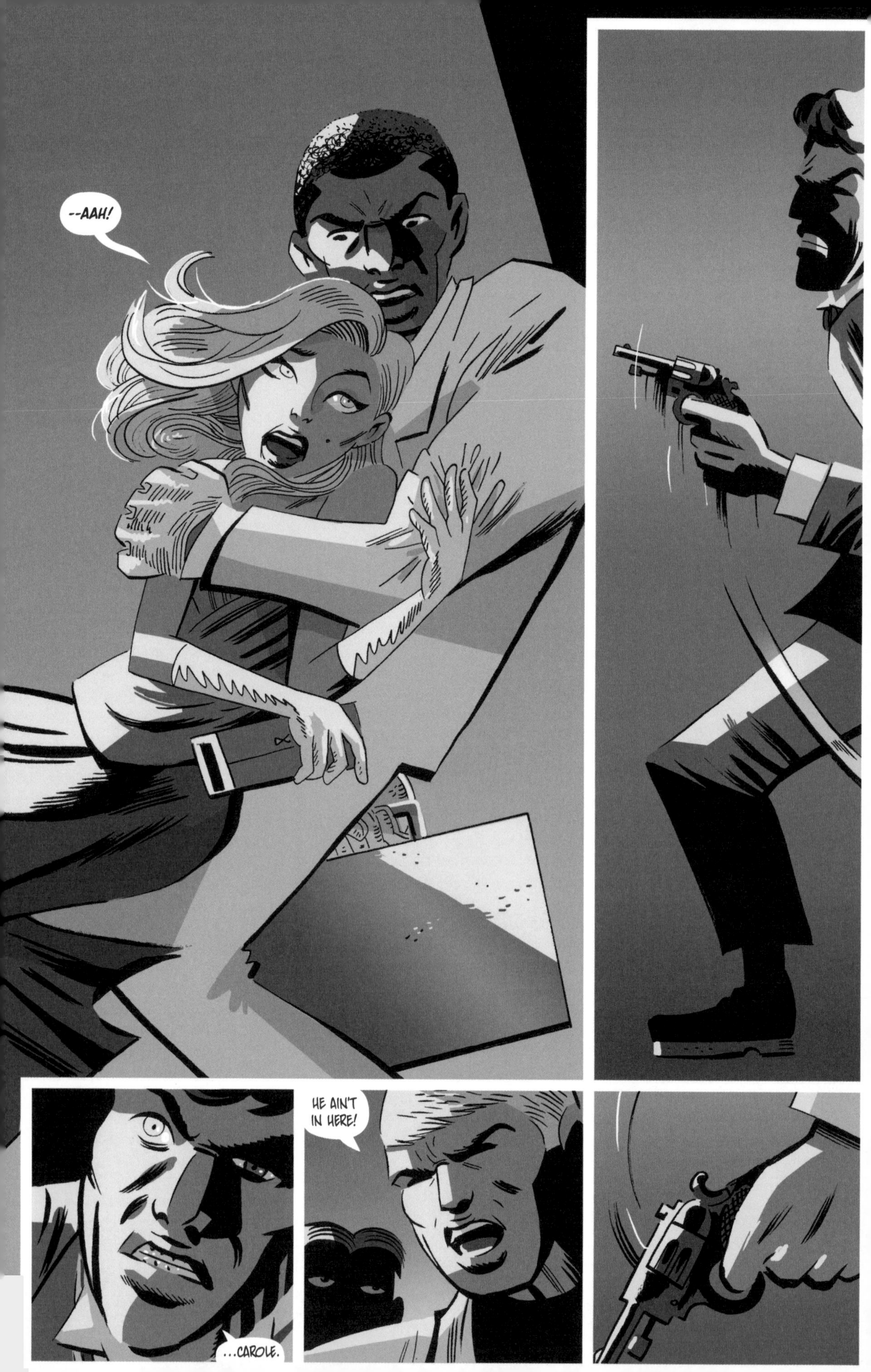
--AAH!
...CAROLE.
HE AIN'T IN HERE!

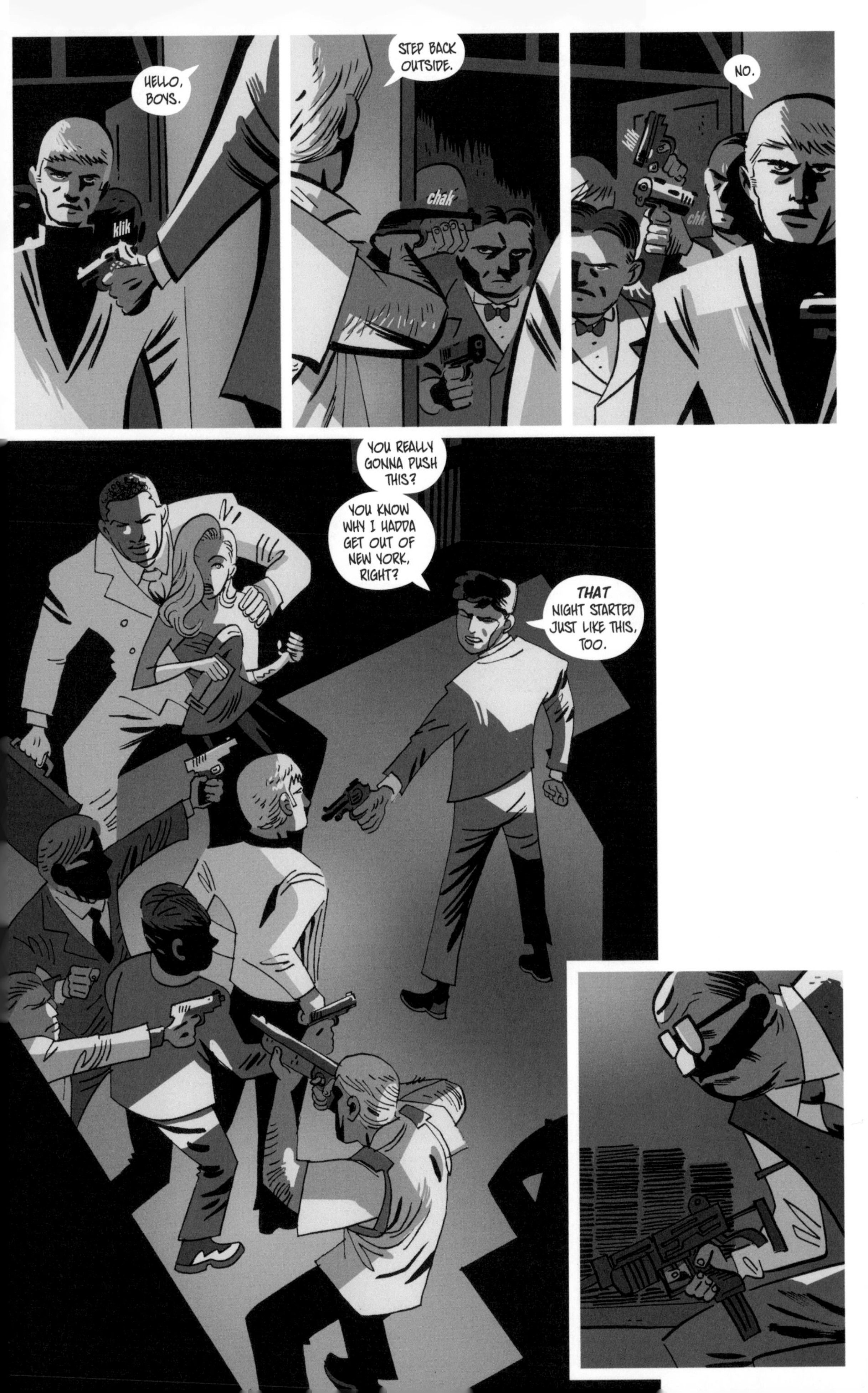
HELLO, BOYS.
klik
STEP BACK OUTSIDE.
chak
NO.
klik
chk
YOU REALLY GONNA PUSH THIS?
YOU KNOW WHY I HADDA GET OUT OF NEW YORK, RIGHT?
THAT NIGHT STARTED JUST LIKE THIS, TOO.

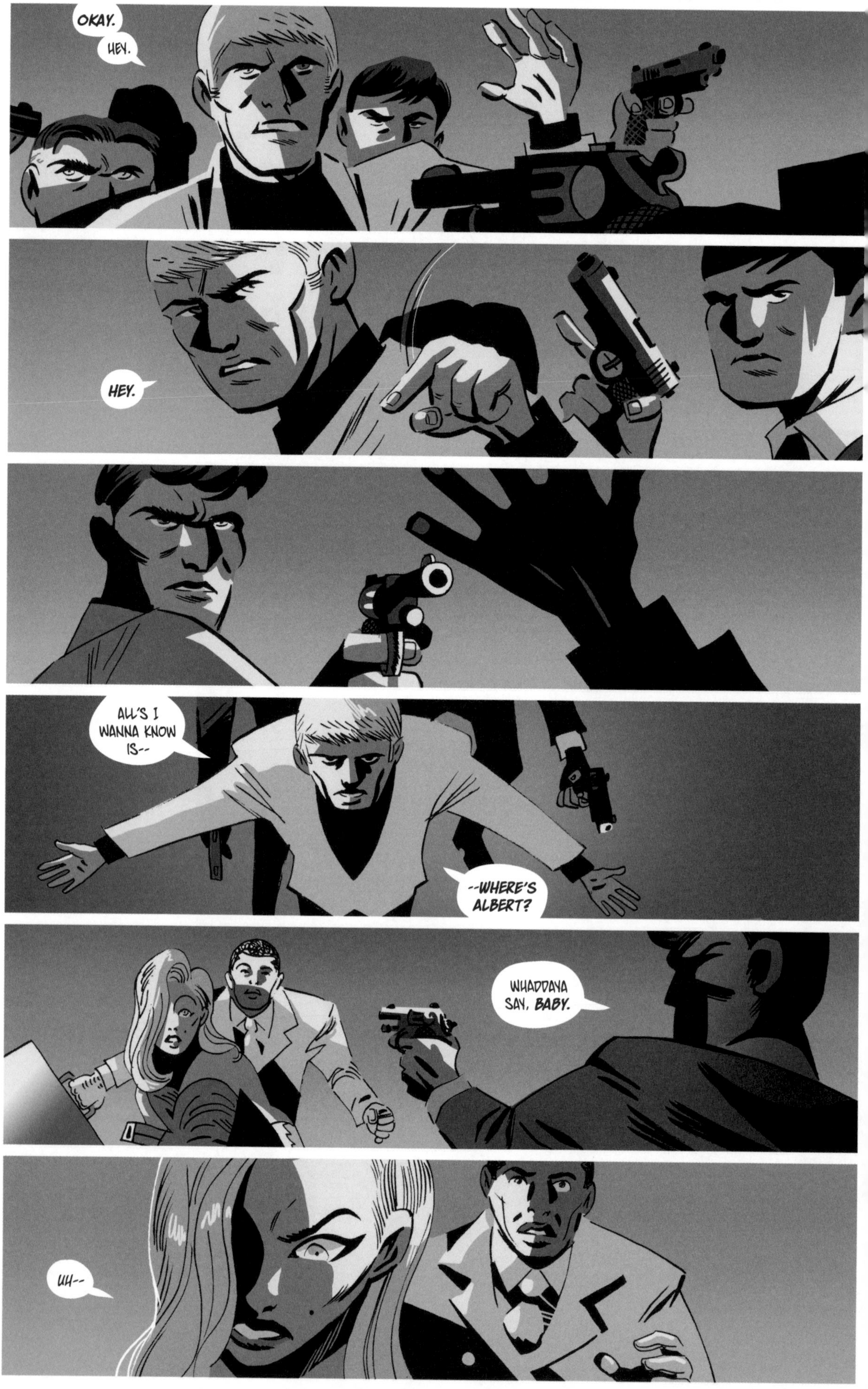
OKAY.
HEY.
HEY.
ALL'S I WANNA KNOW IS--
--WHERE'S ALBERT?
WHADDAYA SAY, BABY.
UH--

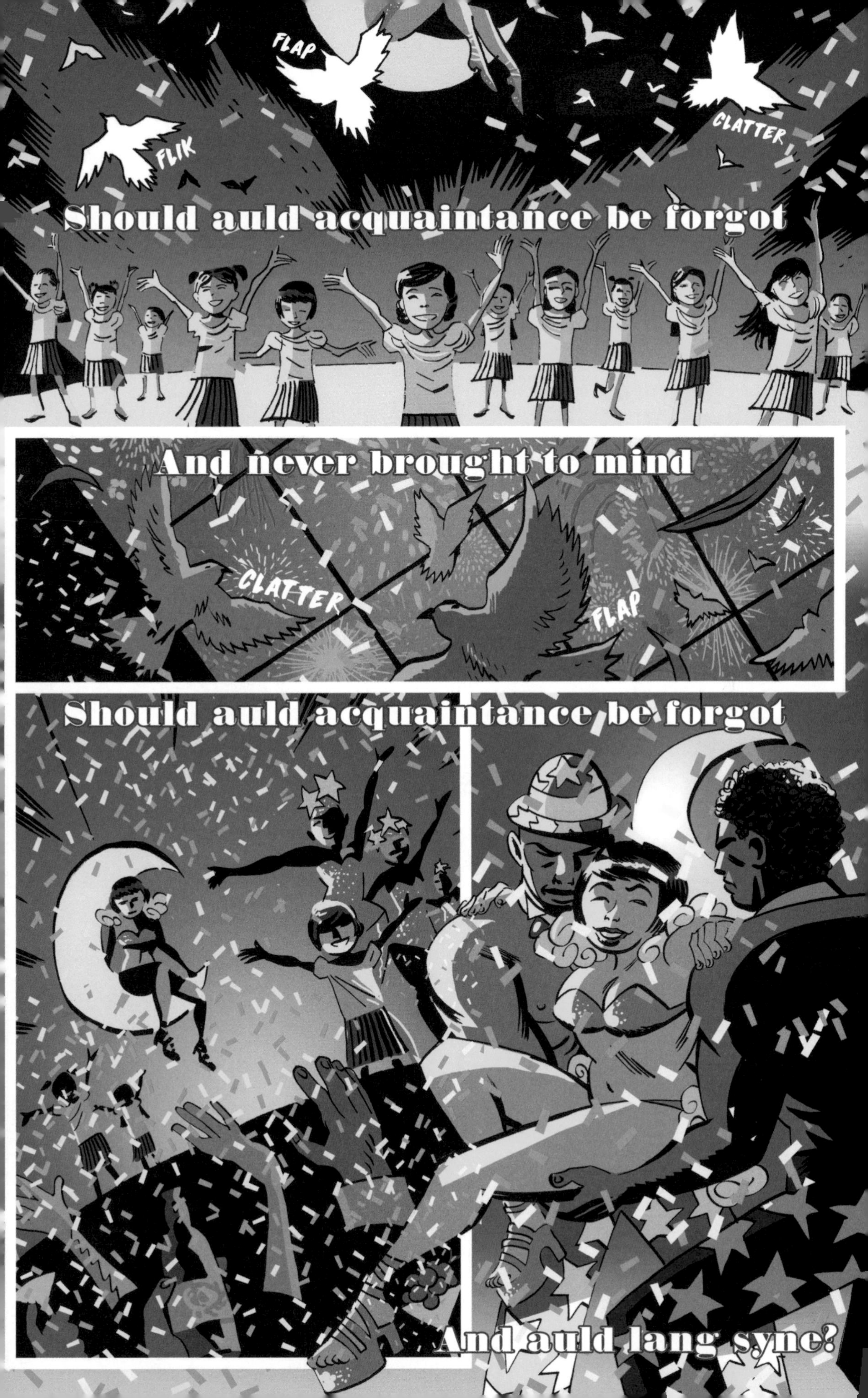
FLAP
FLIK
CLATTER
Should auld acquaintance be forgot
And never brought to mind
CLATTER
FLAP
Should auld acquaintance be forgot
And auld lang syne?

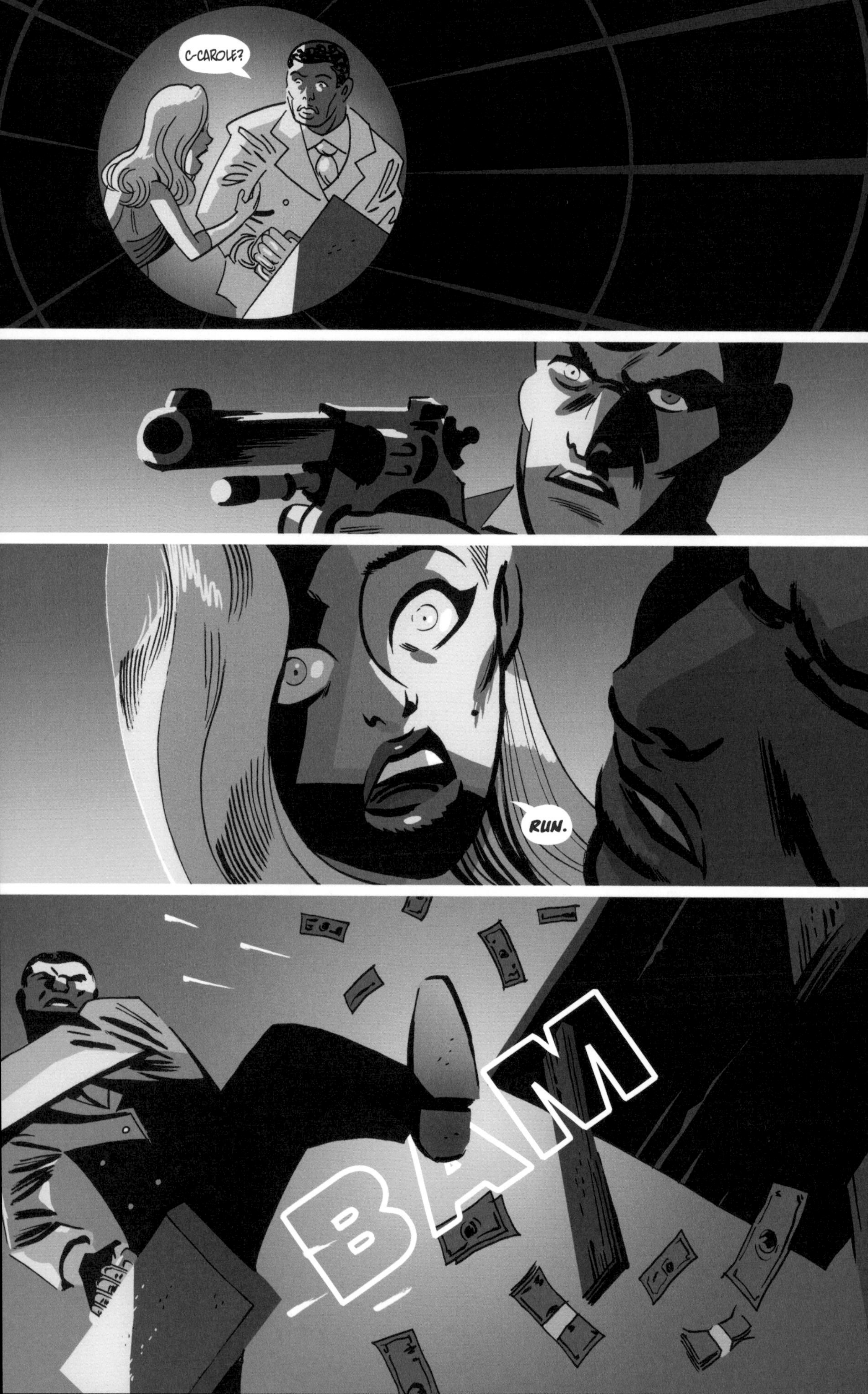
C-CAROLE?
RUN.
BAM

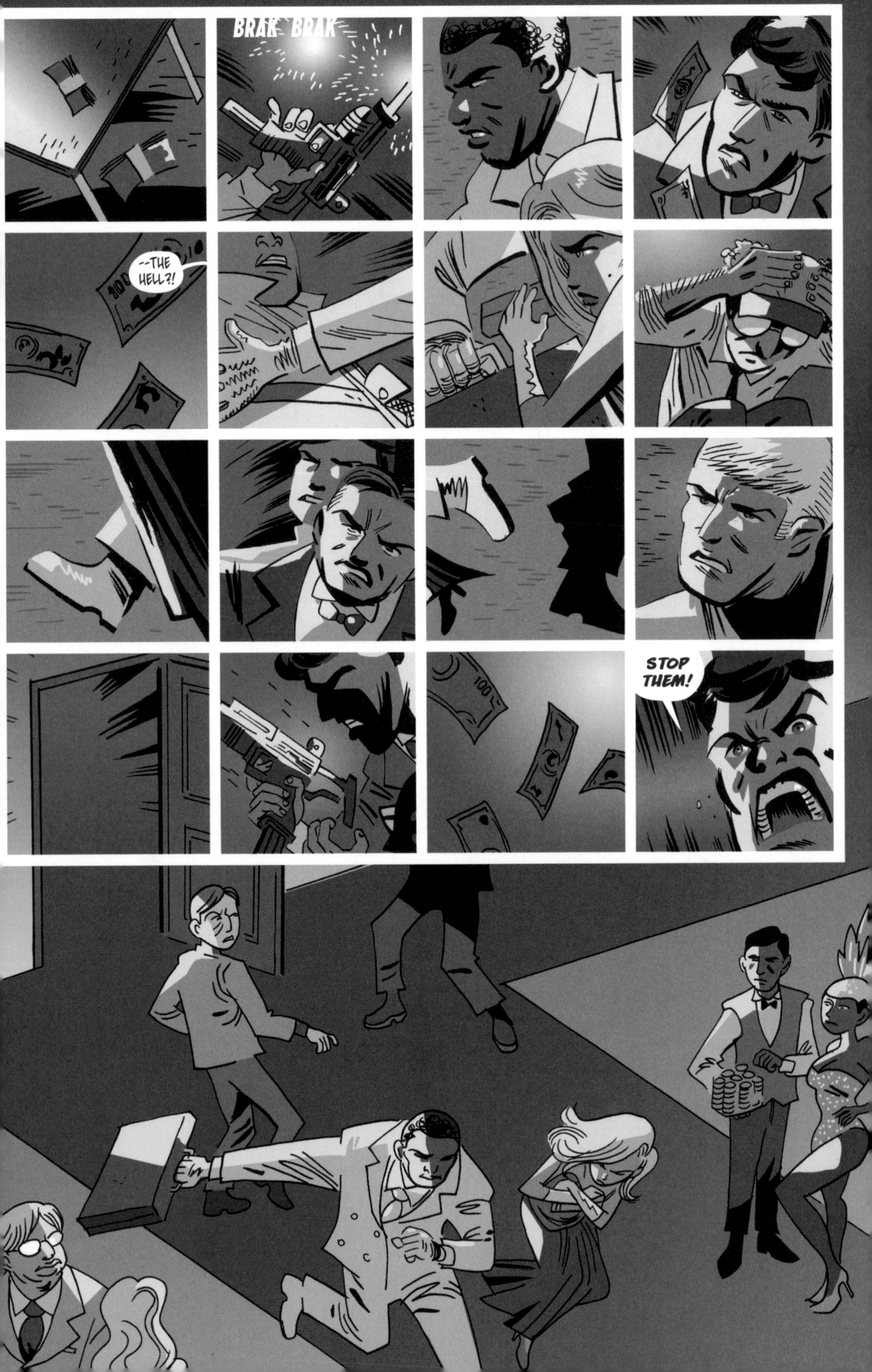
BRAK BRAK
--THE HELL?!
STOP THEM!

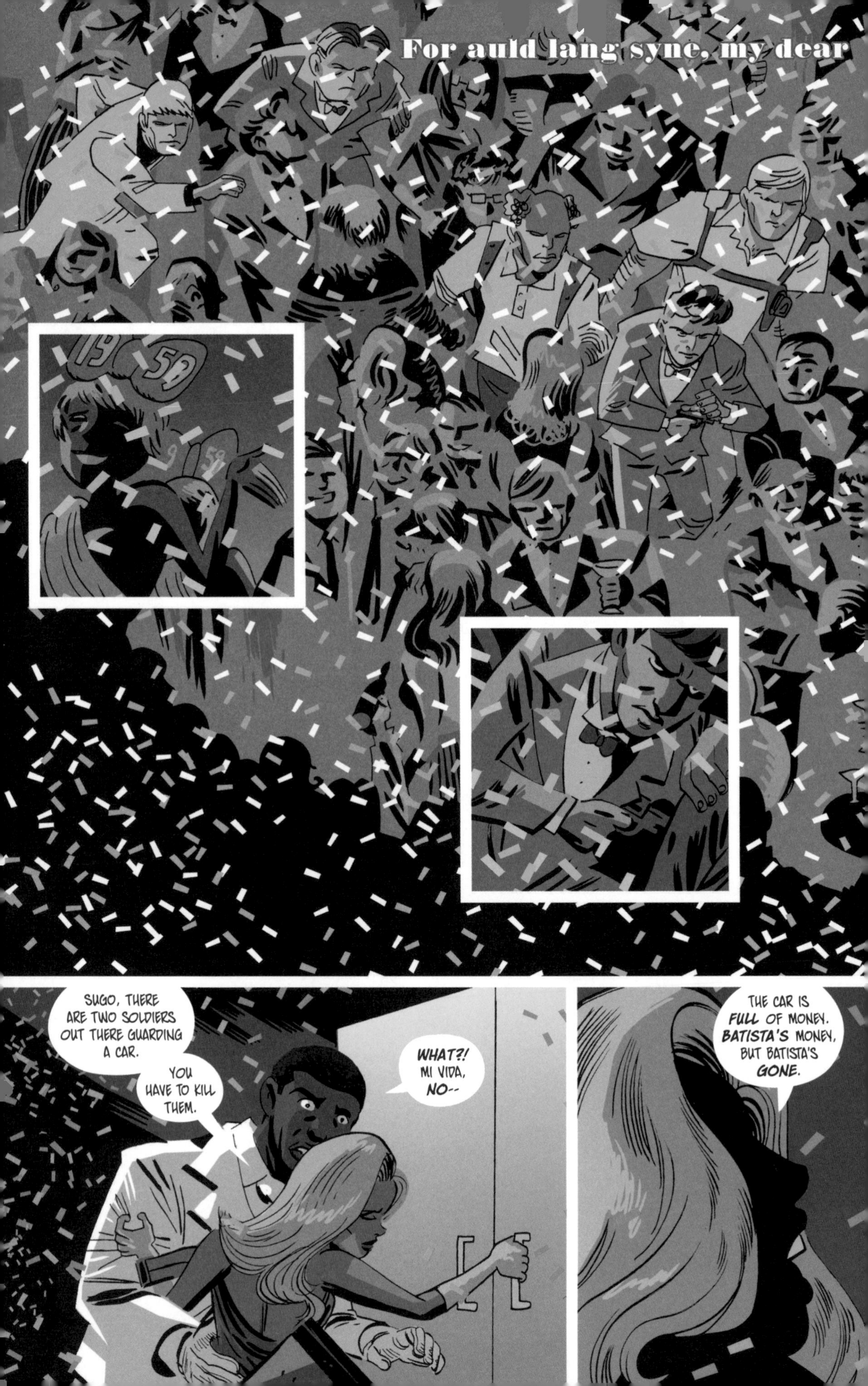
For auld lang syne, my dear
SUGO, THERE ARE TWO SOLDIERS OUT THERE GUARDING A CAR.
YOU HAVE TO KILL THEM.
WHAT?! MI VIDA, NO--
THE CAR IS FULL OF MONEY. BATISTA'S MONEY. BUT BATISTA'S GONE.

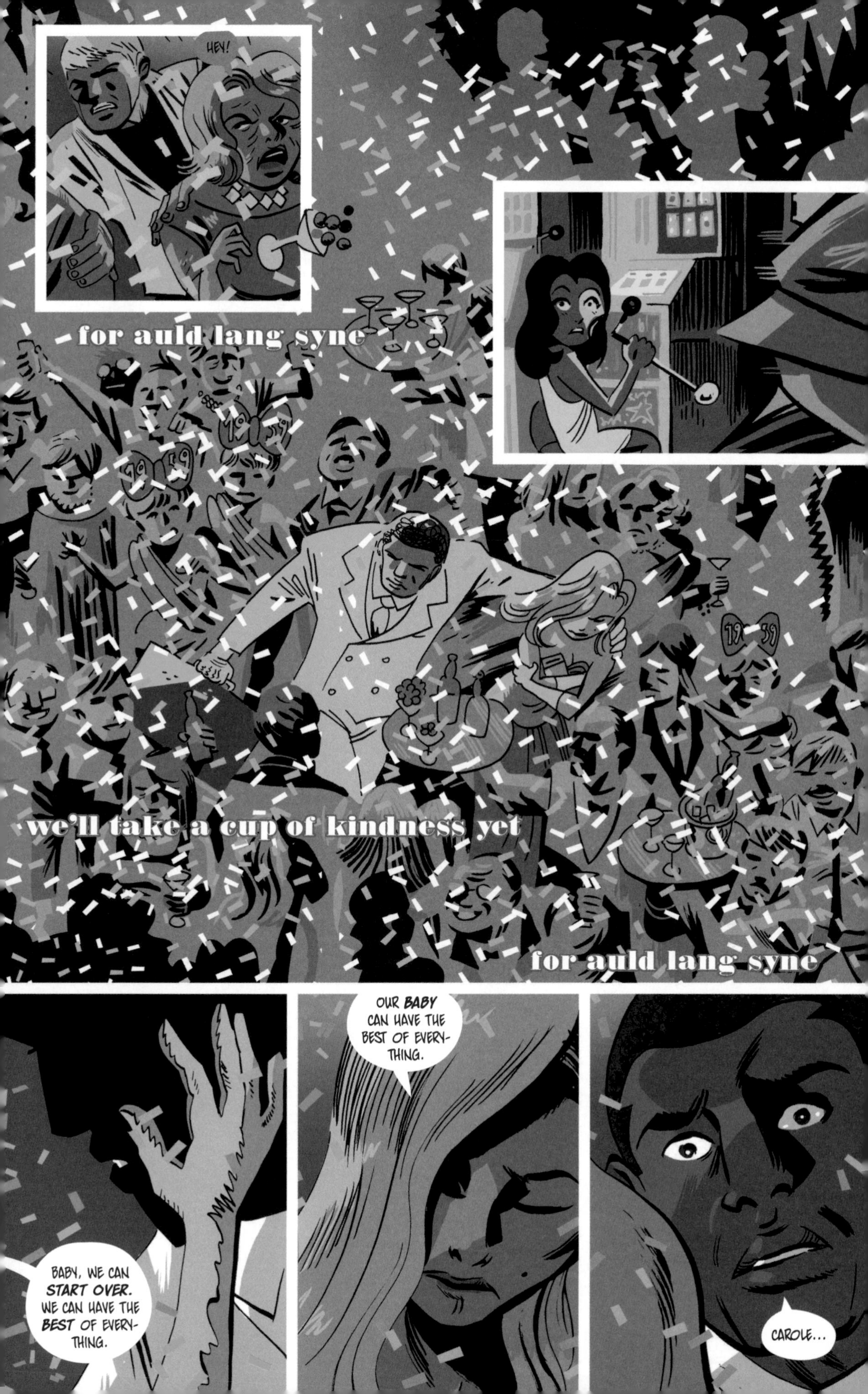

HEY!
for auld lang syne
we'll take a cup of kindness yet
for auld lang syne
BABY, WE CAN START OVER. WE CAN HAVE THE BEST OF EVERY-THING.
OUR BABY CAN HAVE THE BEST OF EVERY-THING.
CAROLE...

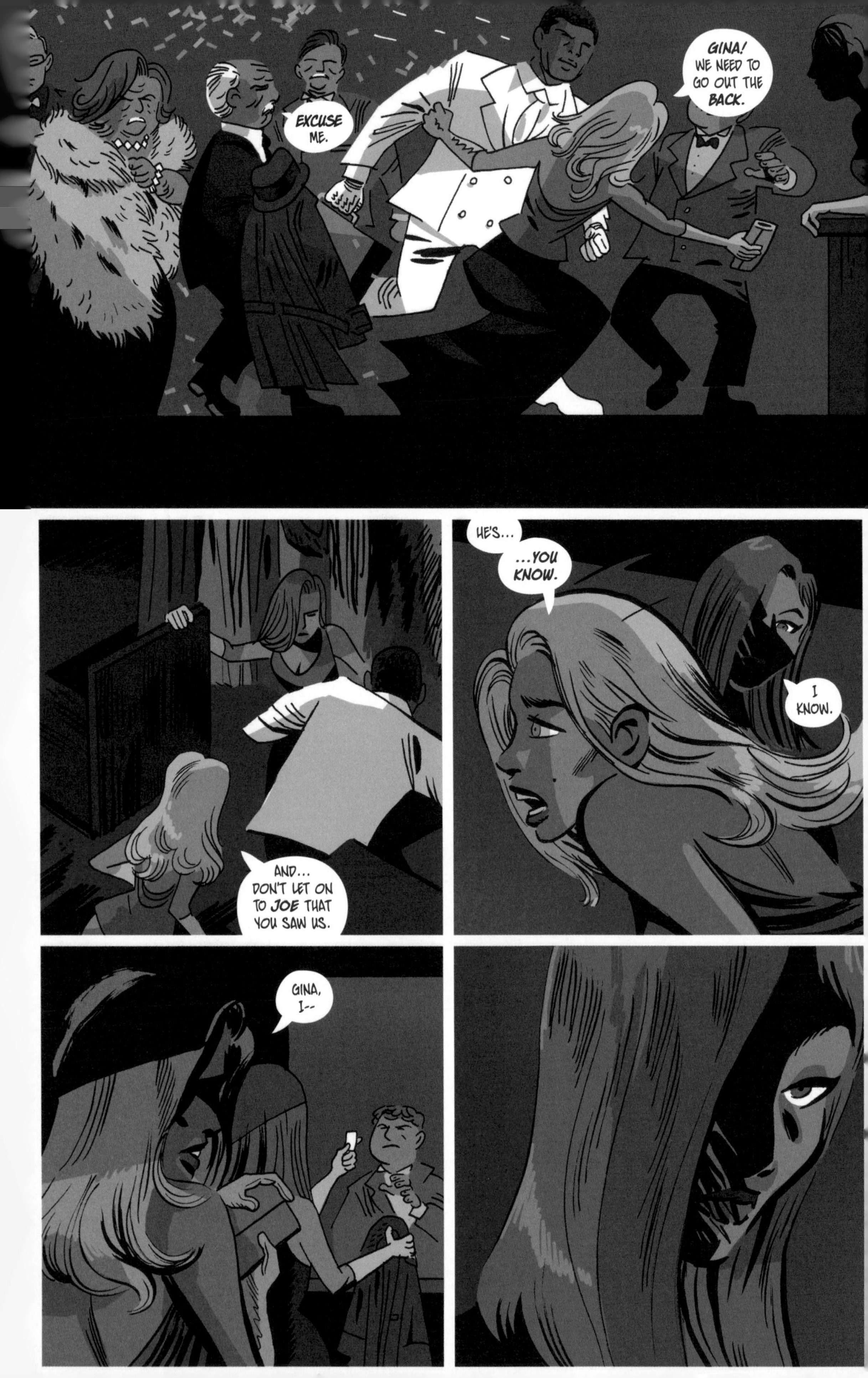
EXCUSE ME.
GINA! WE NEED TO GO OUT THE BACK.
AND... DON'T LET ON TO JOE THAT YOU SAW US.
HE'S...
...YOU KNOW.
I KNOW.
GINA, I--

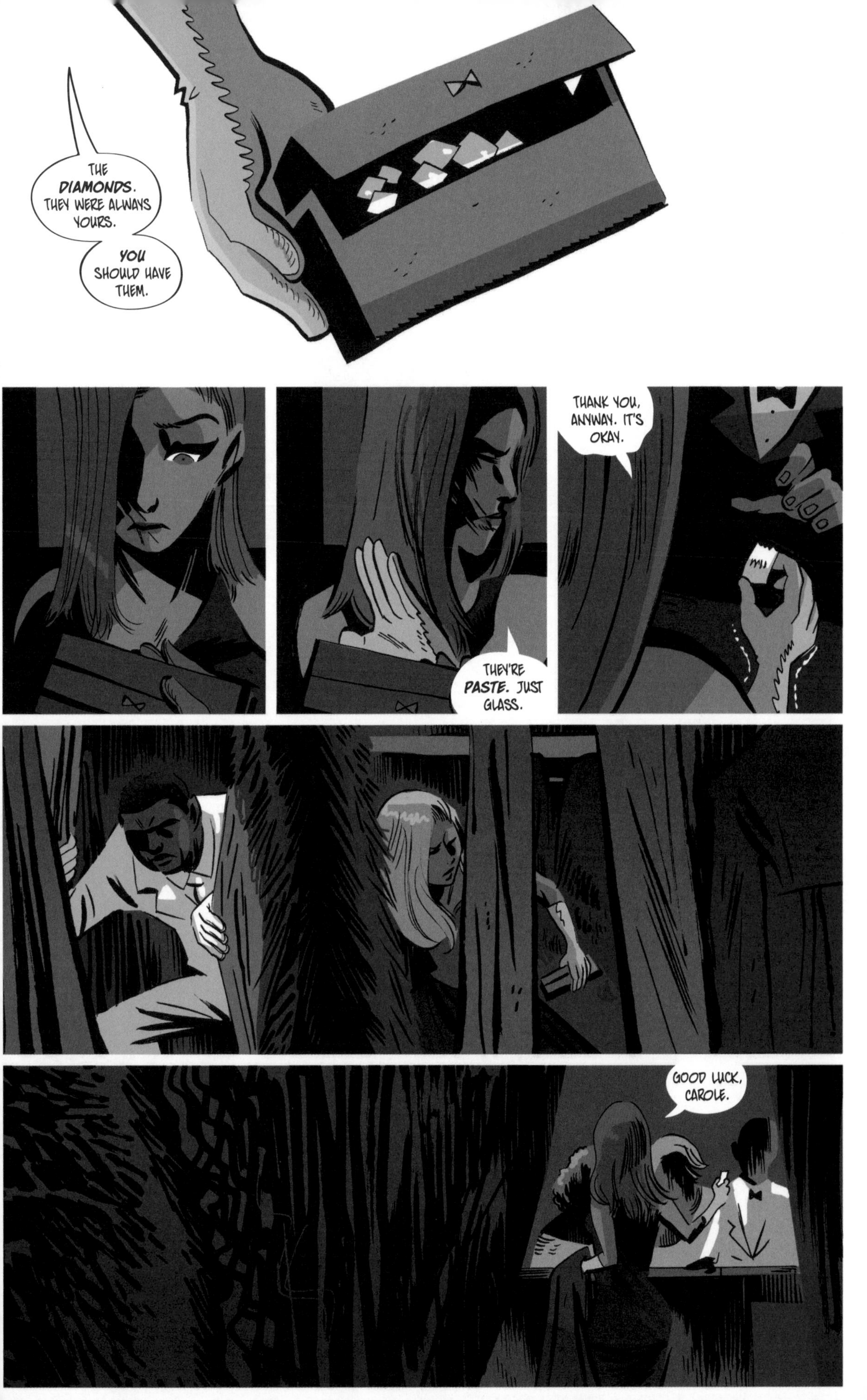
THE DIAMONDS. THEY WERE ALWAYS YOURS.
YOU SHOULD HAVE THEM.
THEY'RE PASTE. JUST GLASS.
THANK YOU, ANYWAY. IT'S OKAY.
GOOD LUCK, CAROLE.

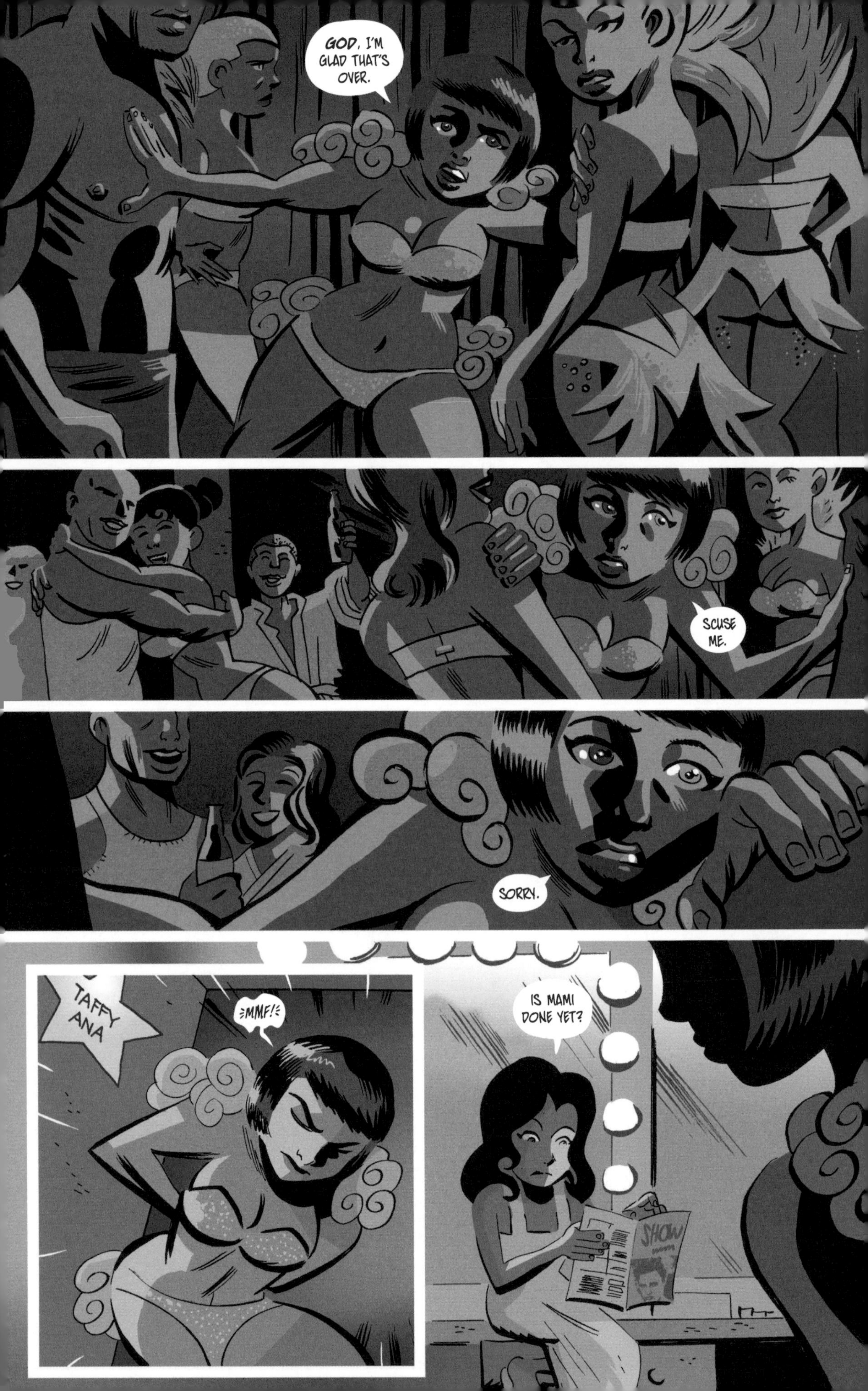
GOD, I'M GLAD THAT'S OVER.
SCUSE ME.
SORRY.
TAFFY ANA
MMF!
IS MAMI DONE YET?
SHOW

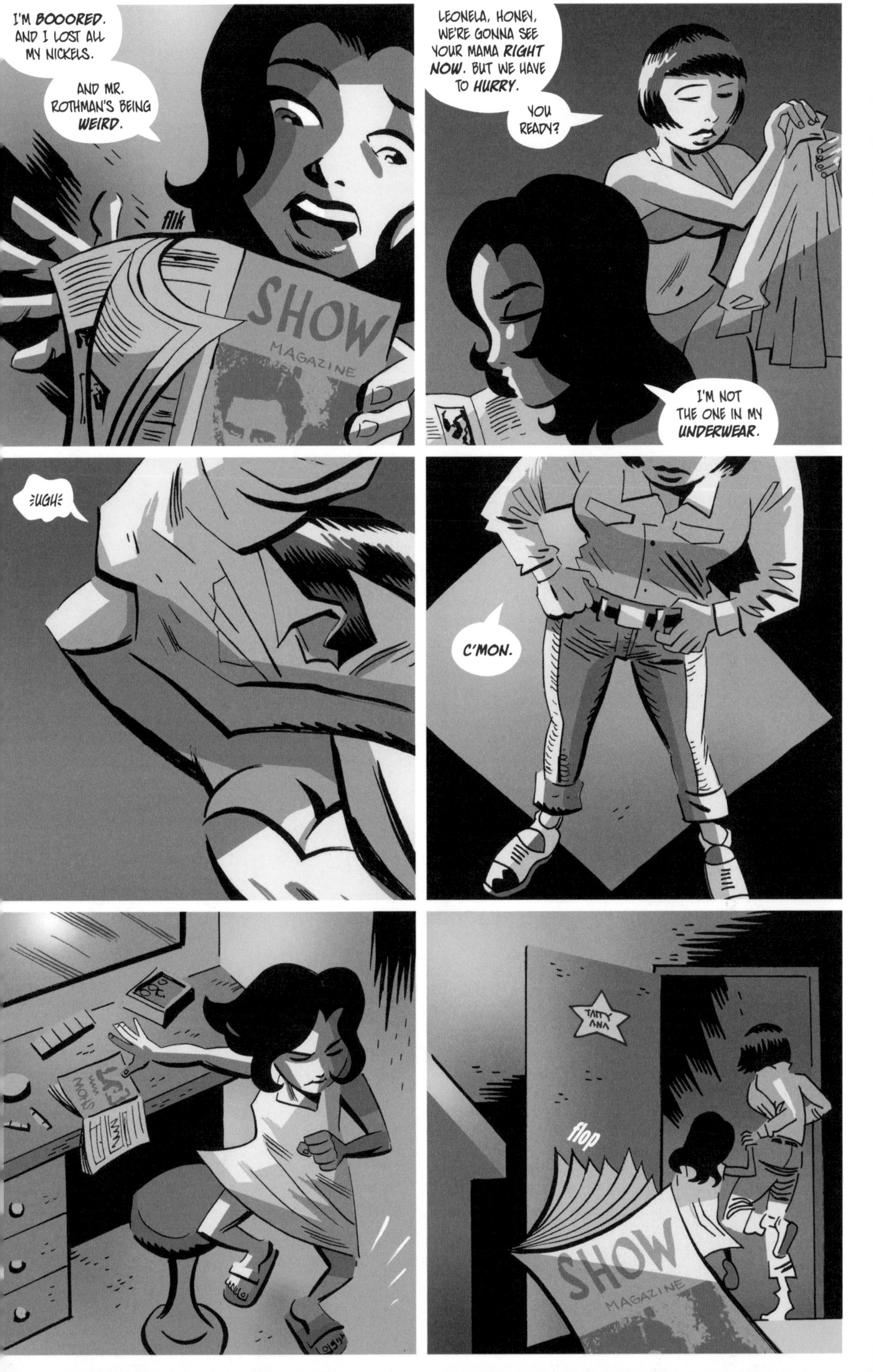
I'M BOOORED. AND I LOST ALL MY NICKELS.
AND MR. ROTHMAN'S BEING WEIRD.
flik
SHOW
MAGAZINE
LEONELA, HONEY, WE'RE GONNA SEE YOUR MAMA RIGHT NOW. BUT WE HAVE TO HURRY.
YOU READY?
I'M NOT THE ONE IN MY UNDERWEAR.
UGH
C'MON.
TATTY ANA
flop
SHOW
MAGAZINE

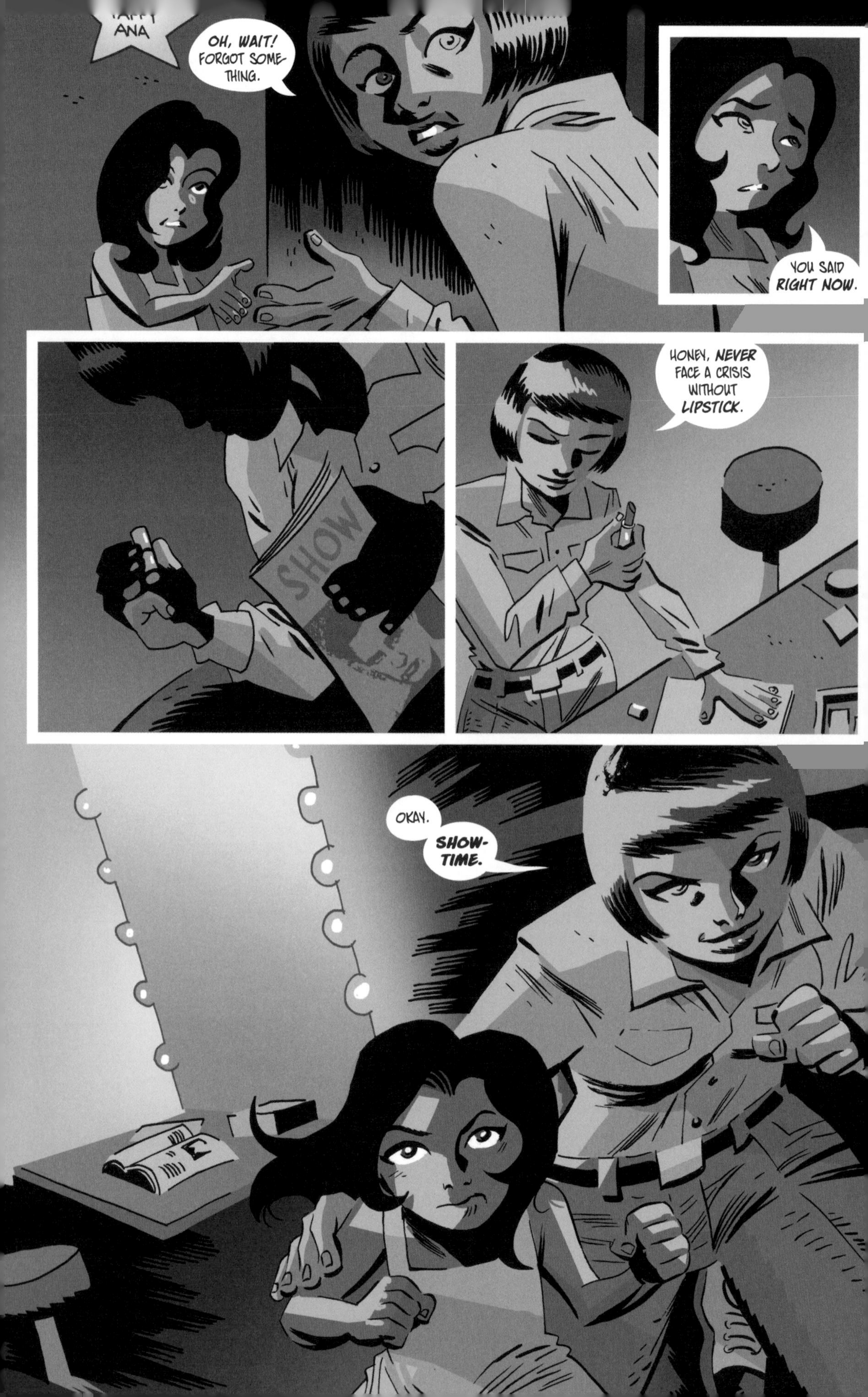
ANA
OH, WAIT! FORGOT SOMETHING.
YOU SAID RIGHT NOW.
SHOW
HONEY, NEVER FACE A CRISIS WITHOUT LIPSTICK.
OKAY.
SHOW-TIME.

1:OO A.M.

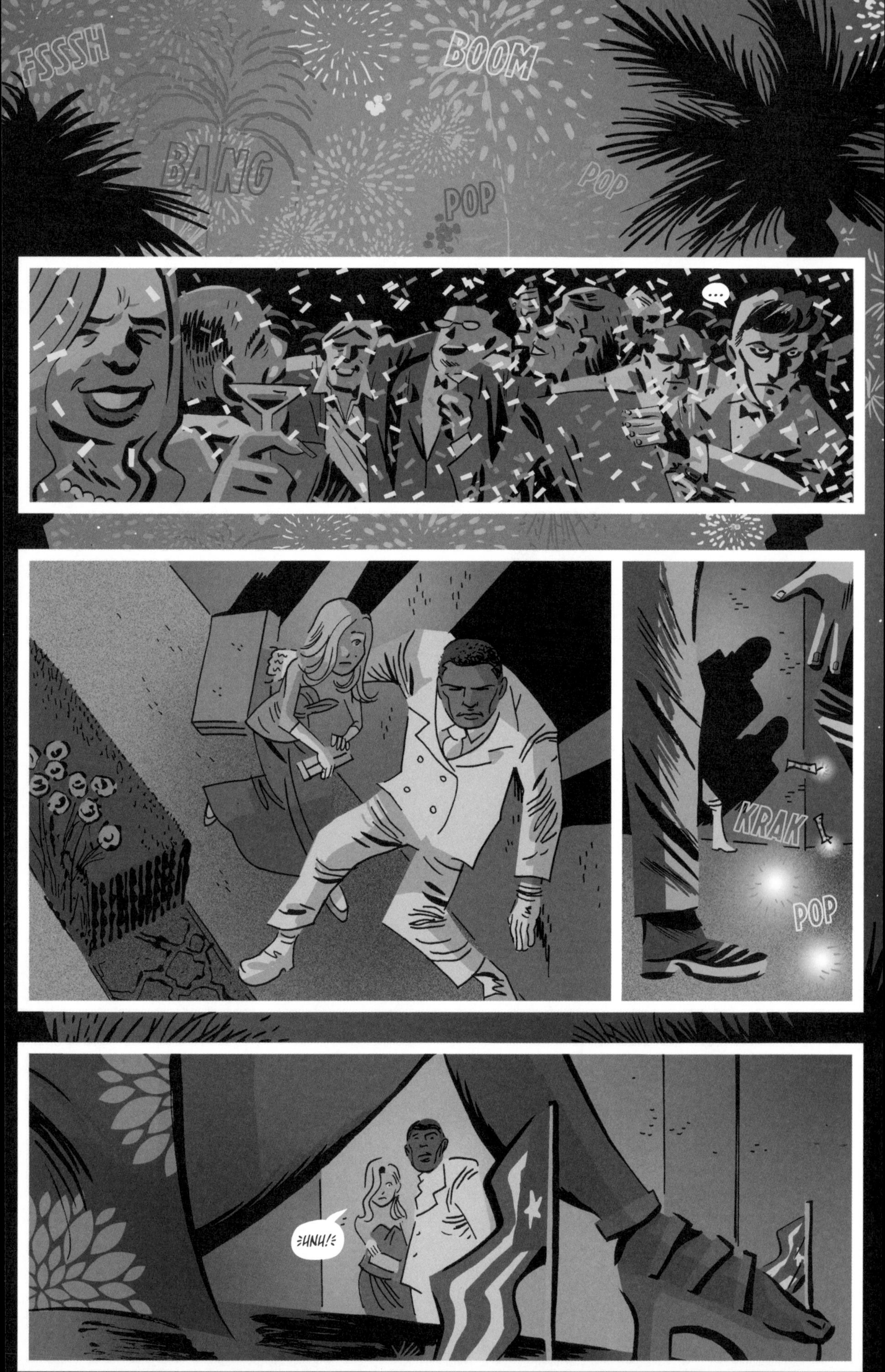
FSSSH
BOOM
BANG
POP
POP
...
KRAK
POP
UNH!

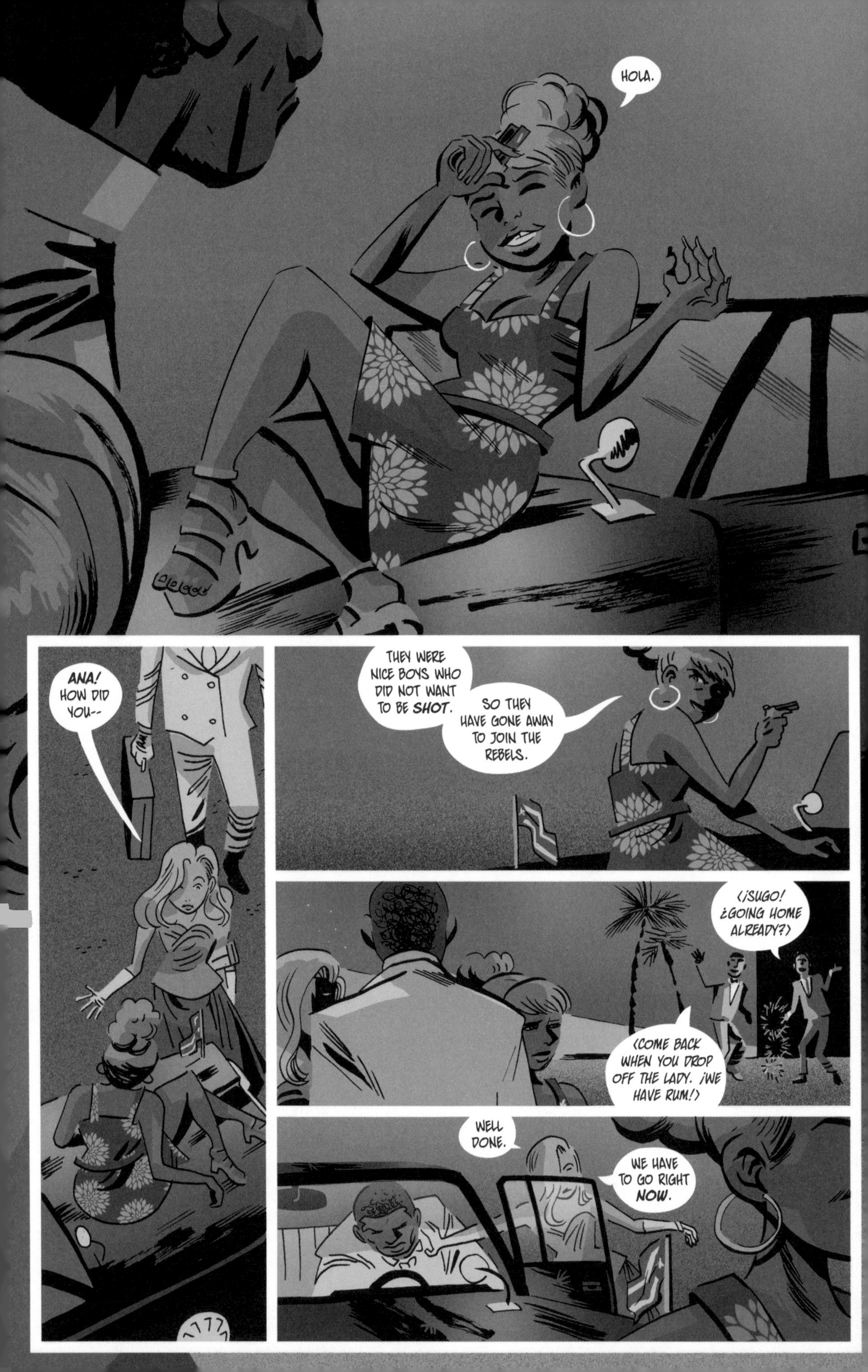
HOLA.
ANA! HOW DID YOU--
THEY WERE NICE BOYS WHO DID NOT WANT TO BE SHOT.
SO THEY HAVE GONE AWAY TO JOIN THE REBELS.
‹¡SUGO! ¿GOING HOME ALREADY?›
‹COME BACK WHEN YOU DROP OFF THE LADY. ¡WE HAVE RUM!›
WELL DONE.
WE HAVE TO GO RIGHT NOW.

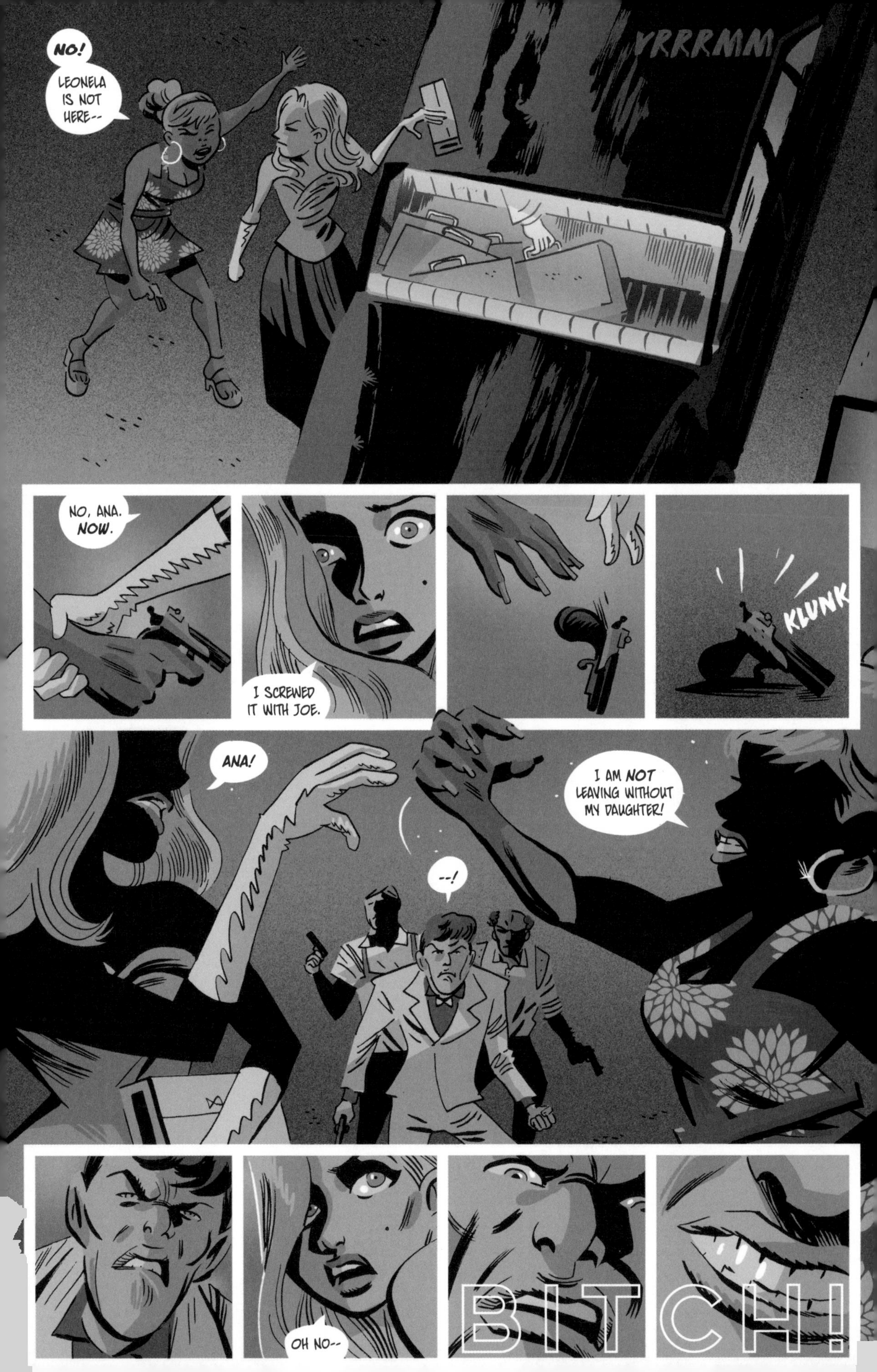
NO!
LEONELA IS NOT HERE--
VRRRMM
NO, ANA. NOW.
I SCREWED IT WITH JOE.
KLUNK
ANA!
I AM NOT LEAVING WITHOUT MY DAUGHTER!
--!
OH NO--
BITCH!

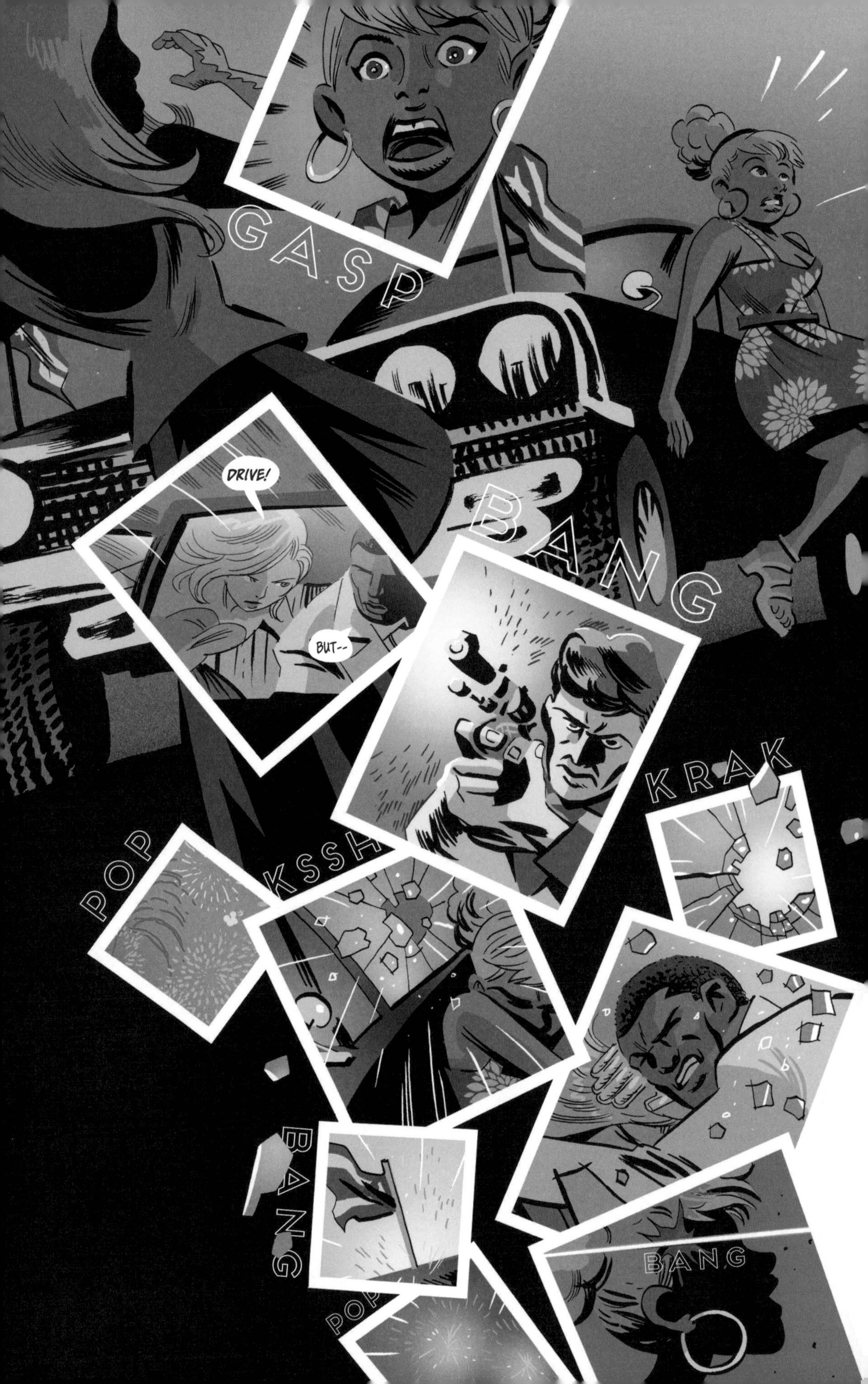
GASP
DRIVE!
BUT--
BANG
KRAK
POP
KSSH
BANG
POP
BANG

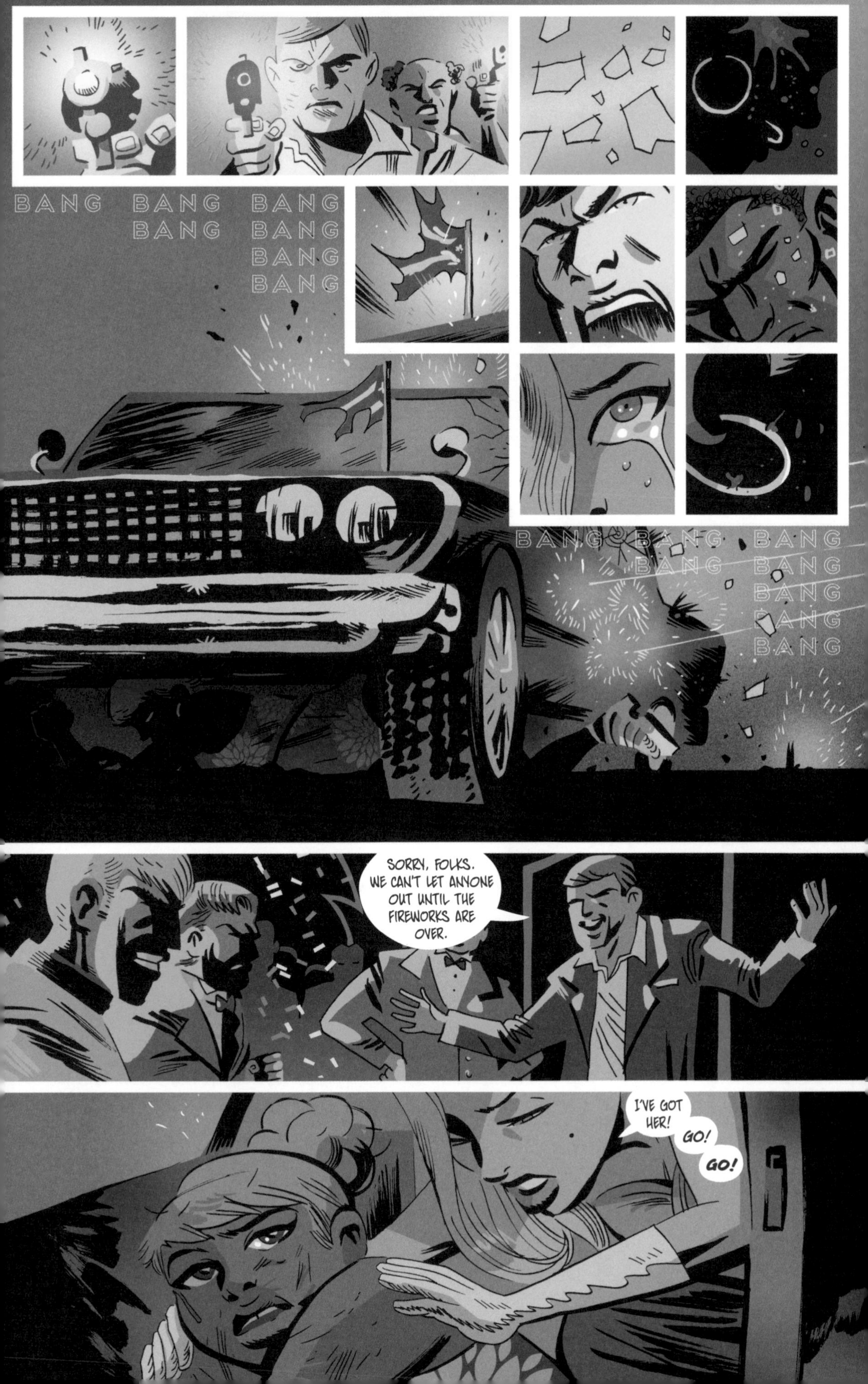
BANG BANG BANG
BANG BANG
BANG
BANG
BANG BANG BANG
BANG BANG
BANG
BANG
BANG
SORRY, FOLKS. WE CAN'T LET ANYONE OUT UNTIL THE FIREWORKS ARE OVER.
I'VE GOT HER!
GO!
GO!

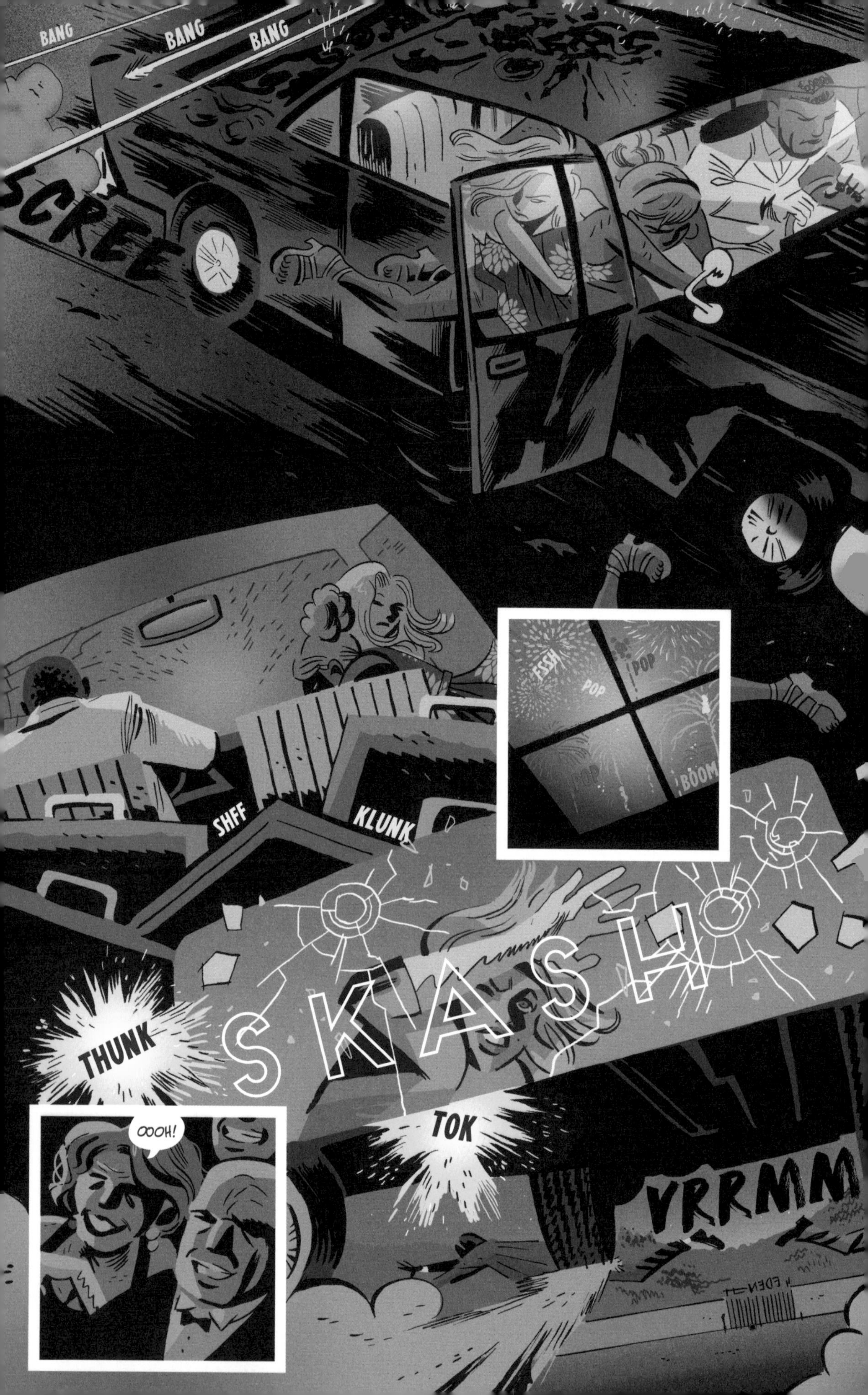
BANG
BANG
BANG
SCREE
FSSH
POP
POP
POP
BOOM
SHFF
KLUNK
THUNK
SKASH
OOOH!
TOK
VRRMM

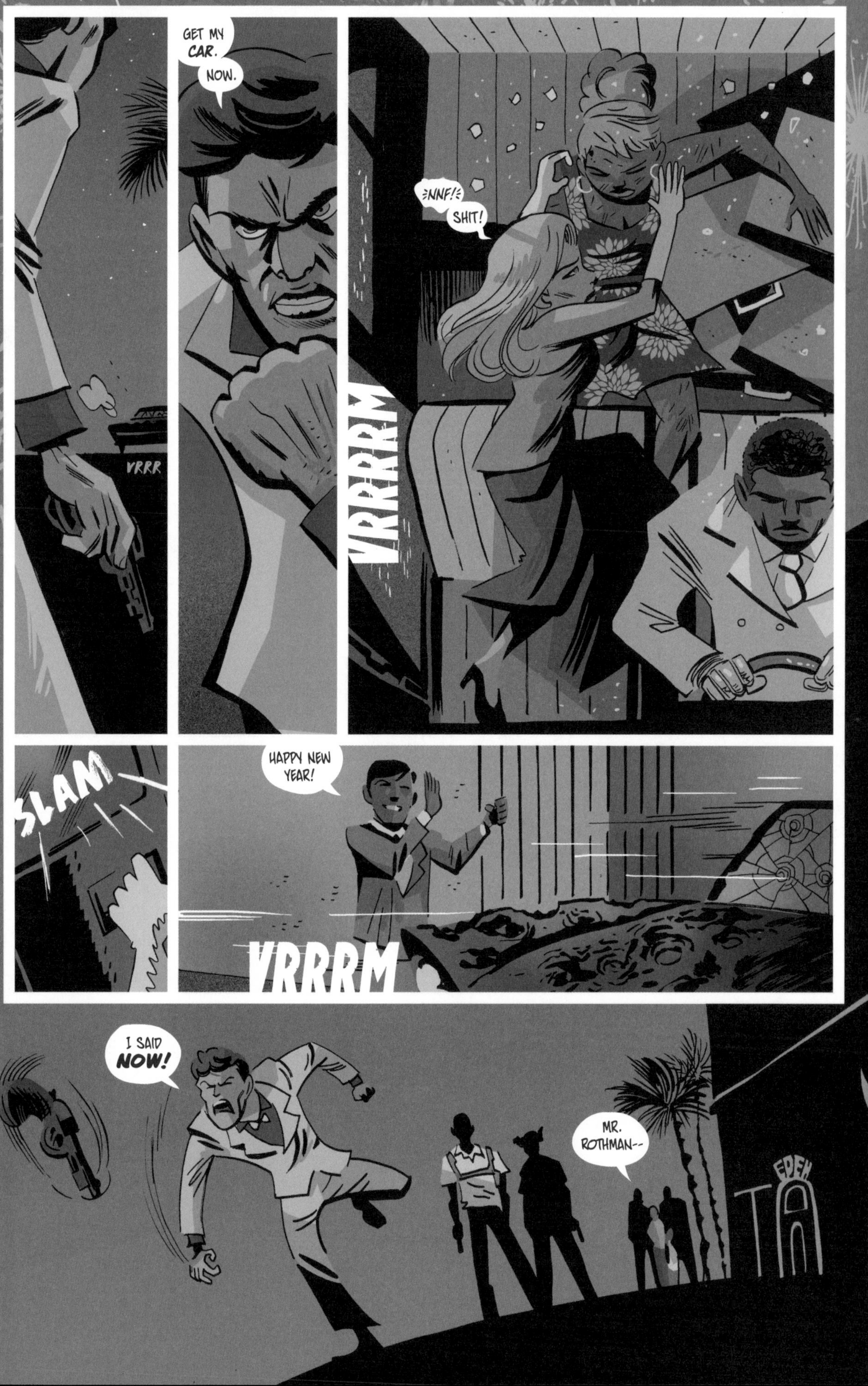

VRRR
GET MY CAR.
NOW.
VRRRRRM
NNF!
SHIT!
SLAM
HAPPY NEW YEAR!
VRRRM
I SAID NOW!
MR. ROTHMAN--
EDEN

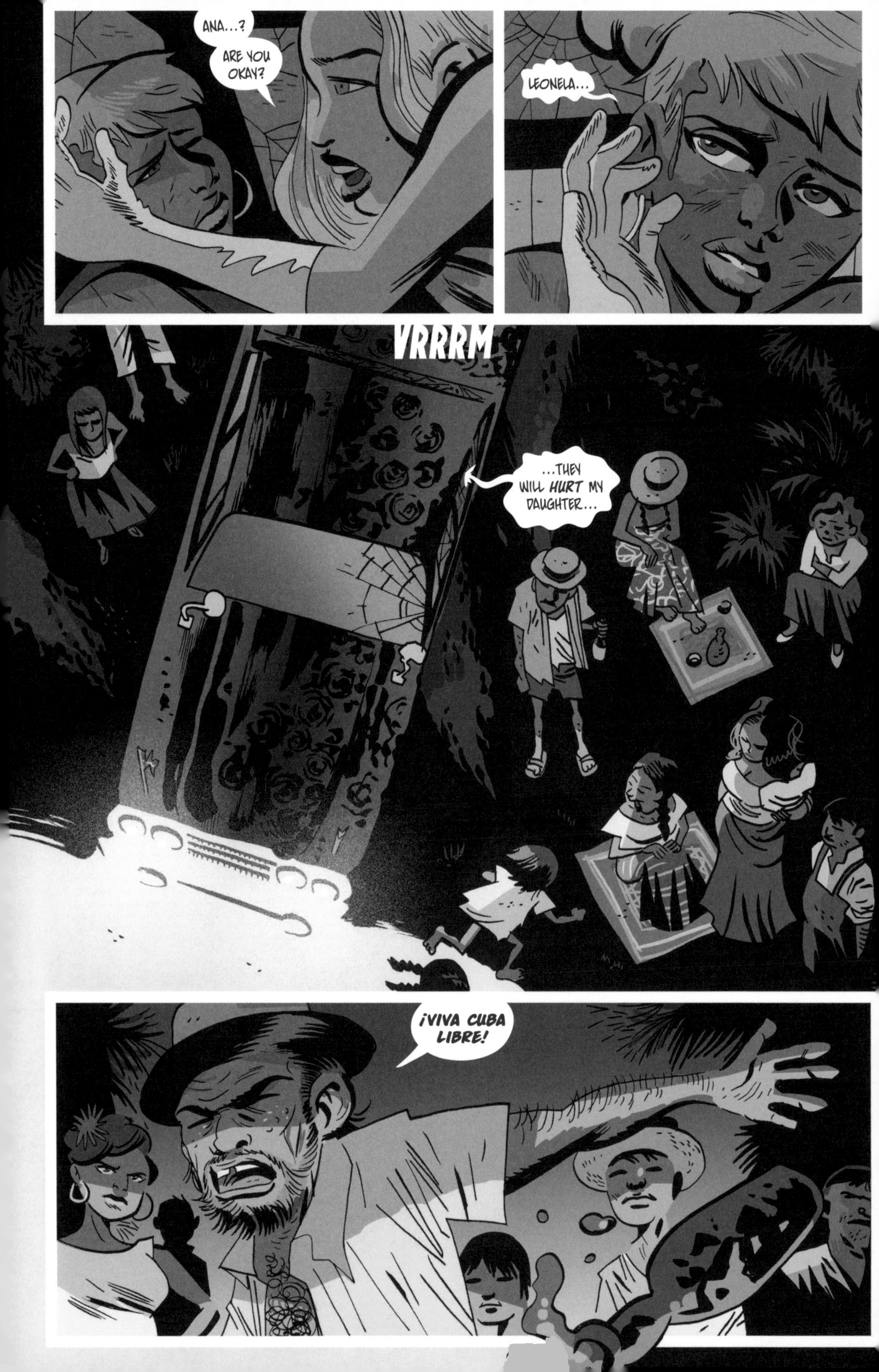
ANA...?
ARE YOU OKAY?
LEONELA...
VRRRM
...THEY WILL *HURT* MY DAUGHTER...
¡VIVA CUBA LIBRE!

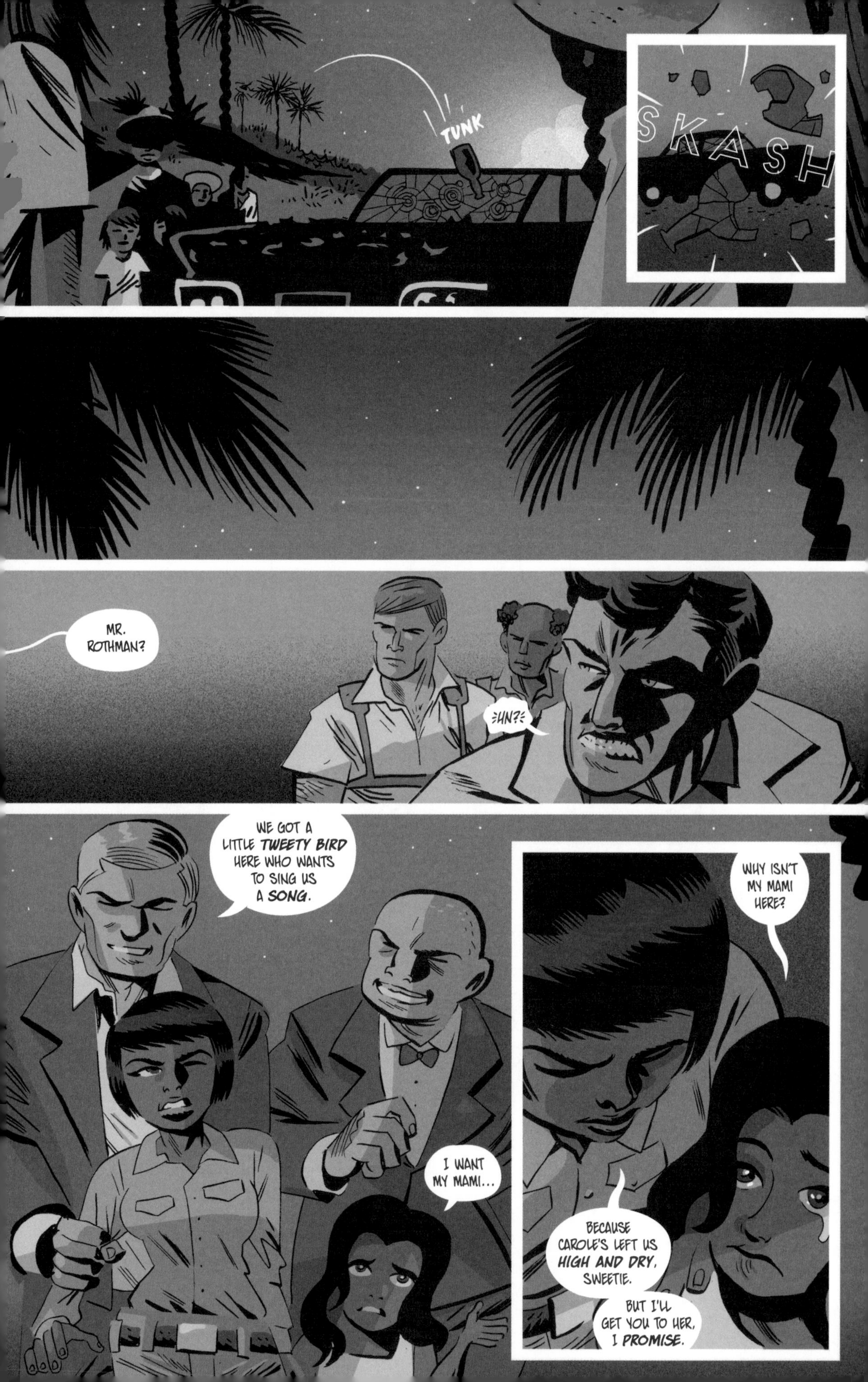
TUNK
SKASH
MR. ROTHMAN?
UN?
WE GOT A LITTLE TWEETY BIRD HERE WHO WANTS TO SING US A SONG.
I WANT MY MAMI...
WHY ISN'T MY MAMI HERE?
BECAUSE CAROLE'S LEFT US HIGH AND DRY, SWEETIE.
BUT I'LL GET YOU TO HER, I PROMISE.

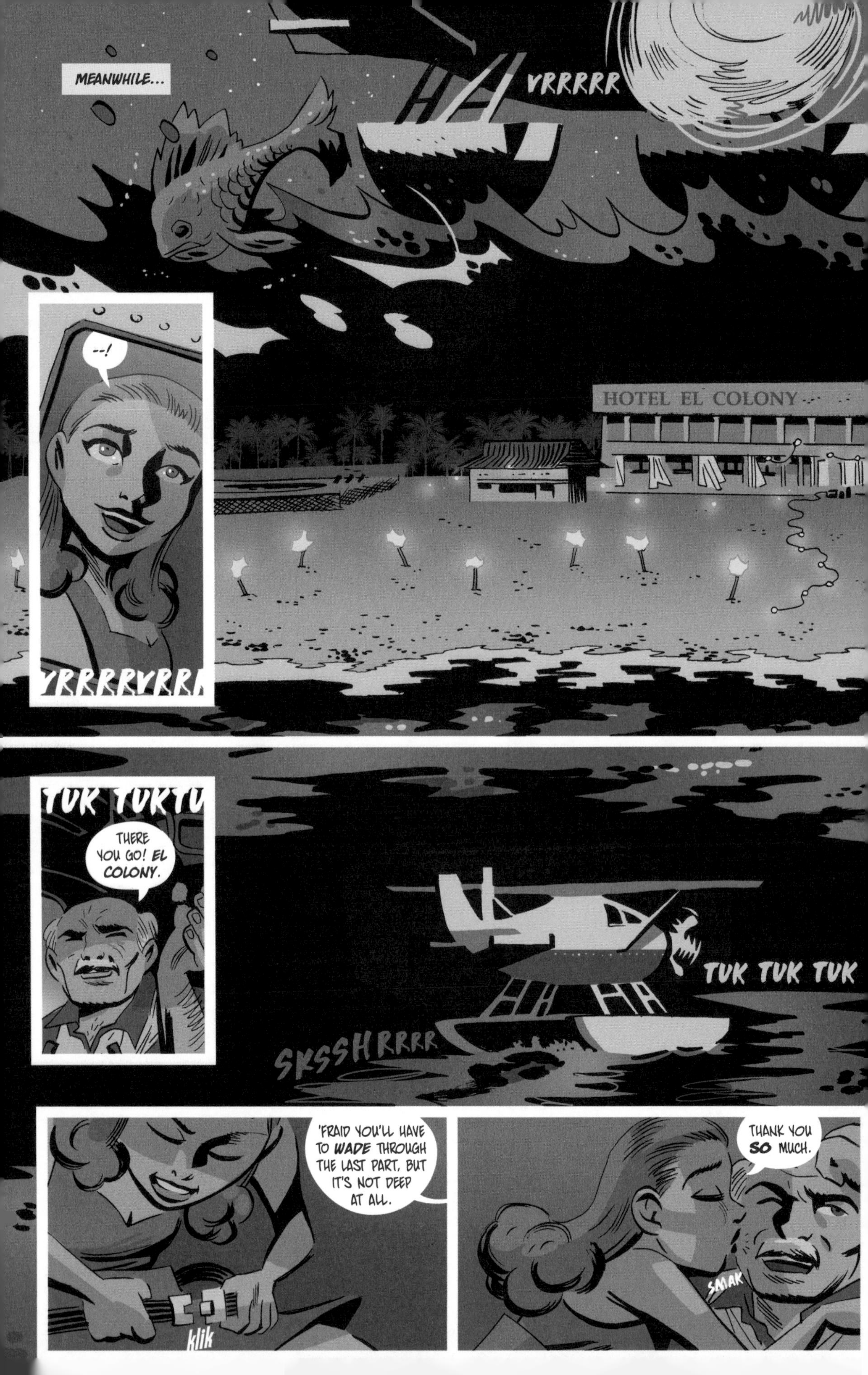
MEANWHILE...
VRRRRR
--!
VRRRRVRRR
HOTEL EL COLONY
TUK TUKTU
THERE YOU GO! EL COLONY.
TUK TUK TUK
SKSSHRRRR
'FRAID YOU'LL HAVE TO WADE THROUGH THE LAST PART, BUT IT'S NOT DEEP AT ALL.
klik
THANK YOU SO MUCH.
SMAK

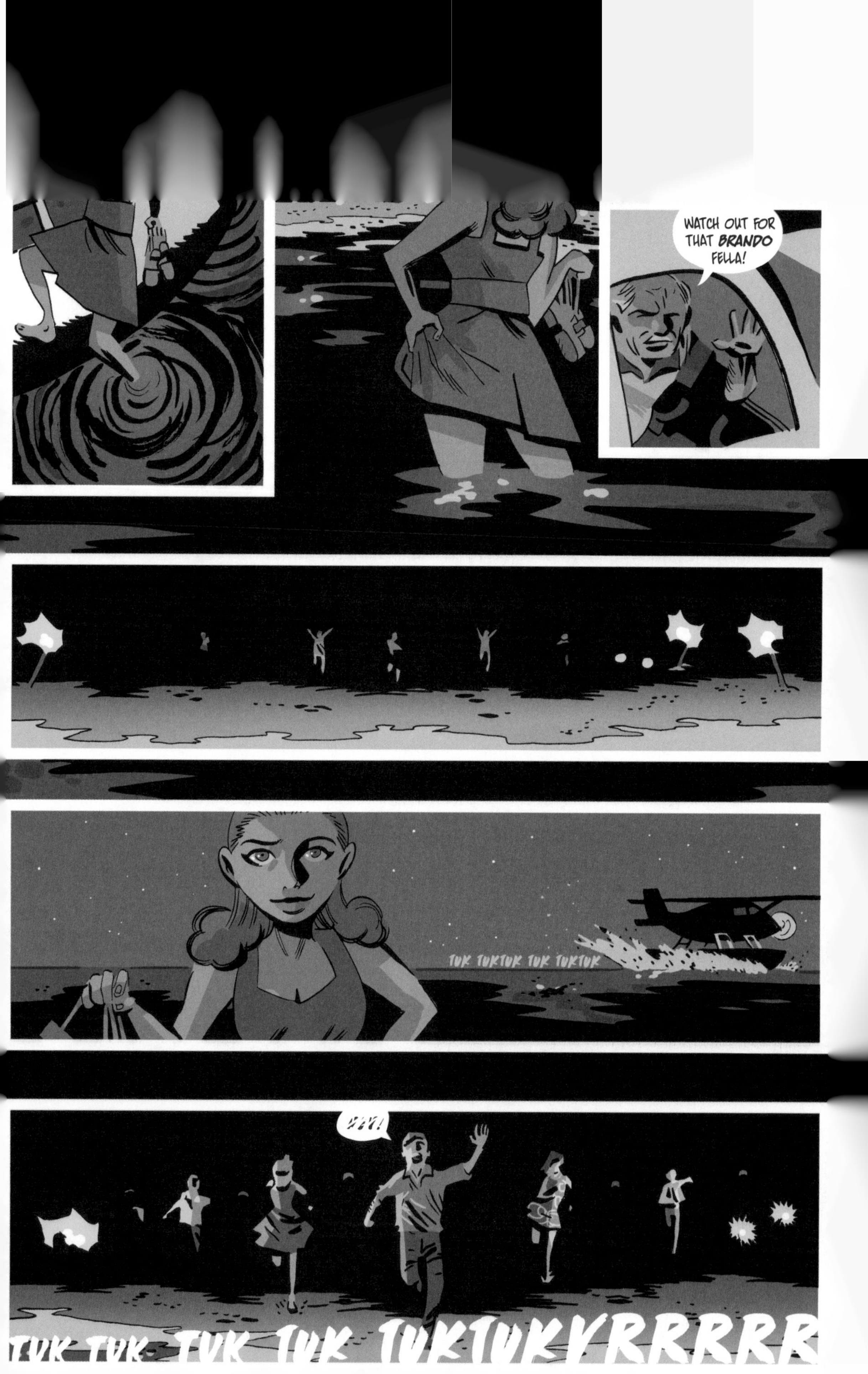
WATCH OUT FOR THAT BRANDO FELLA!
TUK TUKTUK TUK TUKTUK
TUK TUK TUK TUK TUKTUKVRRRRRR

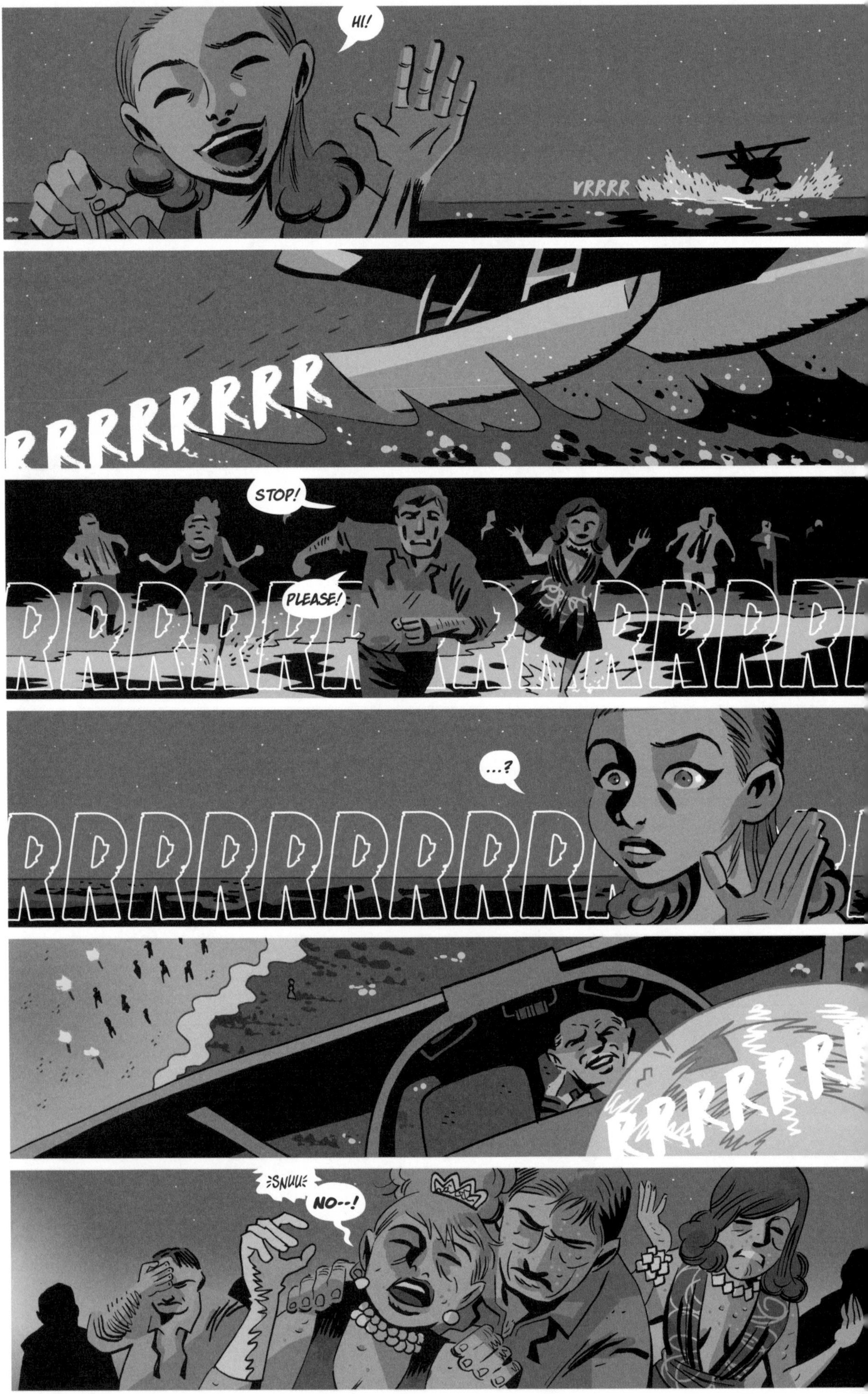
HI!
VRRRR
RRRRRRRR
STOP!
PLEASE!
RRRRRRRRRRRR
...?
RRRRRRRRRRR
RRRRRRR
SNUU
NO--!

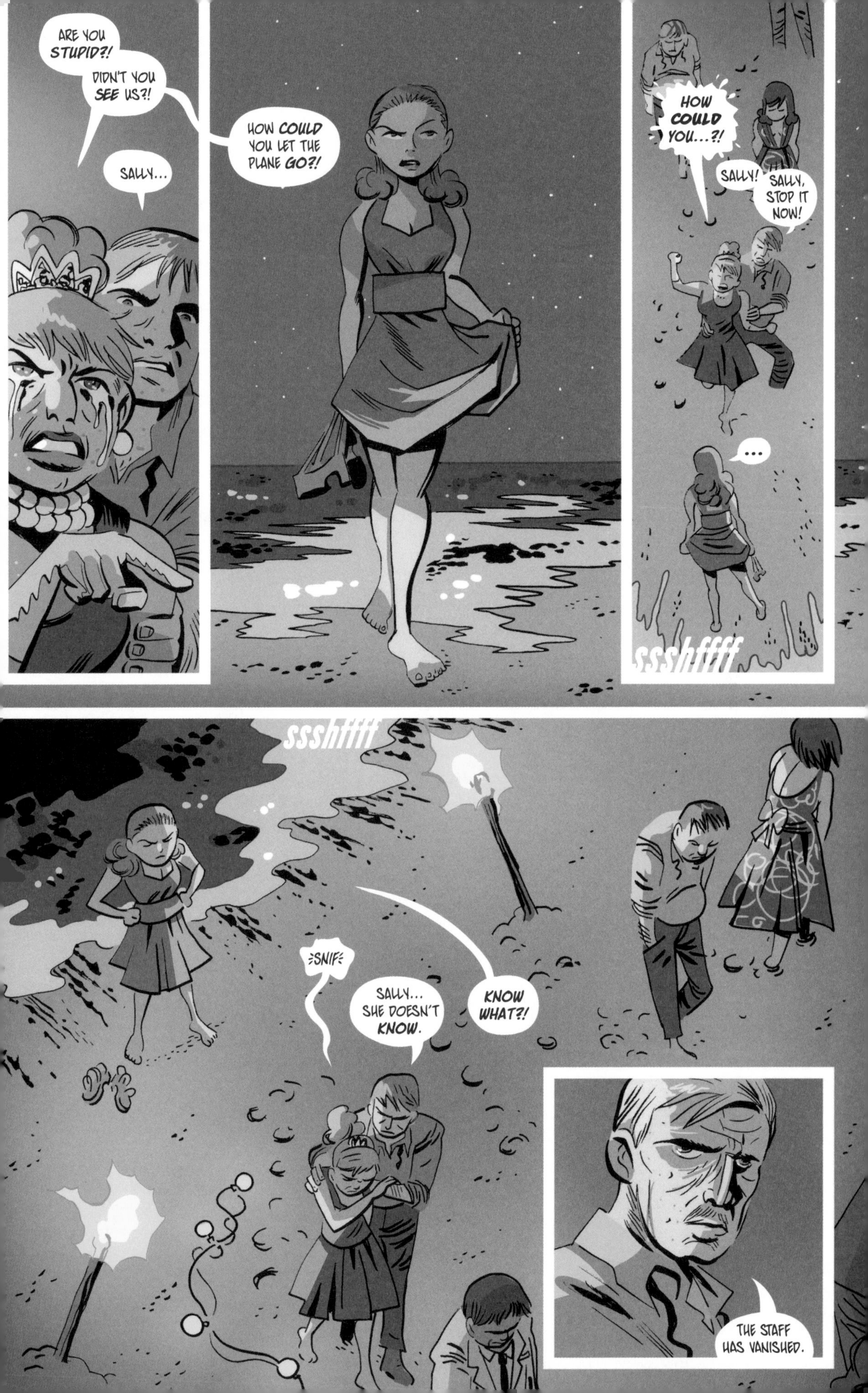
ARE YOU STUPID?!
DIDN'T YOU SEE US?!
SALLY...
HOW COULD YOU LET THE PLANE GO?!
HOW COULD YOU...?!
SALLY!
SALLY, STOP IT NOW!
...
SSSHFFFF
SSSHFFFF
SNIF
SALLY... SHE DOESN'T KNOW.
KNOW WHAT?!
THE STAFF HAS VANISHED.

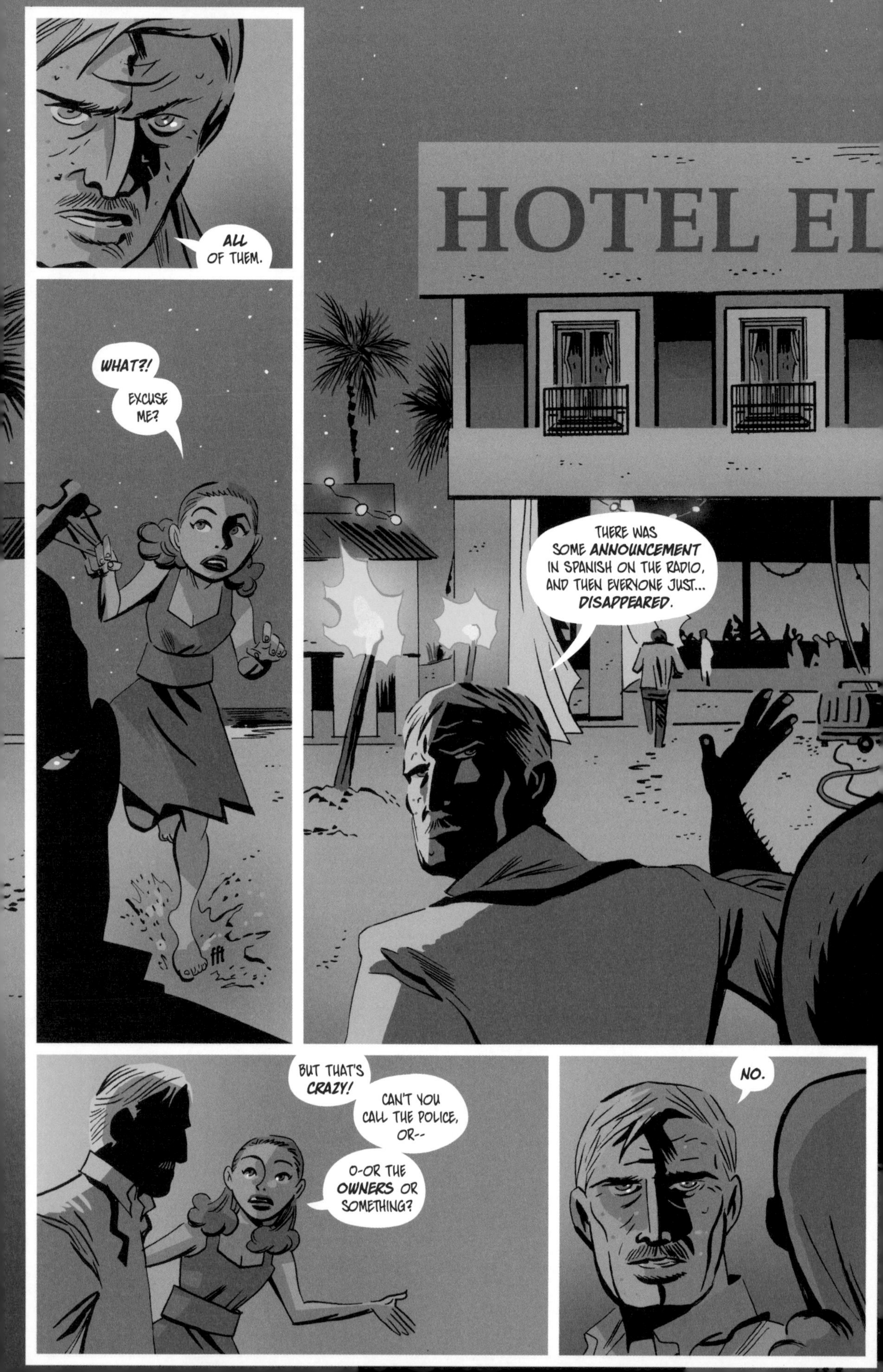
ALL OF THEM.
HOTEL EL
WHAT?!
EXCUSE ME?
fft
THERE WAS SOME ANNOUNCEMENT IN SPANISH ON THE RADIO, AND THEN EVERYONE JUST... DISAPPEARED.
BUT THAT'S CRAZY!
CAN'T YOU CALL THE POLICE, OR--
O-OR THE OWNERS OR SOMETHING?
NO.

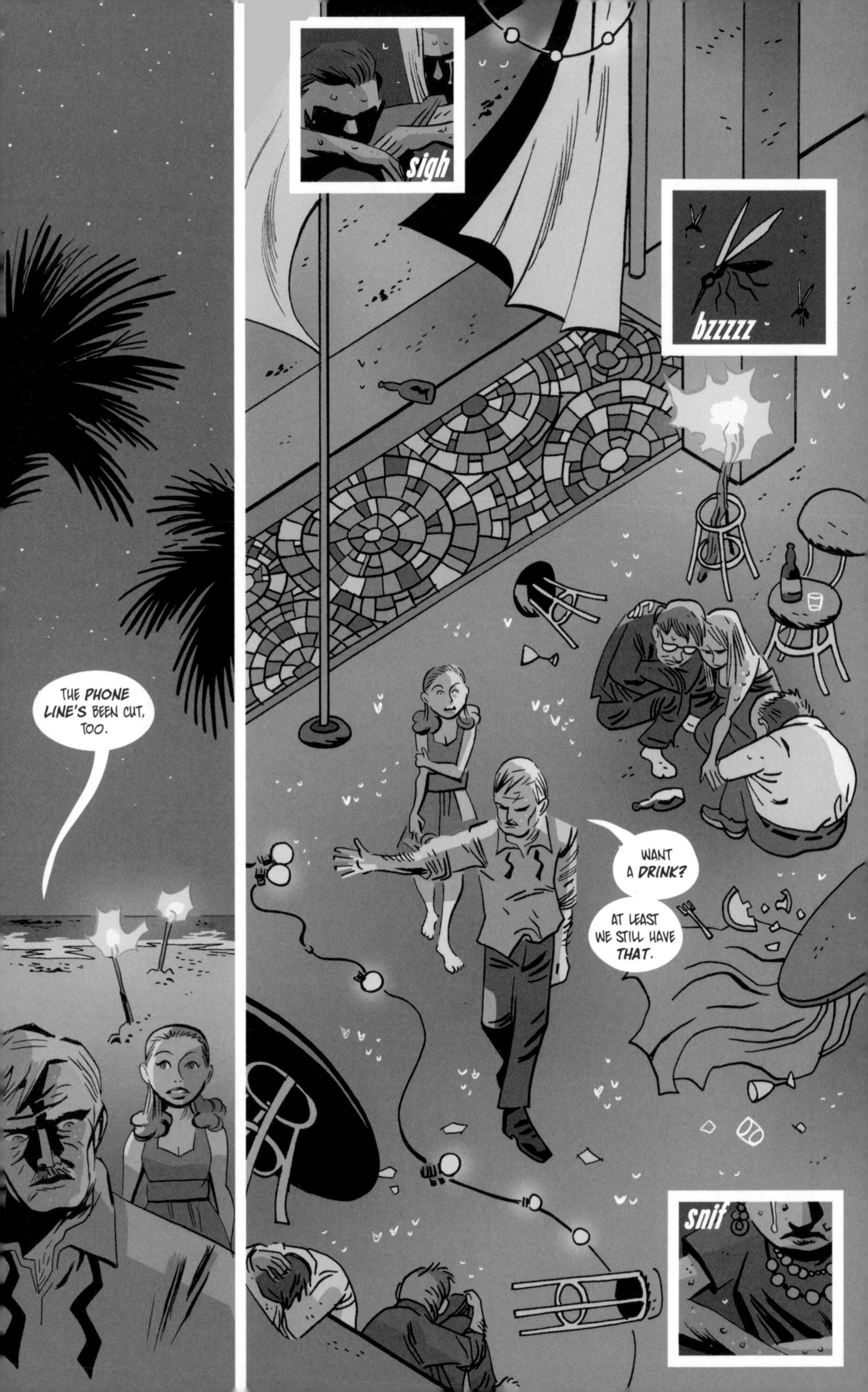
THE PHONE LINE'S BEEN CUT, TOO.
sigh
bzzzzz
WANT A DRINK?
AT LEAST WE STILL HAVE THAT.
snif

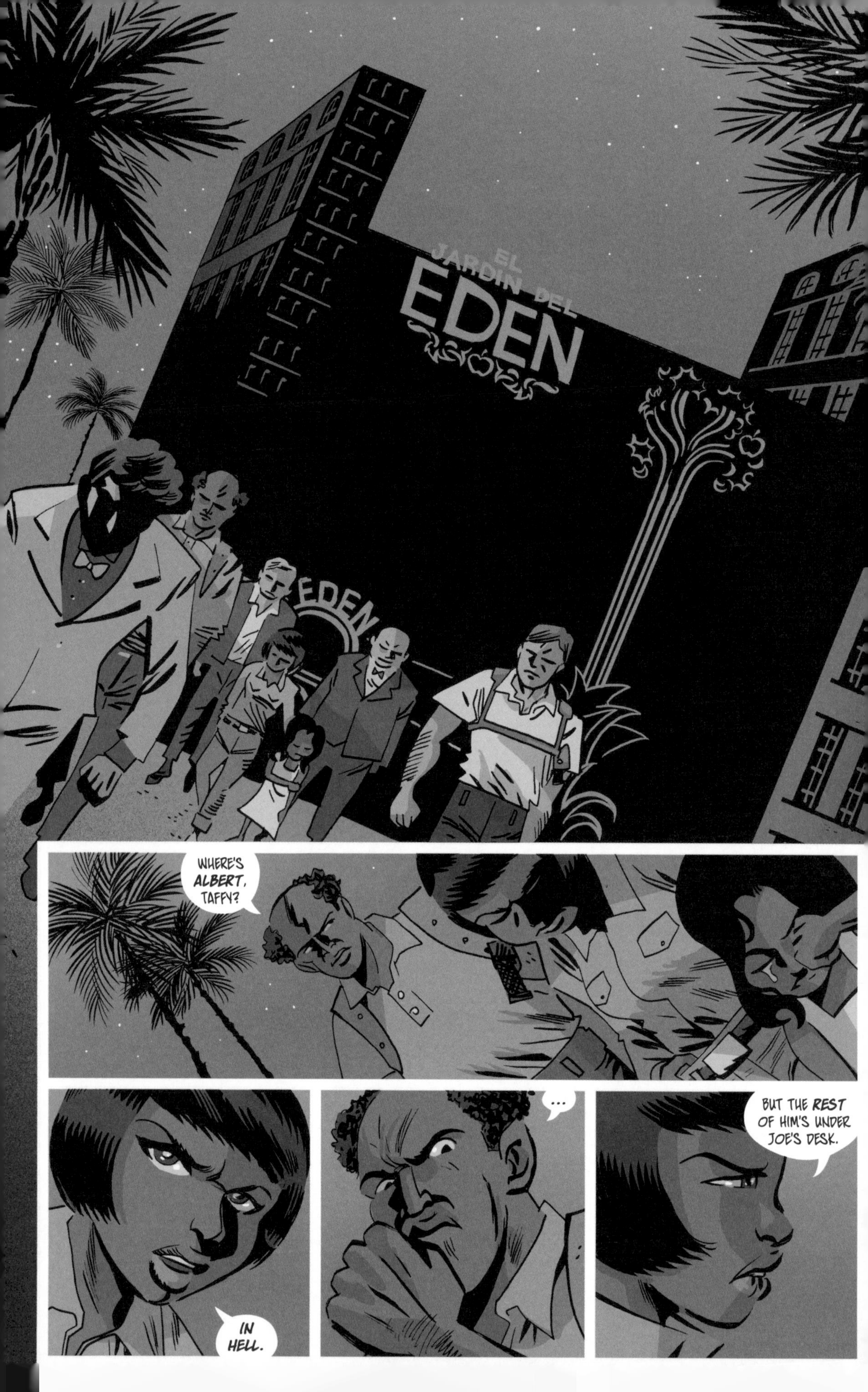
EL JARDIN DEL EDEN
EDEN
WHERE'S ALBERT, TAFFY?
IN HELL.
...
BUT THE REST OF HIM'S UNDER JOE'S DESK.

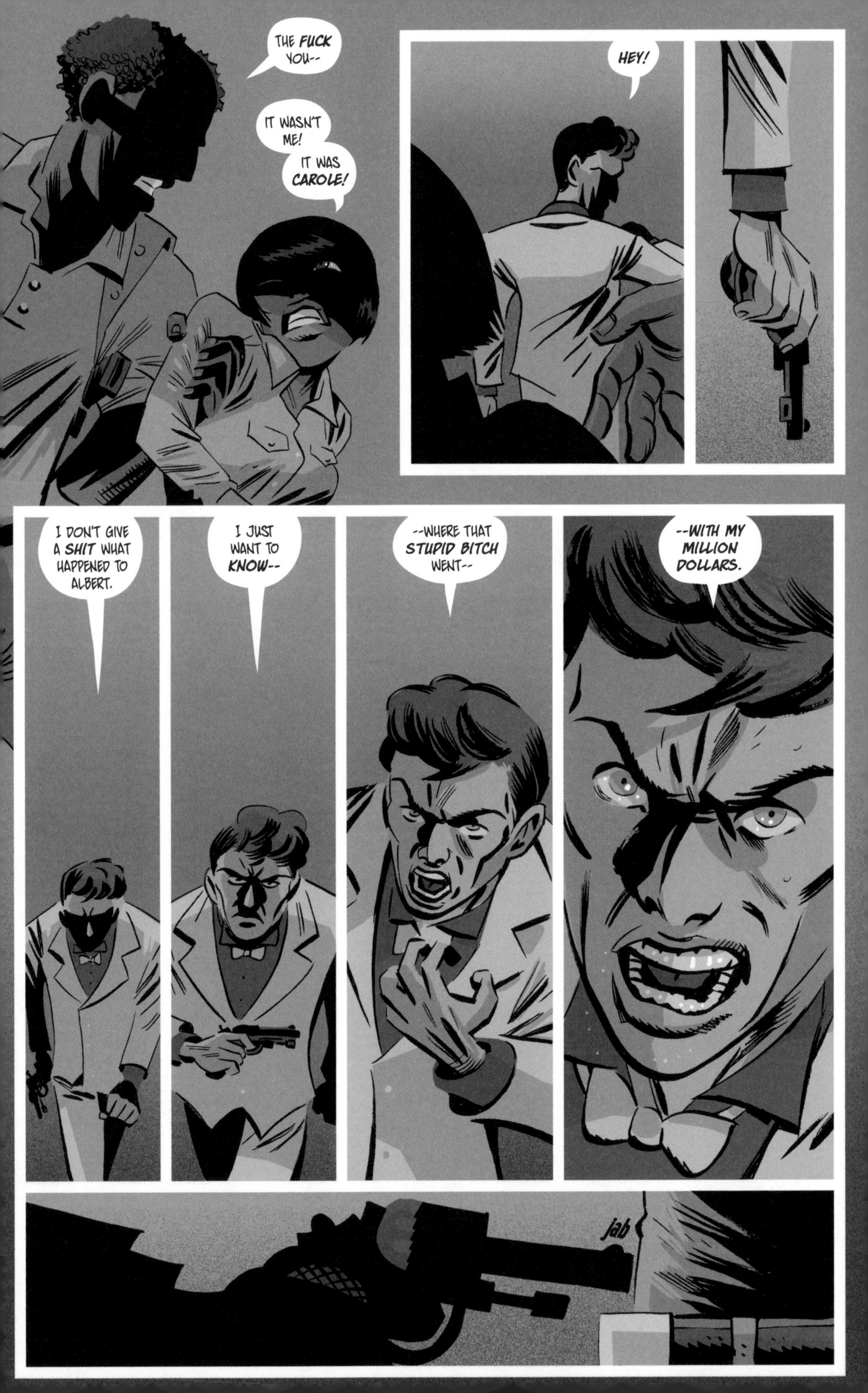
THE FUCK YOU--
IT WASN'T ME!
IT WAS CAROLE!
HEY!
I DON'T GIVE A SHIT WHAT HAPPENED TO ALBERT.
I JUST WANT TO KNOW--
--WHERE THAT STUPID BITCH WENT--
--WITH MY MILLION DOLLARS.
jab

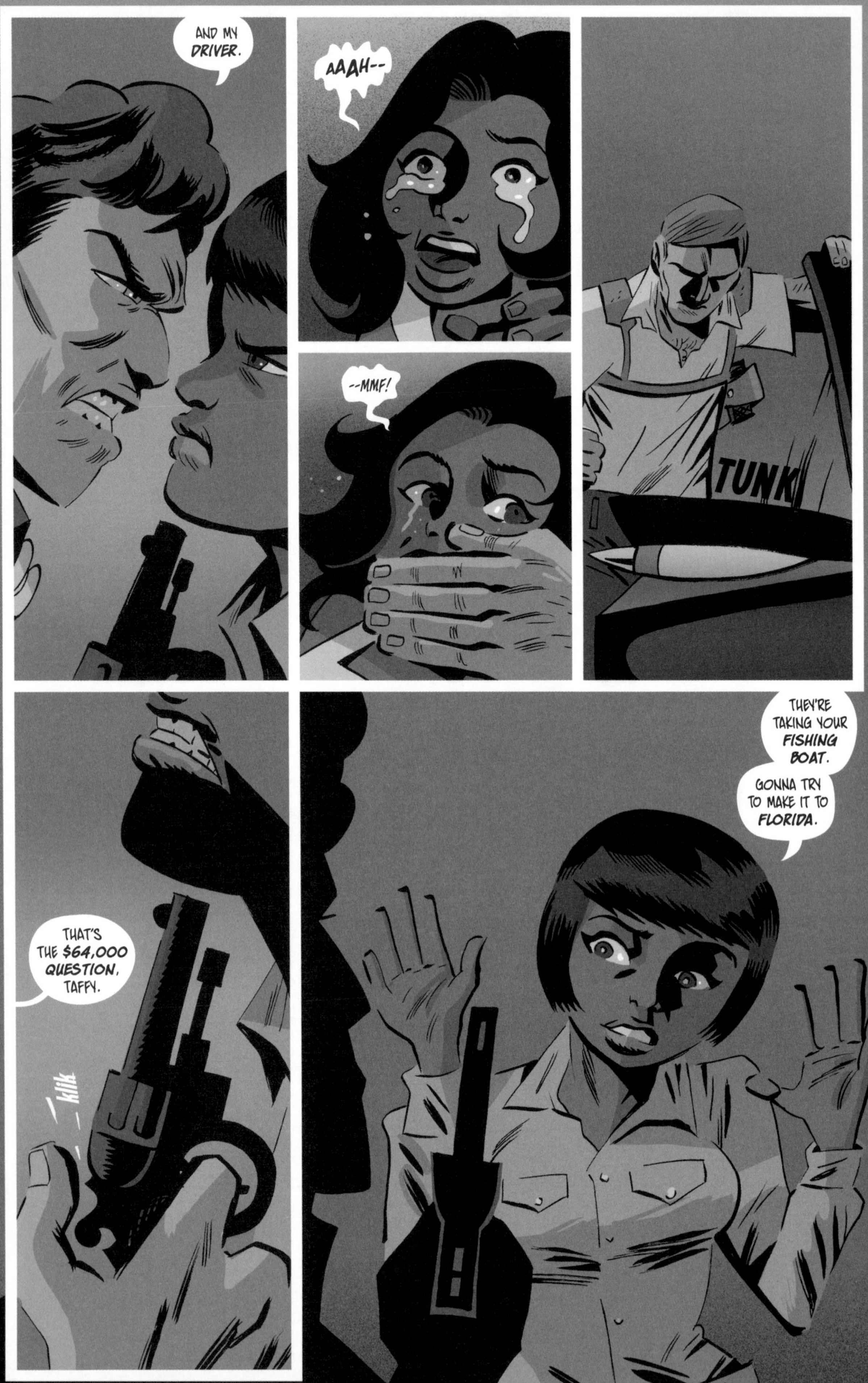
AND MY DRIVER.
AAAH--
--MMF!
TUNK
THEY'RE TAKING YOUR FISHING BOAT.
GONNA TRY TO MAKE IT TO FLORIDA.
THAT'S THE $64,000 QUESTION, TAFFY.
klik

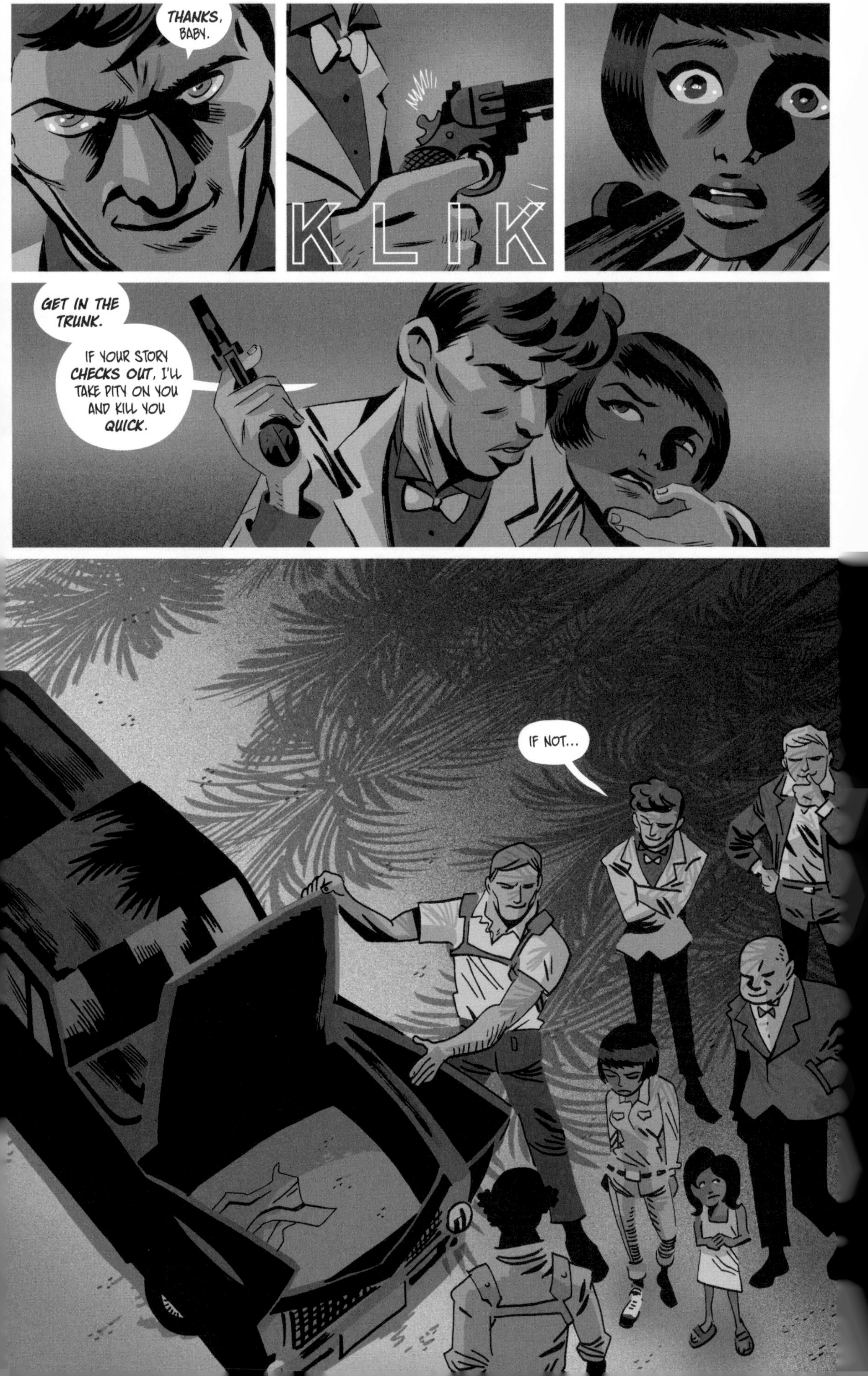
THANKS, BABY.
KLIK
GET IN THE TRUNK.
IF YOUR STORY CHECKS OUT, I'LL TAKE PITY ON YOU AND KILL YOU QUICK.
IF NOT...

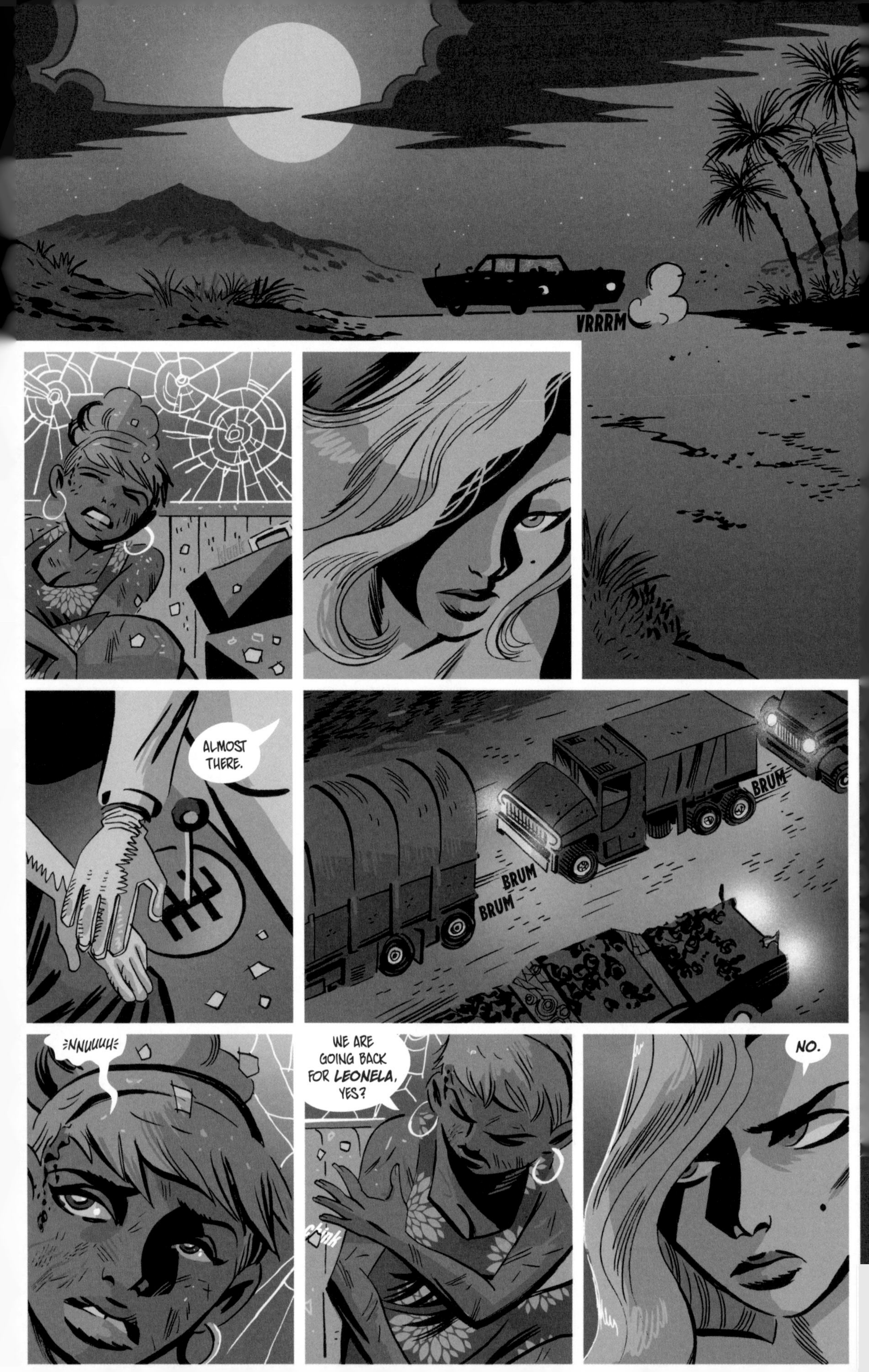
VRRRM
klunk
ALMOST THERE.
BRUM
BRUM
BRUM
NNUUUH
WE ARE GOING BACK FOR LEONELA, YES?
NO.

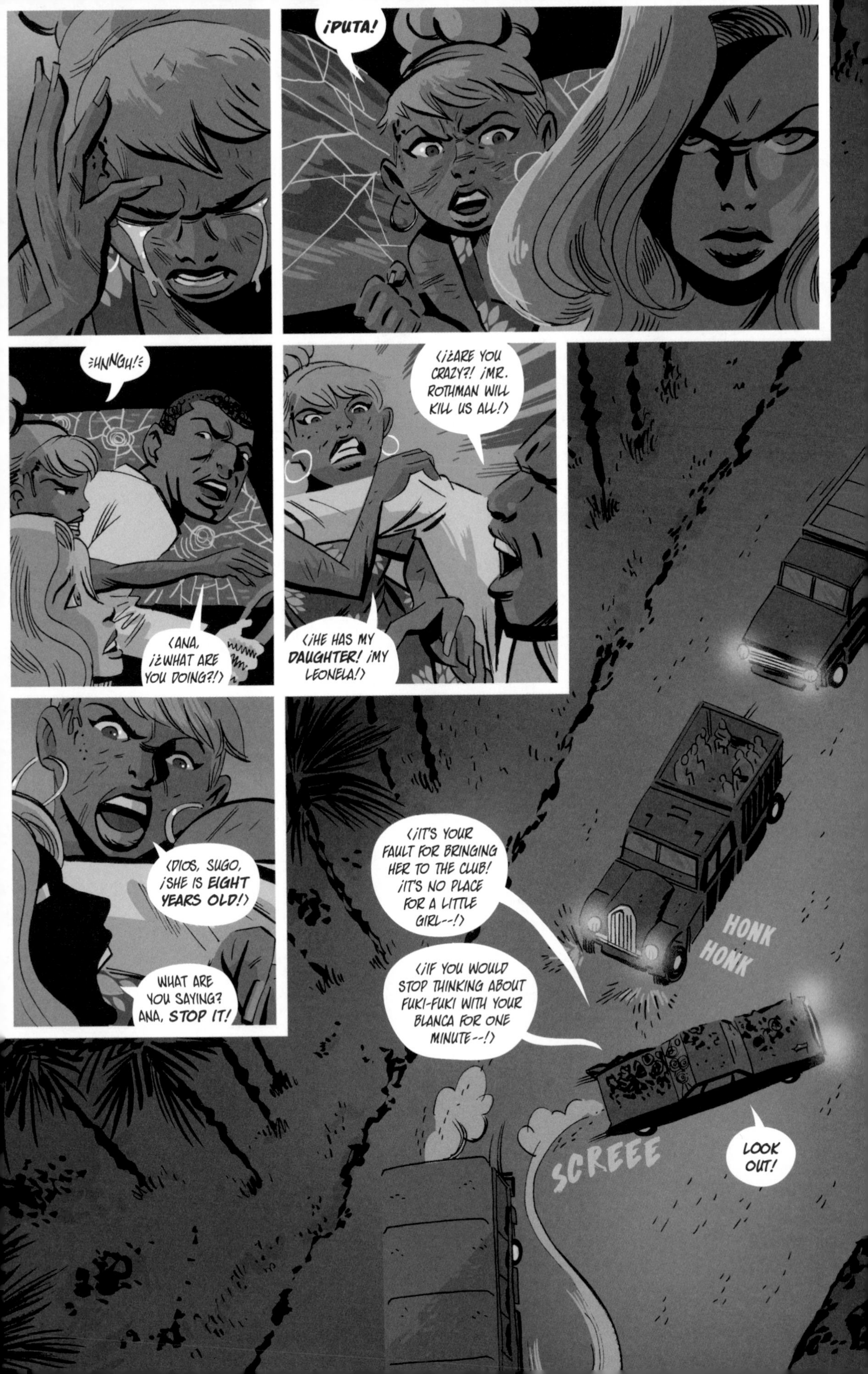
¡PUTA!
≡HNNGH!≡
‹ANA, ¡¿WHAT ARE YOU DOING?!›
‹¡¿ARE YOU CRAZY?! ¡MR. ROTHMAN WILL KILL US ALL!›
‹¡HE HAS MY DAUGHTER! ¡MY LEONELA!›
‹DIOS, SUGO, ¡SHE IS EIGHT YEARS OLD!›
WHAT ARE YOU SAYING? ANA, STOP IT!
‹¡IT'S YOUR FAULT FOR BRINGING HER TO THE CLUB! ¡IT'S NO PLACE FOR A LITTLE GIRL--!›
HONK HONK
‹¡IF YOU WOULD STOP THINKING ABOUT FUKI-FUKI WITH YOUR BLANCA FOR ONE MINUTE--!›
SCREEE
LOOK OUT!

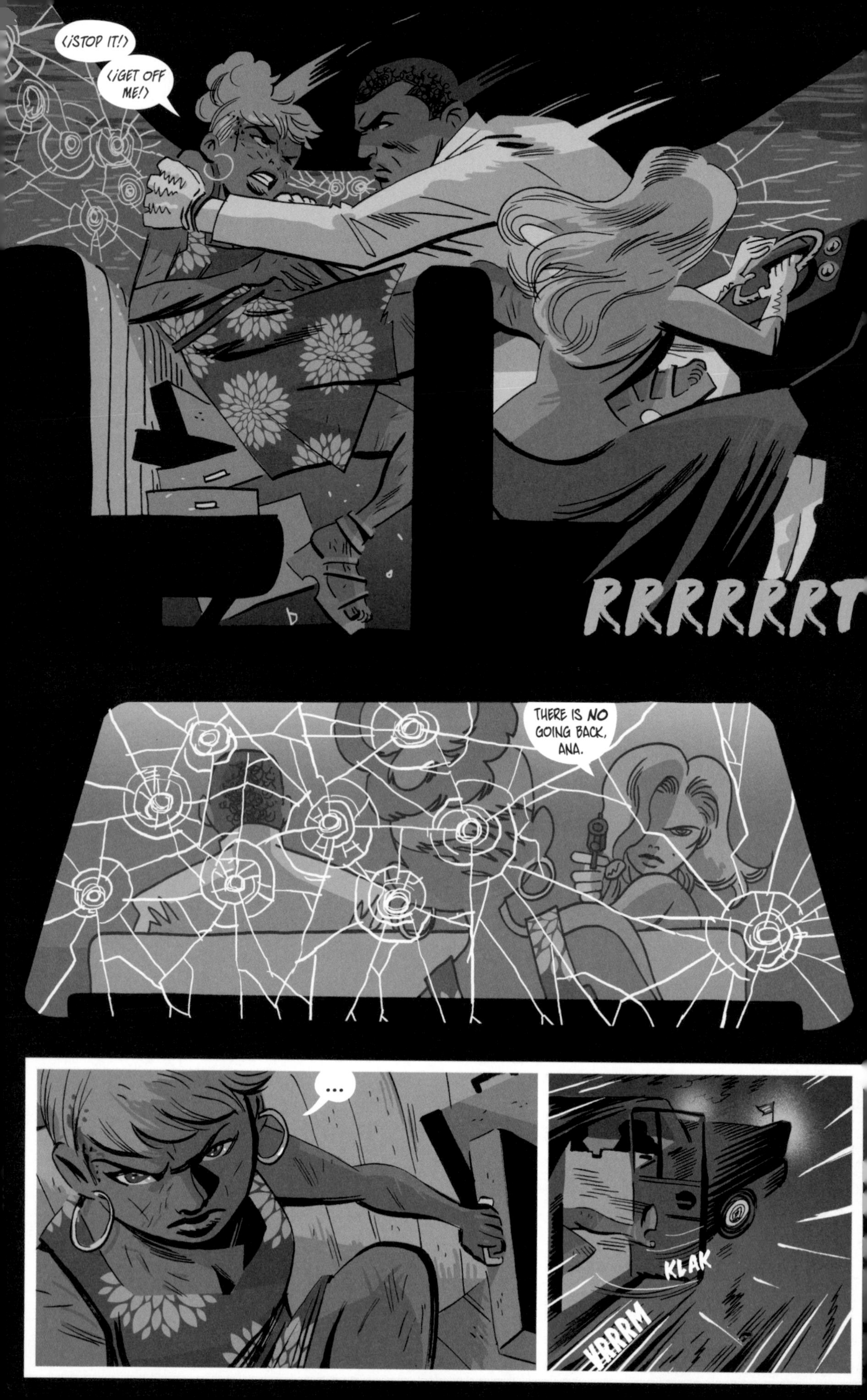

<¡STOP IT!>
<¡GET OFF ME!>
RRRRRRT
THERE IS NO GOING BACK, ANA.
...
KLAK
VRRRM

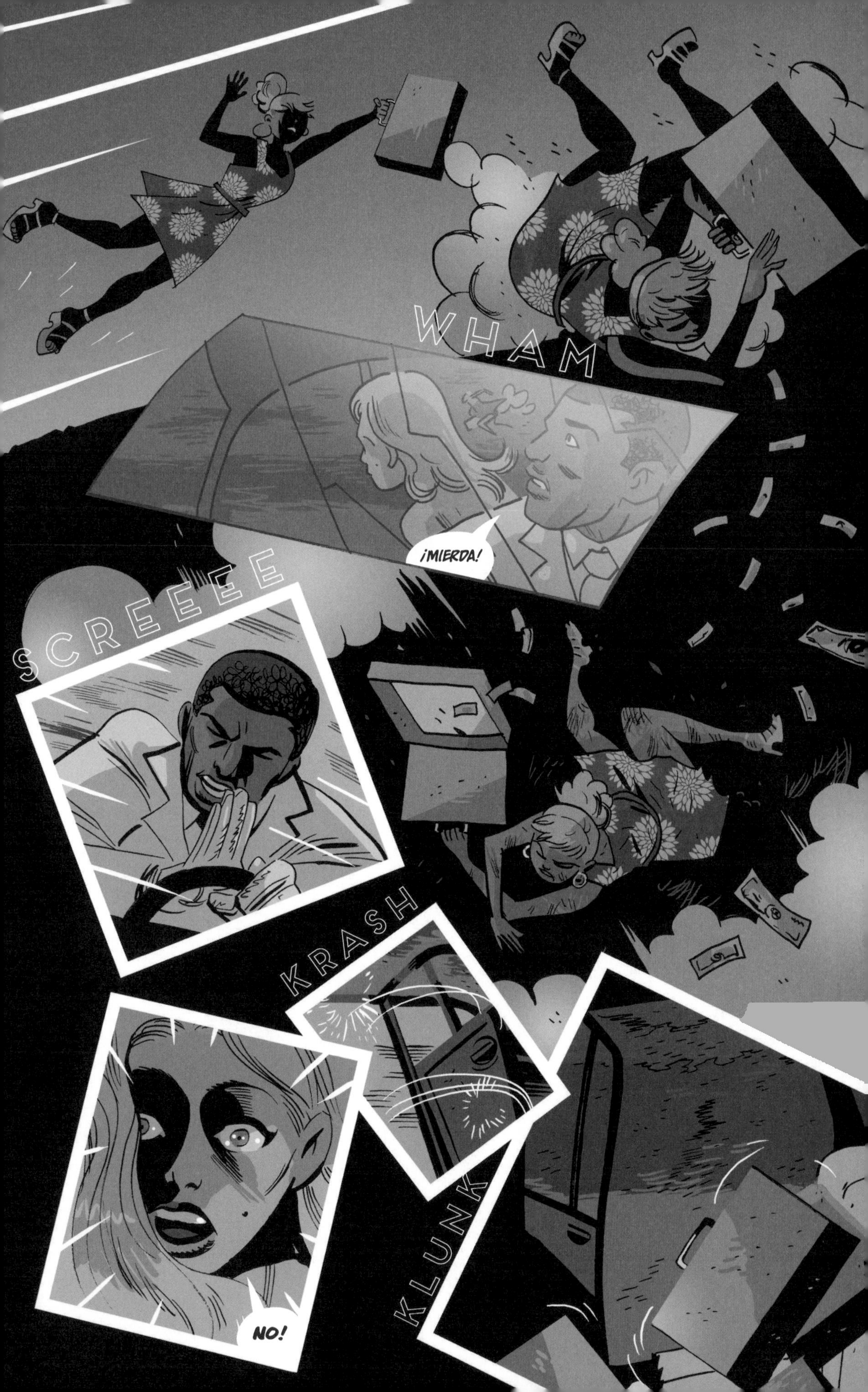
WHAM
¡MIERDA!
SCREEEEE
KRASH
KLUNK
NO!

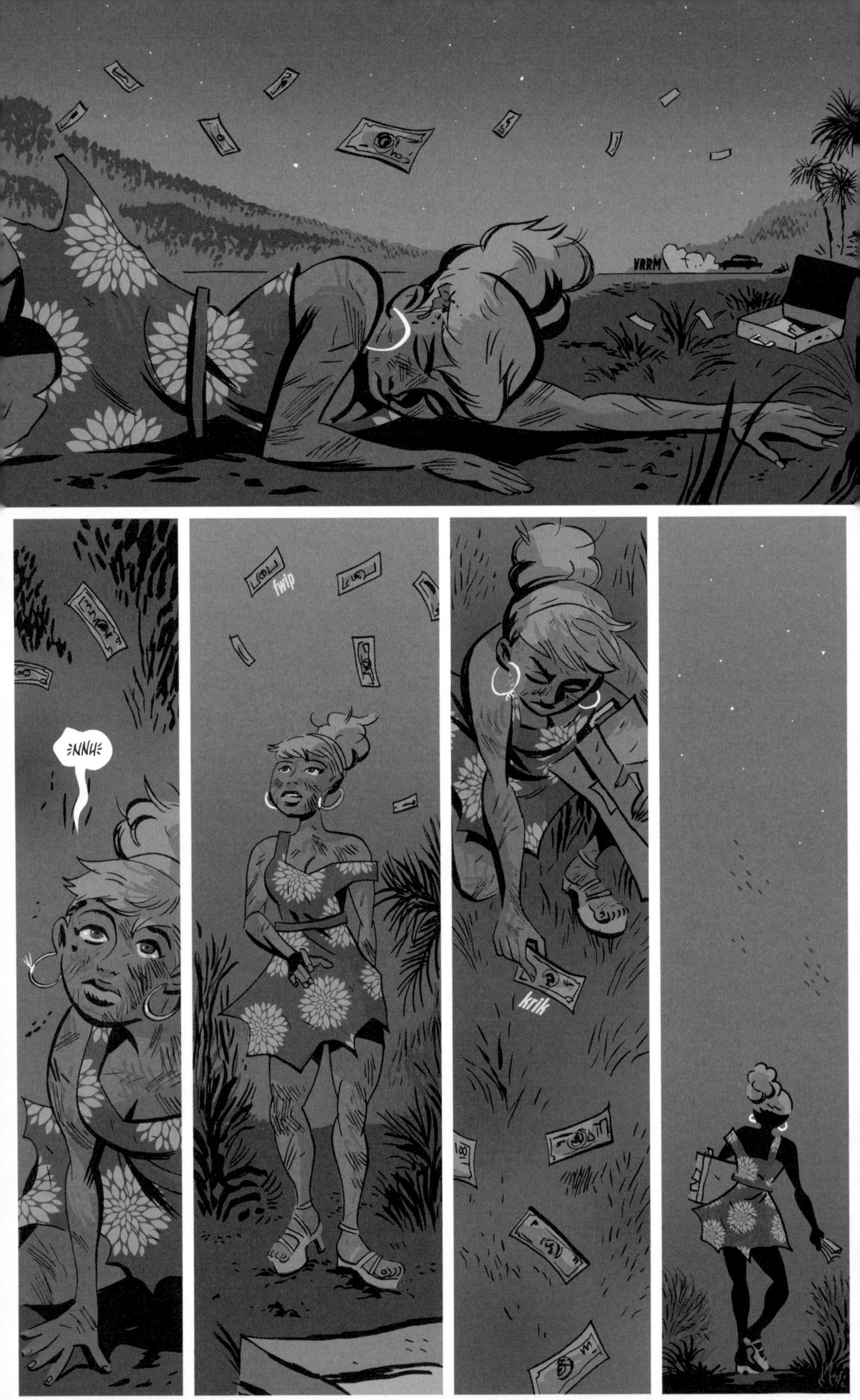
VRRM
NNH
fwip
krik

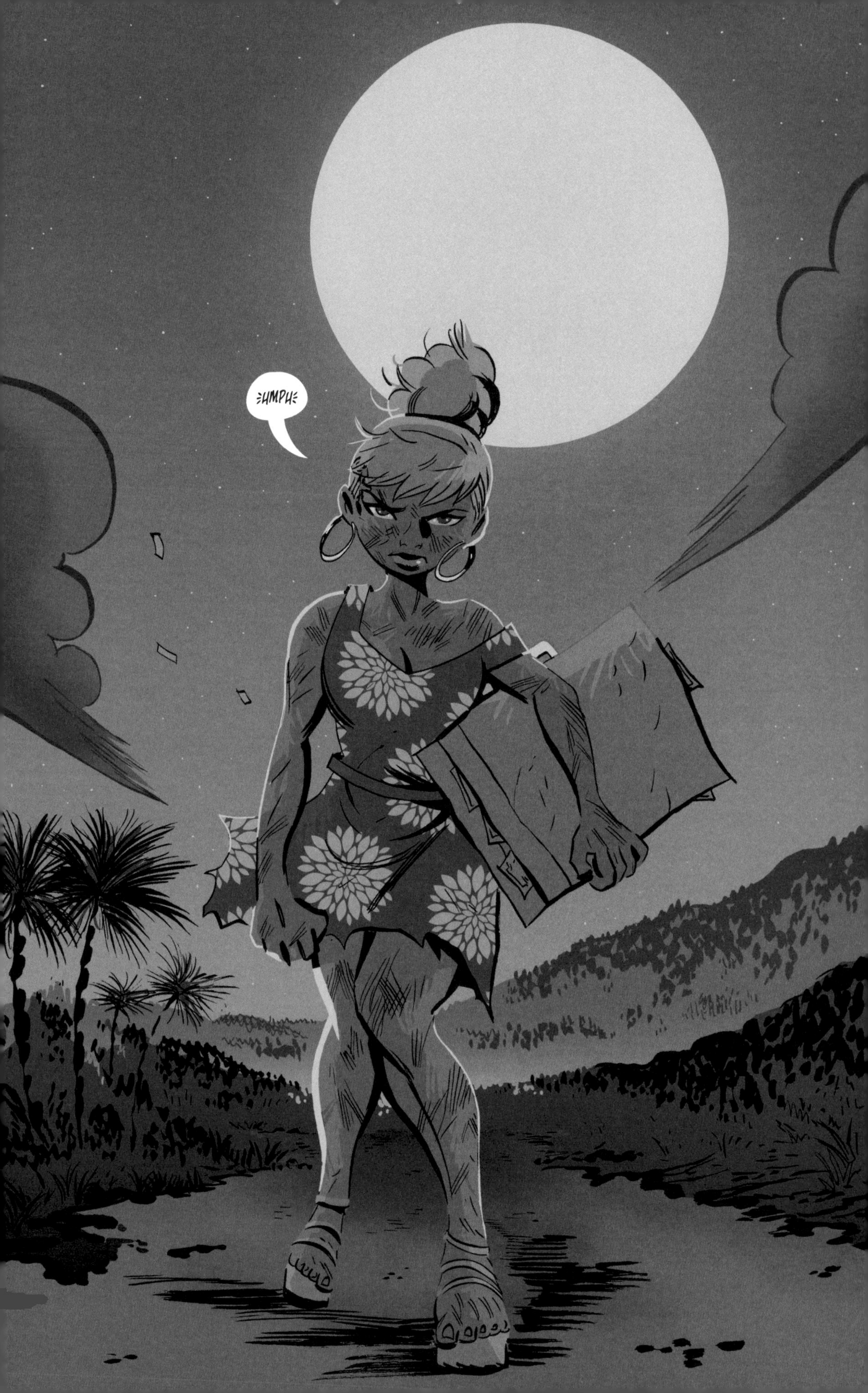
UMPH

2:00 A.M.

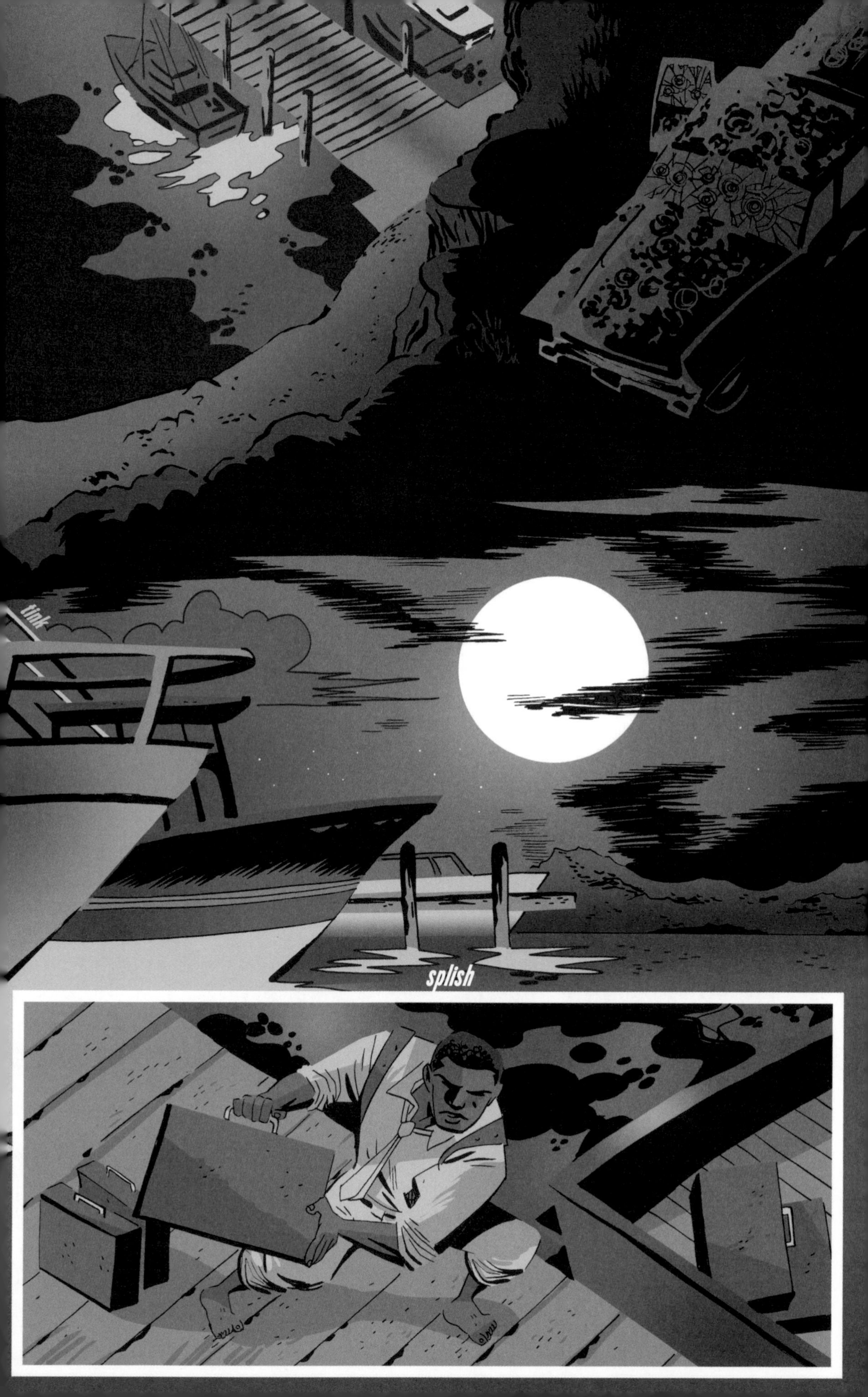
tink
splish

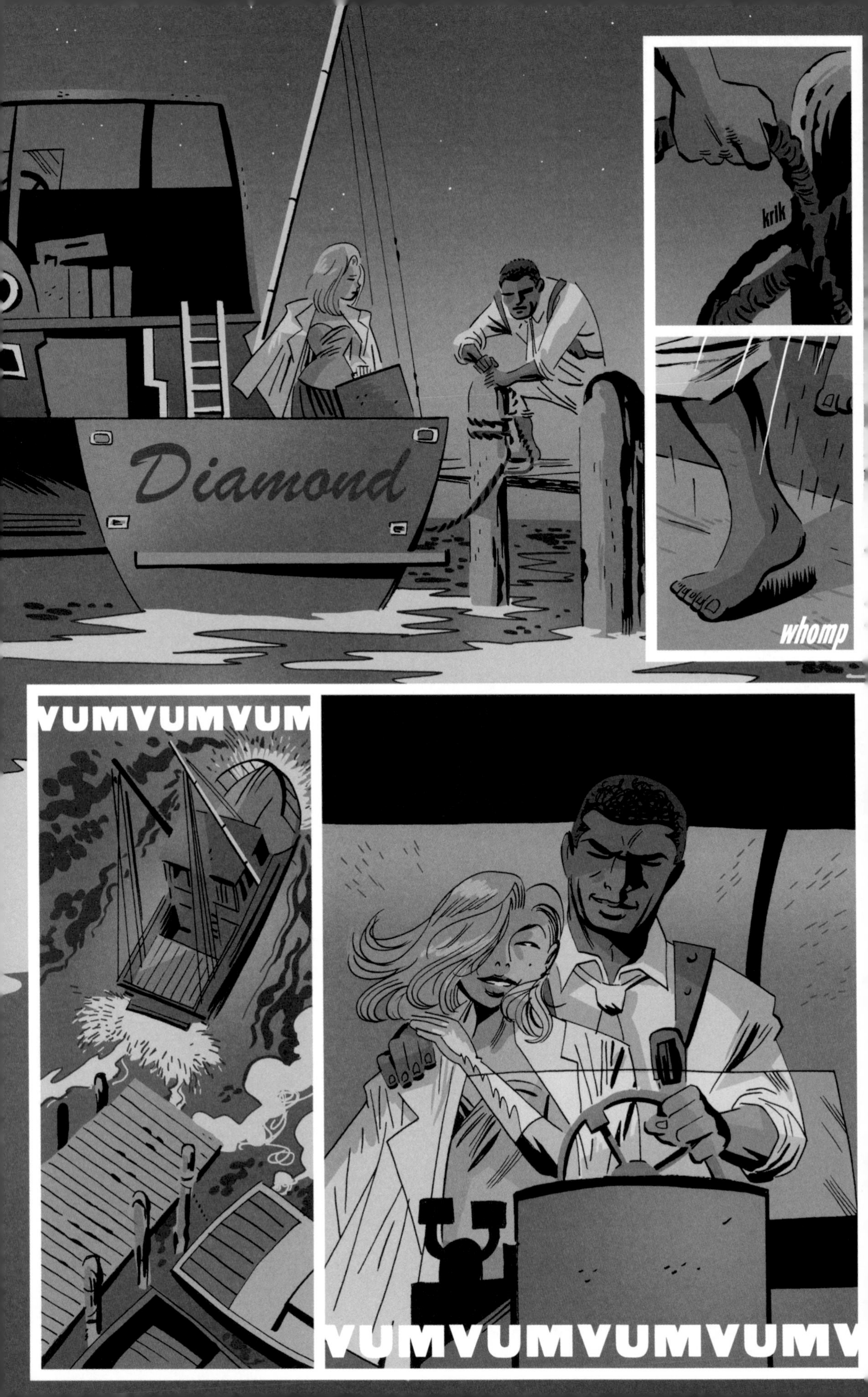
Diamond
krlk
whomp
VUMVUMVUM
VUMVUMVUMVUMV

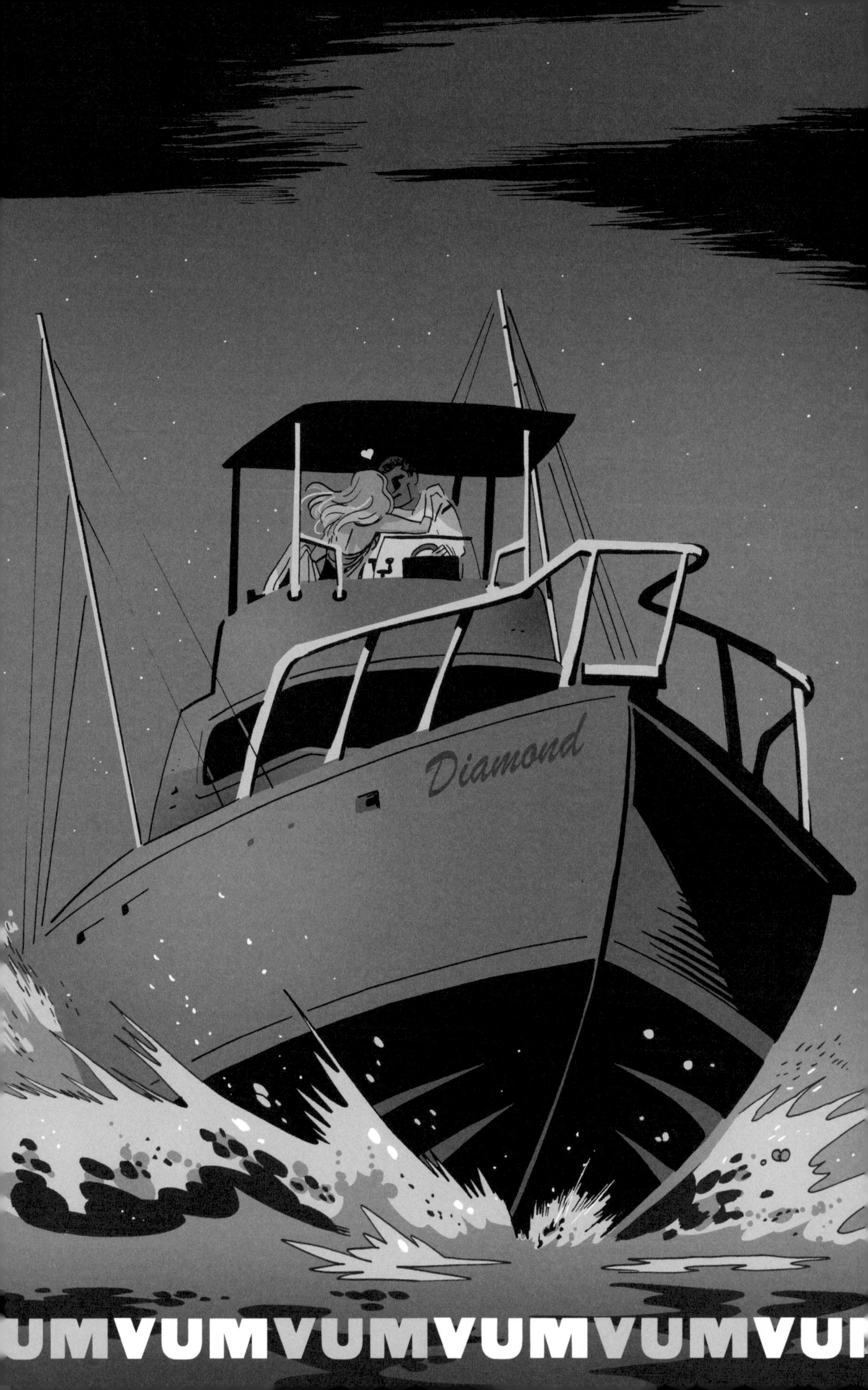
Diamond
UMVUMVUMVUMVUMVUM

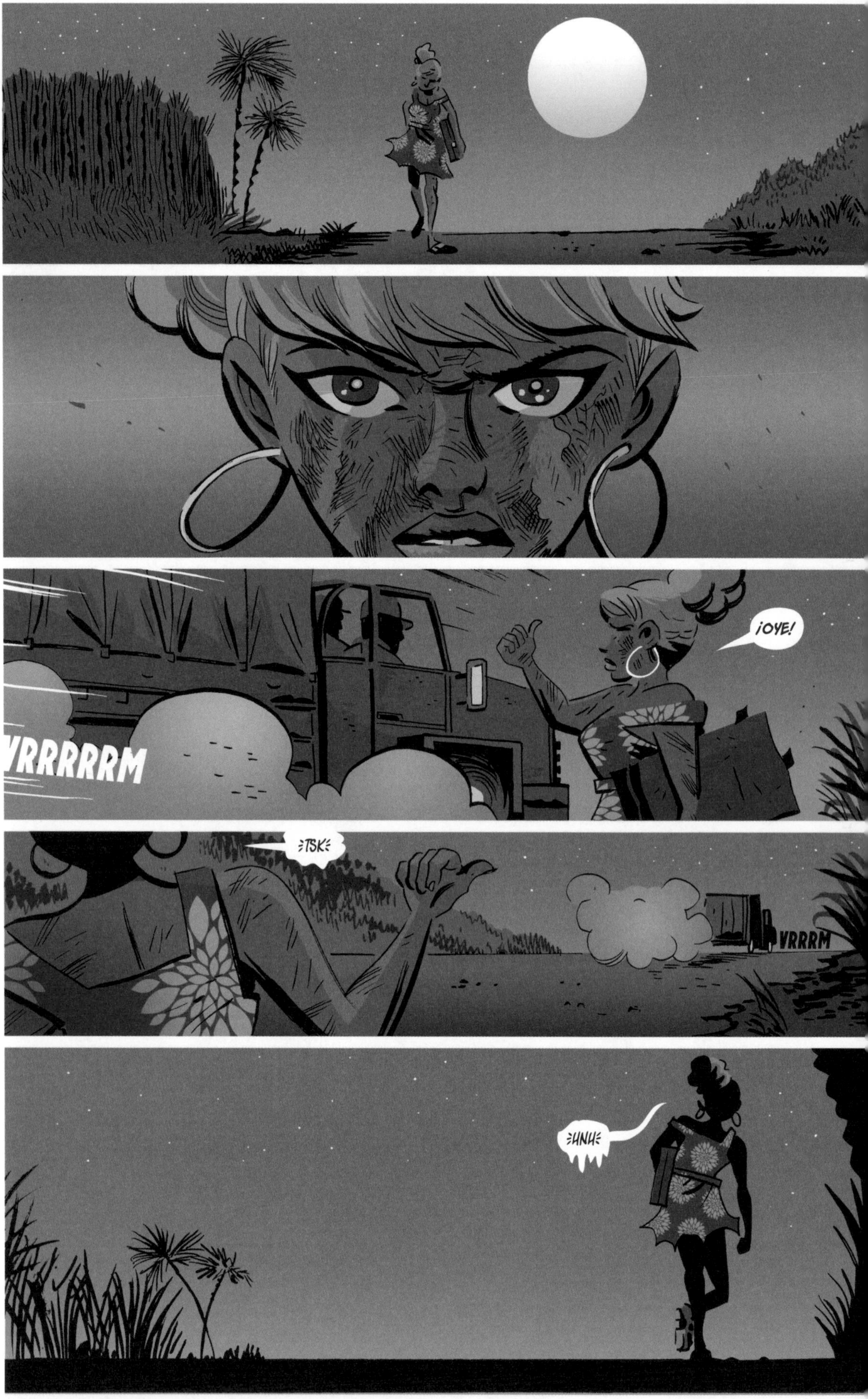
¡OYE!
VRRRRRRM
TSK
VRRRM
UNU

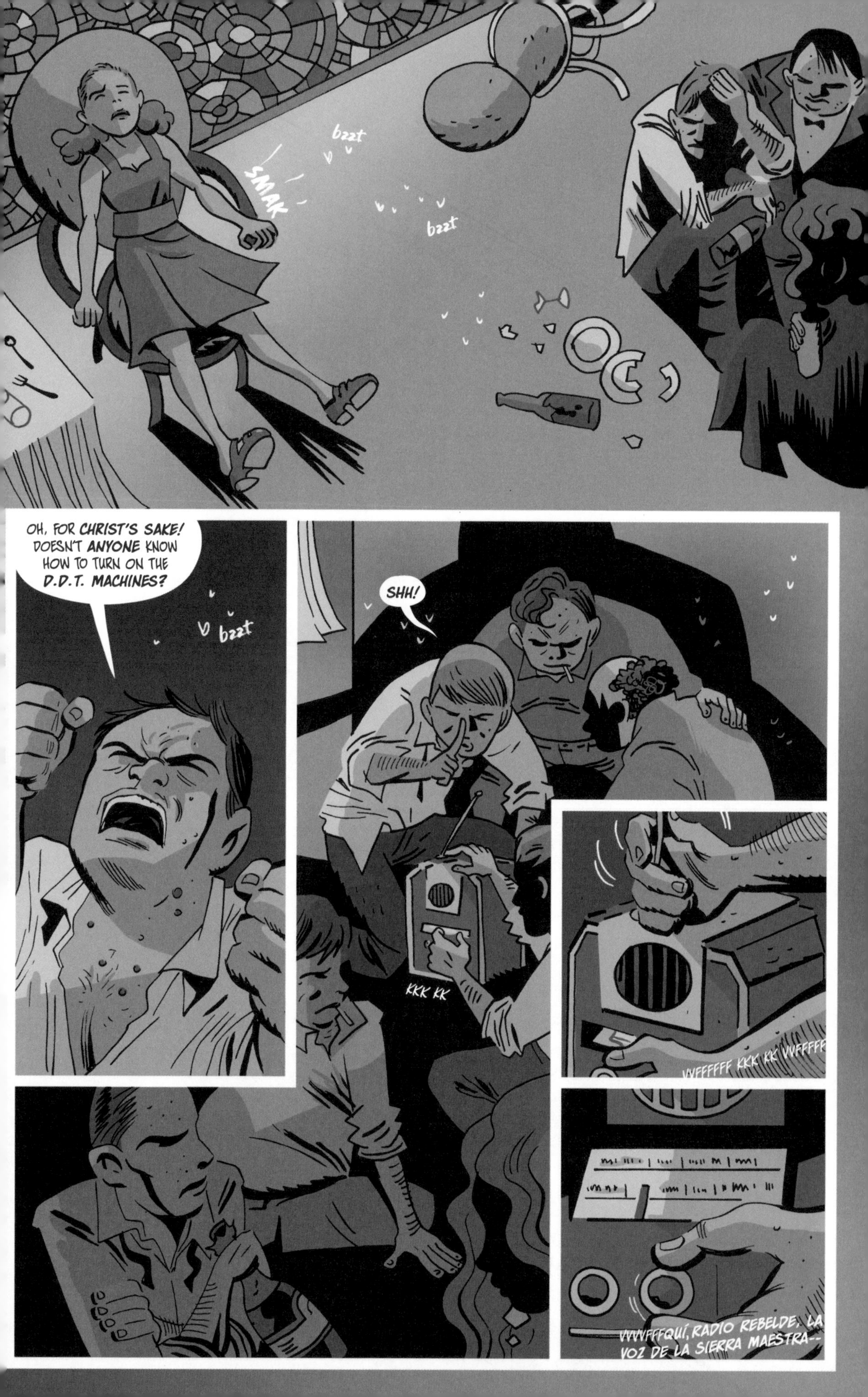

SMAK
bzzt
bzzt
OH, FOR CHRIST'S SAKE! DOESN'T ANYONE KNOW HOW TO TURN ON THE D.D.T. MACHINES?
bzzt
SHH!
KKK KK
VVFFFFFF KKK KK VVFFFFF
VVVVFFFQUÍ, RADIO REBELDE, LA VOZ DE LA SIERRA MAESTRA--

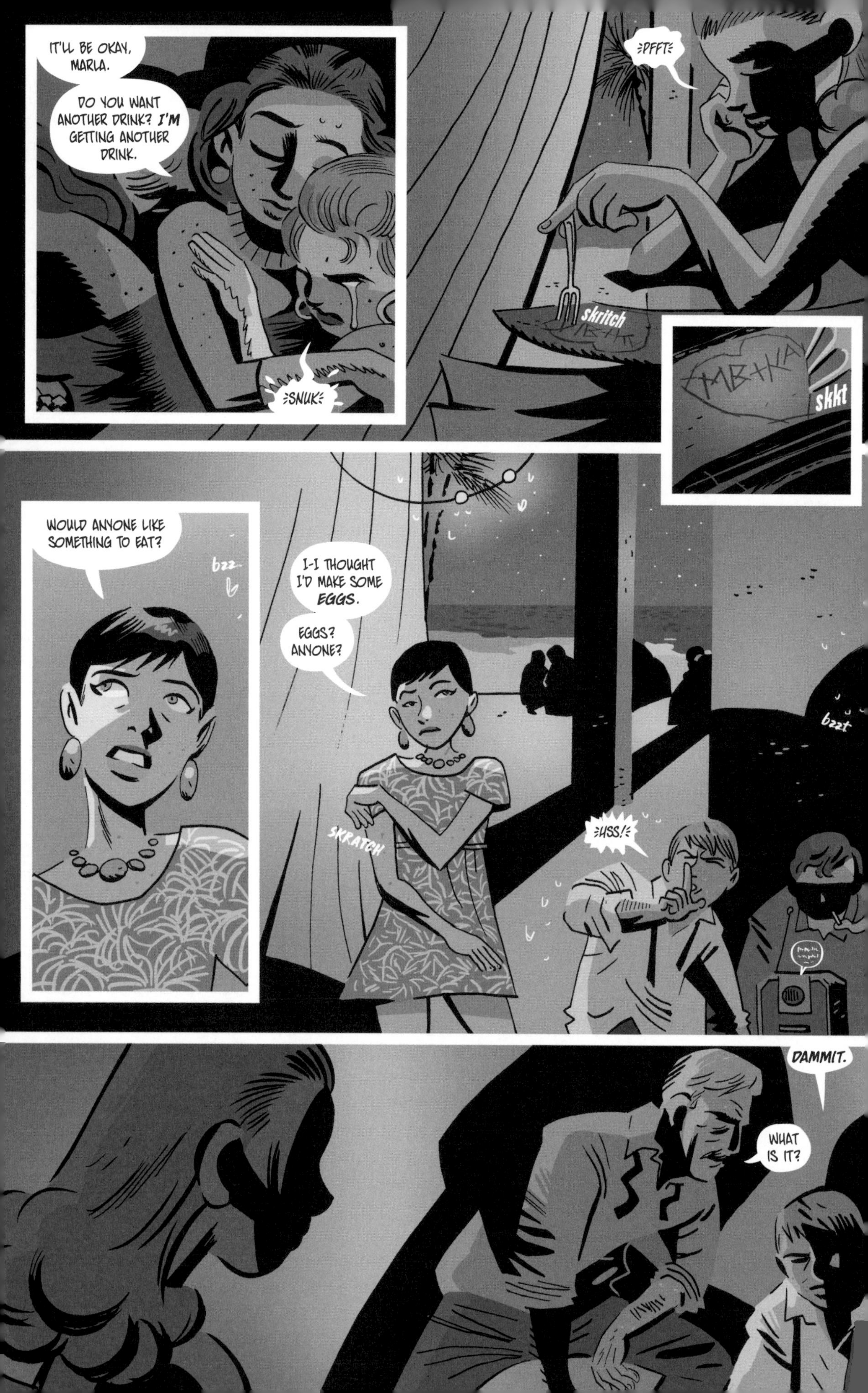

IT'LL BE OKAY, MARLA.
DO YOU WANT ANOTHER DRINK? I'M GETTING ANOTHER DRINK.
SNUK
PFFT
skritch
MB+KA
skkt
WOULD ANYONE LIKE SOMETHING TO EAT?
bzz
I-I THOUGHT I'D MAKE SOME EGGS.
EGGS? ANYONE?
SKRATCH
bzzt
HSS!
DAMMIT.
WHAT IS IT?

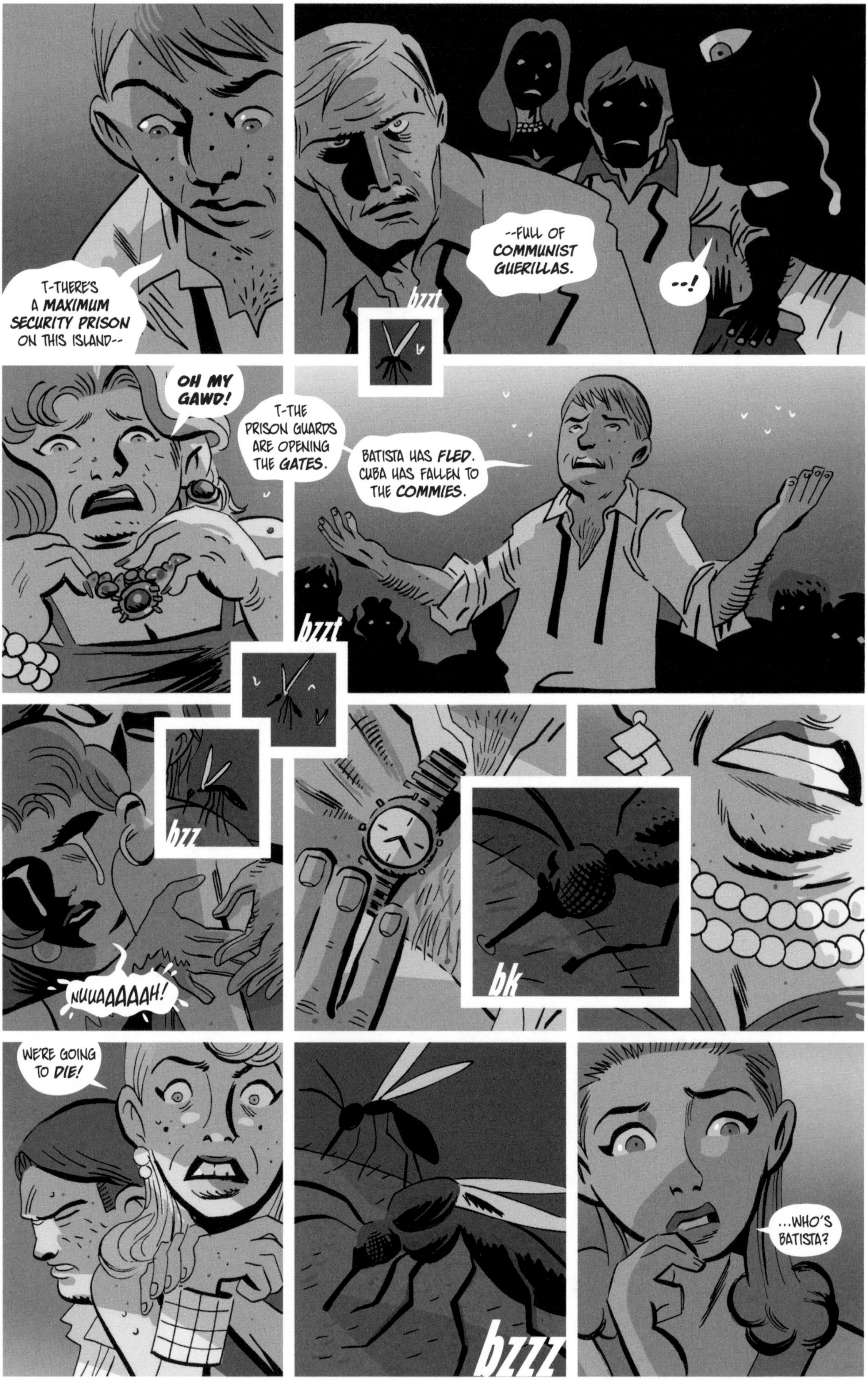
T-THERE'S A MAXIMUM SECURITY PRISON ON THIS ISLAND--
--FULL OF COMMUNIST GUERILLAS.
--!
bzzt
OH MY GAWD!
T-THE PRISON GUARDS ARE OPENING THE GATES.
BATISTA HAS FLED. CUBA HAS FALLEN TO THE COMMIES.
bzzt
bzz
NUUAAAAAH!
bk
WE'RE GOING TO DIE!
bzzz
...WHO'S BATISTA?

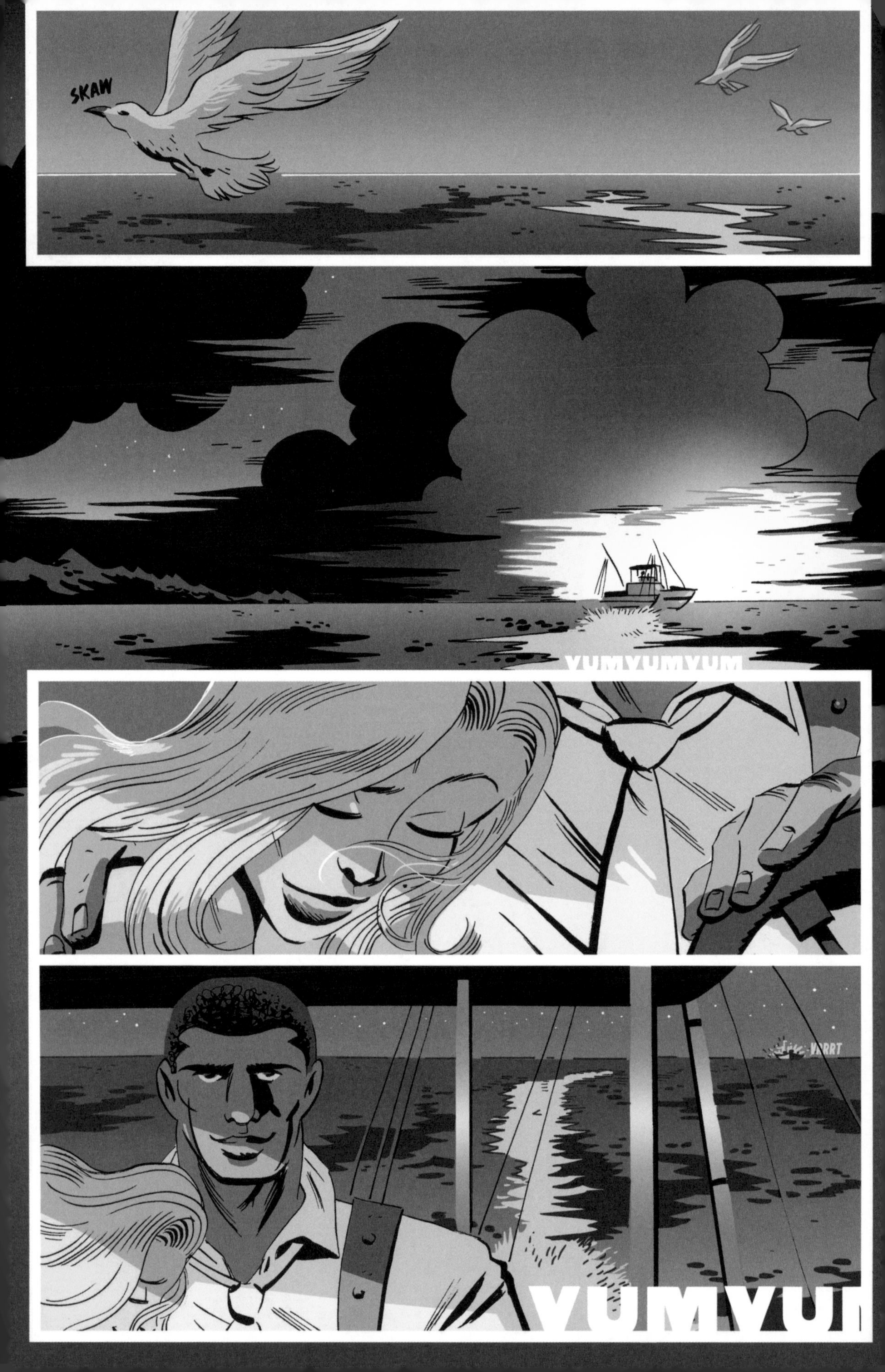
SKAW
VUMVUMVUM
VRRRT
VUMVUM

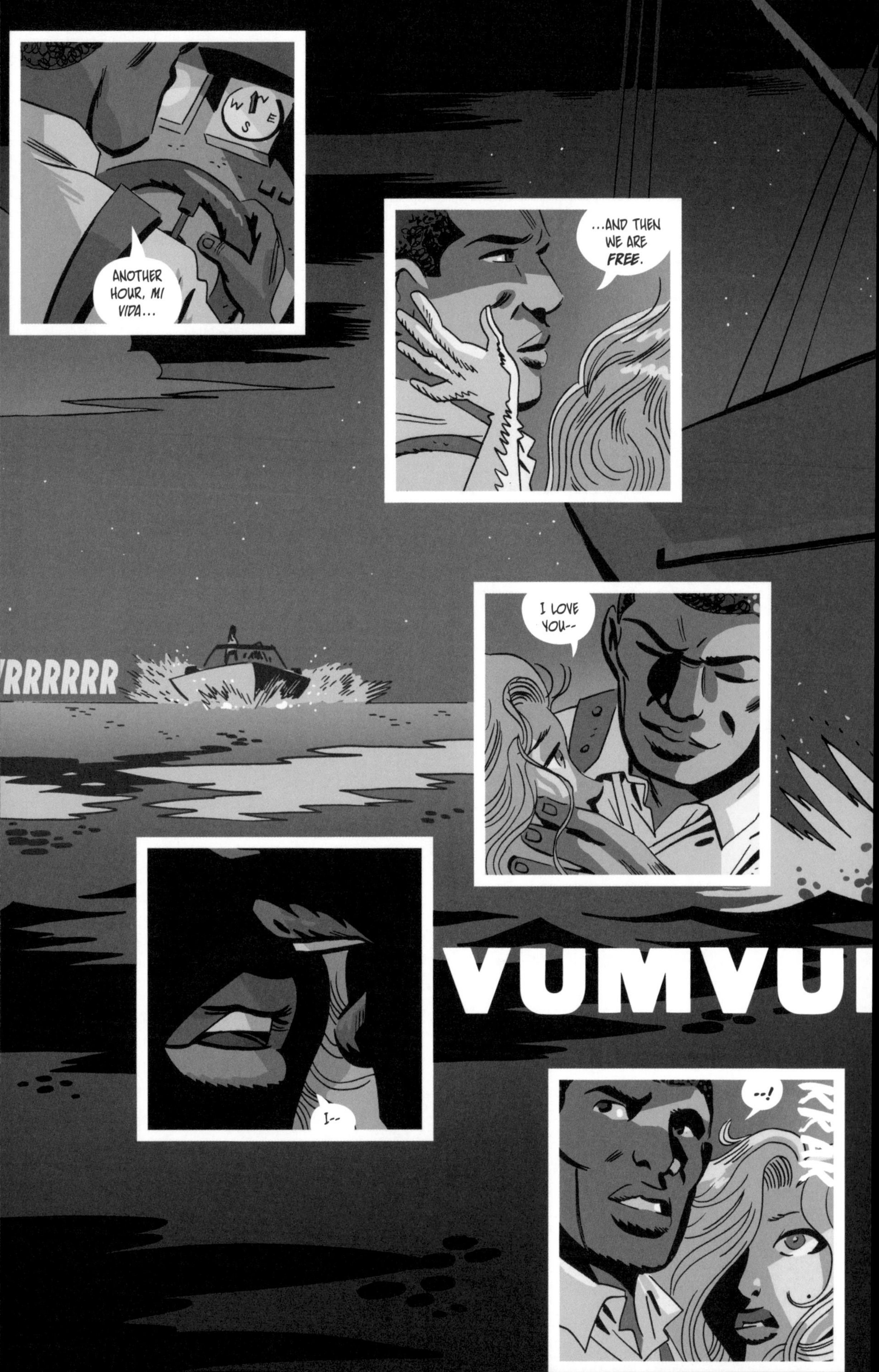

ANOTHER HOUR, MI VIDA...
...AND THEN WE ARE FREE.
VRRRRRR
I LOVE YOU--
VUMVUM
I--
--!
KRAK

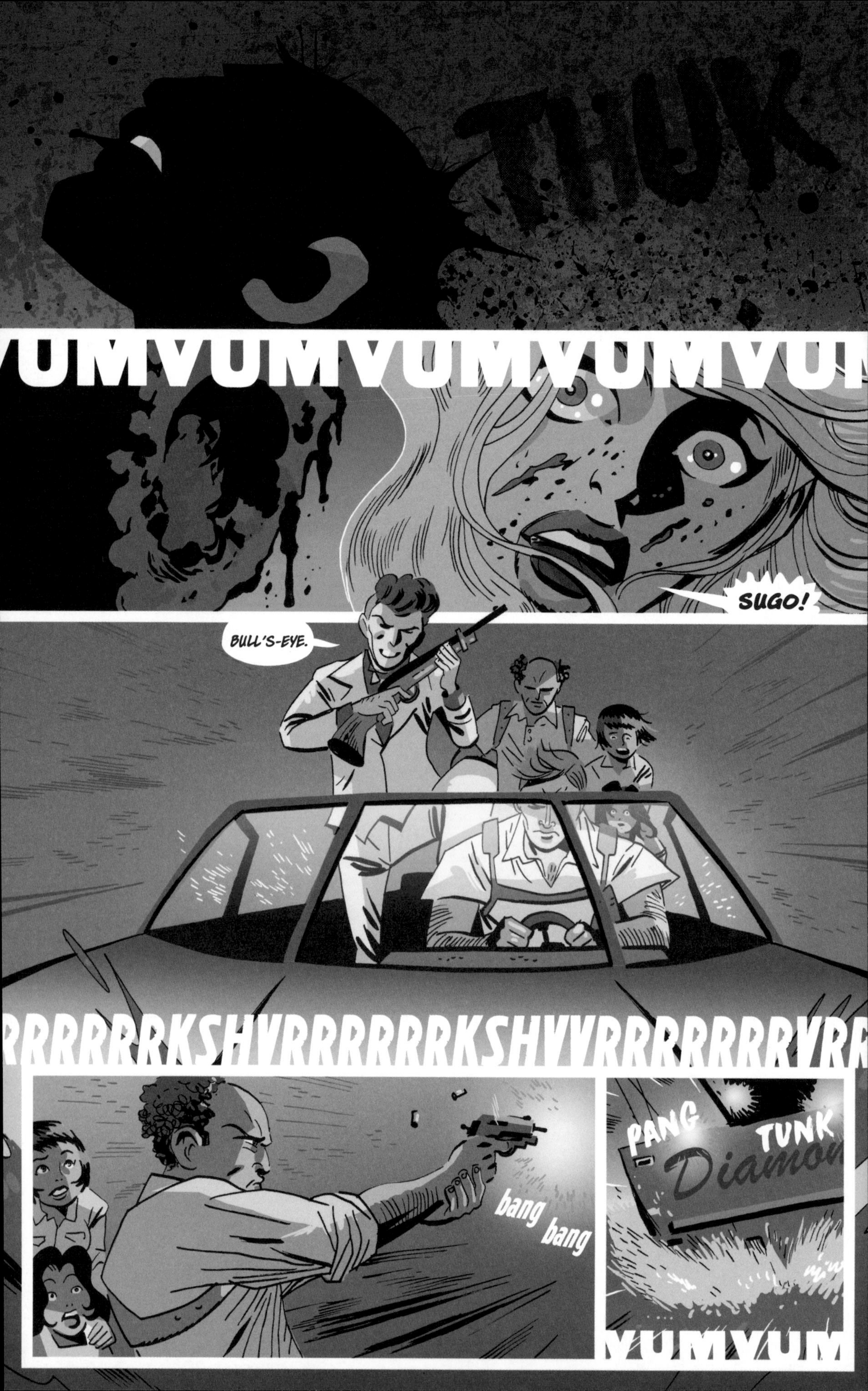
THUK
VUMVUMVUMVUMVUM
SUGO!
BULL'S-EYE.
RRRRRRKSHVRRRRRRRKSHVVRRRRRRRRVRR
bang
bang
PANG
TUNK
Diamon
VUMVUM

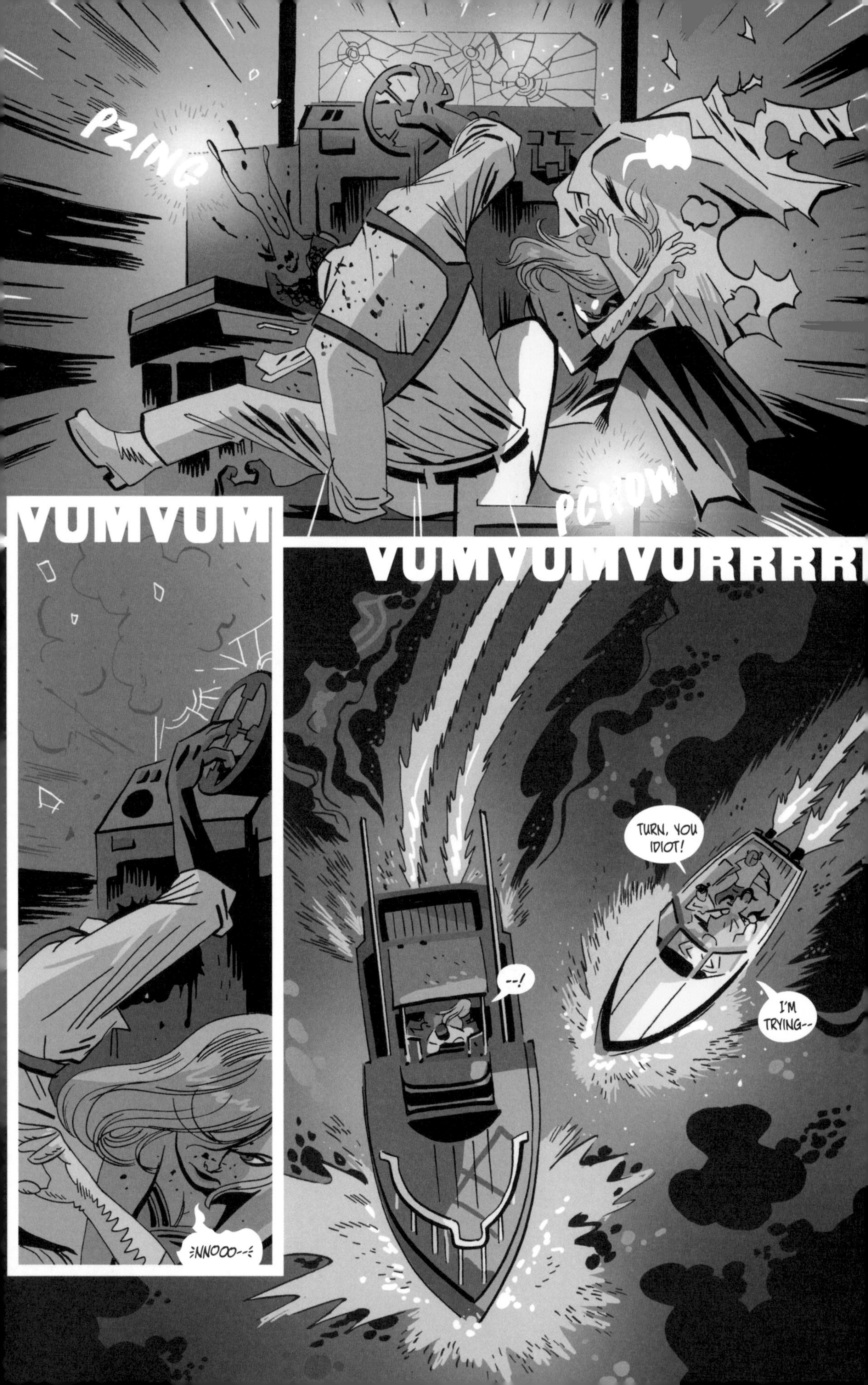
PZING
PCHOW
VUMVUM
VUMVUMVURRRR
NNOOO--
--!
TURN, YOU IDIOT!
I'M TRYING--

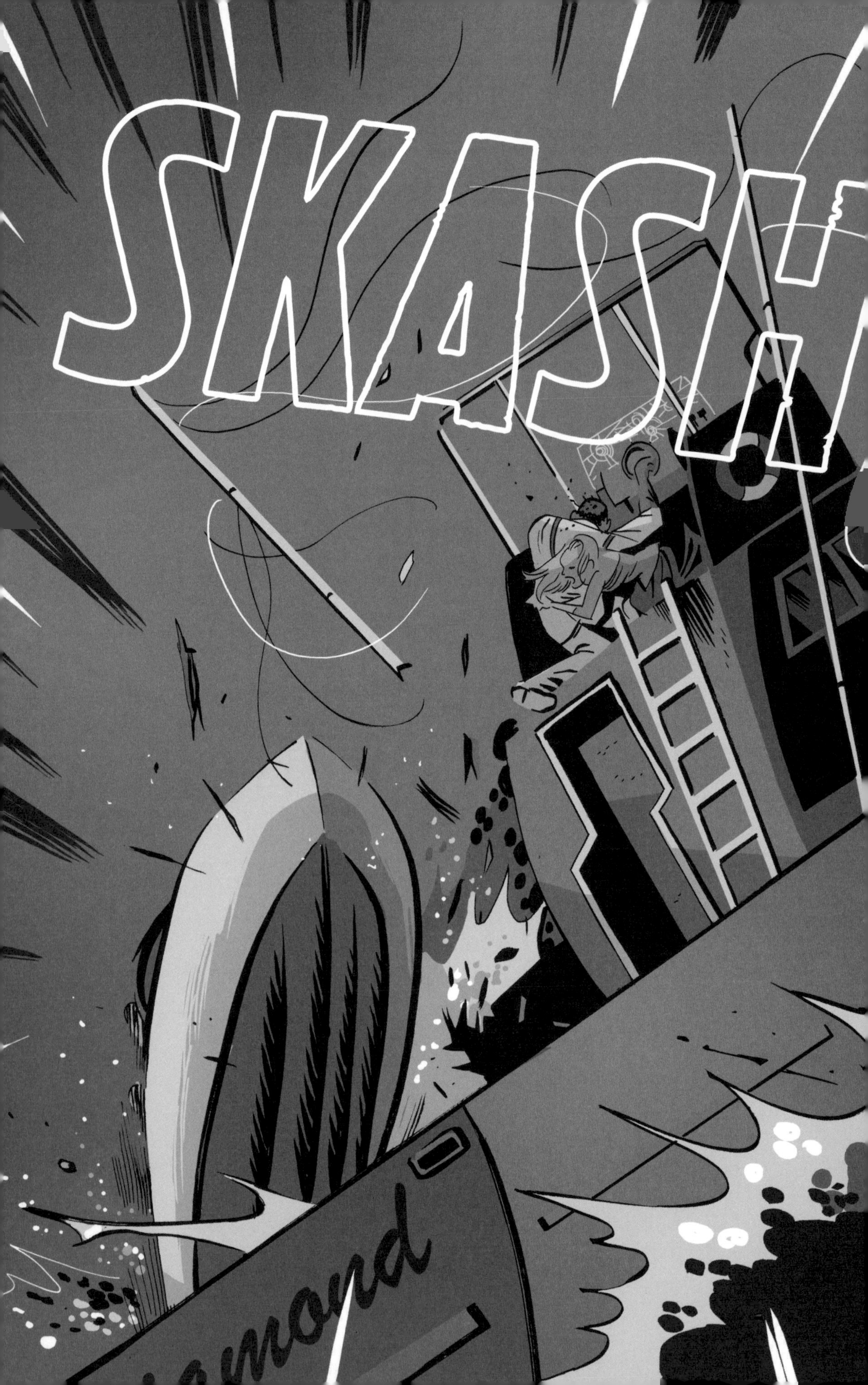
SKASH

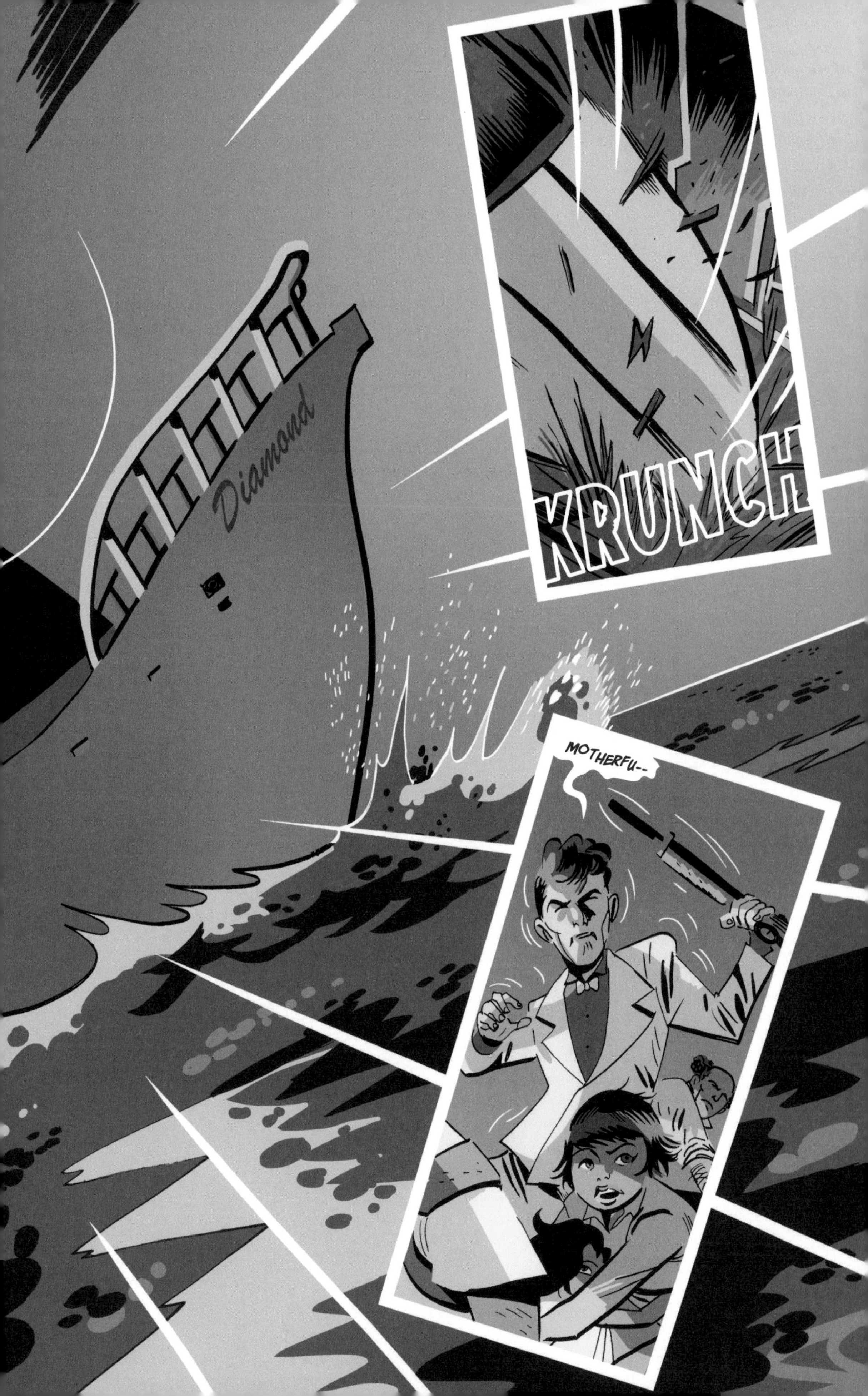
Diamond
KRUNCH
MOTHERFU--

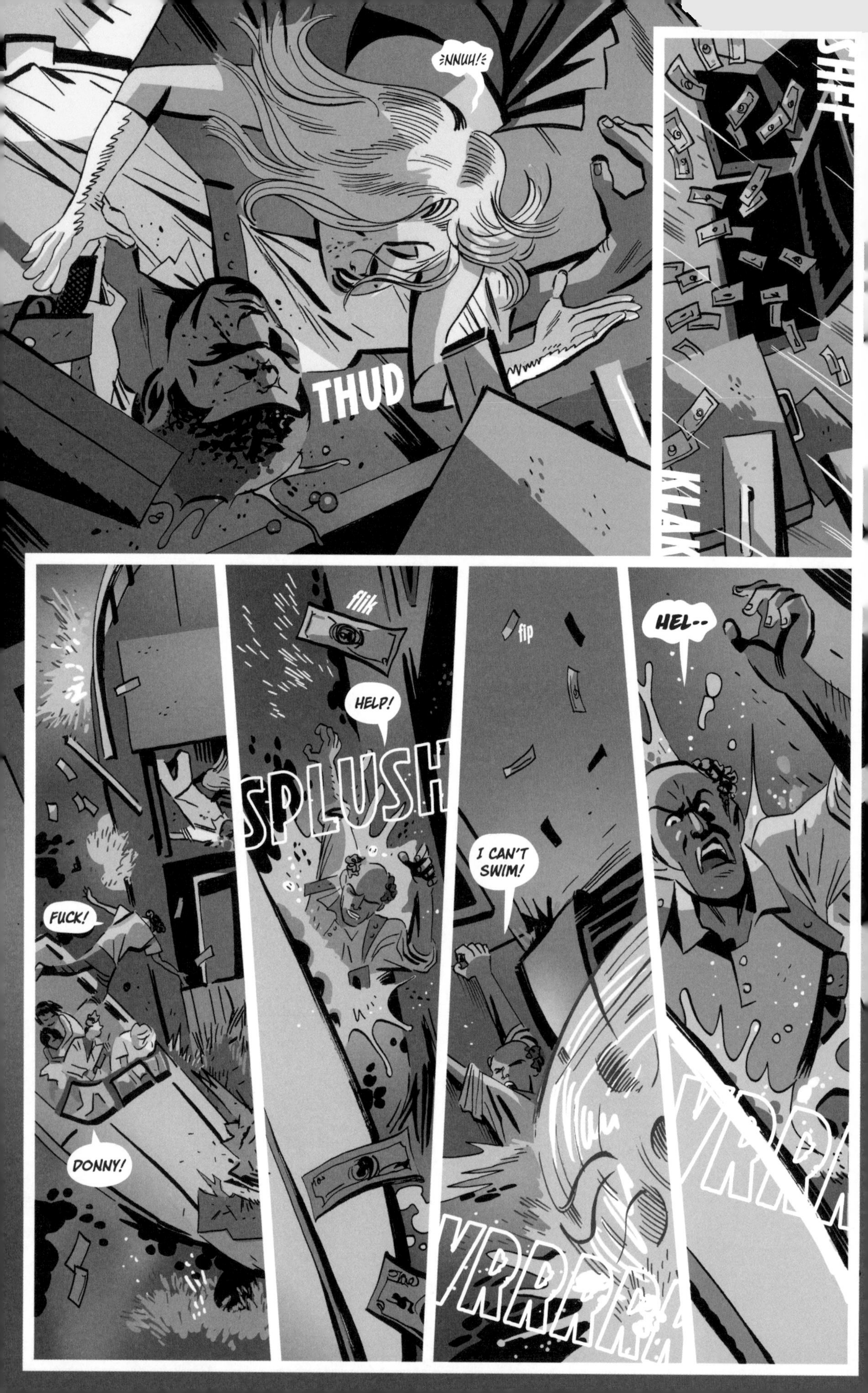
NNUH!
THUD
KLAK
FUCK!
DONNY!
flik
HELP!
SPLUSH
fip
I CAN'T SWIM!
HEL--

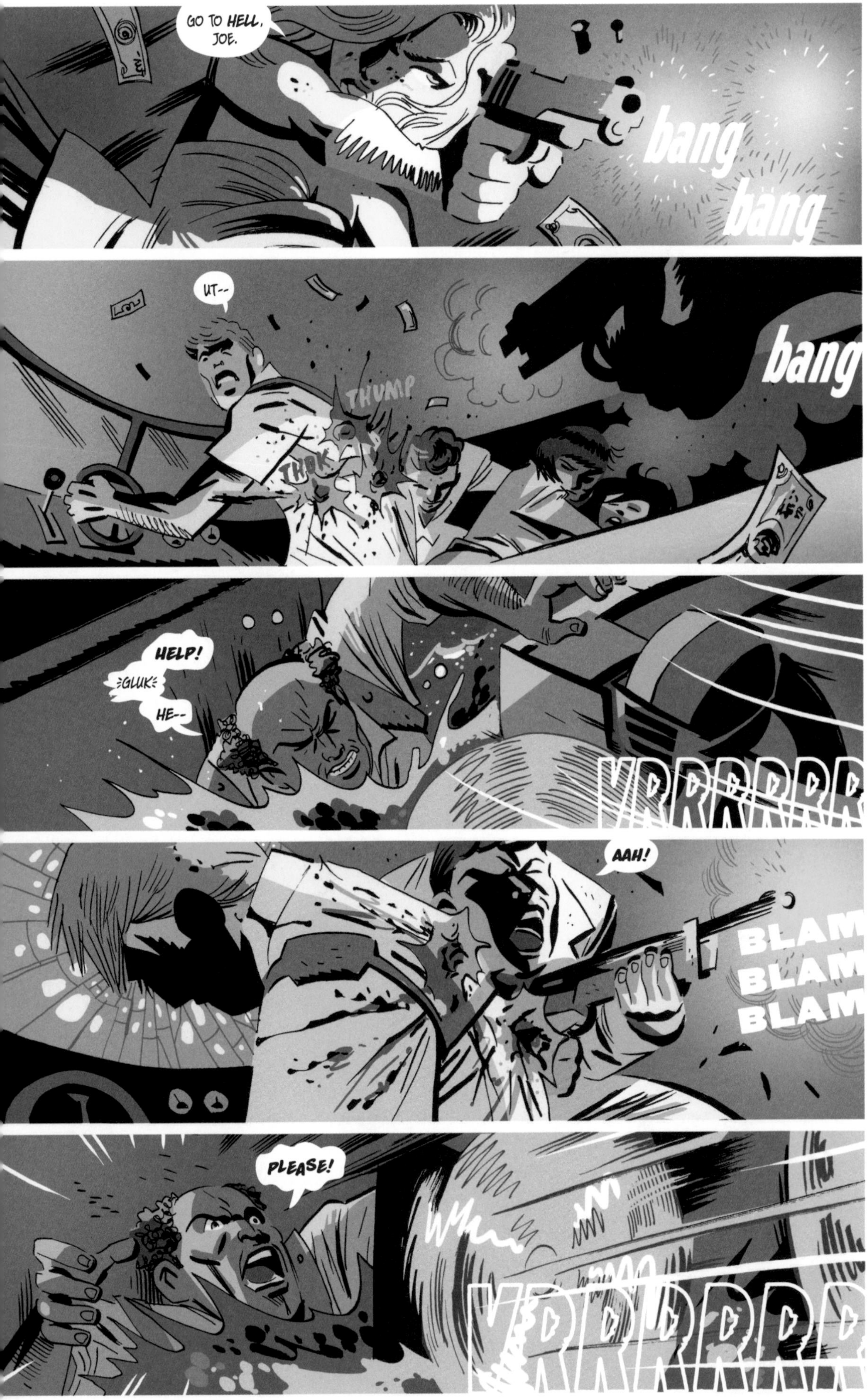
GO TO HELL, JOE.
bang
bang
UT--
bang
THUMP
THOK
HELP!
GLUK
HE--
VRRRRRR
AAH!
BLAM
BLAM
BLAM
PLEASE!
VRRRRRR

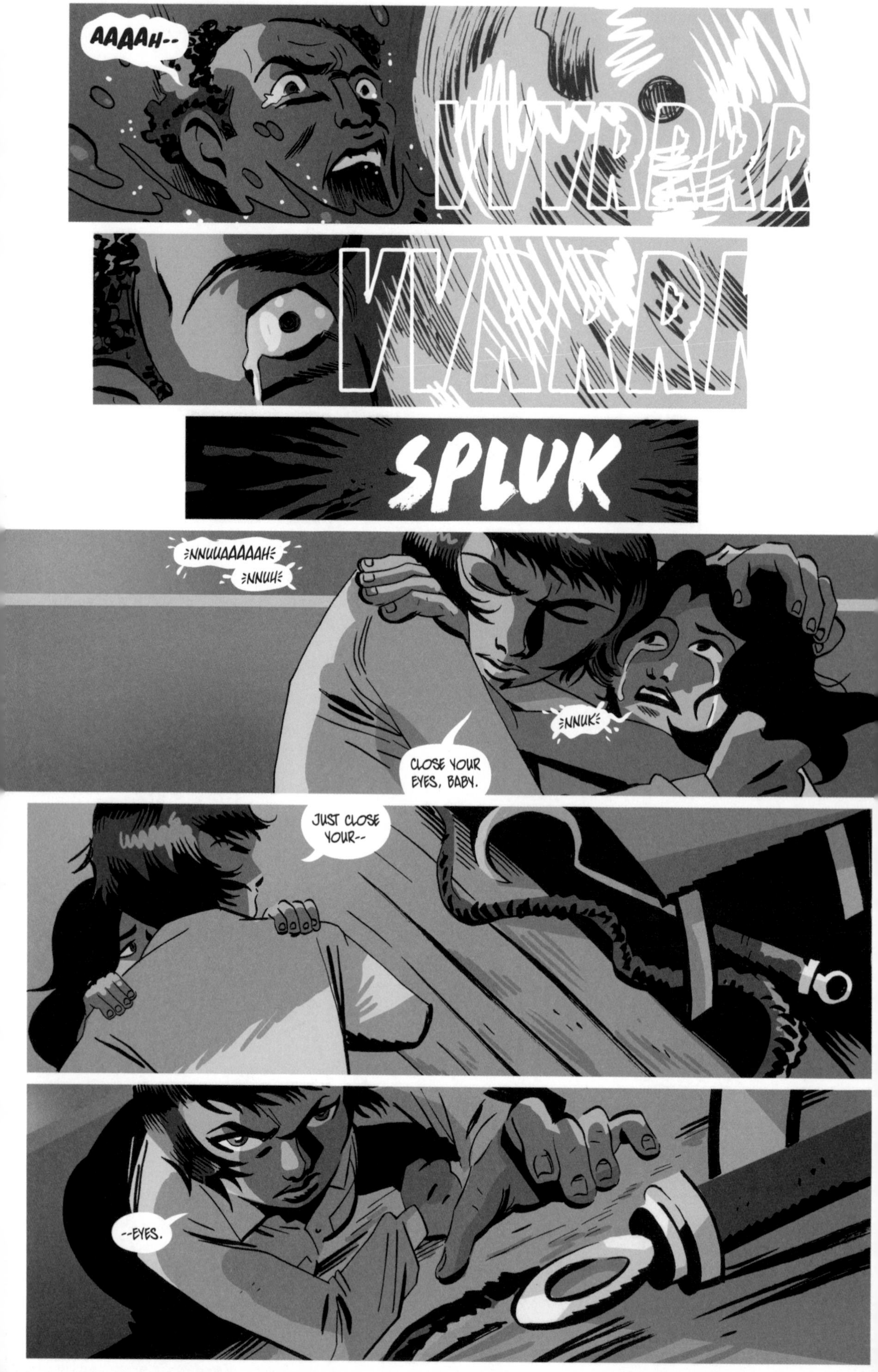
AAAAH--
VVVRRRR
VVVRRR
SPLUK
NNUUAAAAAH
NNUH
NNUK
CLOSE YOUR EYES, BABY.
JUST CLOSE YOUR--
--EYES.

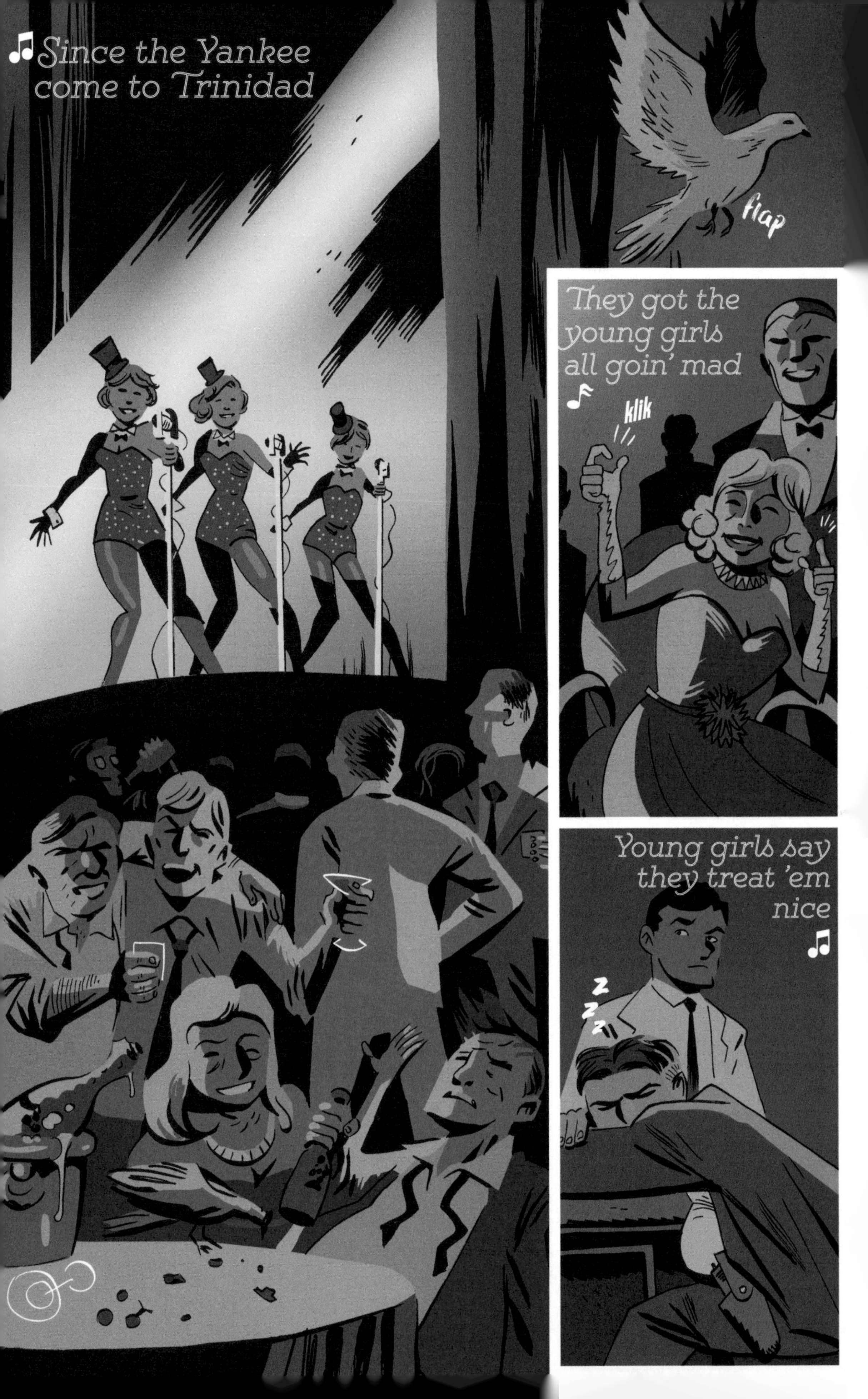
Since the Yankee come to Trinidad
flap
They got the young girls all goin' mad
klik
Young girls say they treat 'em nice
Z Z Z

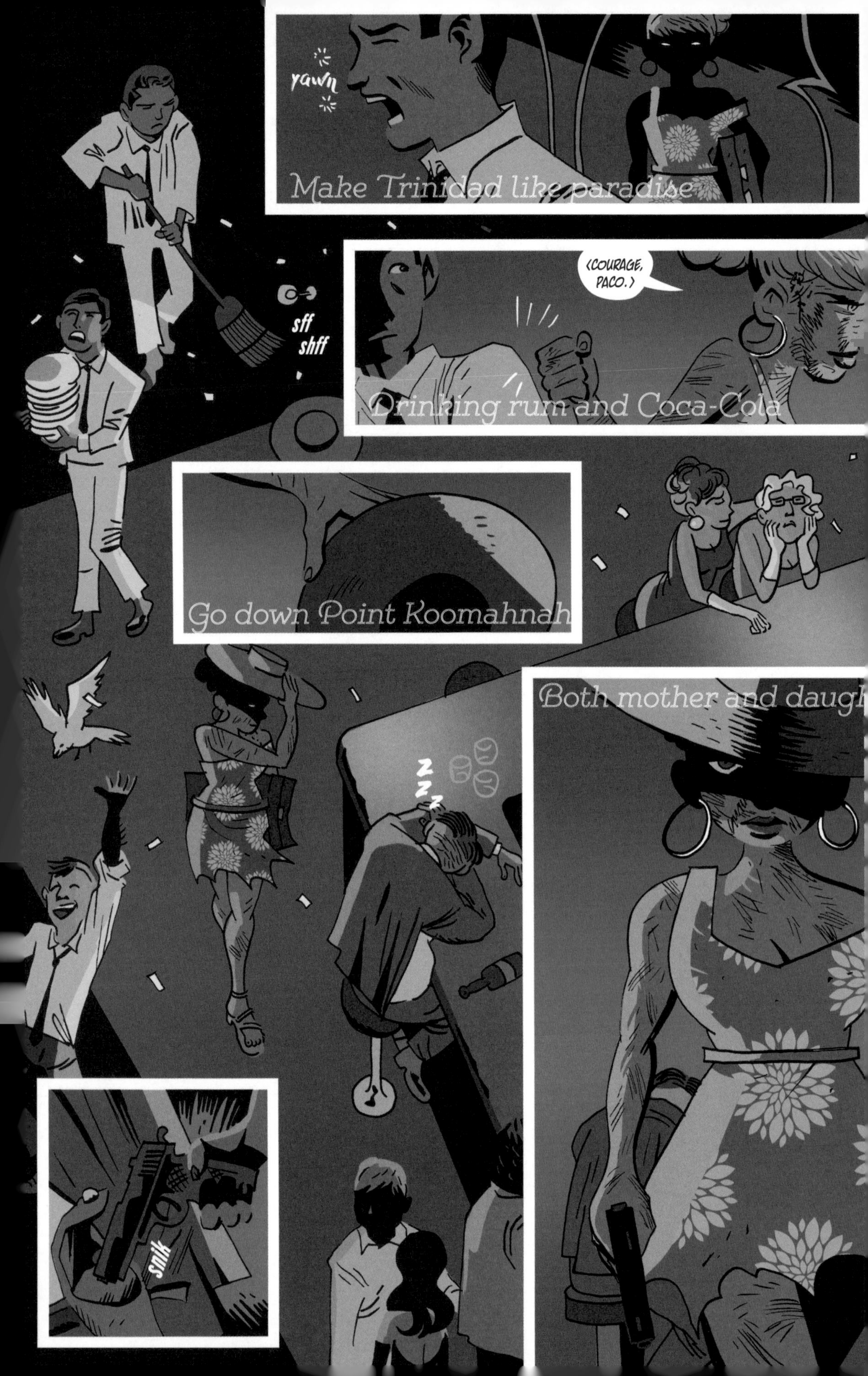

yawn
Make Trinidad like paradise
sff
shff
‹COURAGE, PACO.›
Drinking rum and Coca-Cola
Go down Point Koomahnah
Both mother and daugh
Z Z Z
snik

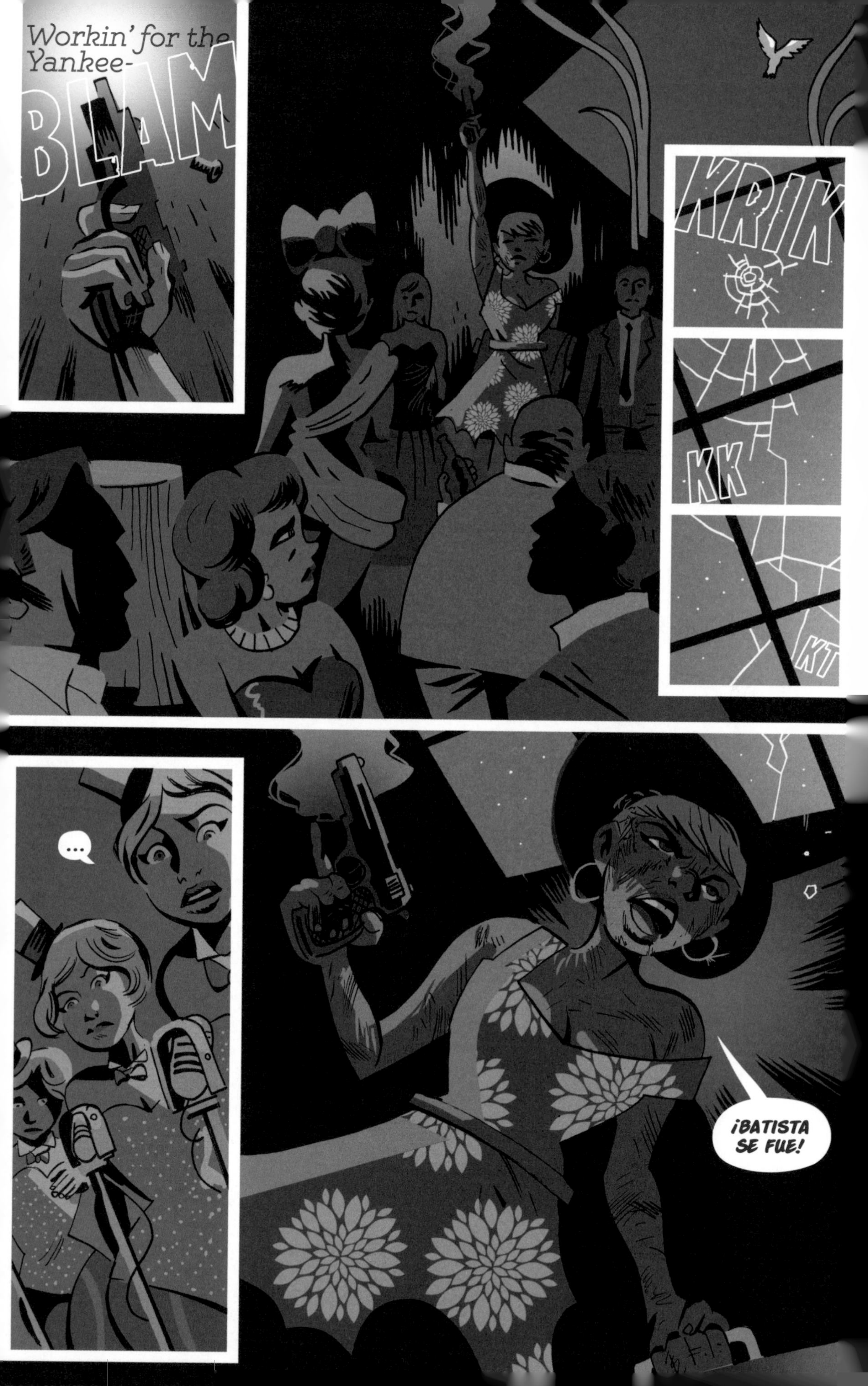
Workin' for the Yankee-
BLAM
KRIK
KK
KT
...
¡BATISTA SE FUE!

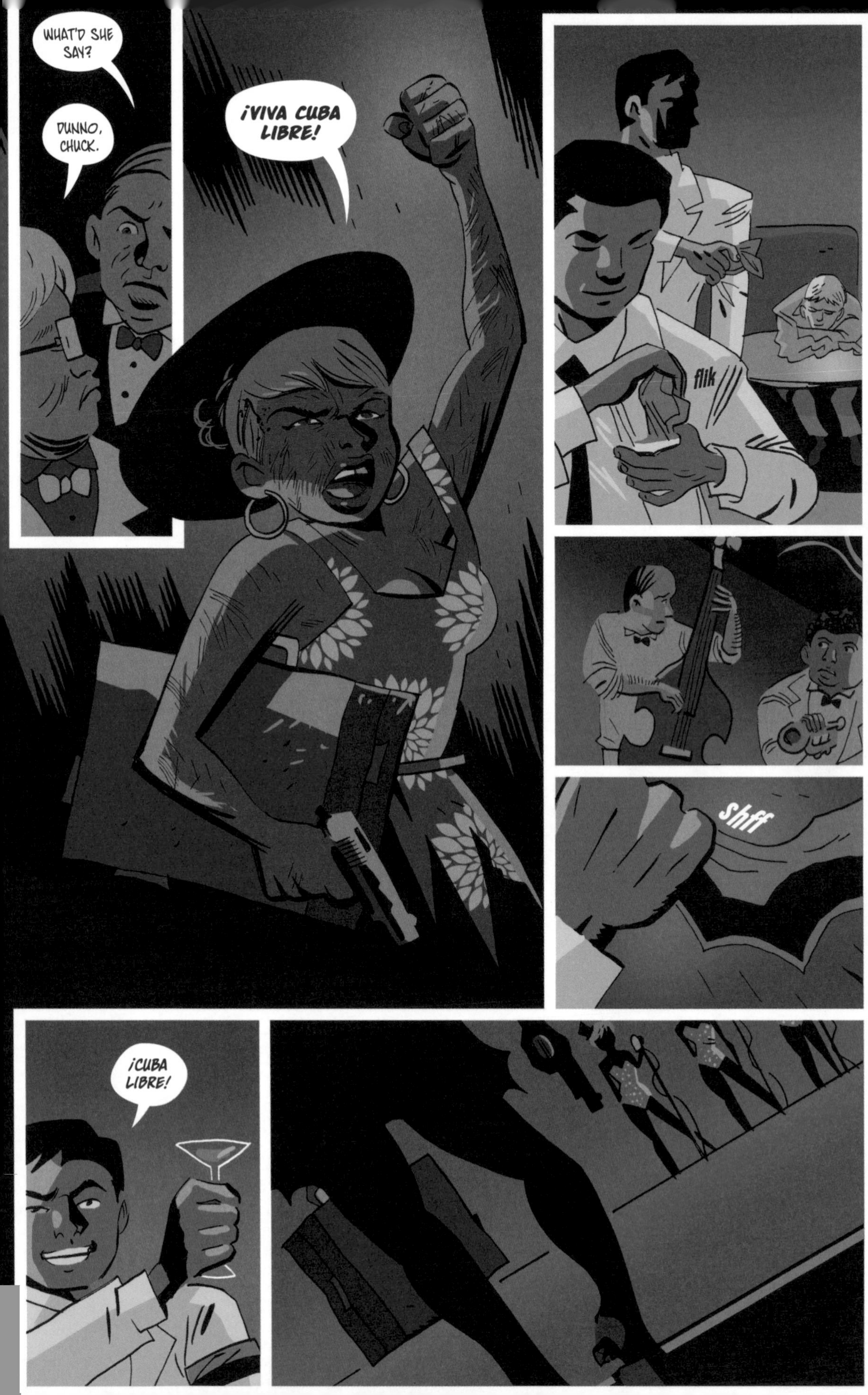
WHAT'D SHE SAY?
DUNNO, CHUCK.
¡VIVA CUBA LIBRE!
flik
Shff
¡CUBA LIBRE!

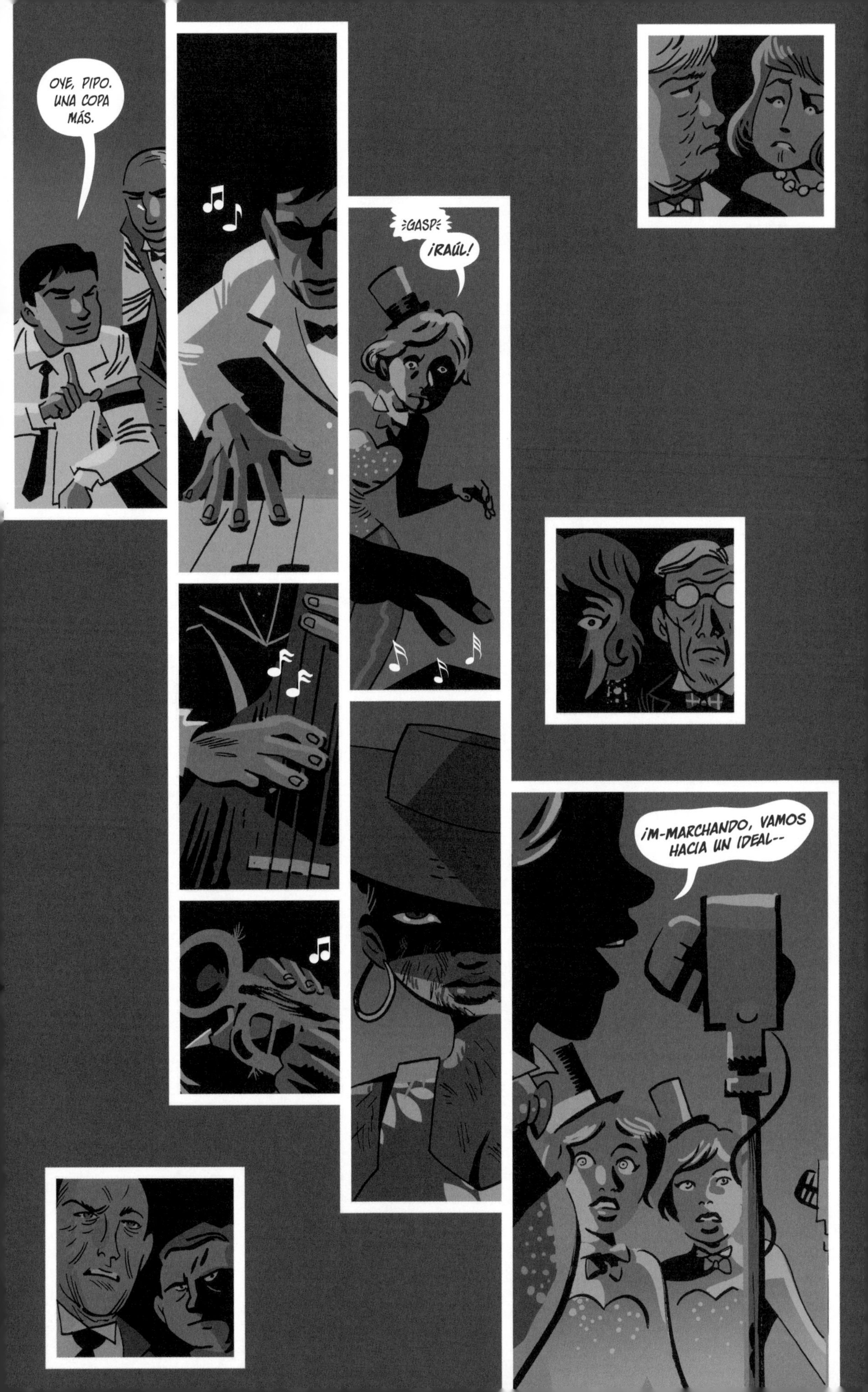
OYE, PIPO. UNA COPA MÁS.
GASP
¡RAÚL!
¡M-MARCHANDO, VAMOS HACIA UN IDEAL--

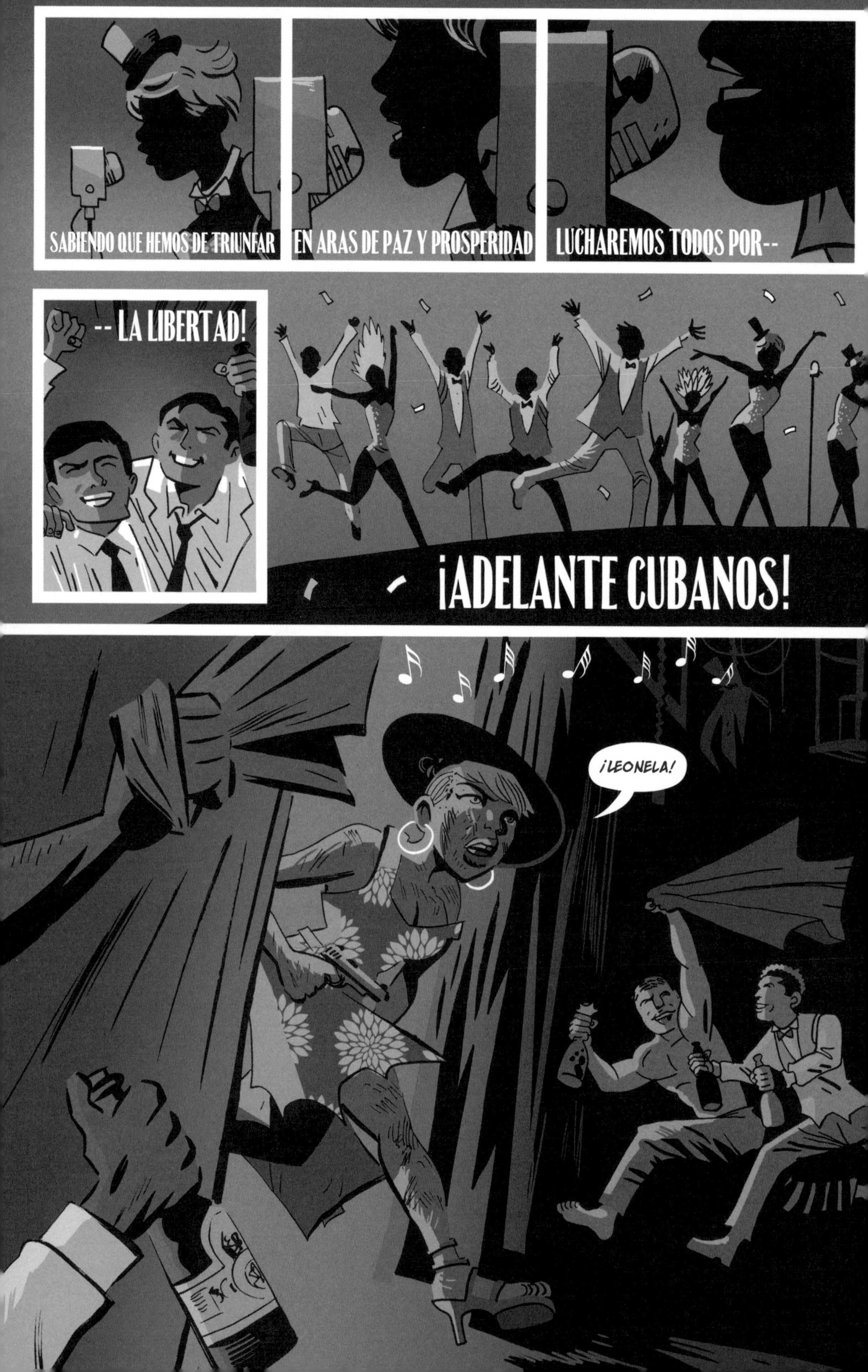
SABIENDO QUE HEMOS DE TRIUNFAR
EN ARAS DE PAZ Y PROSPERIDAD
LUCHAREMOS TODOS POR--
-- LA LIBERTAD!
¡ADELANTE CUBANOS!
¡LEONELA!

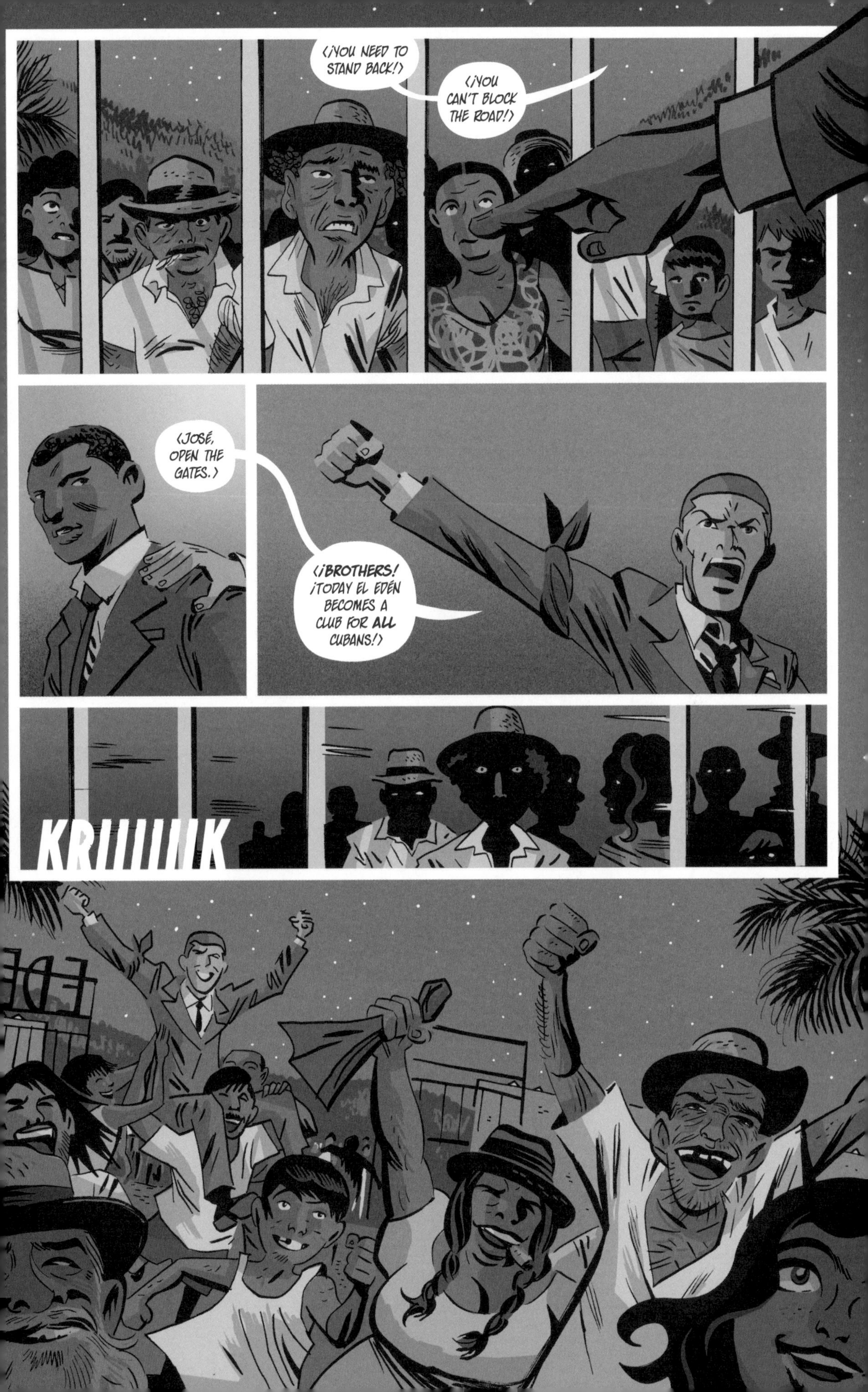

⟨¡YOU NEED TO STAND BACK!⟩
⟨¡YOU CAN'T BLOCK THE ROAD!⟩
⟨JOSÉ, OPEN THE GATES.⟩
⟨¡BROTHERS! ¡TODAY EL EDÉN BECOMES A CLUB FOR **ALL** CUBANS!⟩
KRIIIIIIIK

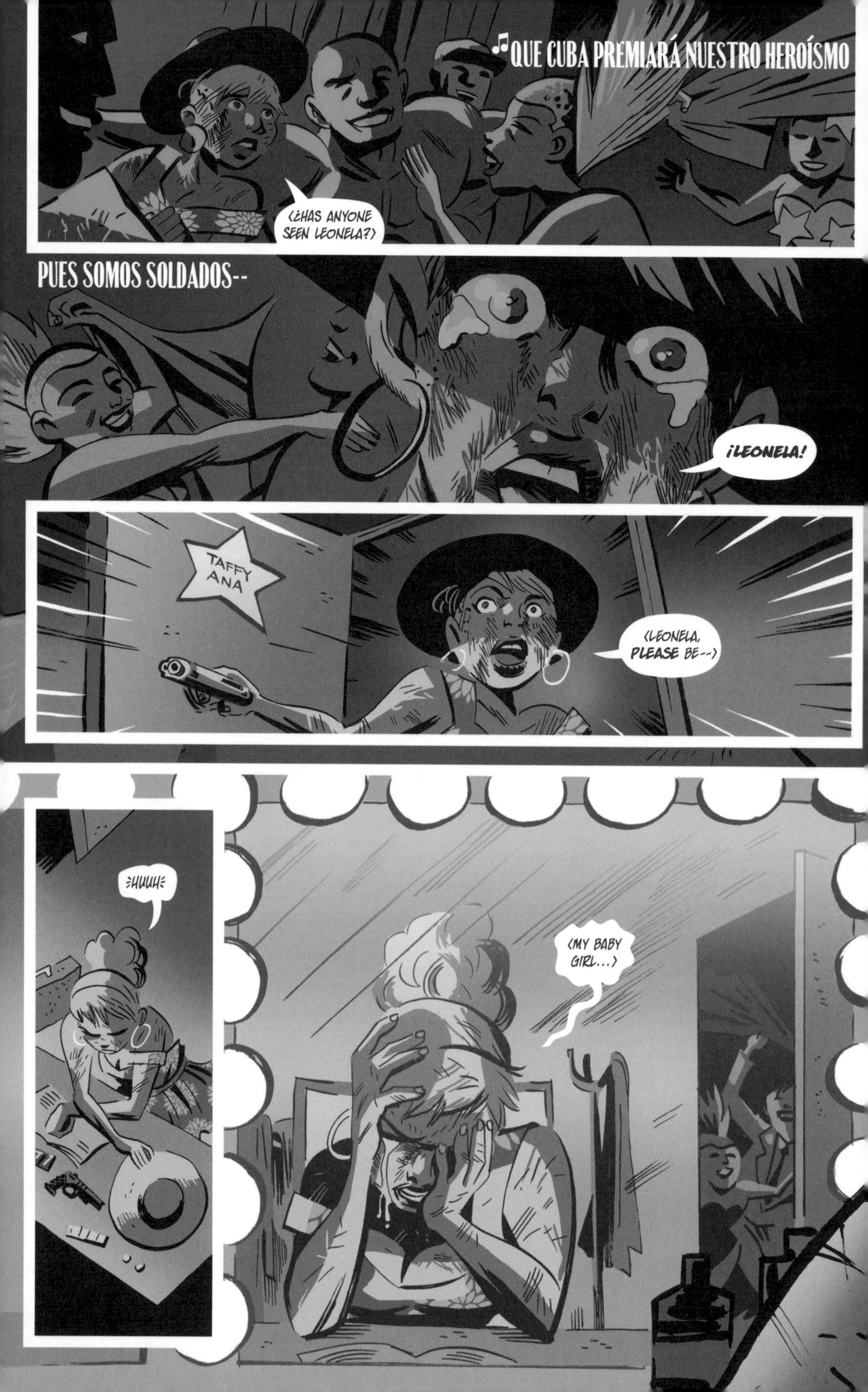
♪QUE CUBA PREMIARÁ NUESTRO HEROÍSMO
‹¿HAS ANYONE SEEN LEONELA?›
PUES SOMOS SOLDADOS--
¡LEONELA!
TAFFY ANA
‹LEONELA, PLEASE BE--›
HUUH
‹MY BABY GIRL...›

5:00 A.M.

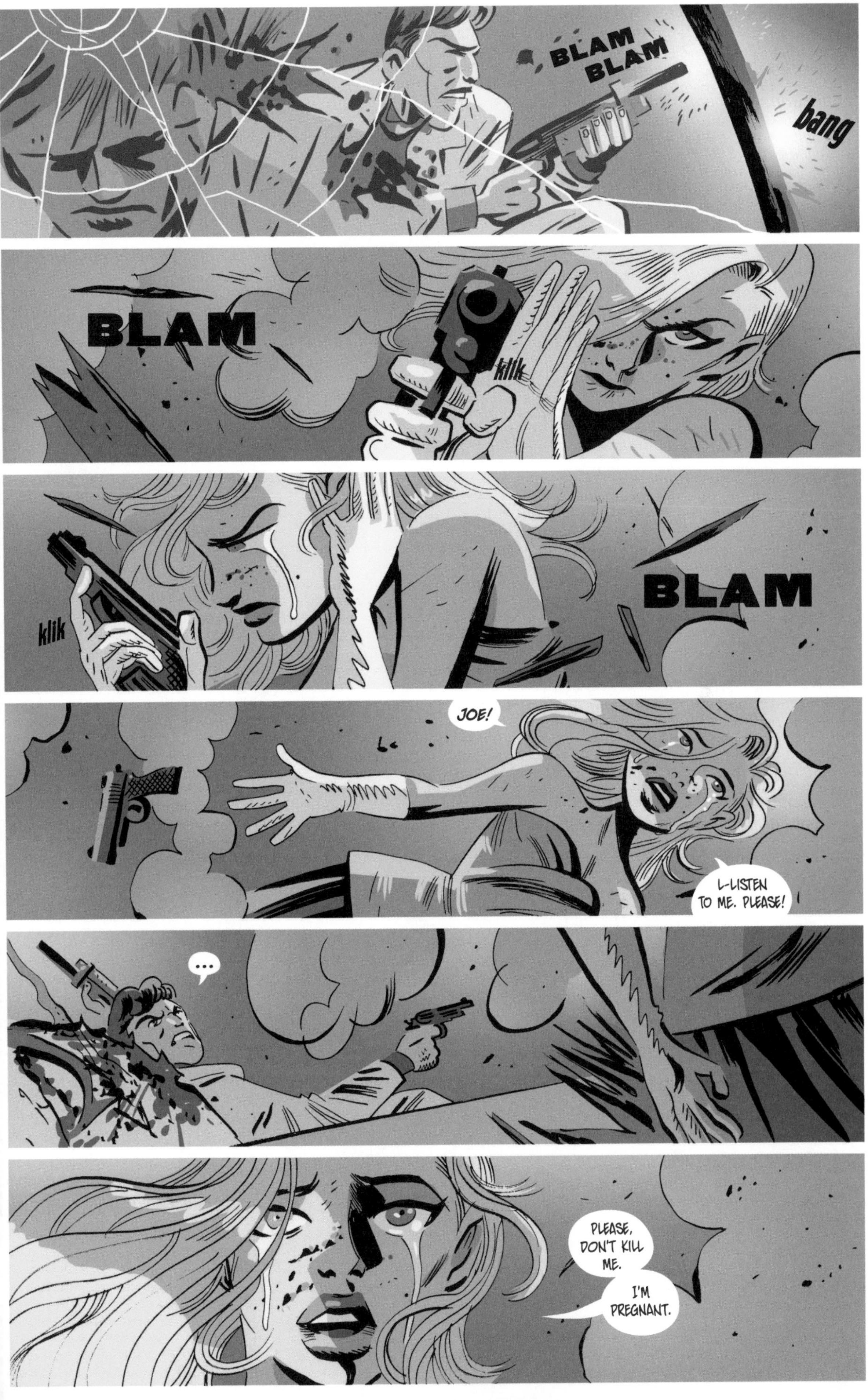
BLAM
BLAM
bang
BLAM
klik
BLAM
klik
JOE!
L-LISTEN TO ME. PLEASE!
...
PLEASE, DON'T KILL ME.
I'M PREGNANT.

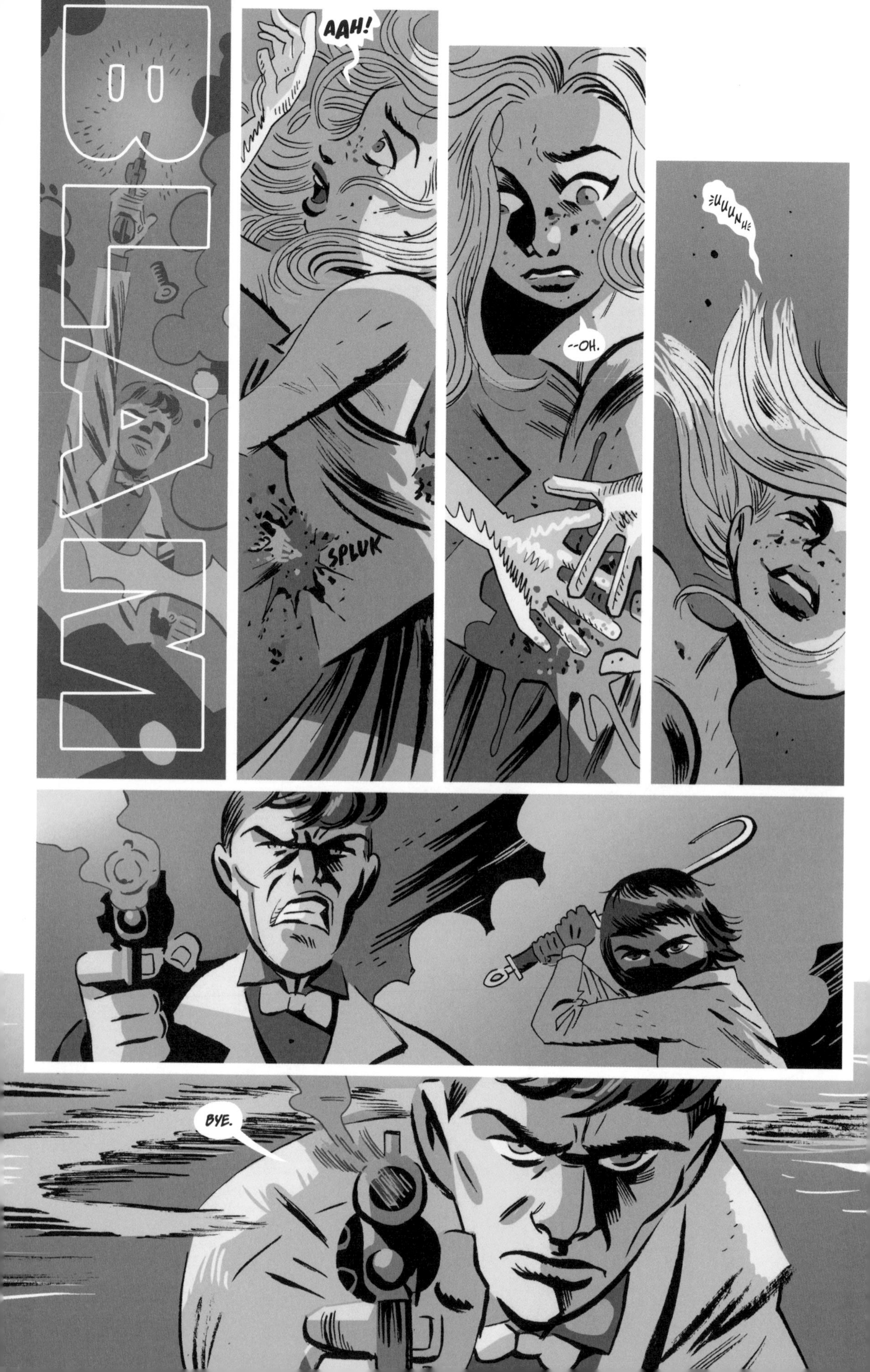
BLAM
AAH!
SPLUK
--OH.
UUUNH
BYE.

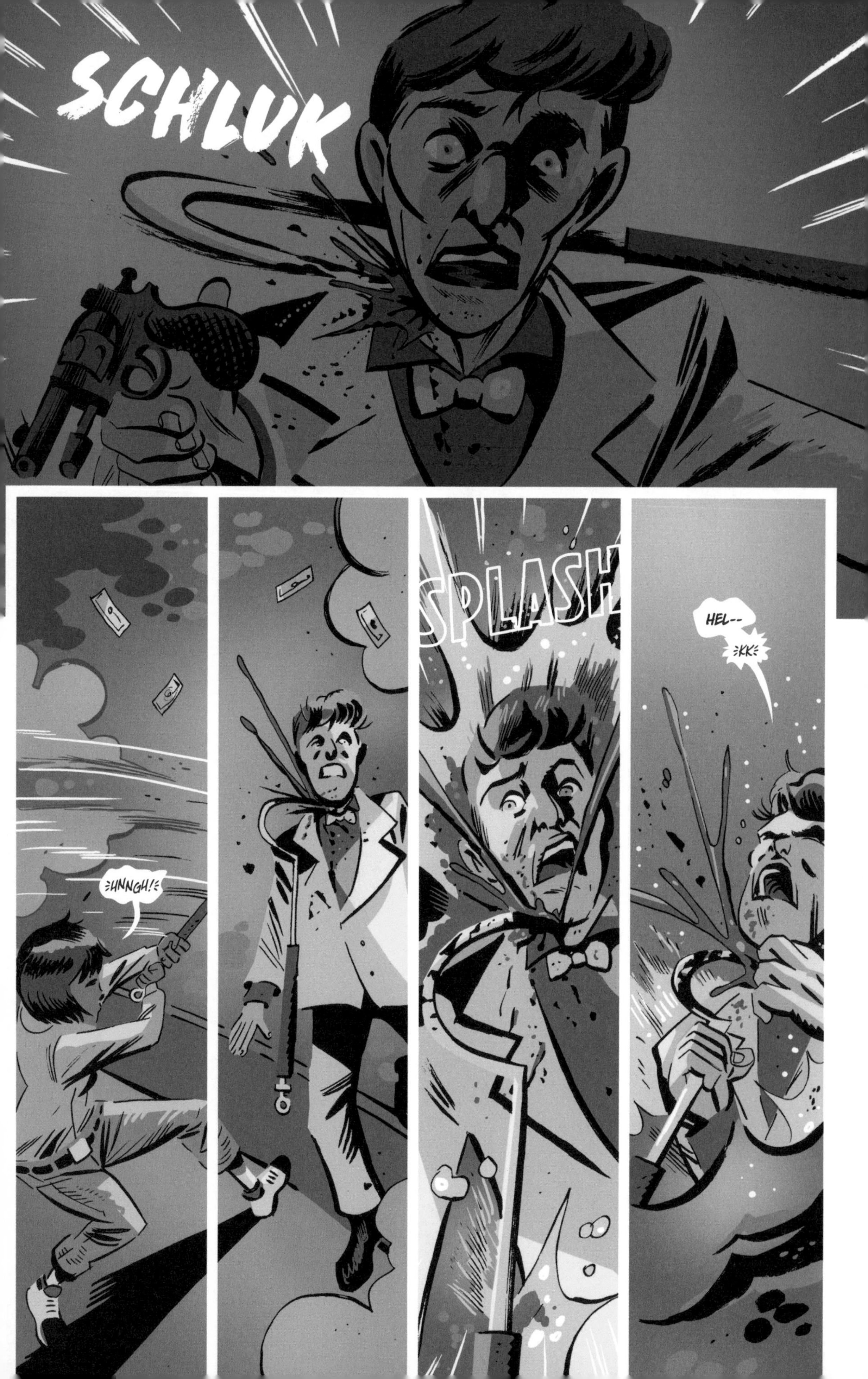
SCHLUK
HNNGH!
SPLASH
HEL--
KK

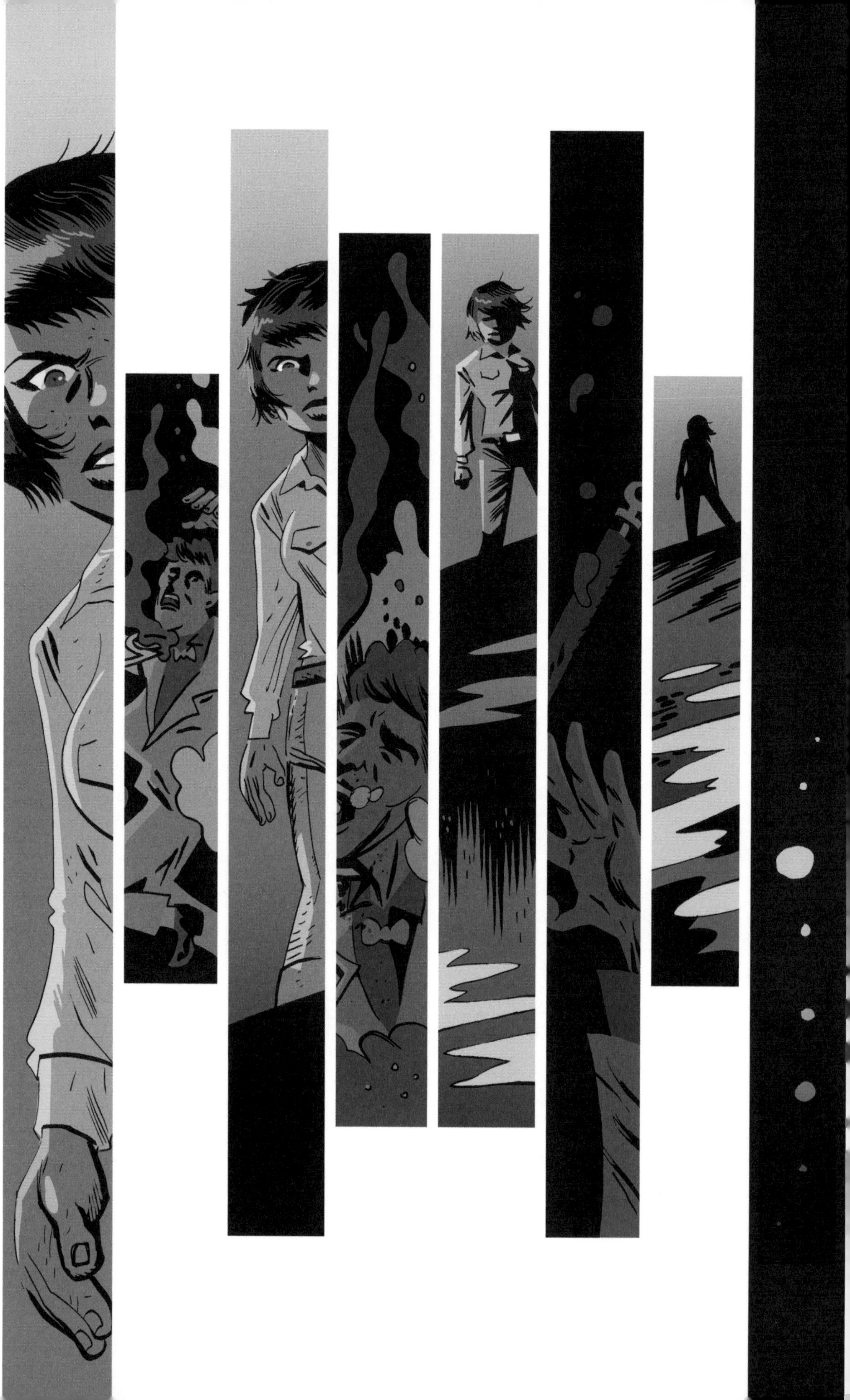

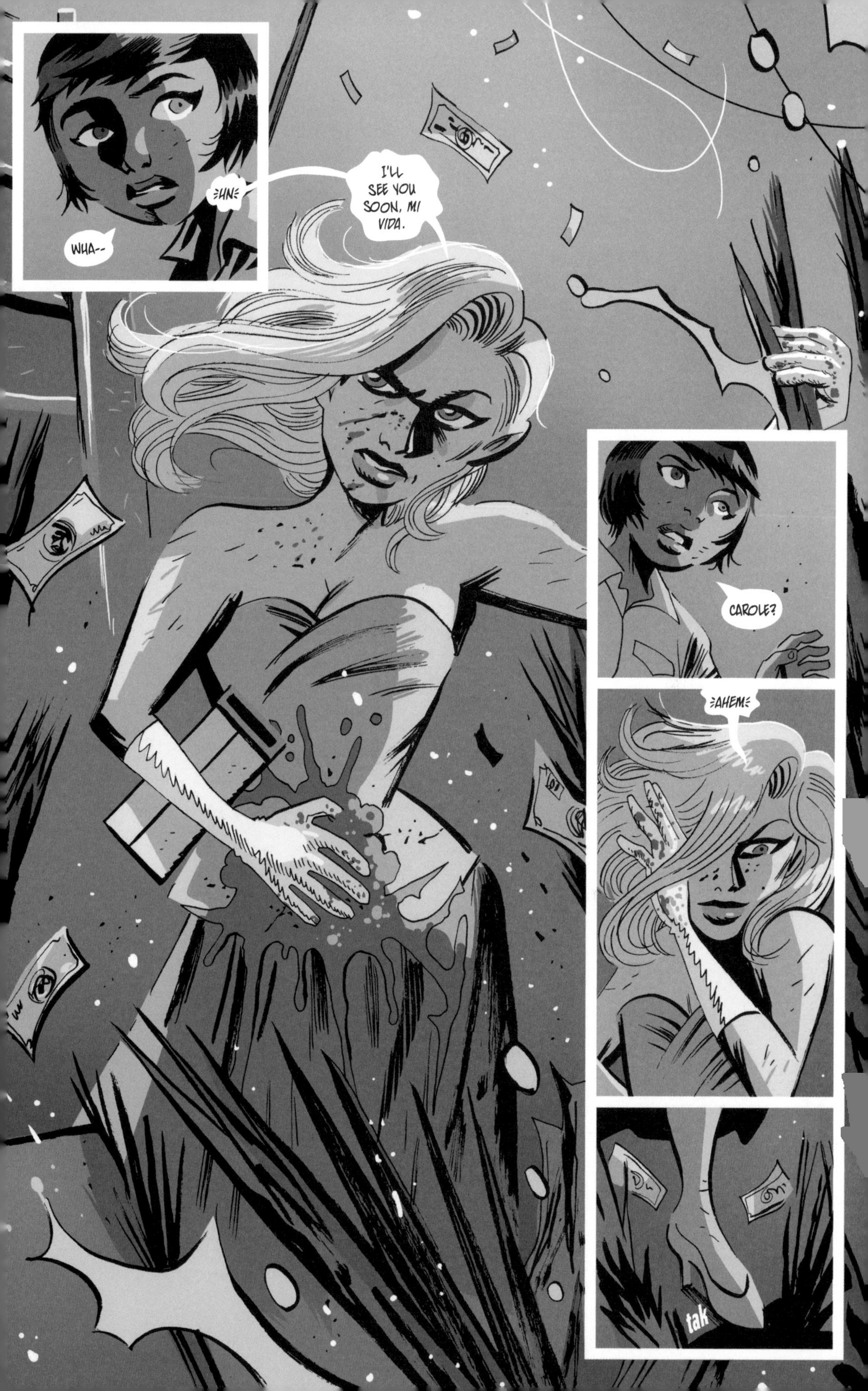

UHN
WHA--
I'LL SEE YOU SOON, MI VIDA.
CAROLE?
AHEM
tak

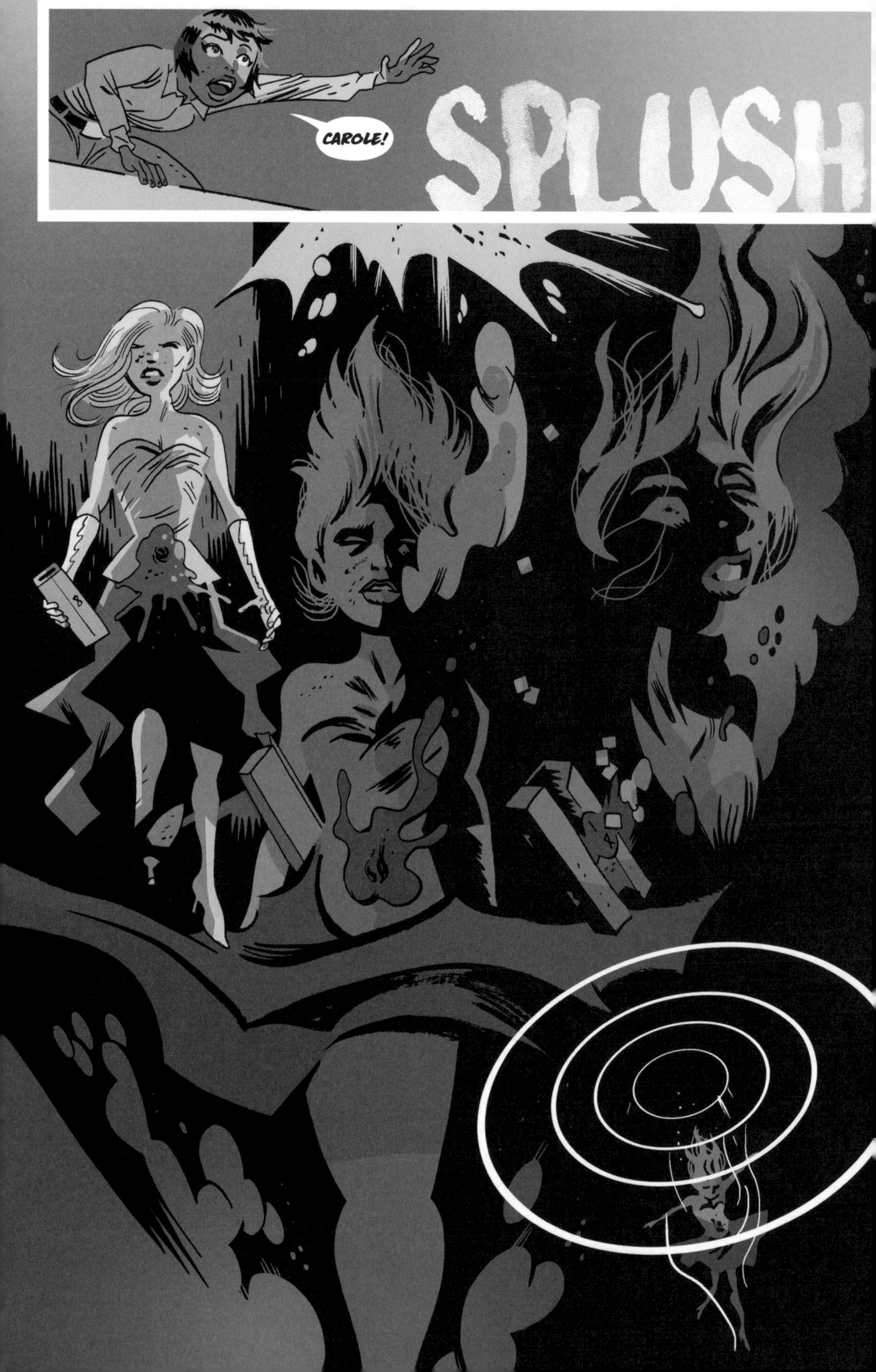
CAROLE!
SPLUSH

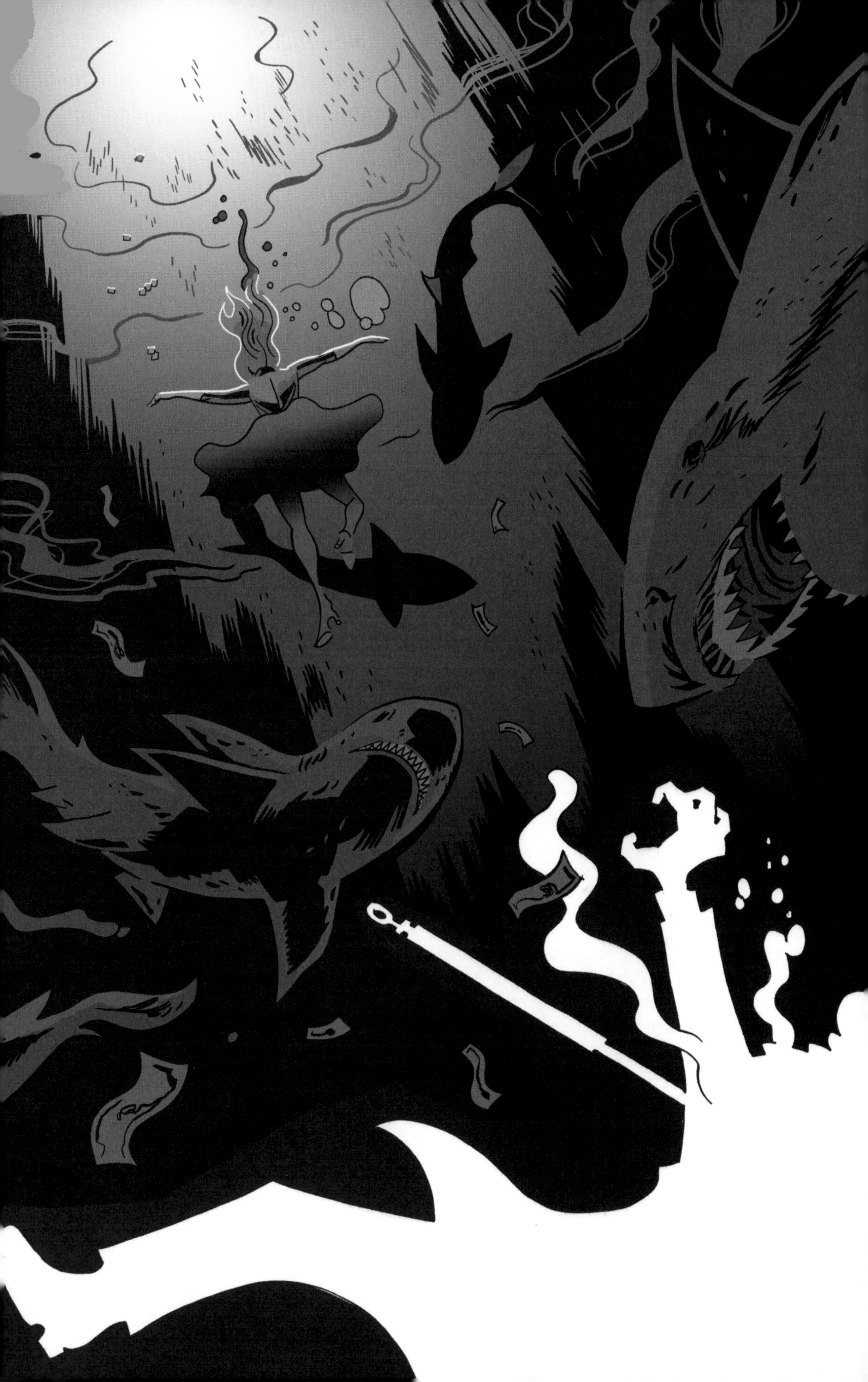

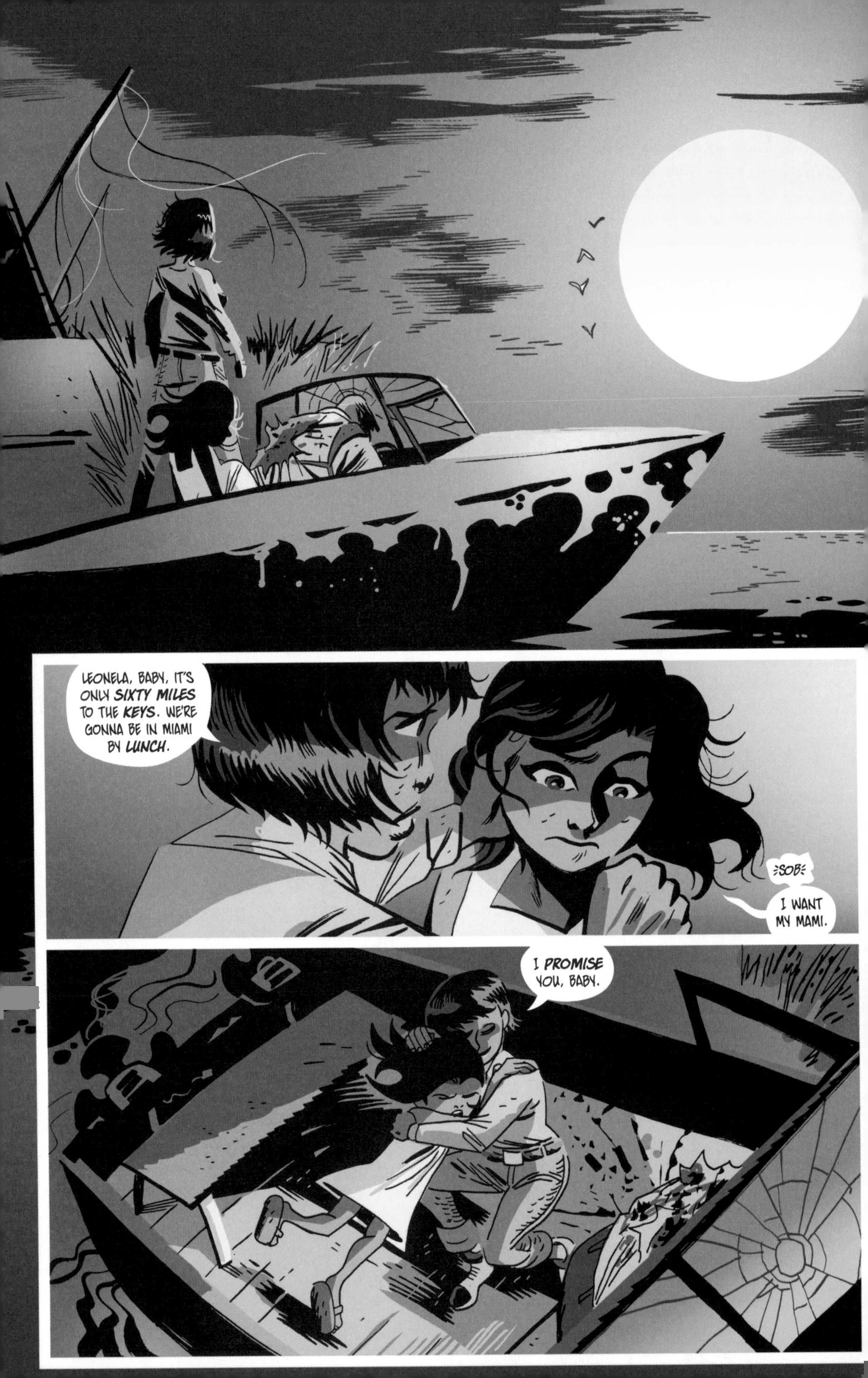
LEONELA, BABY, IT'S ONLY SIXTY MILES TO THE KEYS. WE'RE GONNA BE IN MIAMI BY LUNCH.
SOB
I WANT MY MAMI.
I PROMISE YOU, BABY.

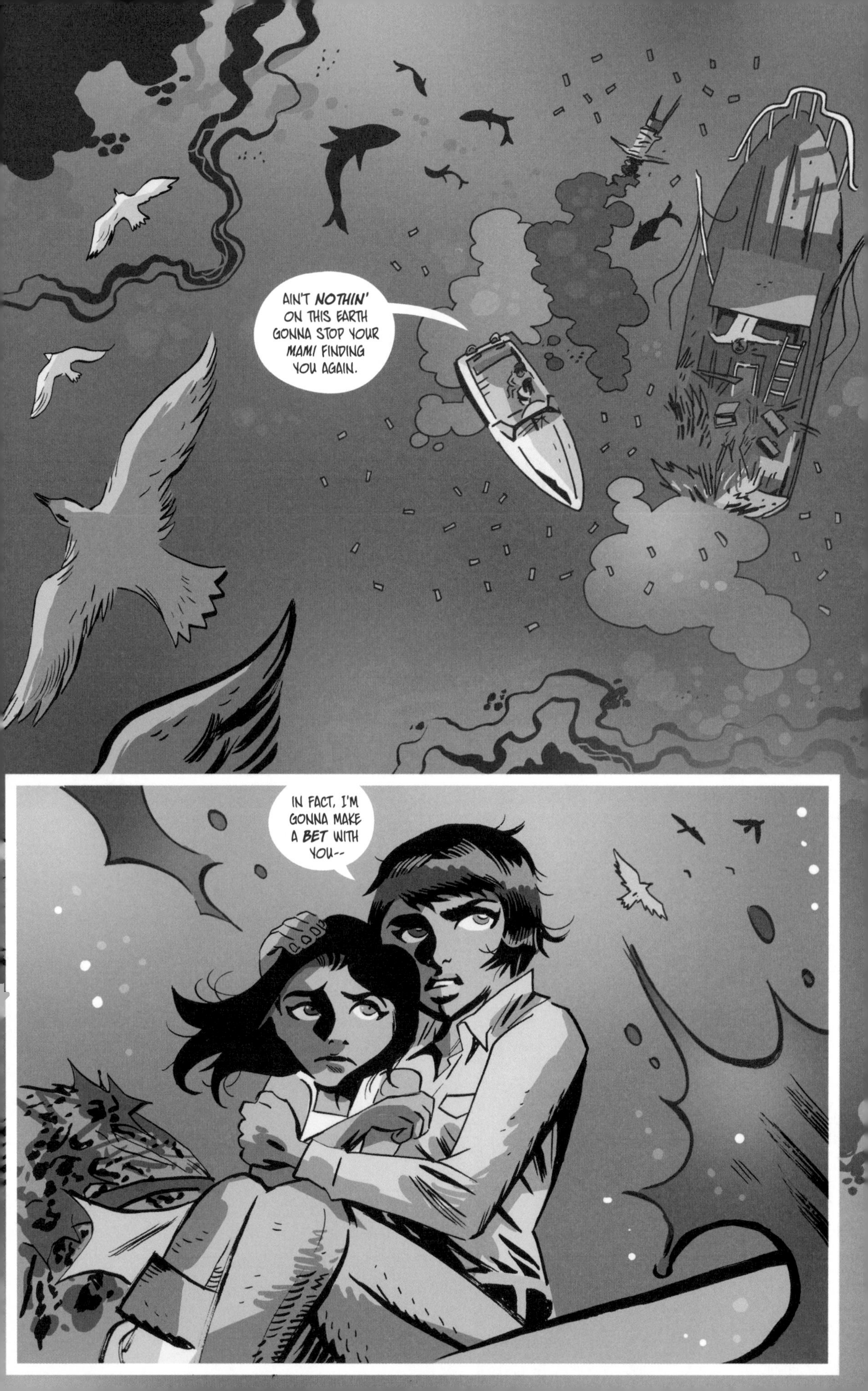
AIN'T **NOTHIN'** ON THIS EARTH GONNA STOP YOUR *MAMI* FINDING YOU AGAIN.
IN FACT, I'M GONNA MAKE A **BET** WITH YOU--

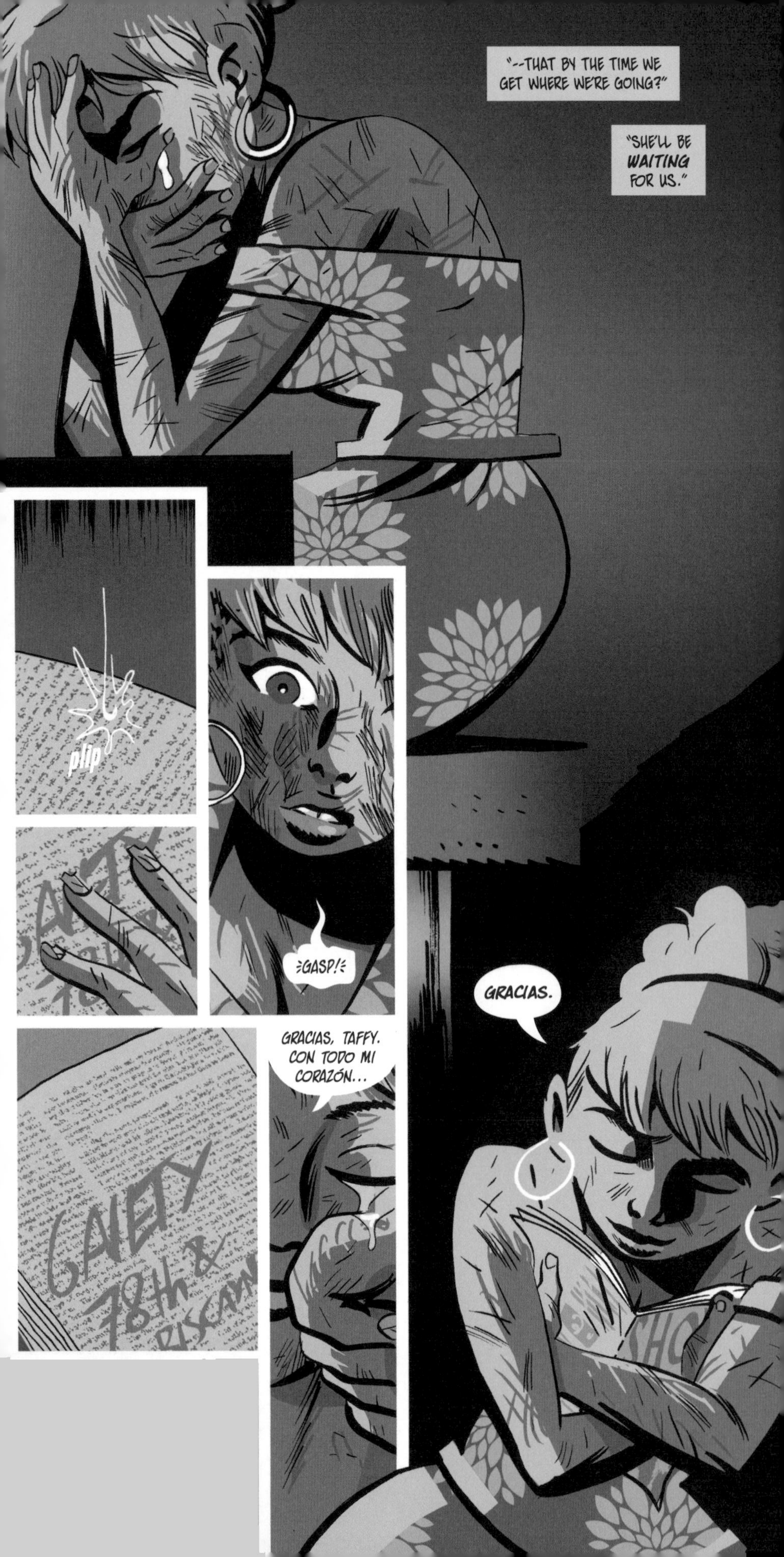
"--THAT BY THE TIME WE GET WHERE WE'RE GOING?"
"SHE'LL BE WAITING FOR US."
plip
GASP!
GAIETY 78th & BISCAYN
GRACIAS, TAFFY. CON TODO MI CORAZÓN...
GRACIAS.

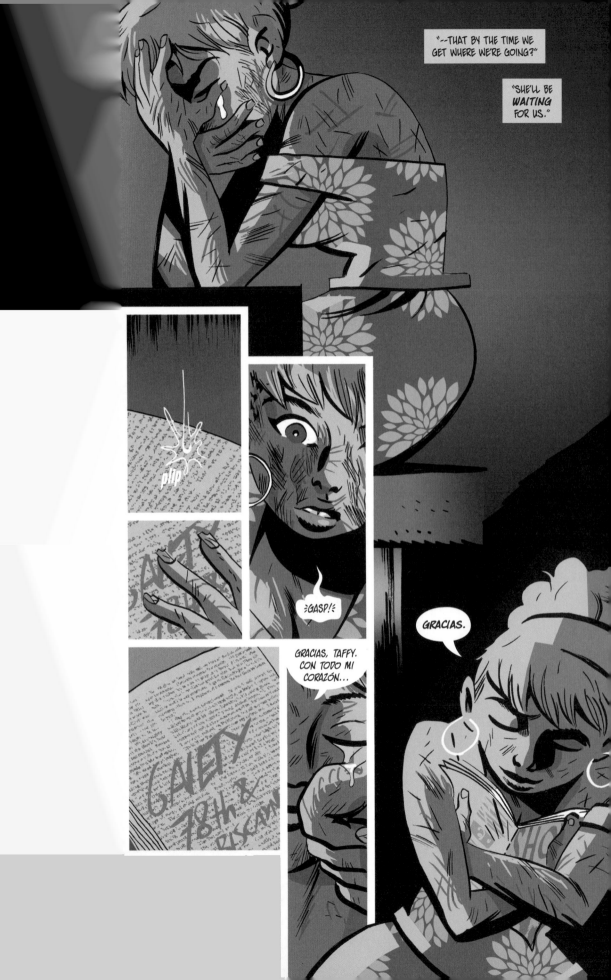

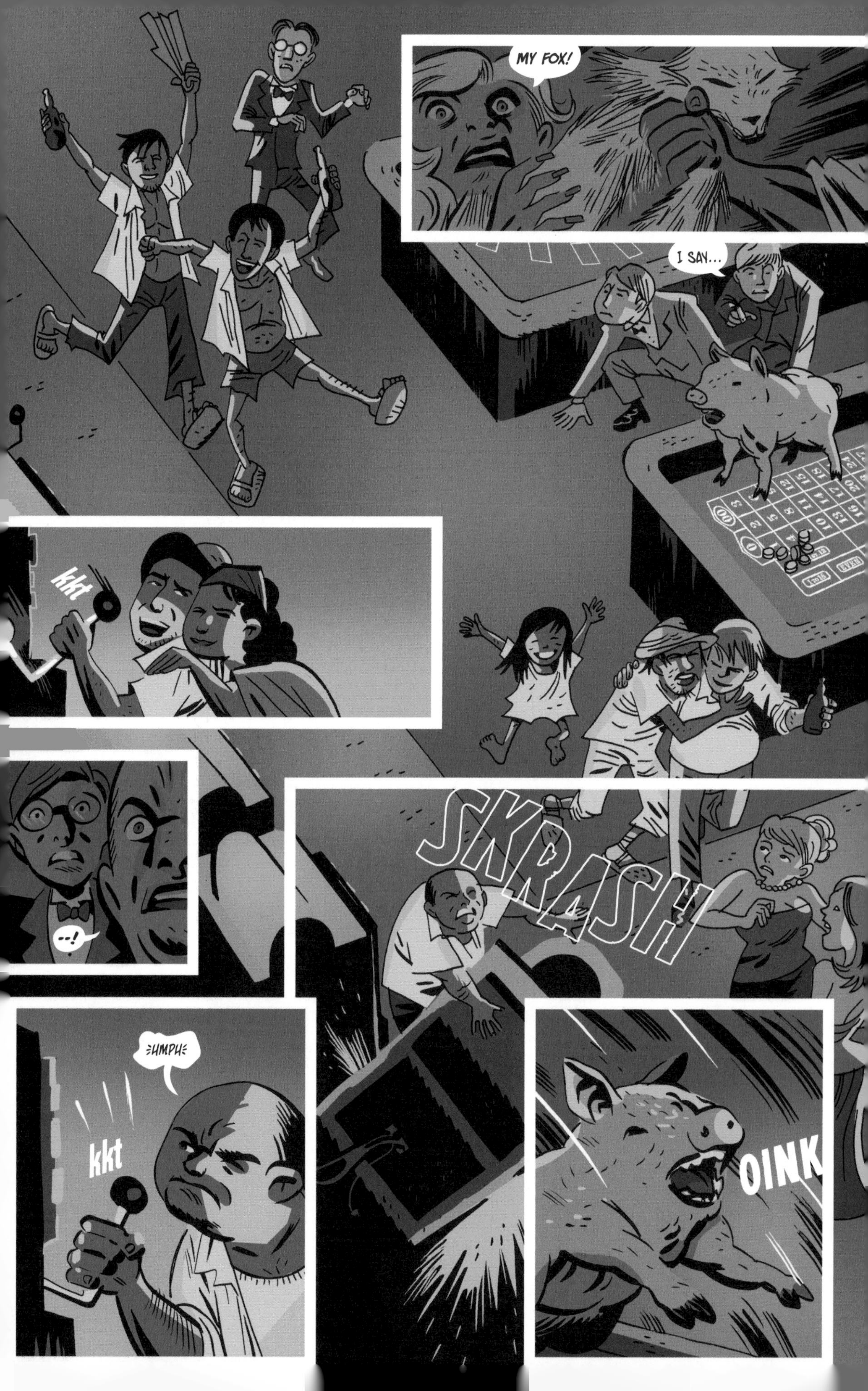
MY FOX!
I SAY...
kkt
--!
SKRASH
UMPH
kkt
OINK

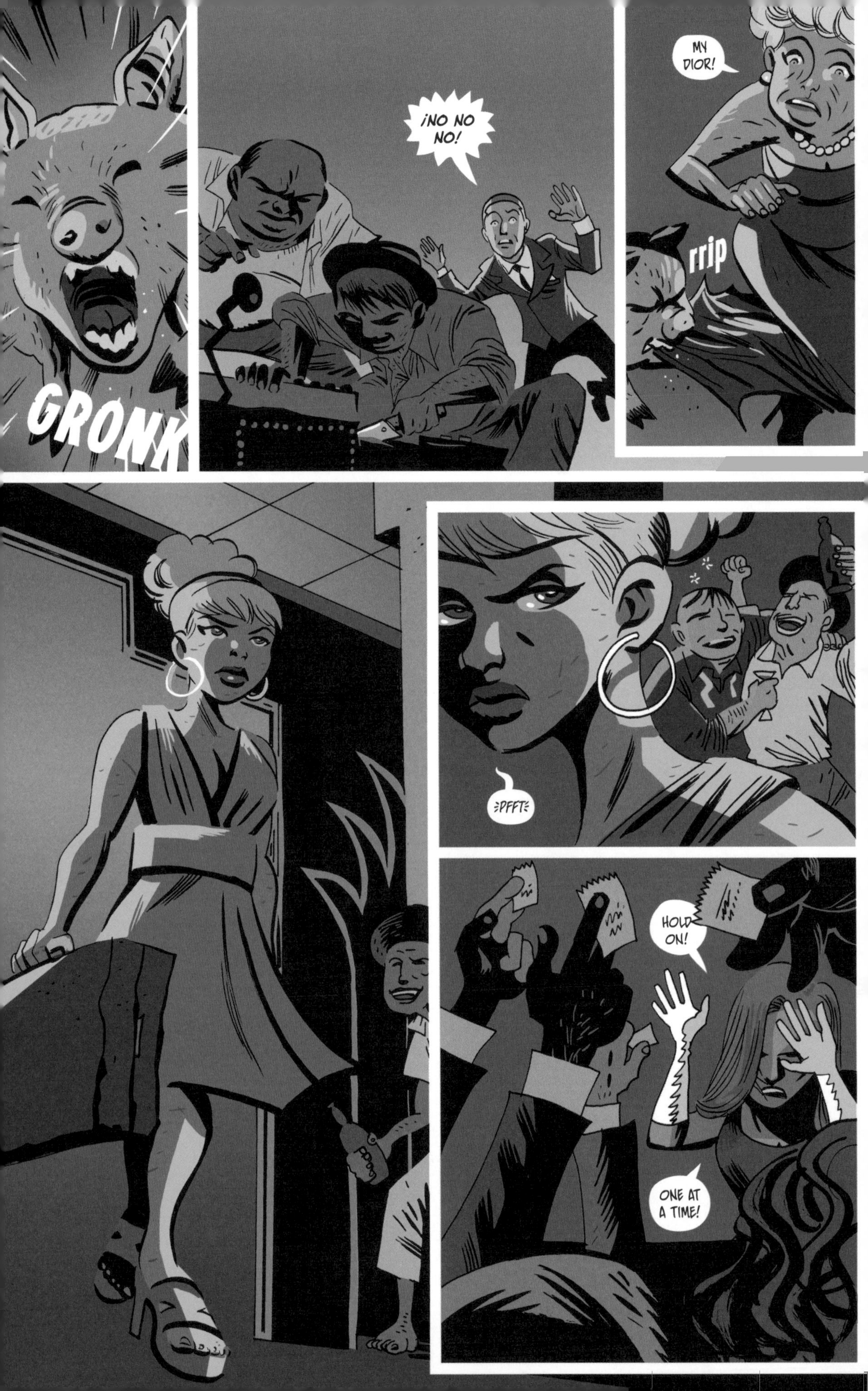
GRONK
¡NO NO NO!
MY DIOR!
rrip
PFFT
HOLD ON!
ONE AT A TIME!

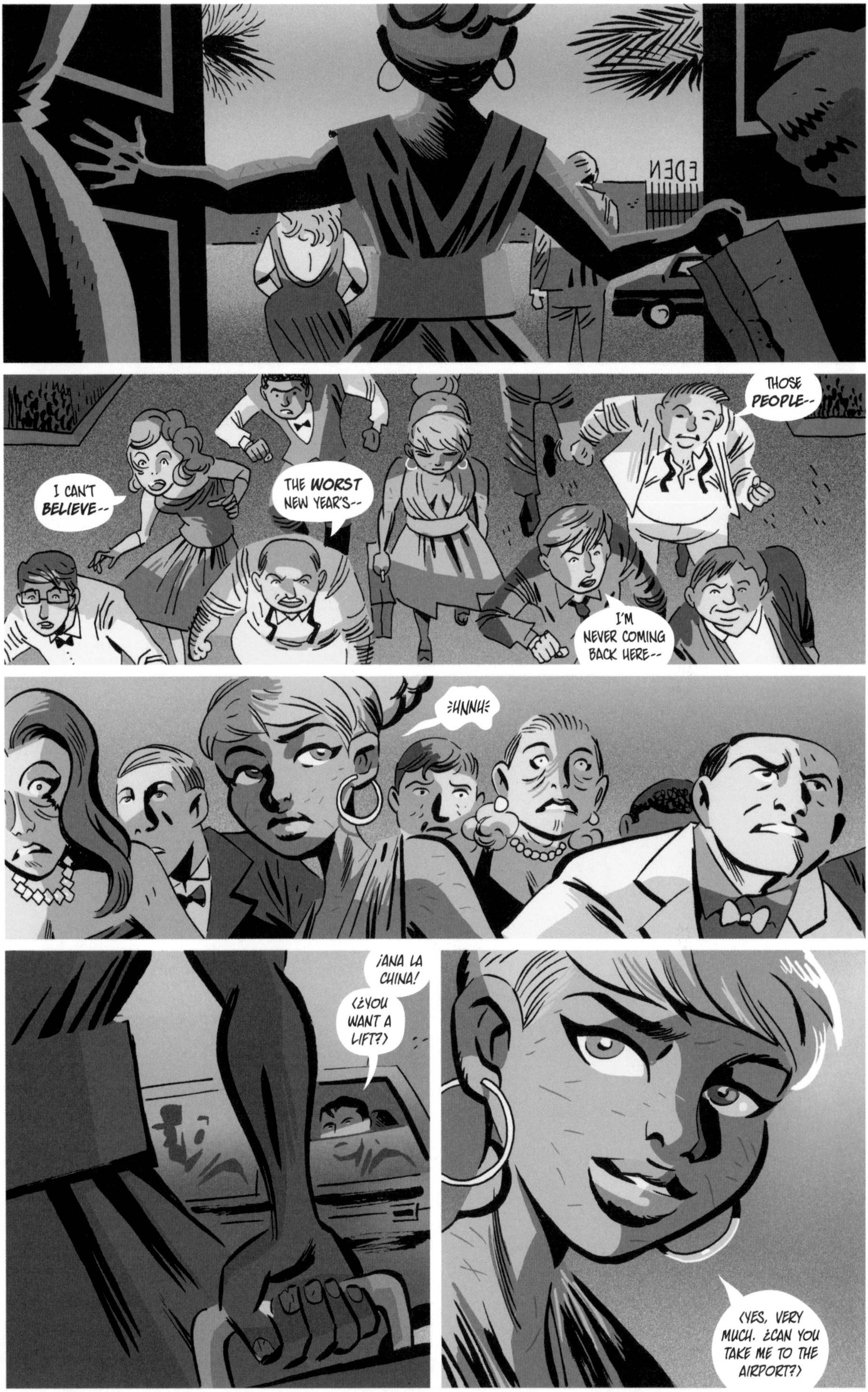
EDEN
I CAN'T BELIEVE--
THE WORST NEW YEAR'S--
THOSE PEOPLE--
I'M NEVER COMING BACK HERE--
UNNH
¡ANA LA CHINA!
‹¿YOU WANT A LIFT?›
‹YES, VERY MUCH. ¿CAN YOU TAKE ME TO THE AIRPORT?›

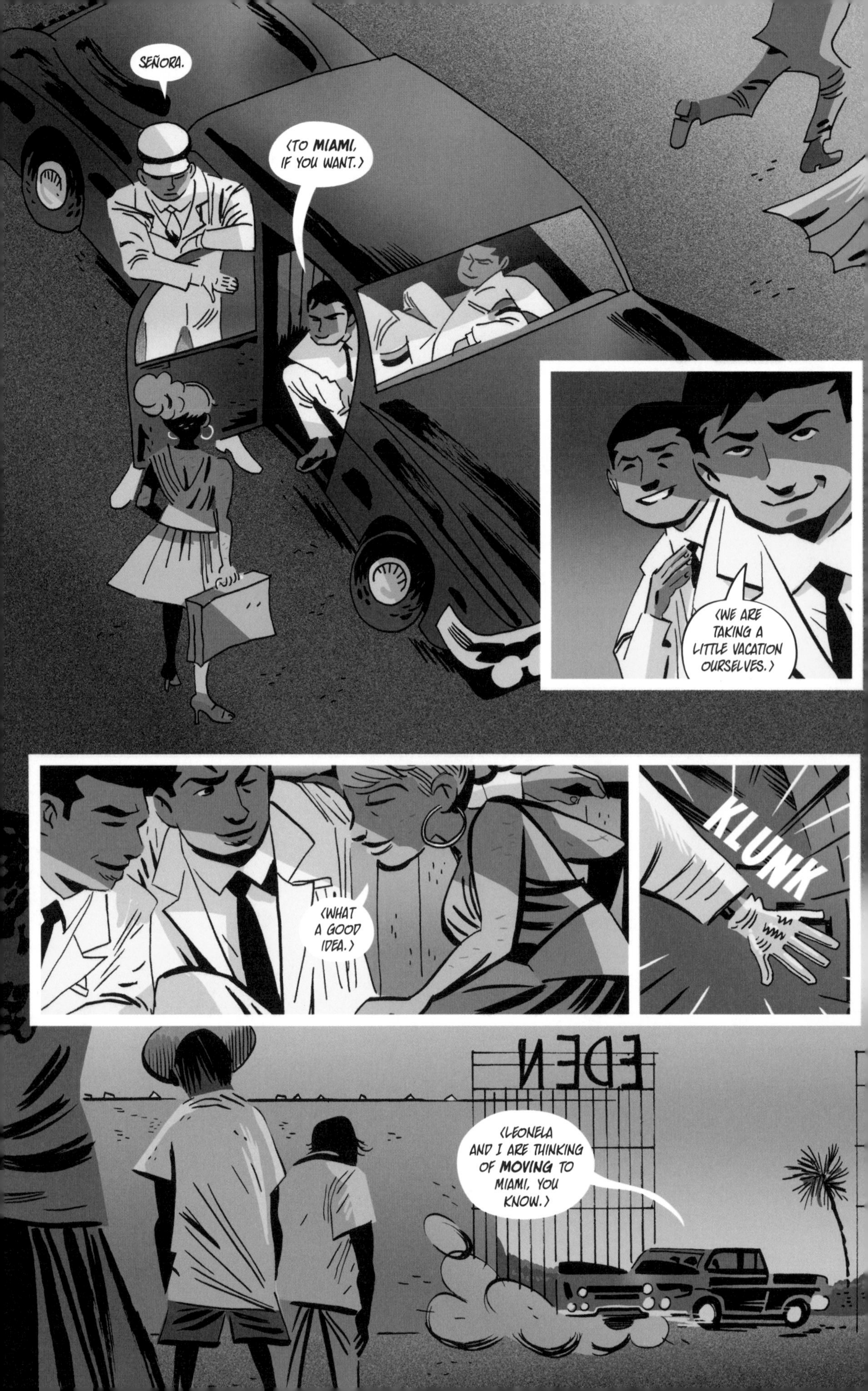
SEÑORA.
‹TO MIAMI, IF YOU WANT.›
‹WE ARE TAKING A LITTLE VACATION OURSELVES.›
‹WHAT A GOOD IDEA.›
KLUNK
EDEN
‹LEONELA AND I ARE THINKING OF MOVING TO MIAMI, YOU KNOW.›

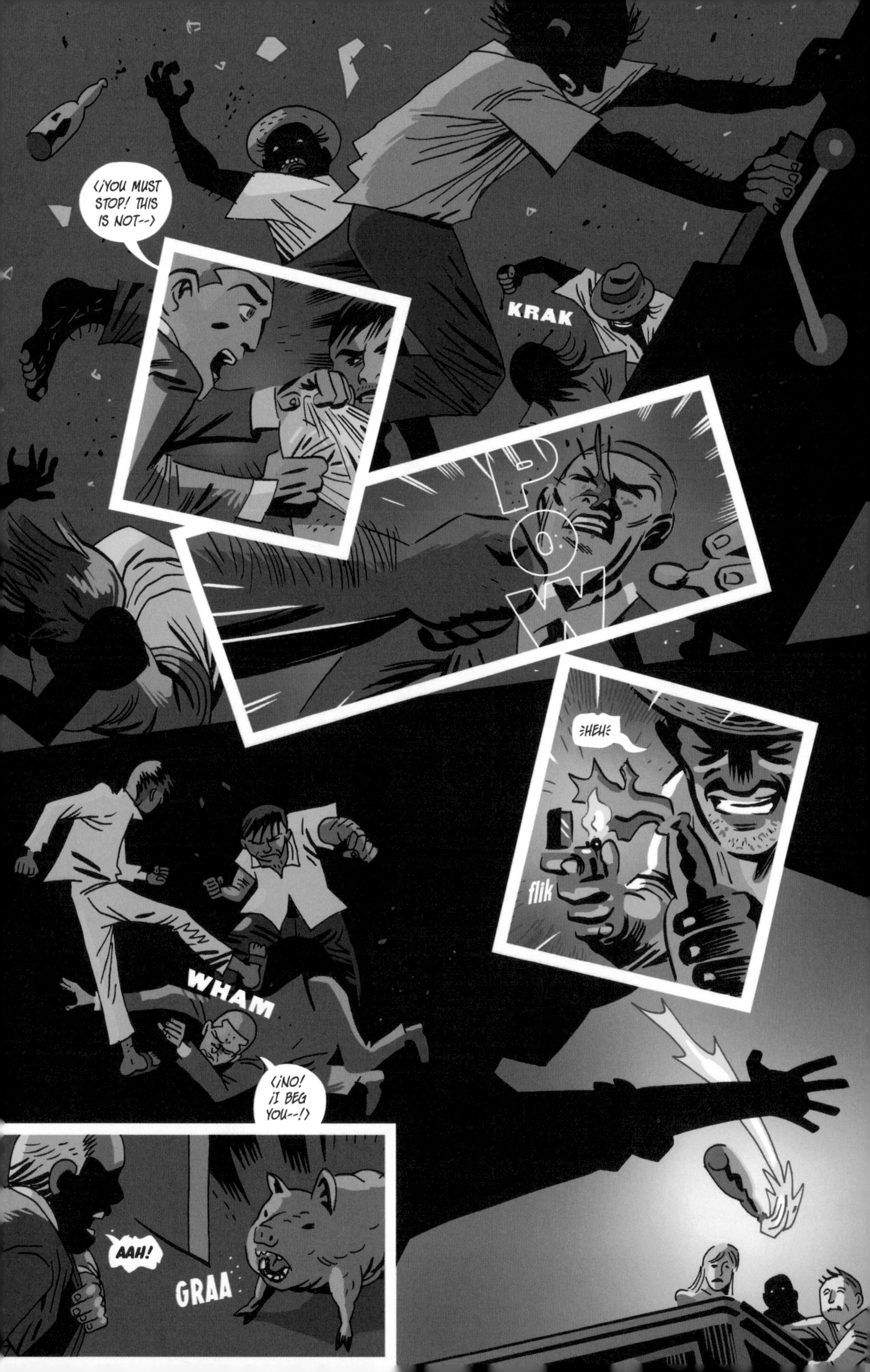

‹¡YOU MUST STOP! THIS IS NOT--›
KRAK
POW
HEH
flik
WHAM
‹¡NO! ¡I BEG YOU--!›
AAH!
GRAA

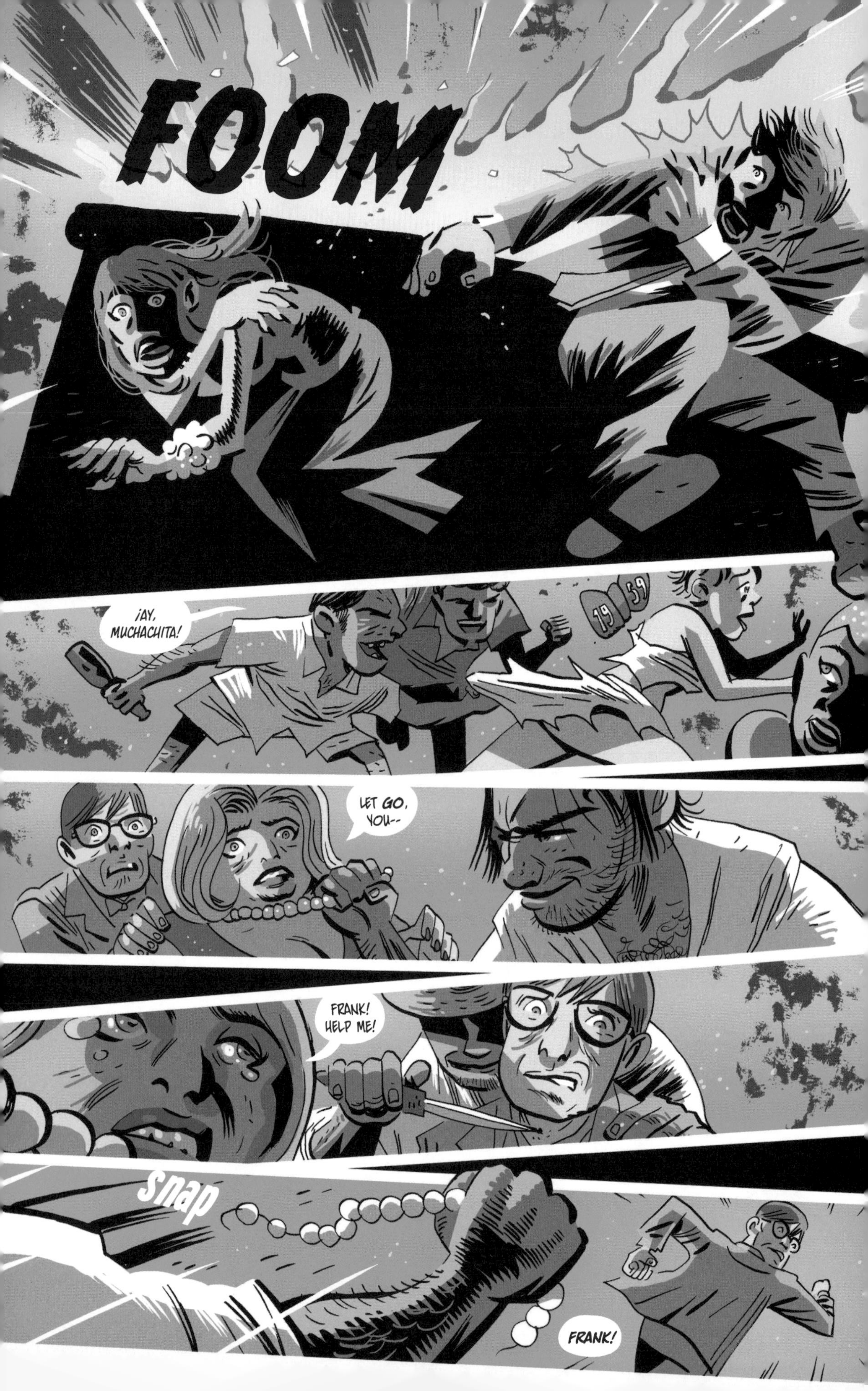
FOOM
¡AY, MUCHACHITA!
1959
LET GO, YOU--
FRANK! HELP ME!
snap
FRANK!

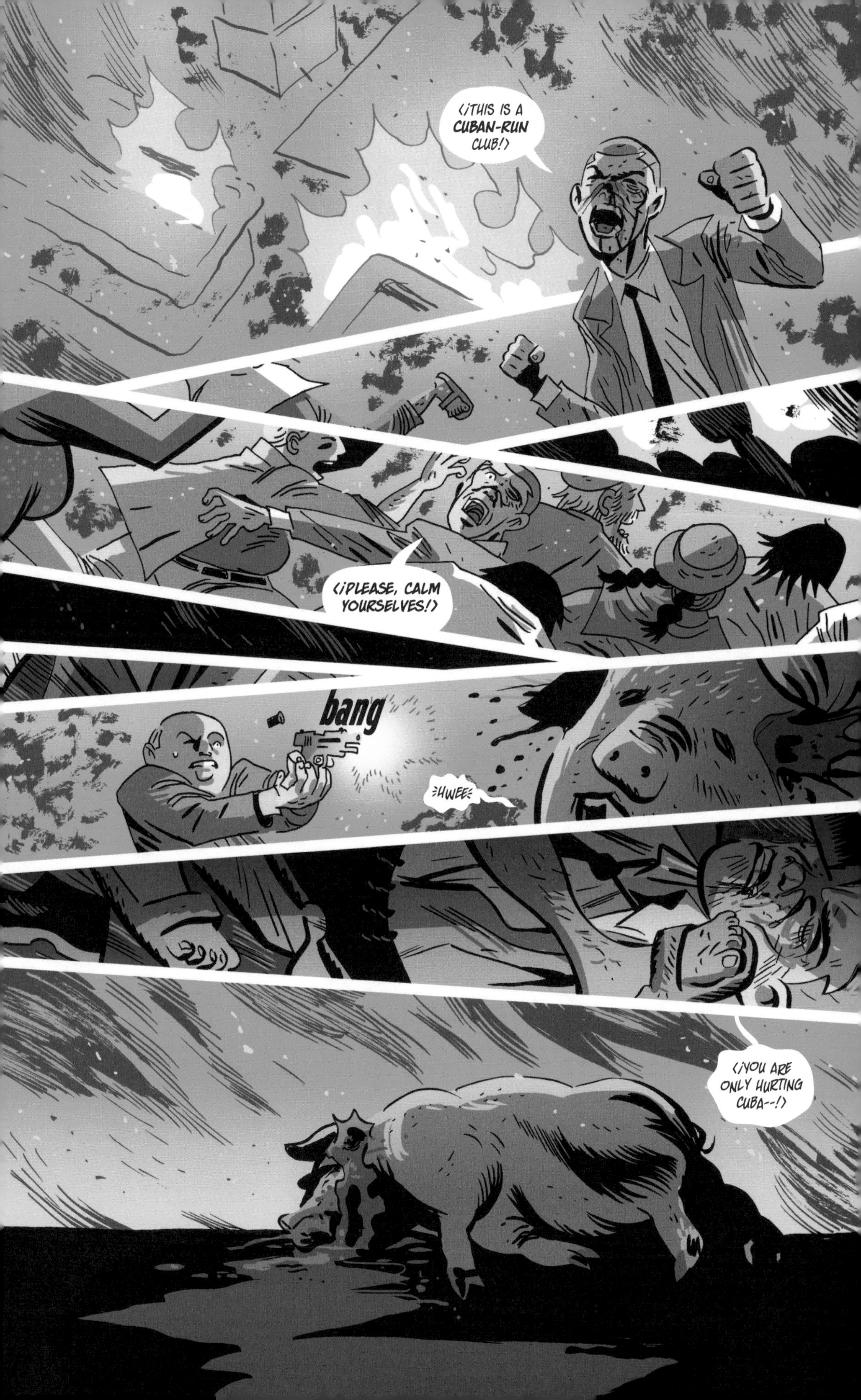

‹¡THIS IS A CUBAN-RUN CLUB!›
‹¡PLEASE, CALM YOURSELVES!›
bang
HWEE
‹¡YOU ARE ONLY HURTING CUBA--!›

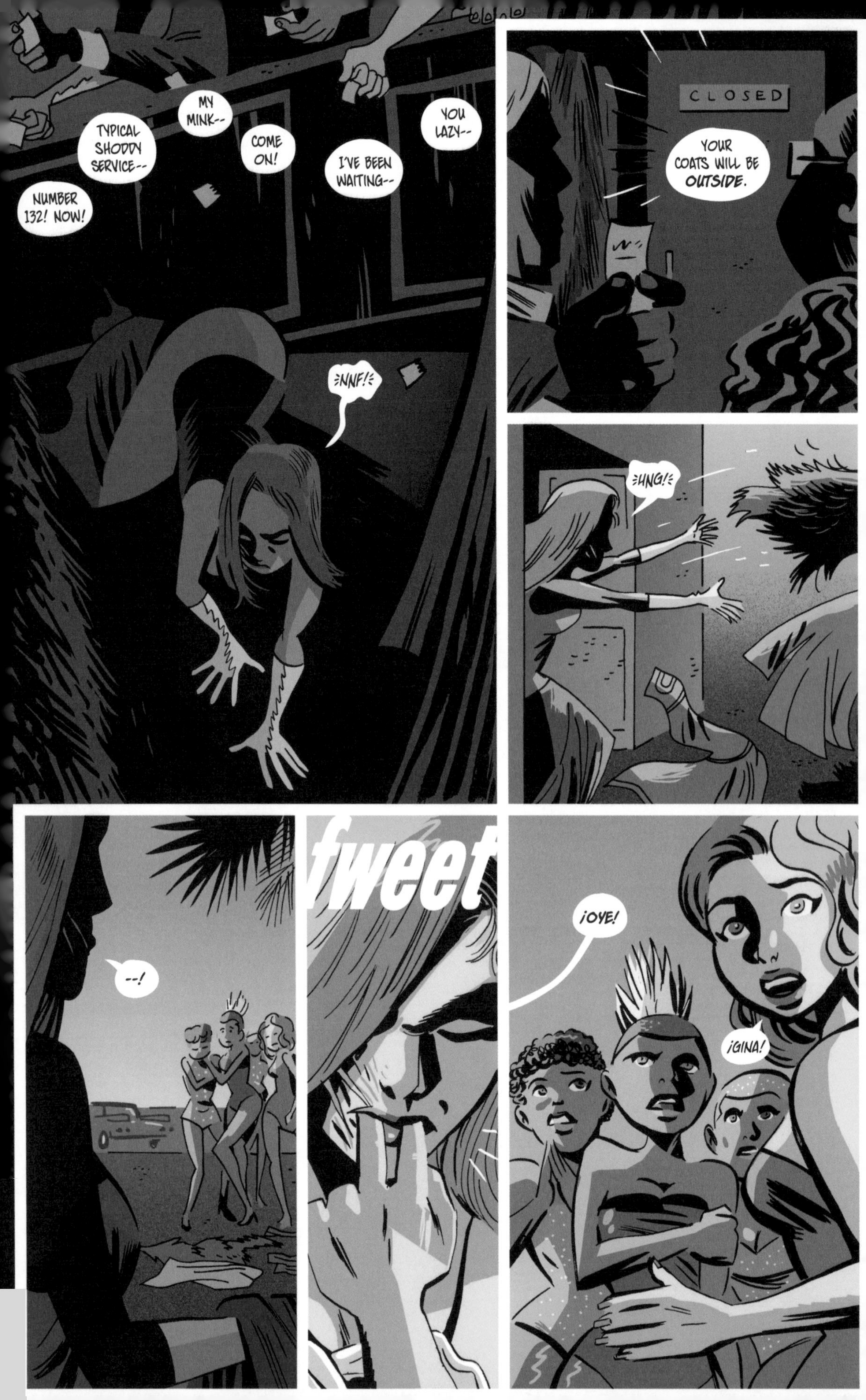
NUMBER 132! NOW!
TYPICAL SHODDY SERVICE--
MY MINK--
COME ON!
I'VE BEEN WAITING--
YOU LAZY--
NNF!
CLOSED
YOUR COATS WILL BE OUTSIDE.
UNG!
--!
fweet
¡OYE!
¡GINA!

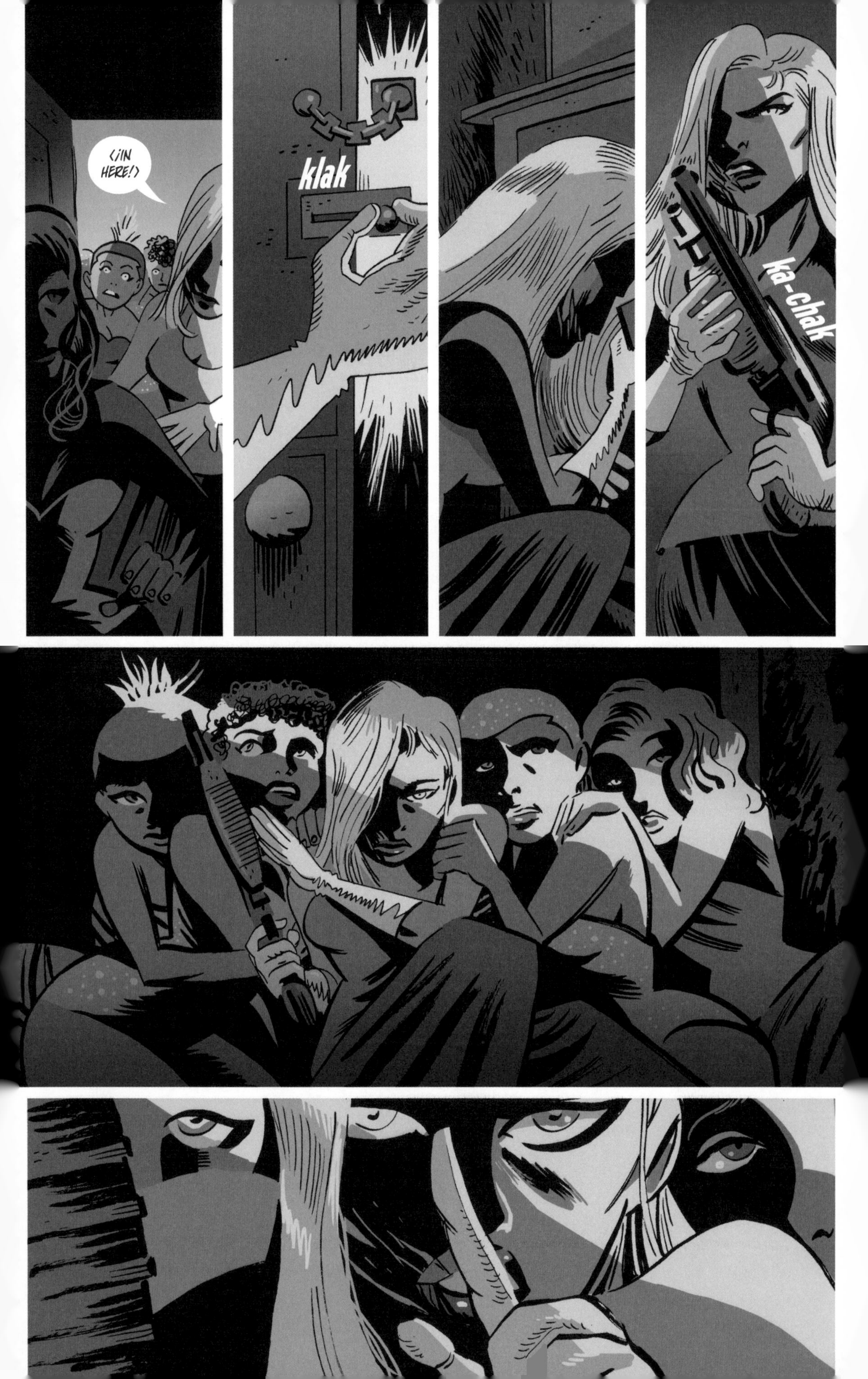
‹¡IN HERE!›
klak
ka-chak

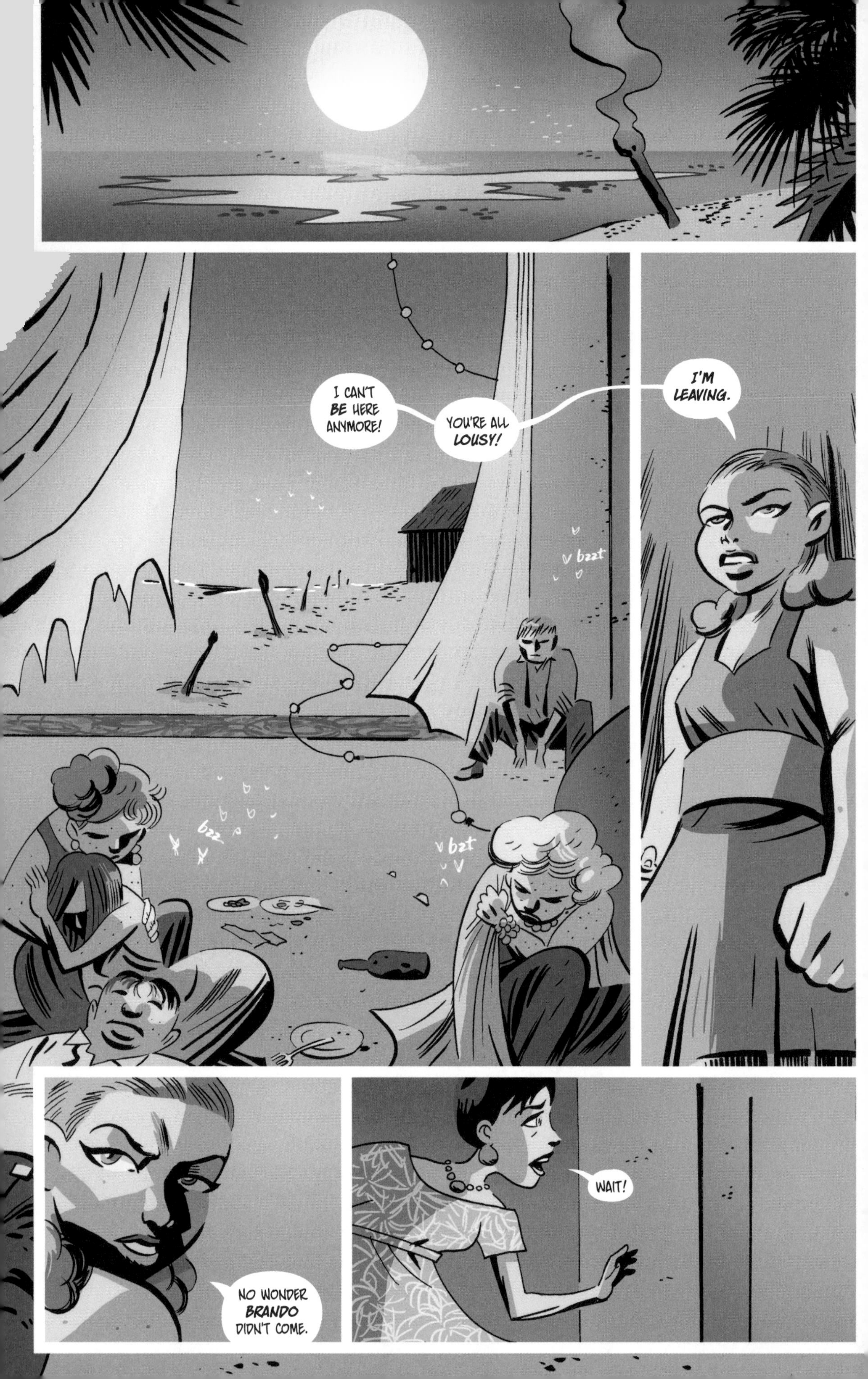
I CAN'T BE HERE ANYMORE!
YOU'RE ALL LOUSY!
I'M LEAVING.
bzzt
bzz
bzt
NO WONDER BRANDO DIDN'T COME.
WAIT!

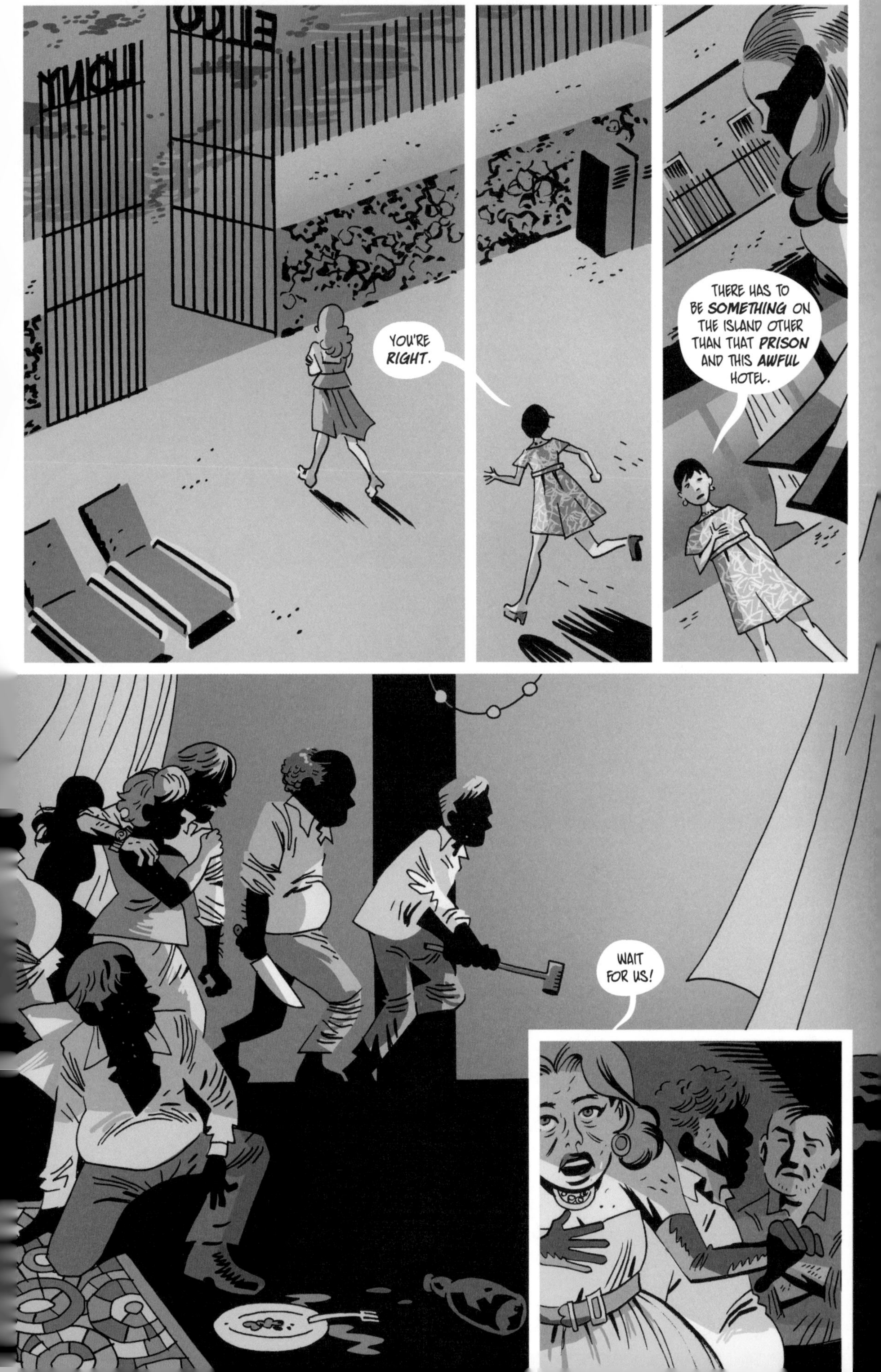
YOU'RE **RIGHT**.
THERE HAS TO BE **SOMETHING** ON THE ISLAND OTHER THAN THAT **PRISON** AND THIS **AWFUL** HOTEL.
WAIT FOR US!

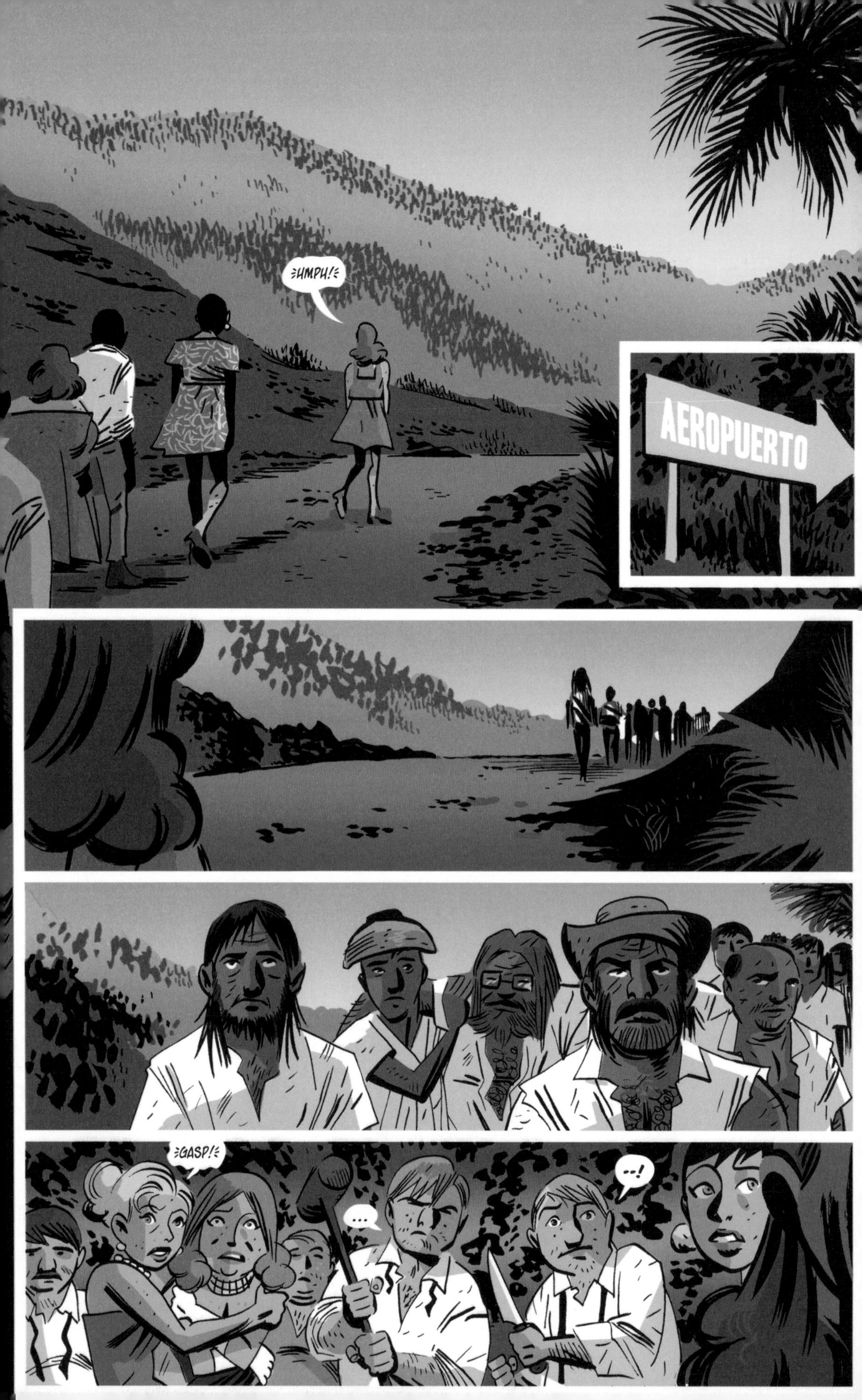
UMPH!
AEROPUERTO
GASP!
...
--!

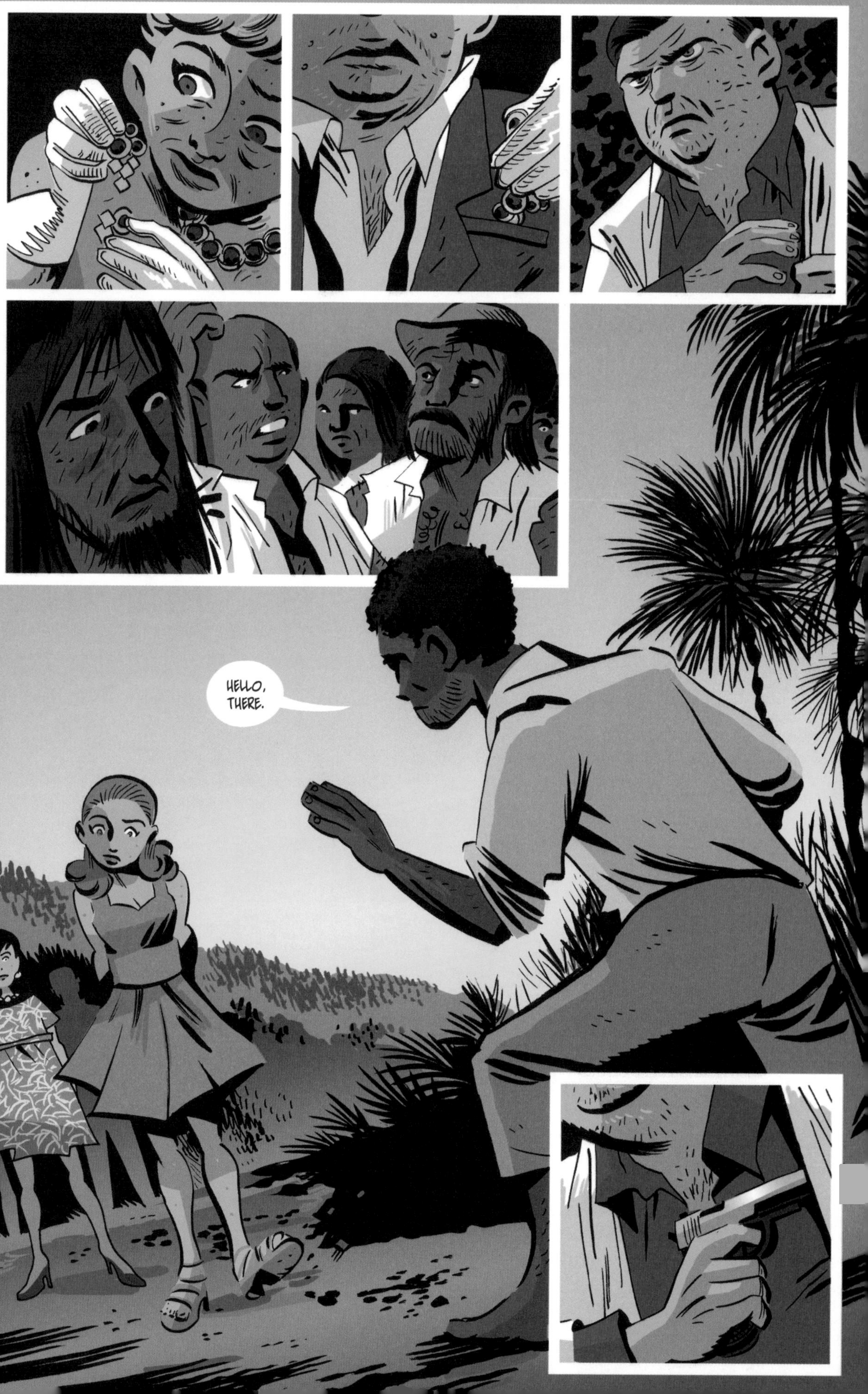
HELLO, THERE.

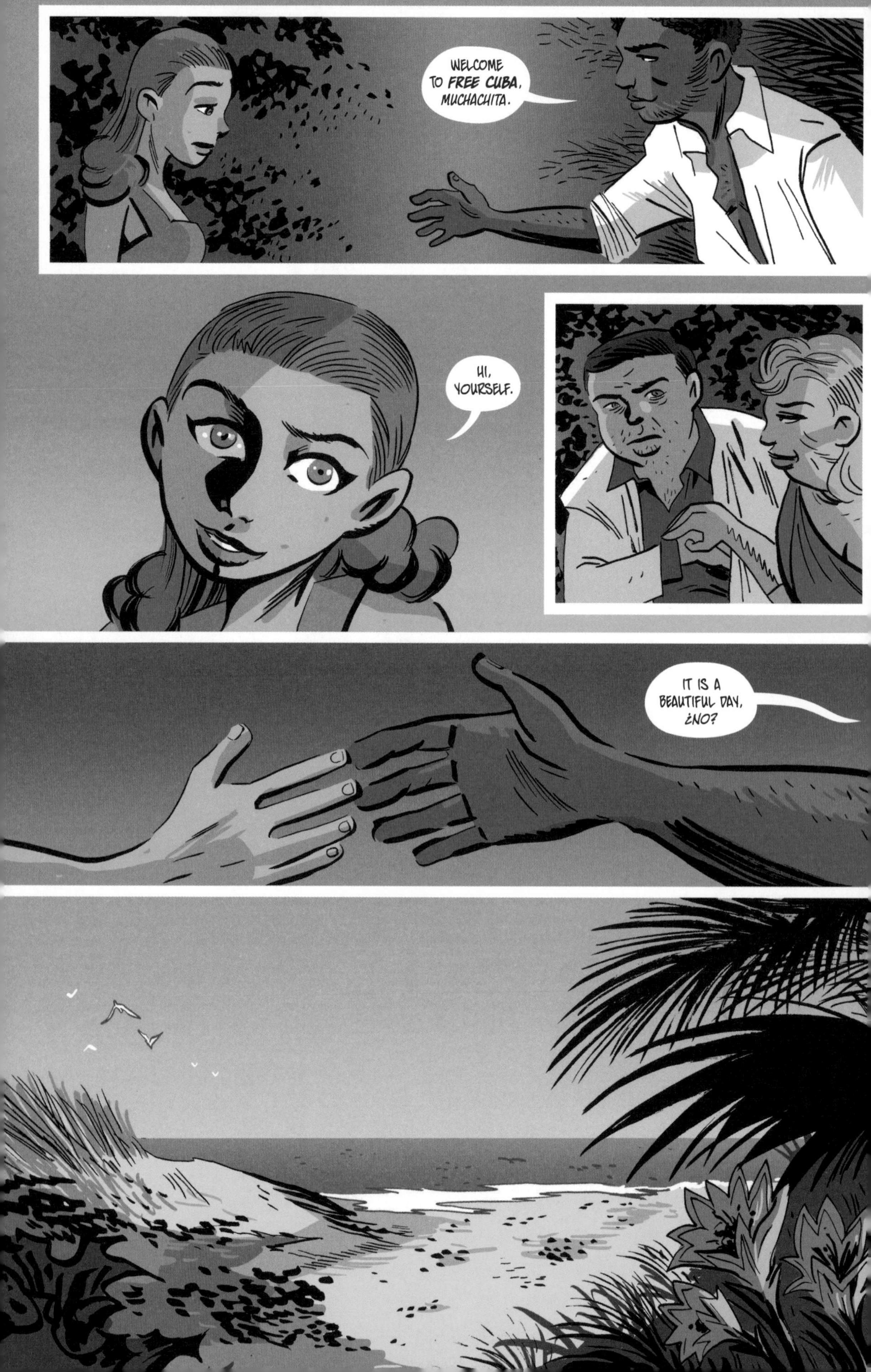
WELCOME TO FREE CUBA, MUCHACHITA.
HI, YOURSELF.
IT IS A BEAUTIFUL DAY, ¿NO?

Gallery 13
An Imprint of Simon & Schuster, Inc.
1230 Avenue of the Americas
New York, NY 10020

First Gallery 13 hardcover edition July 2018

GALLERY 13 and colophon are trademarks of Simon & Schuster, Inc

For information about special discounts for bulk purchases,
please contact Simon & Schuster Special Sales at 1-866-506-1949
or business@simonandschuster.com.

The Simon & Schuster Speakers Bureau can bring authors to your live event.
For more information, or to book an event, contact the Simon & Schuster Speakers Bureau
at 1-866-248-3049 or visit our website at www.simonspeakers.com.

Manufactured in the United States of America

10   9   8   7   6   5   4   3   2   1

Library of Congress Cataloging-in-Publication Data is available.

ISBN 978-1-5011-7681-4
ISBN 978-1-5011-7682-1 (ebook)